CULTIVATING THE PAST,
LIVING THE MODERN

CULTIVATING THE PAST, LIVING THE MODERN

The Politics of Time in the
Sultanate of Oman

Amal Sachedina

CORNELL UNIVERSITY PRESS **ITHACA AND LONDON**

This book has been published in collaboration with the Center for International Regional Studies (CIRS), Georgetown University in Qatar.

جامعة جورجتاون قطر
GEORGETOWN UNIVERSITY QATAR

Center *for* International *and* Regional Studies

First published 2021 by Cornell University Press

Library of Congress Cataloging-in-Publication Data

Names: Sachedina, Amal, 1974– author.
Title: Cultivating the past, living the modern: the politics of time in the Sultanate of Oman / Amal Sachedina.
Description: Ithaca [New York]: Cornell University Press, 2021. | Includes bibliographical references and index.
Identifiers: LCCN 2020050799 (print) | LCCN 2020050800 (ebook) | ISBN 9781501758614 (hardcover) | ISBN 9781501760020 (paperback) | ISBN 9781501758621 (pdf) | ISBN 9781501758638 (epub)
Subjects: LCSH: Material culture—Political aspects—Oman. | Material culture—Social aspects—Oman. | Cultural property—Oman—History. | Oman—Civilization—History. | Oman—Politics and government—History.
Classification: LCC GN406.S23 2021 (print) | LCC GN406 (ebook) | DDC 306.095353—dc23
LC record available at https://lccn.loc.gov/2020050799
LC ebook record available at https://lccn.loc.gov/2020050800

To a formidable advisor and a deeply caring mentor, Saba Mahmood

Contents

Acknowledgments

Officially I am the author of this book. But as a material form that has been years in the making, this work has tied me to intellectual relationships, emotional connections, and learning experiences that have essentially forged its contents. The core issue of this book, the impact of material heritage as part of the state building of a modern nation in the Middle East was first introduced to me during my undergraduate education at Rutgers University in the teachings of Eric Davis and Paul Sprachman.

The seeds they planted found fertile ground many years later in the intellectual environment of the University of California, Berkeley. Classes, tutorials, and long conversations with my advisors—Saba Mahmood, Charles Hirschkind, and Mariane Ferme—became the building blocks for the discovery of scholarly theory, methodology, and unexpected approaches that laid the foundations of my doctoral dissertation, the beginnings of this book project. I was truly fortunate to have them as my primary supervisors and critics. They not only challenged my thinking but found new possibilities in my work. Their judicious critiques enabled me to develop arguments in order to muster up the best work I could. A number of other colleagues read the whole manuscript or parts of it. And their comments produced lasting inspiration that found its way into this work. I am extremely grateful to Adam Gaiser, John Wilkinson, J. E. Peterson, Katayoun Shafiee, Attiya Ahmed, Faiz Ahmed, Bishara Doumani, Chiara di Cesari, Nathalie Peutz, Trinidad Rico, and Jessica Winegar for their astute comments and keen insights. This would also include my colleagues from the Asia Research Institute and the Middle East Institute at the National University of Singapore who attended the workshop for chapter 7, a forum that was extremely productive in facilitating ideas, especially from such colleagues as Zoltan Pall, Mohammed Adraoui, and Nisha Mathew, who gifted me with their incisive thoughts over the course of the workshop and beyond. I thank Engseng Ho and Madawi al-Rasheed for organizing it as well as for their contributing thoughts and comments. Two anonymous reviewers from Cornell University Press have made a decisive contribution to this book and were deftly able to find their way to its weakest points while simultaneously suggesting fruitful ways to strengthen them. I thank them for their productive intervention and careful reading of my work as well as those of my editors, Jim Lance and Clare Kirkpatrick Jones.

This book also embodies my fieldwork in Oman, which spans almost two years. Preliminary research laid the groundwork in the summers of 2006 and 2007. The greater part of the research, however, was done between December 2009 and June 2011. There were subsequent shorter visits in 2015, 2016, and 2017. One of the best schools for learning Omani history, religiosity, customs, and culture in those early days was Ahmed Mukhaini, who not only offered me his friendship but was always ready to direct me toward those avenues that would enable me to acquire a better sense of contemporary affairs in Oman. Internships with the Ministry of Heritage and Culture as well as support from the Ministry of Tourism, Ministry of Awqaf, Directorate of Handicrafts, and the National Records and Archive Authority introduced me to a group of officials and advisors as part of a larger web of state networks who welcomed my work and encouraged me to get a better sense of the ways in which heritage was being organized and deployed as institutions, social practice, and ethics. Their generosity with knowledge and enthusiasm in showering me with pertinent books, pamphlets, poetry, and documents were truly selfless and of indispensable use. In those early days, the guidance of Abdullah Al-Zahli, Marcia Dorr, Birget Mershen, Saif al-Rawahi, Ali al-Mahrooqi, Salem al-Mahrooqi, Hasan Mohammed Al-Lawati, Turkiya Said al-Adawi, Hamad Al Dhawaini, Abdul Wahah Al-Madhari, Moza al-Wardi, Jamal al-Mousavi, Abdulla al-Harrasi, Abdul Wahab al Mandhari, Isam Ali Ahmed Al-Rawas, and Kahlan al-Kharusi was invaluable. In academic circles at Sultan Qaboos University, Muhammed al-Belushi, Muhammad al-Muqaddam, Salem al-Maskri, Ali al-Riyami, Sulaiman Al-Shueili, and Saleh Al-Busaidi were extremely important interlocutors. And I hope the innumerable men and women from various human rights circles are well aware of how much I owe them, especially the Aal Tuwaiya family.

My host family in Nizwa welcomed me into their home with unstinting generosity and enfolded me into their lives and those of their family and friends. My entry into Nizwa society was full of warmth. Both elders and ordinary people were extremely enthusiastic about my work, and their readiness to help me and trust me with their insights and historical perspective was something I had not anticipated. I gratefully thank the people of Nizwa, especially my hosts, for making my research possible. There were those in Nizwa who deserve especial notice, including the officials of the Nizwa branch of the Ministry of Heritage and Culture, Khalfan Al-Sabahi, Jamal al-Kindi, Ibrahim al-Kindi, Sheikh Abdullah al-Saifi and his sons Ali, Muhammad, and Mandhir, Sheikh Al-Khattab al-Kindi, Suleiman al-Suleimani, Muhammad al-Kimyani, and Khalfan al-Zidi. At the University of Nizwa, I greatly benefitted from the generosity of Salim Hamed al-Mahruqi, Ahmed Khalfan al-Rawahi, and Professor Abdulaziz Al Kindi.

The ethnography on the history and lives of the al-Lawati community was fundamentally shaped by the hospitality offered by the family of Zuhair al-Khaburi, whose kindness and unstinting generosity made Oman not just a place of research but a refuge and a home. And there were many in the community who were generous with their time in their readiness to help me, none more so than Batool Bhacker and her family, Shawqi Sultan, Hasan Ali Abdul Latif, Mohsin Juma, Hassan Ali Abdullatif, Maqbool Sultan, Sadek Jawad Suleiman, Bilal Khamis al-Khabori, Baqer bin Muhammad al-Saleh, and Mustafa Mukhtar al-Lawati and his son Muhammad. Their willingness to accompany me on guided tours around the *sur*, join me in stimulating conversations, and trust me with knowledge and memories is one I hope I have faithfully recorded. I thank them all for their kind willingness to meet with me innumerable times in order to give me an insight into the histories and lives of the al-Lawati community. Invitations to attend the *ma'ātim* helped me get a sense of the layered richness of the sur and the types of relationships the site has fostered over time.

I honestly do not know if any of those who enabled me to conduct my research in Oman—Muscat or Nizwa—had any sense of what the final product would look like. I had little sense of it myself. But I do hope they find that this work has been worthy of the trust they put in me. Sections from certain chapters of this book, notably chapters 2, 3, and 4 have been adapted from previously published material. They have appeared in a number of articles including "Nizwa Fort: Transforming Ibadi Religion through Heritage Discourse," *Comparative Studies in South Asia, Africa and the Middle East* 39 (2): 328–43, "Politics of the Coffee Pot: Its Changing Role in History Making and the Place of Religion in the Sultanate of Oman," *History and Anthropology* 30 (3): 233–55.

The writing was done while I was a Mellon pre-/postdoctoral fellow at the American Museum of Natural History, New York. Its setting—as well as lively intellectual exchanges with members of the museum community as part of my project on the cultures and histories of the museum's Middle East and Islam ethnographic collections, especially Laurel Kendall, chair of the Department of Anthropology—helped strengthen my engagement with the writing process. I am extremely grateful for the support that my research received at various stages from a number of academic institutions and foundations. My archival research at the British Library and National Archives in London was supported by an alumni grant from the Institute of Ismaili Studies as well as the Mellon-IHR (University of London) predoctoral fellowship. Fieldwork was funded by the Al Falah Foundation, IIE Fulbright Fellowship, Fulbright-Hays Fellowship, and British Foundation for the Study of Arabia, a faculty grant from Brown University while I was the Aga Khan Visiting Assistant Professor. The writing of this book was made possible through postdoctoral research fellowships with the Middle East Institute, National University of Singapore, and the Institute of Middle East Studies, George Washington University.

The people who I am most indebted to, however, are my parents. Without having the foggiest clue as to what my research was about or what I was doing in graduate school, they served as a lifeline of support and love. My sister, Shadia, was an unfailingly cheerful and staunch supporter, who believed, throughout my most challenging years, that I would be able to bring this project to fruition. At this moment, I can truly say that I am very glad that I could prove her right.

Note on Transliteration

This book uses the system recommended by the *International Journal of Middle East Studies* (*IJMES*) for both spoken and written modern standard Arabic. Terminology using the local dialect was also transliterated, as closely as possible, according to the *IJMES* model. I have at times omitted diacritical marks from certain Arabic words that may be found in an English dictionary. All translations from Arabic to English, unless otherwise noted, are my own.

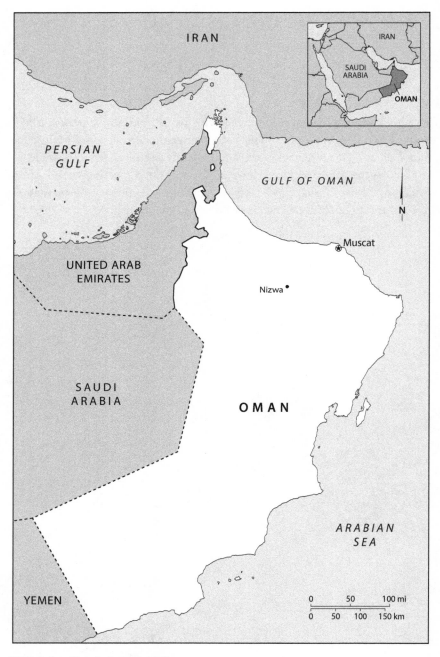

MAP 0.1. The Sultanate of Oman

Courtesy of Bill Nelson

INTRODUCTION
Heritage Discourse and Its Alterities

This book is an immersion into the iconic imagery and discourse of national heritage in the Sultanate of Oman. It explores the significance of the institutionalization of material heritage and the political implications of public history unraveling its sway over daily life among Omani citizens. It came into being in the summer of 2007, during my two-month internship with the Sayyid Faisal bin Ali Museum at the Ministry of Heritage and Culture in Muscat. This small state gallery invited visitors on a journey through the Omani landscape, from the Musandam region in the North, into the interior, and south to the governorate of Dhofar, through a display of fortifications and traditional weaponry. The exhibition followed a chronology, displaying the earliest-known weapons in Oman's prehistory and culminating in nineteenth-century guns imported but covered with traditional Omani silverwork. In writing the exhibit labels, the director emphatically informed me, no mention could be made of anything with political ramifications, including tribes or tribal conflicts. The result was a small museum in which a linear chronicle focused entirely on aesthetic and technical elements of the displays, effectively depoliticizing time-space. This perspective was the object of much contemplative musing throughout my twenty months of fieldwork between 2007 and 2017, as I waded through official files on historic preservation, visited museums and heritage festivals, and accompanied ministry advisors to major forts and citadels in Oman's interior.

One early event was a 2009 trip to Jabrin Fort, a former seat of government for the Ibadi Ya'āriba Imamate (1624–1743). I accompanied a team from the Ministry of Tourism—an American consultant, a Filipino historical conservationist and architect, and a senior Omani official. As we walked through the castle, my

American companion explained that the ministry was establishing the castle as an "authentic" historic site that would give insight into Oman's past through in situ displays.[1] Books, handmade ceramics, wedding trousseaux, and weaponry from the ministry's collections would be exhibited to evoke another age. There would also be cushions and straw mats, apparently the focal point in every room, handmade by the local women's associations to give a sense of "local tradition." Valuable artifacts would be placed behind glass in the many arched niches, their minimal labeling contributing aesthetics and ambiance more than information. The installations were being constructed to convey a sense of each chamber's historical role, leaving an impression of vibrant regional history.

But the Omani past did not make itself felt only in museums, handicrafts, or restoration projects. My daily journeys through the labyrinthine streets of the capital city, Muscat, and regional centers, such as Nizwa, were often lightened by the sight of fortified architecture and national symbols, such as the coffeepot (*dalla*), the traditional trading ship (dhow), and the dagger (*khanjar*) as part of the street scene. As an urban aesthetic, these material forms saturated the urban landscape and were ubiquitous public memorializations of the past. Pictorial history embodied urban geography as colorful mosaic depiction in parks and montages on building facades. On street roundabouts, these and other national emblems regulated the movements of commuters—citizens and noncitizens alike. They appeared as icons in educational and audiovisual media, as national emblems on currency and postage stamps, and as popular design motifs for posters, postcards, keychain ornaments, and finer artistic depictions. These objects of heritage became a highly commodified set of images depicting Omaniness and a visual cascade that inundated public spaces.

Thus, at the heart of the broad sociopolitical and economic transformations that have undergirded Oman's rise as a prosperous oil producer lies another phenomenon in which daily objects and architectures circulate as a visual, discursive mode of cultural production, called *turāth* (heritage). Since Oman's inception as a modern state in 1970, its heritage industry and market—exemplified by the expansion of museums, exhibitions, and cultural festivals and the restoration of more than a hundred forts, castles, and citadels—fashions a distinctly territorial polity, marking Oman as a nation-state.

Even before traveling to Oman, I had perused scholarship and media reports that placed Oman in the emerging Gulf state phenomenon of new heritage enterprises, ranging from camel racing to megamuseums, as the basis for strengthening a national historical narrative and substantiating a sense of citizenness in the postcolonial era (Erskine-Loftus, Al-Mulla, and Hightower 2016, 3). In the Arab-Persian Gulf region, this approach followed the general lines of examining how sociopolitical elites have waded through entangled pasts and disparate relationships, with the help of Western professionals, to entrench a singular sanctioned national history. From this scholarly vantage, the influx of oil revenues in the 1960s and 1970s is seen as having led ruling families in Kuwait, Qatar, the United Arab Emirates (UAE), Bahrain, and Oman to create a network of institutional media—museums, textbooks, heritage festivals, and sports, such as falconry—to forge a national imagination and displace sectarian and tribal affiliations. Media and scholarship construed the politics centered on the region's mass inward migration and regimes of labor and citizenship as playing out through the growing ascendancy of institutional heritage practices, delineating an exclusive citizenship grounded in an indigenous sense of belonging to the Arabian Peninsula and patrilineal tribal relationships in order to differentiate "locals" from the overwhelming number of foreign migrant residents (Samin 2016; Vora 2013).

I had already seen these tensions play out in another Gulf country, Kuwait. Growing up in a society whose great oil wealth had generated its modern prosperity, I was sharply aware that foreign residents and migrant workers greatly outnumbered Kuwaiti citizens and that a ubiquitous but unspoken hierarchy was deeply imbricated in the everyday rhythms of life. This hierarchy was undergirded by sociopolitical status, linked to occupation on the one hand and ethnonationalism on the other (Ahmad 2017). South Asians, for example, were made aware of their low place in that hierarchy through daily interactions that established an autochthonous notion of "Arabness" and the Arabian Peninsula as central elements of Kuwaiti nationality.

Oman was different. There was greater fluidity in the ethnoracial makeup of Muscat and Nizwa, and one was just as likely to see Omanis in lower-income jobs—shopkeepers, supermarket cashiers, or security guards—as Indians or Pakistanis. Moreover, unlike the UAE, Oman offered a public and proud exposition of a rich maritime history and coastal empires as part of the Indian Ocean trade network right into the nineteenth century. Communities of traders, soldiers, and sailors from Gujarat, Sind, Baluchistan, Iran, and the Kutch region had settled along the coast, retaining connections and relationships with their homelands while participating in the creation of diasporic societies, ports, and even new peoples along the Omani coastline and major trading centers. The Omani population remained slightly higher than foreign residents, and Arabic was the official language, but it was not uncommon to hear Omanis speaking Urdu, Baluchi, or Swahili.

The issues animating my exploration of state heritage practices included how underlying assumptions about the past were reworking pre-1970 conceptions of history, religion, and polity. But this question opened up unexpected and unsanctioned lines of inquiry (recall the exhibition labels absent of any markers of tribal identity) about the lives of Oman's varied ethnic groups. I grappled with the ways heritage discourse (and the history it encapsulated) had shaped how the past was reconstructed by different ethnic and tribal communities of Omanis and the manner by which it informed their sociopolitical sense of belonging to a codified national history and its ethical undertones. Although the questions this book examines could pertain to all Omanis, the people whose voices figure in these pages were primarily associated with two communities—groups who differ from each other on the basis of sect and ethnicity: (1) members of different generations of the old Arab scholarly and mercantile families of the city of Nizwa, a city in the heart of the interior of Oman, at the base of Jabal al-Akhdar (Green Mountain) and surrounded by the West Hajar Mountains; and (2) the al-Lawati community, those Khoja and Shiʿa families of Sind origin renowned for their trading networks and business acumen, in Muscat.

Nizwa is about 170 kilometers, or a ninety-minute drive, from the capital city of Muscat. The city once had strategic military and mercantile importance due to its location at a crossroads linking the interior to Muscat and to the southern region of Dhofar. Today, Nizwa is the epicenter of the Governorate of the Interior (ad-Dhākhiliya) and the largest city in the region. It also has a violent history as the administrative capital of the twentieth-century Ibadi Imamate, an Islamic sect distinct from both the Sunni and the Shiʿa. Ibadi doctrine and law claims that the golden age of the Muslim state was during the life of the Prophet and the first two caliphs of the Rashidun, Abu Bakr and ʿUmar ibn al-Khattab. In accordance with the precedent they established, the Ibadi imam was chosen through *shura* (mutual consultation) among the *ahl al-hal wal ʿaqd* (community elders, scholars, and tribal leaders) based on his morality, scholarship, and dedication to Ibadi *shariʿa*. In contrast, Shiʿa imams descend from Ali bin Abi Talib. The Sunni sect has, over time, created a distinctive difference between worldly leaders who were selected via *warathiya* (by descent) and religious-juridical scholarship.

The al-Lawati community, or the Khoja, are Shiʿa families of Sind origin renowned for their trading networks and business acumen. They had long been associated with their fortified enclosure, the *sur al-Lawati* in the port of Matrah, now a district of Muscat Province. The walled enclave once housed a vibrant communal mode of living along the coast of Matrah and remained a flourishing hub of economic activity into the twentieth century. The sur protected the al-Lawati, but it also isolated the community from the rest of the Muscat/Matrah city populace into the late 1970s and early 1980s.

In speaking with members of these ethnic communities, I sifted through memories and fragments of history that were often contradictory. What I pieced together were pasts full of nostalgia, pride, resentment, and exaggeration. My hope was to examine how their understandings of the past were informed by the heritage regime—the vast assemblage of policies, institutions, public discourse, and historic preservation—that developed to manage the material remnants of the pre-1970 past. Through the use of the term *heritage regime*, as Haidy Geismar aptly puts it, the processes at work to discipline the past through reconfiguring its contours foreground heritage as a "form of governance and an experiential domain for citizens" (Geismar 2015, 72; see also Bendix et al. 2012). Her work, moreover, opens an analytical space in which to scrutinize the historical circumstances by which "heritage" has secured ascendancy in shaping people's experiences of the ethical mores of Omani citizenship. But it also forces into view those historic remnants whose pasts may be submerged by the hegemonic discursive practices of heritage, even as they persist through vigorous forms of thought and action.

Thus, as an iterative mode of public history making, how heritage renders the past (in)visible in the public domain does not lie outside Omani history; the construction of heritage is irrevocably context bound. Its full impact as a productive force unfolds within the specificity of sociopolitical conditions. Heritage, as an institutional mode of reasoning out the past and planning for the future—how these temporal dimensions are connected in the present and the sensibilities this rationale engenders—is the lasting effect of premodern governance in the region in the twentieth century: the last Ibadi Imamate (1913–1955) and British informal imperial rule of the Arab-Persian Gulf. To understand the full impact of heritage as a state campaign of intervention and colonization of the local histories of Nizwa and the sur al-Lawati, I work backward, through the pre-1970 era, to examine how the sultanate's heritage project is historically situated as part of the greater context of colonial governance and modern statehood.

Geopolitical and Regional Conflict in Twentieth-Century Oman

In 1913, in response to the informal British governance of the waters and coastal regions of Oman, the Ibadi Imamate reestablished itself in the interior. For 1,200 years, the relatively unknown Ibadi school of shari'a interpretation had periodically instituted the imamate, uniting the peoples of southeast Arabia into a body politic led by an imam. The administrative capital of Nizwa embodied the imamate's authority, and Nizwa Fort was the seat of the imam. Founded on a Quranic world view of "commanding the right and forbidding the wrong" (amr bil-ma'ruf wa nahy 'an al-munkar), the fort's authority was grounded in a concept of the past reaching back to (1) the Quran, (2) the *sunna* (ways and deeds) of the Prophet and his companions, and (3) the formative experiences, words, and deeds of an unbroken line of succession of imams since the early Madinan caliphate. In accordance with Ibadi doctrine, the imam was elected by scholars and elders and given allegiance by the community in his role as administrator of sharī'a. This ideology was premised on the rejection of *jababaira*, rulers who had arbitrarily imposed themselves on the community.

In the early 1900s, this polity emerged in opposition to that prevailing in the coastal areas, where monarchical dynastic rulers, the Al Said, had gradually ceded power to British imperial sovereignty. At the time, Britain supported, among others, the merchant communities from the Indian subcontinent, including the Hindus and the Khojas, and effectively controlled the sea-lanes and coastlines, reconfiguring the nature of political interactions and trade relations among tribes, rulers, and the *'ulamā'* (Jones and Ridout 2015; Landen 1967). A century earlier, Oman had been part of the frontier zone of the British Raj, a crucial entity in the British political system whose policies had consequences throughout the Gulf region.[2] The region was vital to the battle for control of empirewide communications between Britain and India. It was thus instrumental to the balance of power among the European powers and a platform on which "Western civilization" could be extended, even before the discovery of oil.

Dale Eickelman and other scholars have argued that ties between Imam Muḥammad bin 'Abd Allāh al-Khalīlī and Sultan Sa'īd bin Taimur (r. 1932–1970) were strong, despite their conflictual relationship. For example, Sultan Sa'īd offered positions to a number of 'ulamā' of the imamate, who divided their time between the two polities and cooperated in managing border disputes, such as the 1952 Saudi occupation of the Buraimi oasis (Eickelman 1985, 3–24). From the early days of his reign, however, Sultan Sa'īd sought to ingratiate himself to the tribal sheikhs, entertaining them when they came to Muscat and bestowing gifts of money. According to colonial records, he cherished a hope that he would be accepted as ruler of the interior when the imam grew old. On three occasions, he asked the British government for financial and military assistance to subjugate inner Oman by force; the British refused until after the imam's death in 1955 when there was the prospect of oil discovery in imamate territory (British Foreign Office 1987, 1:192).

The prospect of oil resulted in a series of brief, violent conflicts and air assaults in the mid- to late 1950s that ended the imamate period, giving way to a British-backed sultanate and uniting the region under a single polity. The Jabal al-Akhdar War (1957–1959) witnessed the final expulsion of imamate forces, their eventual exile to Saudi Arabia, and the sultan's suzerainty over the Omani interior, uniting the region as the Sultanate of Muscat and Oman (simplified, after 1970, to the Sultanate of Oman). In 1968, the sultanate began receiving regular oil income. A 1970 coup ousted Sultan Sa'īd bin Taymur in favor of his son, Sultan Qaboos, marking the beginning of the *nahda*, or Omani "renaissance."

This period witnessed the first material integration of Oman's interior, including Nizwa, with the capital, Muscat, through the centralized civic infrastructure of modernization and state building. This period was also marked by reverse migration; thousands who had left to seek employment or education in South Asia, East Africa, and other parts of the Gulf in the 1950s and 1960s returned with their families to form a new bureaucratic class of professionals and civil servants. Many were members of merchant communities, such as the Khoja, whose ancestors had settled in the Muscat/Matrah coastal region and were neither Arab nor Ibadi but became Omani citizens.

This study is thus situated within the paradoxes unleashed by the conflicts and contestations of two very different modes of governance, the temporal logic underlying each one, and their sociopolitical implications. It focuses on (1) the Ibadi Imamate, established within a tribally organized community, intimately linked to the broader framework of the *umma*, a theologically invoked space that enabled Muslims to embody Ibadi sharīʿa as the practical juridical system by which they were governed and practiced daily moral and ethical mores; and (2) the modern, territorially bounded nation-state, entrenched within a linear chronicle and organized around a calendrical pre-Islamic (rather than sacral) timeline, which culminates in "traditional" ways of life that infuse and direct the past, present, and future of the nation-state. At this juncture, analytical questions may be posed that privilege an alternative set of issues: How have ideas about the past and its proper form and practice secured the categories of *tradition* and *religion* in the Omani public domain today?

In Ibadi Oman, imamate authority was undergirded by an ethical mode of living directed toward divine salvation and implementing God's law on earth. It was predicated on the Quran and the sunna (ways and deeds) of the Prophet and his companions, in accordance with ideas about their exemplarity, as interpreted by the Ibadi school of law and doctrine. Even as the notion of the umma assumed an idealized egalitarian order, the sharīʿa community of the imamate recognized and worked within a sociopolitical order structured around hierarchies grounded in tribal lineage, occupation, and wealth. These elements of a sharīʿa tribal sociality have not only persisted but have been reconfigured by heritage practices. This Islamic sectarian tradition, which predominated for more a millennium, is still in evidence in the citadels and walled residential quarters that dot the landscape.

Through the 1900s, the fort, the dalla, and other forms were anchored by two temporal rationales and arranged around the social and political singularities of two distinctive notions of history, each conforming to the authoritative ways of life of two regimes that have occupied the region. These objects and sites come to embody different institutionalized experiences and concepts of time, implicit in how they are put to quotidian use. Their shifting roles result from a historically contingent outcome shaped by the intersections of institutions, power, and knowledge that underpin the sovereignty of two entities: the Ibadi Imamate (1913–1955) and the sultanate (1970–present). In the twentieth century, Nizwa Fort (as the juridical and administrative center of the imamate) and the dalla (in its utilitarian function as coffee server) forged an ethical mode of sociality and living, predicated on the divine, through engagement with the Quran and a critical history grounded in the virtuous conduct of exemplary figures. This history delineated the ways through which the governing institutions of the imamate were forged.

The fort's spatial divisions generated practices linked to the three key functions of the imamate: administration, military headquarters, and the hall of justice (*barza*). These functions were enjoined by a past oriented toward evaluating acts as part of a world view centered on fulfilling God's design. The dalla, in its utilitarian role, was integral to the *sabla*, a daily forum for local governance widely prevalent in Nizwa before the nahda era. Coffee and dates were necessary components of sabla practices as men gathered to read and discuss the Quran and prophetic histories and to mediate quarrels and settle affairs. Like the fort, the quotidian role of the dalla in the imamate era turned on a history anchored to the exemplary lives, primarily moral in nature, oriented toward God and divine salvation.

For Nadia Abu El-Haj (2001), in Israel the very act of excavating the land as part of an institutional and community enterprise produces a material culture and carves out a landscape with the concrete signs of a particular historical vision. In Oman, establishing the nation-state from the physical remains of the imamate has involved objects like the dalla and sites such as Nizwa Fort in part of a "purification" process that separates their material forms from the sharīʿa practices that defined their significance for the Ibadi Imamate.[3] Set within the rubric of heritage, the complex operations that disjointed these forms include processes of collection, preservation, interpretation, and display that refigured these once utilitarian objects into artifacts monuments, architectures, and exhibitions (Kirshenblatt-Gimblett 2004). Redefining and reworking the past produced a new historical experience compatible with the civic values of citizenship, modern education, and professional life. The work of heritage processes has acted as a temporal force to formulate a new set of conceptual categories. *Culture* and *civilization* now anchor the past in ways that engage directly with the regional political and religious struggles the sultanate has been confronting for forty years, from socialist nationalism and Islamist movements to the travails and exigencies of modernization in national life.

Since 1970, the transformation of these imamate objects and sites into heritage substantiated Oman's transformation into a nation-state and a united sultanate. This process of "liberation" opened a space to reconfigure the material of the Ibadi Imamate, transforming the boundaries between politics and religion and remapping the terrain of the imamate to that of the Sultanate of Oman. These objects become signs; their pictorial and graphic capabilities are arranged to generate historical experiences in accordance with the modern political and moral order. As iconic imagery and museum pieces, these became fixed to an immaterial set of civic values and ethical principles (entrepreneurship, mutual support, hospitality, social solidarity, and innovation) that embody the nation-state. Material forms lose their integral relationship with social exchange grounded in authoritative exemplars from the past, toward one of representation. The object now stands as an index to historically concrete ways of life and the values they impart, becoming directives for efficacious future actions. The collection and display of material objects carves out a national history tethered to a narrative that becoming Omani has been a chronological process of working the land and its resources. Its trajectory is progressive as it moves from a simple (Stone Age) mode of living to one that is increasingly complex (nineteenth-century Indian Ocean empires), culminating in a nationalist revival of traditional modes of life as a moral inheritance.

The foundations of the state now rest on a new periodization of history. A new conception of time is institutionalized in how past, present, and future relate to each other and organize the present and its senses of flux or stability. It enters the domain of modern wo(man), where the effacement of those histories, whose juridical and ethical-moral bases are founded on a divine text and analogies of exemplary figures from the Islamic past, give way to a more centrally regulated mode of historical consciousness, rooted in a humanist world and the productive force of labor that now anchor the Sultanate of Oman.

This temporal undertaking transforms the relationship between politics and religion by distancing the citizen from problematic imamate doctrine, which centered on an elected imam and an exemplary history. The divine gives way to a history premised on the secular political rationality of the nation-state through a national rubric amenable to modern-day needs. A telos of divine salvation and its substantiation through sharīʿa law and doctrine break down in the face of an alternative ideal—living in ways consonant with the civic virtues of a hereditary sultanate. The transformation of Ibadi Islam seems inseparable from the process of redefining institutional public history to conform to modern political and moral nationhood.

The construction of the heritage project in modern Oman has thus also necessitated the reconfiguration of the public domains of history and Islam as seemingly autonomous, erasing any awareness of the sociopolitical and ethical relationships that once characterized Ibadi Islamic rule (1913–1958). The result is the transformation of a formerly sharīʿa society through practices of progressive historicity. In constructing a pedagogical public space, visual commemorations of historical memory incorporate time, history, tradition, and religion, providing the context within which territorial space is reworked and establishing the corporeality of a nation-state and a modern-day sultanate.

But the fundamental contrast in the sovereignty of the two dominant polities that prevailed before Oman's inception as a bureaucratized nation-state has left a residue of too many historical tensions and lingering contradictions to be neatly encased in heritage rubric. These include the violent final overthrow of the imamate with the support of a colonizing power, which resulted in the imprisonment of senior 'ulamā' and judges who had represented the community, and the visible signs of the imamate that indelibly mark the region. In shaping a historical consciousness through submersion and containment, a new polity, the Sultanate of Oman, is substantiated.

Through examining pre-1970 colonial archival material and historical scholarship (Landen 1967; J. Peterson 1978; Wilkinson 1987), it became increasingly apparent that the mode of history that emerges from institutional heritage purposefully excised certain experiences, even as it sought to remake differences by embodying national unity by emphasizing co-option and inclusion. The outcome appears to be a landscape increasingly denuded of tribal networks, differential kinship, and emphases on genealogy, occupation, and status. In the process of cultivating a distinctive relationship to history, heritage discursive practices emplotted a visual, cumulative narrative that was foundational to the guarantee of civil and political equality. It also revealed how such a heritage regime was predicated by both the constraints and possibilities of what was sayable and doable within the rubrics of a national history. Heritage as a mode of reasoning out the relationship between past, present, and future was organized around the problem of reconfiguring Ibadi Islam, effacing tribal hierarchies, and managing ethnic differences in ways that normalized the lifeworld of a modern sultanate. Simultaneously, elisions of the histories of slavery, tribal mores, and ethnic communal pasts like the Baluchi or Khoja, as well as those pertaining to British informal governance of the region in the nineteenth and twentieth centuries, were built into the concept of turāth. These histories were occluded from official view. Yet it is still possible to understand how they instantiated the operation of history making through their persistence in contemporary Omani life.

Growing awareness of Oman's colonial history and the violent end of the imamate in the late 1950s led me to ponder how material objects and sites now embedded in institutional practices of public history were shaping people's historical consciousness and sense of time. These would be communal groups who were part of the violence and conflicts that tore through the region in the 1900s— the long-established families of Nizwa and the diasporic al-Lawati community. This was important to understand, especially given people's habitation of an alternative temporal rationale into the 1970s. The tangibility of the national landscape, with its forts, *souqs*, and everyday objects like the dalla, created an emotional and historical resonance that the nation-state was actively co-opting. I wanted to examine how daily interactions with these sites and objects—through discourse, imagery, or their physical presence—became integral to the ordinary histories and memories interwoven into contemporary existence. I also wanted to consider other histories that had been effectively silenced by a hegemonic heritage discourse that reduced the act of "becoming an Omani" to a matter of laboring over its land and sea resources. Submerged pasts ranging from slavery to tribal hierarchical genealogies and the specificity of ethnic histories continue to cast long shadows, shaping contemporary Omani life through the growth of modern institutions, a capitalist economy, a national drive toward Arabization, and the propagation of a desectarian Islam through mass media and schooling.

I tracked Nizwa Fort, the dalla, and the sur al-Lawati across their quotidian roles and their significance in the twentieth and early twenty-first centuries. Their material forms became the focal point for a study of their embeddedness within the pervasive domain of state heritage and its institutional matrix of practices, the registration of how this hegemonic relationship relates to ordinary Omanis' modes of reasoning out the past, and the actions they took in accordance with that reasoning. On the one hand, there were those in Nizwa who had been staunch supporters of the imamate and whose sense of the past was conditioned by the ethical and historical discourse of Ibadi Islamic tradition. On the other, the al-Lawati in Muscat/Matrah had been staunch allies of the sultan and British against the imamate.

Nizwa is still considered emblematic of the "golden age" of the Ibadi Imamate from the eighth to the twelfth centuries and celebrated through heritage discourse as *bayḍat al-Islam* (the seat of Islam).[4] However, the twentieth-century imamate was rarely mentioned in the official histories. Over approximately two years (between 2009 and 2017), while staying with a local merchant family in Ghantaq, one of the city's oldest residential quarters, I learned what had happened in Nizwa over that period and how Nizwanis engaged their own sense of history in the present. I was introduced in the surrounding neighborhoods and included in household routines, visits with larger kinship networks, and regular meals in their homes. This mutual goodwill was deeply shaped by larger political regional forces; my being Pakistani and Muslim greatly facilitated the community's acceptance of my long-term residence and the ease with which I was enfolded into the daily activities of my host family. Living with them and sharing their lives also gave me a better sense of how a city of thousands could still seem so intimate. I could appreciate how long-standing networks and relationships created a face-to-face community that was continually reaffirmed through visits based on reciprocal obligations, a birth, a death, or a move to a new home.

It continually amazed me how so many in Nizwa knew each other—especially among the long-standing families—if not in person, then by reputation and name. Through these networks, I tracked the social and political interactions between residents and the city's key monuments and studied how local memories and histories, textual and oral, played out with forms of national imaginaries and global tourist narratives. This involved moving outward from the city's historic center, with its nexus at the fort, souq, and its oldest residential quarter, *harat al-'aqr*, toward the religious scholarly and mercantile families and tribes of the city who had once governed the region as part of the imamate. Many of these families had a scholarly lineage and had been renowned for their learning and work as judges and advisors under the Ibadi Imamate. Their members were now in the upper echelons of government or state-sponsored higher education. Many of the voices that appear in this book were born in the 1930s and 1940s and recalled the days of the imamate and the time of civil war and hardship in the 1960s, before the nahda era. Others were born in the mid-1960s or later; their voices articulate their parents' and grandparents' stories as well as a sense of how the past has been shaped by changes in the political present. My interviews and social visits included people from a range of backgrounds and livelihoods, from retired guards and judges to taxi drivers and shopkeepers, government officials, teachers, and venture capitalists.

From these interactions, I learned Nizwanis were subjected to heritage projects in Muscat and Nizwa. Modern roads had transformed the distance between the two cities from a journey of several days during the imamate era to a quick, ninety-minute car ride. People frequented the capital for work, school, and play. Many families with roots in Nizwa lived in Muscat, returning regularly to visit. My study of contemporary Omanis' interactions with the material traces of the past uncovered emotional ties, forms of consumption, political agency, social institutions, and ethical orientations toward history that were deeply shaped by state heritage and conservation projects, but in ways that were often incongruous with the state's telos of cultivating the "good citizen."

Like the forts of the interior, the aesthetic appearance of the al-Lawati fortified enclave, the sur al-Lawati, has been incorporated into the public spectacle of discursive heritage. Yet, their history right into the 1970s was tied to their origins on the Indian subcontinent and Shi'i geographical heartlands in Iran and Iraq. Among the al-Lawati community in Muscat/Matrah, I spent time wandering the sur, attending Shi'a *majālis*, and collecting life histories from middle- and upper-middle-class community members, including community elders, merchants, bureaucrats, teachers, journalists, and human rights activists.

An exploration of how members of both ethnic groups stake claims on the past provides an entryway toward exploring how the Nizwanis and the al-Lawati express their understandings of historical subjectivity in ways that are informed by being citizen-subjects and members of an Other indexed by ethnicity and religion. What became increasingly clear was that in the midst of the material plenty brought about by the oil boom, different ethnic communities were informed by state institutional techniques designed to regulate Omani subjects by organizing them into tribal kinship categories. Lineage purity anchored to tribal genealogical histories of the Arabian Peninsula became an integral component of state belonging, even as ethnic and religious differences were neutralized through the production of a national history rooted in "Omani civilization" and a "desectarian" Islam.

Set within these two paradoxical discursive constructions, the past as an integral component of nationhood is fraught with tensions that arise as individuals navigate the knotty terrain of community formation and an ethical sense of selfhood. Inasmuch as official practices of history assume the process of creating a territorially bounded homogeneity through the construction of a normative historical narrative, this has not led to assimilation among the populace. Instead, commitment to the virtues of shared values deployed by heritage discursive practices and a compulsion toward tribal lineage become springboards for divergent ways of relating to institutional histories, as different communities of Omanis enter these interactions from differential positions about what nationhood means to them.

Relating to heritage sites and objects develops through the pattern of ongoing experiences as part of the pragmatics of daily living. Negotiation with official histories and unofficial collective memories tied to a sharī'a past are enfolded into intensive debates among Nizwanis about the mode of moral-ethical living to be assumed in modern life. These debates are rooted in a variety of seemingly disparate experiences, the asymmetrical impact (unemployment, high cost of living) of modern state-driven socioeconomic change, social and political discrimination along tribal lines, and how the taint of slave ancestry influences marital choices. The al-Lawati, in turn, foreground their ties to the sur in justifying national belonging on a tangible level through their role as a mercantile elite whose labor has maintained Oman's prosperity for more than a century, even as the "lineage game" plays out in their daily lives through the politics of ethnic differentiation, Arabization, and class antagonisms between the al-Lawati and other ethnic communities.[5] Simultaneously, however, the sur is reworked as a religious space in ways that reinscribe inhabitants' sense of national "difference" as being Shi'i with alleged origins in the Indian subcontinent. Heritage thus becomes constitutive of a dynamic field in which religious, ethnic, and historical differences are worked and reworked in ways that produce new relationships with the material past. Heritage ceases to be a space of historic conservation insofar as these operations are inextricably tied to the ongoing transformation and construction of new possibilities for experiencing and acting on the past.

Scholarly Assumptions about Time in Oman

In scholarly writing on Oman's history, the shift from the Ibadi Imamate to modern nation-state building is usually addressed in terms of a polarizing rupture and discontinuity. Such writings map Oman's twentieth century onto its proximity to Western modernity. In effect, Oman's recent past assumes a series of binaries in which such terms as *backwardness, isolationism, tribal anarchy,* and *xenophobic religiosity* are strung together to contrast with the post-1970 *renaissance, modernization,* and *enlightened cosmopolitanism.* Titles such as *Oman and Its Renaissance* (Hawley 1977) and *The Reborn Land* (Clements 1980) encapsulate familiar official (state-sponsored) and unofficial narrative frameworks, a shorthand with which Western discourse represents Oman's late twentieth century.

In scholarship and popular literature, elucidating the contemporary era in Oman as a time of enlightenment necessarily entails the counterinvocation of a "traditional" imamate and the bleakness of zealous religiosity, tribalism, and poverty, albeit constituted as the markers of a bygone era. Oman has been explored primarily through the concept of the nahda—the "awakening" or "renaissance"—wherein Sultan Qaboos's accession to the throne in 1970 and new oil revenues established a modern state whose political organizations have forged nationwide modern educational institutions. This includes a far-reaching program for local health centers and clinics, a seemingly inexhaustible supply of government jobs, the construction of civil and urban infrastructure, and the organization of a private sector. A modernized and Westernized polity comes into view, one that has fundamentally reconfigured people's daily lives, relationships, and sociopolitical subjectivity.

Set within this teleological framework, Mandana Limbert's (2010) eloquent work explores Omanis' daily experiences and understandings of the nahda. Moving beyond a study of oil wealth in terms of statecraft, she deftly examines how the people of Bahla in the Omani interior understood the transformations in infrastructure, sociality, water, and connections with East Africa and absorbed these oil-produced changes by comparing their present to a past of "political instability and poverty" (3). In Limbert's study, state heritage is recognized as part of the infrastructural changes that have forged the notion of a national past. In a vivid analysis of Jabrin Fort through the eyes of Grandmother Ghania, she describes a sense of complete alienation from what the fort had become: "Ghania had been interested in seeing the house that she had heard so much about, of occupants who had directly influenced the governance of Bahla. . . . Instead there was a museum, almost empty, rebuilt and completely unreal . . . no longer part of the daily workings of the town" (26–27).

From this perspective of what Limbert describes as a growing emptiness between the rebuilt fort and the townspeople, one sees a binary structuring the impact of heritage on inner Oman, a textualized history that characterizes the state's official narrative against a premodern, organically inhabited memory, lived and embodied in communal relationships. Heritage practices are conceived as an ideological, artificial reconstruction that brings about only an alienation, increasingly removed from lived experience (Limbert 2008, 83–103). The experiential memory gives way to a fundamentally engineered historical sensibility, ultimately resulting in a sense of collective loss.

The appeal of this reasoning is considered along the lines of Eric Hobsbawm and Terence Ranger's (1983, 7–13) argument on the "invention of tradition." Through a paradigmatic process of inclusion and exclusion, architectures and objects in the region are construed as an evidentiary terrain in which a new mode of history is put to work toward authenticating novel practices and concepts—the nation-state, the people, and a ruling family—even as alternative modes of history are eliminated (Chatty 2009; Cooke 2014; Davis and Gavrielides 1991; Erskine-Loftus, al-Mulla and Hightower 2016; Exell 2016; Fromherz 2012; Khalaf 2000; Limbert 2010). In this analysis, heritage becomes an instrument that state elites deploy to destroy old ways of life and facilitate the emergence of new ones, while substantiating national legitimacy through promoting new forms of tradition as part of modern living. In other words, heritage practices are often considered byproducts of power struggles to shape collective memory and state ideology or means of mitigating conditions under rapid social change. Heritage is thus prone to being construed as a masking strategy that obfuscates reality (R. Harrison 2013; Smith 2006).

For Allen Fromherz (2012, 13), a more complex and conflictual history lies beneath the modern infrastructure of Qatar's urban builtscape, with its multistoried buildings, hypersupermarkets, five-star hotels, and a pervasive, almost mundane sense of serenity. Infrastructure, linked to history making, is a superficial effect of modernity, striking to the visitor but superfluous to the realities of Gulf societies. "True" historical knowledge, or rather "critical" history, exists prior to the processes of manipulation and dissemination that make up popular state discourse. With this set of presuppositions, the very act of selection under the aegis of the Gulf state becomes a political and psychological problem to be understood and resolved. The concept of history itself is at stake here, as it becomes the yardstick for assessing a state's modernity.

For Fromherz (2012, 16–17), the self-realization that the citizen of Qatar acquires "when they start assessing their own history critically and not according to the agenda of nation and Emir" leads to a psychological catharsis, paving the way toward a "fully experienced modernity" that is assumed to be a given. Any form of selection or manipulation is more than simply erroneous; conceded as a failure of modernity, it is understood as a potential deception that, when unmasked, will lead to the recognition of the self—a sign of a full modernity where complexities and conflicts prevail. Although Fromherz uses the word "critical," there is an assumption that this alternative, "more objective" mode of history is better able to convey the problems of modern life to the citizen, who is cushioned from its full effects by the state bulwark and its capacity to regulate history and tradition as a condition of daily living. The supposition is that within this alternative mode of history, one conceived as closer to that of the modern West, there lies the means toward truly grasping the "paradoxes of living in the now" (Fromherz 2013, 15–16).

Yet this understanding begs the very question as to whether there is any history that is not, by its constitution, selective. Fromherz's assumption that there is a "more objectively detached" history is never put into conversation with a scholarly literature that has problematized the very notion of the historical fact. Archival documents, excavated objects, or the material accoutrements of past daily life are the evidentiary sources for constructing a history. To fall into such a rubric in the first place, they are necessarily weighed down by modes of understanding and frames of inquiry. Such filtering and arrangement processes shape historical narratives in accordance with the work they are obliged to do, premised on larger historically and culturally grounded academic, political, and scientific institutional interventions (Hirschkind 1997a, 16–17). Any type of history, then, is necessarily conditioned along certain assumptions.

Such analytic approaches enforce a binary mode of thinking about the role of heritage practices in society. Binary contrasts such as mask/reality and inauthenticity/authenticity entrench a perspective that public participation (for example, visiting a museum) is mere rhetorical performance that should either be taken literally, embraced as an integral part of the national past, or with a strong sense of improbability, as something ideological that is not integral to daily living.

These scholarly writings raise important issues about the relationship between the exercise of power and knowledge, but they implicitly frame heritage practices as undermining any possibility of getting at genuine memories. Such an understanding assumes commonalities among the Gulf states, which become interchangeable, with "similar phases of professionalization, bureaucratization and commercialization" (Peutz 2017, 725) and in their emphasis on explaining how heritage works through "the values of the desert, Quran . . . immaculate white *disdasha* [male traditional tunic], stylized camel racing, miniature coffee cups" (Carapico 2004, 23). Such works call on scholarship to tear at the surface of institutional heritage in the Middle East to expose the constitutive role of institutions and actors of empire and nation building in giving rise to a state-driven heritage industry. Heritage is deemed a politicized tool, and the call goes out to get at the "true" history behind the fabrication.[6]

Stripping the mask away, as a growing trend of Gulf scholarship implies (Al-Rasheed and Vitalis 2004; Fromherz 2012), will generate oppositional histories, producing counterhistoriographies that enable participatory challenges and debates to the normative understanding of the past. Unofficial alternative histories, leaflets, magazines, and online forums that circulate in the region and beyond are valorized as resisting official versions of events by overturning narratives that have long secured the position of the nation-state. "True" historical knowledge, or "critical" history, is considered the key to liberation and the attainment of a self-realization free of the authoritarian mantle of the state. Local social and economic histories, the "voices" of subaltern memories, are posited as unproblematic means toward critiquing hegemonic forms of official history in order to establish an oppositional counterpart.

This approach to framing an inquiry correlates with a liberal positioning of the self-realized individual in opposition to the authoritative practices that define a community. The disciplinary regime of heritage practice is conceived as a constraining obstacle that represses personhood rather than a medium of productive possibilities that may generate the articulation of goods, virtues, and experiences internal to a normative understanding of tradition, history, heritage, and culture. Those subject to these history-making practices in their everyday lives are assumed to be self-constituted, autonomous human beings who are not so much shaped by a historical consciousness as much as subdued into either passively receiving or actively opposing the significance of heritage.

An Alternative Understanding

Studying heritage in the Gulf by tacking back and forth between such dichotomies as domination versus resistance and hegemony versus differentiation indexes how historical knowledge produces and maintains power relationships in ways that instantiate state governance and political authority. During my ethnographic fieldwork, however, I was repeatedly struck by how the institutional circuits of heritage discourse ceased to align with the explanation of being an instrument of state ideology, a "shoddy or sanitized form of history" (Peutz 2018, 7). Instead, public history had spilled out of heritage institutions to become constitutively enfolded into people's daily lives as part of a complex ethical and political way of being, thus forging a new normative reality. Omanis were voicing sentiments and advocating modes of political and ethical action in ways that cannot be mapped onto a polarity of repression/resistance. With the advent of the nahda, Oman's "renaissance," a new institutional mode of history has emerged that goes beyond truth and falsity to produce the effects of truth. I offer the following example, a rather amusing account that, for me, powerfully encapsulates the naturalization of heritage discourse among Omanis.

The account is one I heard from an archaeologist at Sultan Qaboos University. In emphasizing the changes he had seen in people's attitudes in what was once Ibadi Imamate territory, he recalled the story of a farmer from Ibra, in the Ash-Sharqiyah governorate of Oman. It was 2006. The farmer had traveled to the region of Shina in another governorate, al-Wusta, where the archaeologist was digging with his team. The farmer saw a large rock whose form he rather liked—a perfectly ordinary rock, but he liked its shape and color, so he sent for workers to take it to his farm in Ibra. The people of Shina witnessed the event and immediately told the archaeologist, also complaining to the wali (governor) that someone from another region had taken an important rock. The resulting uproar created something of a national incident; the Ministry of Heritage and Culture even sent a specialist to evaluate the rock's importance.

Laughing, the archeologist summarized his thoughts on how the national heritage project has transformed historical consciousness: "People of Oman originally used to break the famous ancient beehive tombs in the graves [at the World Heritage site of Bat in the northwestern governorate of al-Dhahirah]. They would break the slabs over the graves and build houses. . . . Today, they are upset because this man cut rocks in far-off mountains, which were nowhere near the beehive tombs. They assumed the rock was important. This is a huge [*ha'il*] difference in attitude. The level of consciousness . . . has gone up [*tataṣāʿud*]."

This account demands we restrain the impulse to "unmask" in order to take more seriously the disciplinary framework of heritage discourse and imagery in shifting people's conception of time and history as part of the nahda. It directs our attention to conceptual changes in the meaning and role of history as a lived reality among ordinary people in the former imamate territories. According to the archaeologist, a sense of the past and its vestiges among Omanis have been transformed; where once they saw building materials, they now see precious markers of the past that require safeguarding. His story intimates that state heritage practices have gone beyond representation to become generative, reworking Omani sensibilities about time as part of larger sociohistorical processes at work in the region. This book takes his assumptions seriously—that part of the experience of the nahda in the quotidian is marked by new conceptions of historical time that have subverted older notions of history. State heritage programs and policy making, in other words, produce a new temporal and political space in which modes of living modern lives have been fundamentally transformed.

The realm of heritage is approached not merely in its ability to instill ideologies, thus downgrading its truth to a function of state power and manipulation, but in its transformative potential to shape the perceptual habits of its audience. Material forms and their circulation through education and publicity assume an iterative aesthetic pedagogy that cultivates everyday civic virtues, new modes of religiosity, and forms of marking time, defining the ethical actions necessary to becoming a modern Omani through a framework of tradition. This systemic dissemination has been productive for organizing discussions on Omani history and emotional sensibilities and directing certain kinds of actions among state officials and laypeople alike. It becomes a series of spaces marked by people's contemplative thoughts of the past as they visit or work in museums, restored forts, or other history projects; pass historic sites in their daily life; and indulge in such routines as making coffee or baking bread, buying handicrafts to decorate their homes, or embarking on private ventures to preserve the past. Through these mundane activities, people are cultivating a broad awareness of time and place and an emotional sense of belonging and ethical mores through the deployment of the language of heritage. Prescribing a particular authoritative relationship with the past becomes the ground on which new citizen-subjects are created but is also a complex site where alternative modes of history and temporality from the pre-nahda era—imamate past, tribal hierarchies, and ethnic histories—become entangled and give rise to new sources of contestation. To the extent that historical critiques as utterances or actions among ordinary people would need to be intelligible as sociocultural or political interventions, one needs to understand how laypeople's principles and experiences of history are continually reworked as a productive force through being conditioned by available institutional forms of address about the past in order to render these critiques socially legible and authoritative (White 1987, 14).

Tradition and Heritage as Grounds for Change

While I agree with Limbert's analysis that reconstruction of the past has emerged as a new mode of governance in nahda Oman, my project looks more closely at how the sultanate's heritage discursive practices have authoritatively restructured the conception and role of imamate history in ways that inhabit the present, sustaining an active effect on the configuration of religion and community in the nation-state. Contingent historical circumstances and manners of relating to material sites and objects among Omanis as part of the process of subjectification cannot be reduced to a masking strategy, coercion, or mere absorption. My approach dovetails with an alternative framework that enables understanding the forcible impact of institutionalized history making through its ability to foster affective ties and intimacies in ways that reproduce heritage as a mode of governance, even as it may serve to generate transformative political and ethical effects.

In her work on the politics of environmental conservation on the World Heritage site of Socotra in Yemen, Nathalie Peutz (2018) explores how the process of instilling the language of natural heritage, through discourse and material institutions, acts as the generative basis for recuperating the discursive grammar of heritage for the production of new forms of grassroots political empowerment. Soqotrans sought to reorient the focus of heritage from the natural environment to culture in order to make claims for their indigenous language and way of life in the midst of social and political upheaval. Overlapping to some degree with Peutz, Chiara De Cesari's work (2019) explores how heritage initiatives in Palestine, through advocating for historical conservation and urban rehabilitation projects in the occupied territories, consolidate their claim to sovereignty and rights over these lands, even while the discursive language of heritage instantiates new provisional and innovative modes of local governance. In relating to the logic within which material objects and sites have been co-opted by the Omani state, we see how heritage making lays claim to the uniformly common tie of citizenship and its civic values through the act of labor in ways that do not merely exert institutional authoritative power. Labor also becomes the generative site among Omanis to claim rights of citizenship and sameness by addressing the social and economic inequalities brought about by state-driven modernization, ethnic and tribal hierarchical discrimination, and the persistent taint of slave descent in ways that mobilize and harness alternative understandings of the past. In their banality and resourcefulness, conformity and alterity to national institutional historical narratives and expressions, these acts of interpreting the material past are entangled with everyday living and become unexpected sites for the study of politics of history and memory.

Multiple Rationales of Tradition

A chief problem in studying discursive constructions about the past in the Gulf region is problematizing the notion of *adāt wa taqālīd* (customs and traditions) among locals, in this case Omanis. A primary scholarly approach to the concept of tradition has been to view it within a dichotomous framework: if modernity is associated with creativity, choice, and adaptability, tradition is a static repetition of habits handed down from the past and inflexible to conscious modification. In this understanding, the two concepts appear coconstitutive, sustaining a bifurcated set of normative assumptions: the invariable repetition of the past, in opposition to a modernity premised on continual change. This concept of tradition appears to exist only to naturalize the Western modernist conception of homogenous time (Agrama 2012, 13–14).[7]

This assumption prescribes to tradition a static quality, ultimately incompatible with a fundamentally changing future (Koselleck 2004). As Dipesh Chakrabarty (2000) suggests, the narrative of progress constructs, in its deployment, kinds of difference that become anachronisms. Although progress lies at the heart of modernity projects, the persistence of the past in traditions, objects, or languages can pose challenges to the agency of the living. In this progressive temporal narrative, the past can be abandoned as a burden incommensurable with a changing future. Alternatively, it can be allowed to persist through recalibration to the imperatives of secular rule (Koselleck 2002, 115–31). The question is, what type of refiguration must occur for tradition to cease being an obstacle to modernity? How should the past be "correctly" understood and deployed to facilitate an Omani modernity?

In examining these questions, I build on the pioneering perspective of Talal Asad (2003, 222–23), who explores "the way time authoritatively constitutes present practices and the way authenticating practices invoke or distance themselves from the past" through how it reinterprets forms of history and memory. I interpret Asad's words to suggest that there may be an alternative set of analytic questions to pose for the notion of tradition. This involves a closer examination of the perception of continuity—the frame through which the past's relevance to the future is interpreted, the modes through which it is translated, and the grammatical bases that delineate the possibilities of (and the limits on) what can be said and done with respect to the past. What is at stake in such a formulation is how ideas about temporal linkages (between past, present, and future) change and how these relationships structure a living past. These queries overlap with those of Reinhart Koselleck (2004, 3), who directs attention to the tensions between the space of experience and the horizon of expectation to examine "how, in a given present, are the temporal dimensions of past and future related?"

Sundering the simple binary between "tradition" and "modernity," Alasdair MacIntyre's (1984) study of tradition emphasizes that how the past is experienced becomes part of a living relationship with the present and may be of particular value in opening possibilities. A living tradition is part of a "historically extended, social embodied argument concerning the pursuit of goods" (MacIntyre 1984, 222) that constitutively defines what is "proper" in the context of a community and delineates how moral logics enter into the practices of everyday lives. This perspective is evident in a growing body of anthropological literature on ethics and religion and its relationship with temporality, practices, and pedagogy (Asad 1993; Hirschkind

2006; S. Mahmood 2005). Tradition, in this sense, becomes part of a reflection on the past that is constitutive of a set of prescriptive practices whose performance enables the generative unfolding of a specific type of subject and sense of personhood. These scholars recognize that the virtues, experiences, and categories that are considered internal to the pedagogical practices of practical, scholarly, and embodied forms of knowledge also connect practitioners across temporal domains.

The past ceases to be a cyclical repetition of cultural prescriptions or a veneer of stable continuity whose symbols act as a vehicle to facilitate the dynamic present. Instead, it becomes fundamental in grounding an ongoing, discursive set of engagements into doing the moral and epistemological work of pursuing established ideas about the "good." The outcome is a set of embodied practices through which these understandings and their histories are enacted in the pursuit of such a telos. The past is no longer an unchanging substance but rather a distinctive way of imagining history's relationship to the present and future that engenders specific practices and styles of argumentation and critique. It is the very stuff through which change can occur.

Attuned to the connections between past, present, and future in twentieth- and twenty-first-century Oman that underlie the different "regimes of historicity" (Hartog 2003) that anchor the authority of the Ibadi Imamate and the Sultanate of Oman, this approach goes beyond a study of how discursive modes of history and history making are enacted and subverted to examine how authoritative temporal logics, institutions, and imaginations are experienced in northern Oman. Simultaneously, this study answers Rodney Harrison's (2013, 9) call for a greater focus in heritage studies on "the affective qualities of material things and the influences the material traces of the past have on people in the contemporary world."

The trajectories of these objects, the values they embody, and the uses to which they are put as material indexes of history become active to shifts in historical knowledge, periodization, and its transformative implications on the nature of polity, sovereignty, and ethical practice among the populace. But they have done so, in Webb Keane's (2016, 10) succinct words, as "ethics that run quietly through ordinary everyday activities." Systemically disseminated through repetitive patterns to emphasize new perceptions of history and experiences of tradition in, for example, museums, textbooks, media, and street sculptures, these objects and sites produce "ethical affordances" (Keane 2016, 27–32). As ethical affordances, they yield an embodied knowledge that feeds into people's evaluations of their sense of self and decision making about how they want to live or should live. However, the role these objects play in sustaining a national ethical tradition among Omanis does not necessarily imply that they are wholly integrated into the singular logic of state heritage practices and visual iconography. Daily interactions with these sites and objects direct our attention to how socialized senses of history and ethics are being nurtured through state heritage discourse and toward desires that impinge on the work of heritage. These processes power alternative collective memories that may exist only as fragments but make possible distinctive forms of critique and suggest alternative ethical modes of living (Pandian 2008). This pushes us to consider how the ethical practices deployed by objects and sites are not merely "goods" that are internal to the discursive and visual logics of heritage. Rather, the intensity of the "ordinary effects" of these material forms (Steward 2007) for Omanis lies in their ties to other discursive practices—global tourism, religiosity, economic and political regulation, and development as part of state building. It is within these entangled practices and their contradictory logics that Omanis pursue judgments on how to live ethical lives.

Heritage Work in Oman

Ibadi Imamate's establishment in 1913 was considered to be a culmination of three processes: (1) the British regulation and blockade of trade in enslaved people and arms into the region, (2) the active presence of British troops and naval squadrons, and (3) increasingly strident protests against what was widely considered the tyrannical regime of the British-supported sultan. Chapter 1 looks at these policies, exploring the ways in which they were understood and acted upon according to two distinctive concepts of historical time. The first was the British understanding of progressive historicity that, buttressed by imperial gunboat diplomacy and the steamship, aimed to extend "civilization" across the region. This understanding entailed total transformation of the land and social order to leave behind the "tribal anarchy" and "xenophobic religiosity" of the past. The second was the Ibadi Imamate's, in which tradition, in accordance with Ibadi sharīʿa, was not the enemy of change but the ground on which change could occur. It was undergirded by a history that held that everyday interactions and relationships were grounded in the Quran and could be assessed with reference to exemplary forms of justice and morality from the past. Everyday virtues, such as reciprocity, generosity, or forbearance, were considered as the ongoing articulation of disciplined practices and moral criticism based on time-honored discursive models. But a discursive and affective engagement with history also included calls for a revolution to overthrow sultanic rule, whose authority stemmed not from sharīʿa but from a Christian power, the British. Historical logic not only grounded the intent behind the rise of the last Ibadi Imamate (1913–1955) but also was incorporated into thought and action by both sides to condition a moral relationship that brought about a confrontation of cultures with different modes of conceptualizing the relationship between religion and politics.

Chapter 2 focuses on two forms of material heritage once integral to the governance of the twentieth-century Ibadi Imamate: Nizwa Fort and the dalla. These modes of governance were presided over by the hulking contours of the fort, in its role as sharīʿa adjudicator, and circulated by the form and function of the dalla as part of daily social interactions in the sabla. The past became a knowledge that was read, recited, and debated while being sedimented in an embodied disposition. Through daily readings and discussion, local affairs and conflicts were addressed by honing a relationship to the past that cultivated and amended disposition, thought, and action on the basis of exempla. It was a past that was primarily moral, oriented toward God, and grounded in tribal mores and Ibadi doctrine and practice. Both material forms facilitated a history that held that life's interactions and relationships could be sanctioned and critiqued based on past forms that also held templates for future action. This conception of history formed the foundation of religiosity, law, governance, and ethics.

The roles of manuscripts, objects, and buildings during the imamate underwent a drastic transformation as they were inscribed into the discursive and visual idioms of heritage production and linked to the broader nation-state project. Oman before the systemic dissemination of heritage and Oman after are different entities. Chapter 3 looks at the public spaces that have come into being; museums, heritage festivals, monuments, street montages, and exhibits have heralded the nahda in a dual sense—an epochal break from the past, even as they celebrate the "return" and the immanence of this history in the present. These values and principles have fundamentally reorganized historical experiences and cultivated new sensibilities and emotional links, providing the context for shaping the nation. In the process, the mode of museal representation that is heritage cleaved the temporal assumptions of sharīʿa time and its relations to the past. The materiality of objects and sites, including sharīʿa manuscripts and mosques, assume an iterative, pedagogical mode of representation through which historical-national claims, histories, and heritage objects substantiate the sultanate. It may assume such intimacy as wearing the Omani disdasha, even as it climbs to the heights of widely mediatized historic discourses and aesthetics around "national day" spectacles. These material effects cultivate everyday national civic virtues and new forms of religiosity and of punctuating time, defining the ethical actions necessary to become an Omani modern citizen through the framework of tradition. Heritage discursive practices work toward absorbing tribal hierarchical differences as well as sectarian and ethnic variability and transforming them into sameness.

This new mode of historical experience also becomes the site for the reconfiguration of the Ibadi religious imagination and affinities. This is felt in the emergence of new arrangements in religion and politics cultivating the new citizen-subject, now versed in belonging to a territorially bounded nation-state. Set within a new conceptual vocabulary of "culture" and "civilization," the doctrinal specificity of Ibadi Islam is politically defanged, erasing any awareness of the sociopolitical and ethical relationships that once characterized imamate rule and British informal governance, paving the way for a hereditary sultanate.

In the liberal West, although heritage becomes fundamental to the project of defining and living the modern, it is still carefully delineated within a separate realm labeled "heritage" (R. Harrison 2013). Boundaries between past and present create a sense of contemporaneity, while providing distinct ways to endorse the perception that the past is irrevocably past, safely categorized as "tradition" or "nostalgia." Liberalism emphasizes the self-owning individual, free from the confines of custom and tradition, capable of achieving moral and intellectual autonomy. In Oman, meanwhile, the presence of heritage dismantles temporal boundaries; past and present flow together, inextricably grounding the ways in which the modern is lived. The past still registers as having claims on the present and the future, even though an exemplary, authoritative history is no longer the basis for directing them. The prospect of an ever-changing and uncertain future is now understood as the locus of authority on which the past and present are calibrated. It is on this basis of organizing time that history becomes a transcendental anchor.

Limbert (2010, 10) observes that the Bahlawi construe Oman's future in terms of uncertainty, "with the expectation of an oil and Sultan-less future." She is referring to an awareness of an indeterminate, open future, due to heightened sensibilities about the precarious nature of oil reserves in Oman and questions about the succession of a childless sultan.[8] Endorsing this sense of instability among Omanis, I examine how the state has increasingly institutionalized this understanding of a precarious future in the wake of encroaching Westernization, economic strains, global reductions in the price of oil, and geopolitical struggles to define Islam. In the face of such variables, the state mobilizes a past that aims to shape citizens' desires and daily practice in ways that allow them to confront unpredictable encounters by orienting practical reasoning in the face of the unplanned.

A historically grounded ethical mode of reasoning is being instilled as part of citizenship, one that is capable of adapting to uncertain socioeconomic and political conditions through being rooted to fundamental ethical virtues and principles that define the national past. Tooled with the right techniques of ethical discipline, as chapter 4 elucidates, by way of education, mass media, and museums, citizens are conceived as containing the deportment to navigate the tides of modernization by filtering their changing circumstances through heritage as a lived reality, made of values and principles that define proper conduct and established by the more positive aspects of Oman's past. For the state, history ceases to be merely a matter of abstract cognition; the past becomes constitutive of the evaluative capacities deemed necessary for the citizen to be continually immersed in through daily acts of modern living.

The historical sensibilities cultivated by the state were ideally meant to transform the relationship between the government and its population and create a uniform and stable sense of equality. What emerges from ethnography (chapters 5, 6, and 7), however, is that even as this new historical consciousness imposes a normative way of living modernity, it is continually undermined through entanglements with alternative logics of governance. The very act of establishing a historical grammar in the public sphere involves gaps and contradictions. Tensions emerge with the state's efforts to work through hierarchical forms of belonging—buried by state heritage projects—such as (1) regulating socioeconomic material transformations and their uneven effects on social interactions, (2) managing tribal kinship relations, and (3) ethnic differences. These disjunctures lie at the core of what passes as a unifying history and temporality, opening space for contention and debate. Simultaneously, the creation of critique within the space opened by heritage institutions further entrenches heritage discursive practices through the questions it raises about the social impact of conservation projects, the role of Islam in a tribally oriented society, and tensions between ethnicity, history, and politics.

In Nizwa (chapter 5), socioeconomic instabilities and their effects are powerfully shaped by the felt gap between national historical narratives and the utopian aspirations and civic values that are intimately associated with them. Among laypeople, the language of heritage becomes a discursive medium and a practical enterprise for economic and political claims making through such ethical principles as social solidarity, generosity, and interpersonal consultation, which are continually undermined by the state's restructuring of the urban fabric of the city. Through tracking people's relationships to the old residential quarters, the fort, and the souq of Nizwa, I examine how this contradictory state of affairs has opened a space for alternative memory practices that invoke the Ibadi Imamate, while acting as a broader critique of the sultanate's governance practices.

Developments in mass education and political participation in Oman as a nation-state have substantiated claims of a homogenous history, where each citizen is integrated into the state through a system of legal rights and obligations. For many Omanis, specifically those of *mawla*, or "client," lineage (versus free "Arabs")—due to their patrilineal descent from enslaved people or members of a historically subjected tribe—the structural transformations that have led to mass urbanization, education, and welfare have also resulted in a rise in status and occupation. The nahda also led to the abolishment of slavery (chapter 6), including the use of the term *mawla*, as part of the operation toward creating a united citizenry. However, many Nizwanis (and others) construe state management of tribal hierarchies and kinship ties to be in direct contradiction to the state's discourse of a common history and culture. Moreover, the importance of genealogy is officially sanctioned by a recalibrated sharīʿa, now relegated to the domain of family or personal status law, through the principle of *kafāʾa*, or equivalence in marriage. This paradox has produced widely acknowledged tribal discrimination in the workplace and in marriage. It has also resulted in fiery debates about the relationship between the Islamic discursive tradition, differential status accorded by tribal genealogies, and intermarriage in ways deeply informed by the lived realities of nationhood, including liberal notions of equality, human rights, and capitalist modernity.

Chapter 7 explores the sur al-Lawati, the fortified enclave of the al-Lawati, a non-Arab, non-Ibadi mercantile community historically oriented toward the British Raj, staunchly allied to the pre-1970 Muscat sultanate, and grounded in a Shiʿi geography. This community has been incorporated into Oman's national historical narration and iconic imagery. Their differences with the Arab and Ibadi population are managed through the state's governing logics of a common history and tribalization, even while these institutional mechanisms apportion the space in which one emerges as an Omani citizen. This dense assemblage of key elements both limits and opens possibilities for political engagement and participation in state planning and policy making. These terms of reference formulate the space in which the "differences" that sum up the al-Lawati are managed within the community and with outsiders, defining the terms of their political and religious belonging and the referential basis by which they participate in public life (outside the sur) versus private life (inside the sur).

Even though the forms heritage assumes in Oman may seem familiar, inasmuch as they are global, their significance is best understood within the parameters of a regional history. People's mundane engagements with the traces of the material past are subjected to hegemonic visual and discursive practices, even as their understandings turn fluid as they are subjected to changes in the region, such as those that gave rise to the Arab Spring protests of 2011 and the economic downturn of 2014, and struggles over the definition of Islam as manifested by the rise in Islamist reform movements and sectarian divides. In recent years, these momentous changes have embedded themselves in how Omanis relate to the material past as part of daily living.

Drawing all these threads together, my project shifts the conceptualization of history from an intellectual exercise to a governing intervention that has actively transformed people's daily lives through refiguring religious and political realities. In Oman, "inhabiting" heritage forms the nexus of competing modes of engagement with material objects and landscapes, even as it mobilizes the very different anxieties that this history offers. Material forms produce a unique register for the exploration of the embodiment of multiple temporalities while destabilizing the modernist notion of time and its ties to global conservation practice. In studying the modes through which people relate to them, new possibilities arise in the ways objects and sites may articulate distinctive geographic, temporal, and epistemological spaces that are enabled by but not reducible to socio-political forces.

REFORM AND REVOLT THROUGH THE PEN AND THE SWORD

In May 1913, the Arab tribes in the Omani interior rose up in rebellion against Sultan Faiṣal bin Turkī (r. 1888–1913) and elected Salim ibn Rashid al-Kharusi as imam, establishing the last Ibadi Imamate (1913–1955), an entity that had been almost fifty years in abeyance. This act effectively created two governing bodies that held sway over a much-contested region—the imamate in inner Oman, with its capital in Nizwa, and the Sultanate of Muscat, supported and enabled by the British along the coastal regions, with its centers in Muscat and Matrah.[1] This was a climactic moment in the colonial struggle. The British were attempting to secure geostrategically important communicative routes to the British Raj at a time when imperial influence in the Arabian Peninsula had reached its zenith.

The British and the Ibadis alike perceived the rise of the imamate as the culmination of three active policies. First was the regulation and blockade of trade in slaves and arms, which the Ibadis saw as permitted in Islam. Second was the presence of British troops and naval squadrons in Oman. Finally, the general economic circumstances, already exacerbated by the First World War, were characterized by a blockade on all goods into the interior and enforced duties paid by all ships passing through Muscat—part of Britain's economic pressure on the crucial date trade, engaged by the increasingly strident rebels in the interior.

This chapter argues that the rise of a resistance movement among the Omanis who rallied around the revival of the Ibadi Imamate resulted from two types of temporal consciousness that gave rise to distinctive modalities of action and ways of being: (1) a distinctive religious movement that sought to establish an imamate grounded in Ibadi doctrine and law and (2) British geopolitical maneuverings to secure the Indian Ocean trade networks. Each temporal project differed in its understanding of the nature of historical change. The restoration of the Ibadi Imamate was a utopian ambition that addressed the external onslaught on daily living brought about by British imperial interventions in Omani affairs from the mid-nineteenth century onward. The uprising called for overthrow of the sultan's regime, widely considered arbitrary and "corrupt," and ousting of the British, on whom the sultan increasingly depended. As the political agent and consul Major L. B. H. Haworth conceded in Muscat, "his government is so bad that to continue to support it in its existing condition is nothing short of immoral."[2]

However, to understand the conceptualization and nature of the Ibadi state that arose from the 1913 rebellion, we must also examine the competing temporal vision of the colonial administrators who were attempting to transform the coastal region by rendering it consonant with the geostrategic goals of safeguarding the Raj and fulfilling such liberal goals as suppressing the slave trade. Through analyses of the temporal assumptions embedded in textual narratives, ranging from colonial correspondence to historic texts that were widely disseminated in the imamate, I have found that even as each endeavor unfolded within divergent senses of history, each vision was constitutively implicated in the other, in terms of both material constraint and imaginative possibilities of defining an enemy and acting accordingly. Implementing these two visions of the future culminated in a series of imamate conquests of the interior over the next two years, including the forts of Nizwa, Izki, and Samā'il. Despite repeated warnings, the imamate tribes attacked, convinced that the war with Germany would keep the British government from its obligation to support the sultan. In April 1914, owing to interior tribes' forays into the coastal areas, where large numbers of British Indian merchants were centered, the ports of Barka and Qaryat were bombarded by the HMS *Fox* and the HMS *Dartmouth* (Persian Gulf Political Residency 1873–1957, vol. 7, 41). Tribal incursions ended in a rout in Muscat in 1915, when they faced Indian army troops at Bait al Falaj Fort. On January 7, British reinforcements arrived—950 men of the 102nd King Edward's Own Grenadiers and the 95th Russell's Infantry—furnishing a protective shield for the towns of Muscat and Matrah and fulfilling an 1895 guarantee to the sultan that no attacks would be allowed on these towns, whatever differences the sultan might have with the tribes (Persian Gulf Political Residency 1873–1957, vol. 7, 105). The guarantee extended to the Batinah coast in the northwest.[3] Until 1955, however, the rebels had complete control over Oman proper and an organized government. They remained thereafter in undisputed possession of Oman, posing a constant threat to the coastal towns and cities. In his correspondence, as will be noted below, Haworth leaves little doubt that the Ibadi tribes could have taken the coast, if not for the British garrison at Bait al Falaj and the presence of British gunships along the coast.

This vision of the imamate promised to restore a mode of governance grounded in the will of God, as embodied in Ibadi sharīʿa, part of a sectarian tradition that had predominated for more than a millennium. Guided by that ubiquitous injunction *amr al-maʿrūf wa nahy ʿan al-mūnkar* (commanding the right and forbidding the wrong), it undertook the return of an imam who, in accordance with the fundamentals of Ibadi doctrine, would be elected through consultation by the ahl al-hal wal ʿaqd (leading scholars and tribal leaders of the region) rather than through seizure of power. Justice would once more be conducted in accordance with the opinions and rulings of the ʿulamāʾ (scholars and jurists) and grounded in the Quran, the exemplary words and deeds of the Prophet (sunna), his companions, and the righteously guided imams across the ages. The British would be driven into the sea, and God's law would return. Arms and ammunition would once more be sold in Muscat, slave dealing would prosper, and wine and tobacco would no longer be sold. In temporal logic, the imamate movement was tethered to a recursive vision of restoration and renewal.

Yet these aspirations existed side by side with equally complex visions articulated in the textual correspondence and reports of colonial administrators and soldiers, who sought a complete innovation of the Omani coastal region's religiosity and sociopolitical order—a more linear vision of progress. In this vision, reconfiguration of the coastal regions would come about through harnessing technology (gunships, steamboats, and the telegraph) and financial instruments (loans). These were embedded in a set of underlying assumptions that necessitated radically transforming the mode of governance in the Omani coast by "developing" it in unprecedented ways that not only were amenable to long-term British imperial interests in the region but also aimed to create a new "man," transformed by new institutions put in place by the British to ensure an institutionally durable rule under the sultan rather than the instability of tribal war.

Developing a Futurist Vision of the Sultanate of Muscat

Colonial correspondence of the early twentieth century is replete with descriptions of the Ibadi revolt as "retrograde," an "outburst of religious fanaticism," or "xenophobia" that expose their own implication in the material predicament of the besieged Ibadi tribes. When British officers described late nineteenth-century and early twentieth-century Oman as "divisive," "uncivilized," "piratical," and "backward," they were describing the effects of sociopolitical and economic conditions that were largely due to their own exploitative governance of the region.

Although Oman was not a formal colony, it fell within a sphere of influence that encompassed the Arab-Persian Gulf region.

Absorbing Oman into a narrative of universal history, British travelogues, correspondence, and official reports describe the Arabs of the Oman region through the matrix of antitheses: civilization and barbarity, Christianity and Islam, modernity and a "traditional" ahistorical cycle with "constant fighting and trouble especially when one imam or sultan died and another was elected."[4] The fundamental assumption of tribal chaos and infighting became a habitual way of thinking about the region, spurring the 1895 British declaration of unequivocal support to the sultan (whoever he might be) through the use of naval force against any tribal sheikh who threatened the stability of the coastal zones (Bailey 1988, 3:326). According to Haworth, the "principle of self-determination" for the tribes of Oman could be allowed only "based on some signs of movement towards progress . . . and the interest of civilization must be the deciding factor"[5] Oman's past, which was also its present, did not align itself with the expectations underlying this understanding of progress filtered through Indian spectacles.

Oman was just 1,600 kilometers from the port of Surat, where the East India Company first established itself (only a little farther than the distance between Muscat and Kuwait). Having eradicated the French threat in the nineteenth century, Britain's interests in the early twentieth-century Gulf region were primarily strategic—safeguarding the telegraph lines along the Arab Gulf coastlines, speeding communication between London and India (Muscat had a cable station on the route between Karachi and Aden, Yemen), and ensuring the safety of British shipping lanes to Persia, Iraq, Muscat, and India.[6] These were the primary routes for the British India Steam Navigation Company from the late nineteenth century onward, incorporating major Gulf ports such as Basra, Qatif, Manamah, Muscat, and Dubai on the way to and from Bombay.

Once a necessary commercial port of call / central entrepôt in the Gulf trade networks, Muscat's importance had waned with the introduction of steam power. This faster means of transport was fundamental to the imposition of an imperial trading and communication regime that was favorable to British strategic interests, as competition from the steamships reduced the profitability of Oman's local shipping fleet. Most of the transport trade that Muscat had once catered to the smaller Persian and Arab ports had disappeared, owing to the direct visits of steamers from India and Europe to these ports (Persian Gulf Political Residency 1873–1957, vol. 7, 103).

The opening of the Suez Canal in 1869, which cut shipping time from months to weeks, played a significant role in overall British policy for ensuring the safety of the British Raj, as the stability of shipping lines in and around the Arabian Peninsula assumed paramount importance (Landen 1967; Onley 2007; Wingate

1959). Progress in Oman was thus tied to the region, becoming part of the buffer zone for the defense of India. In the aftermath of World War I, control of Muscat, through a stranglehold on the Gulf, assumed even greater importance in view of British commitments in Iraq.[7]

Thus, on the one hand, the British government's attitude in the late nineteenth and early twentieth centuries was to abstain from involvement with dynastic disputes or intertribal feuds and wars (Saldanha 1906, 13). This informal mode of colonial governance was considered an "improvement" over direct rule, inasmuch as "a country is improved by the advice and development of its own internal powers rather than by its absorption and by its direct management"[8] On the other hand, "civilizing" the Arab-Persian Gulf necessitated a cleansing and reorganization to ensure the pursuit and enforcement of measures that would define the relationship between Oman and British informal governance. Measures against slave trafficking and piracy and regulation of the traffic of arms and armaments thereby towed the region into the broader space of exchange that defined the civilizational flow that enabled the Indian Ocean's imperial trading and political networks. This entailed preventing the "disturbance of maritime peace" and protecting "the interests and property of British subjects" (Saldanha 1906, 13). Accordingly, it was considered preferable for the British political resident to recognize, protect, and entrench local coastal rulers and "customary" rule, holding these rulers responsible for their subjects' transgressions rather than enforcing the treaties. This was one of the primary tools in the British bag of imperial political strategies: the recognition and protection of local chiefs and rulers (Mamdani 1996; Newbury 2003). As they saw it, implementation of their policies was easier with a few malleable rulers than navigating the tribal groupings, with their sheikhs and their variable relationships. Their "independent" status notwithstanding, these regions were as integrated into British imperial rule as formal colonies. Internal "self-development" involved heavy-handed imperial intervention on the coastlines that led to forcible transformations of everyday social, political, and economic lives, and not only on the coast.

In other words, the British government was unwilling to extend its power beyond the reach of its naval gunships (Persian Gulf Political Residency 1873–1957, vol. 7, 64). These gunships, which could turn an attack into a surrender through their very presence, forged the constitutive unit of what was the most powerful force in the region. At the behest of the British political resident, the Gulf Squadron of the Indian Navy (later the Royal Indian Navy) presided over the Gulf as a British lake, with no real rivals in the region.[9] With the entry of steam as a crucial mode of modern power in the development of the Gulf region, Oman increasingly existed through the categories and actions that emerged through its relationship with Great Britain, whose support was decisive to the continuity of the

Āl Bu Saʻidi dynasty. These transformations were the direct consequence of a series of defined imperial interests that sought to modernize the Gulf through Britain's position there—the economic and technological modernization of the Arab-Persian Gulf region, the banning of the slave trade, and the regulation of arms trade and gunrunning.

Presided over by the British in 1861, Oman's legal separation from Zanzibar effectively created two sultanates, while destroying a once powerful integrated economy. This left Oman dependent on its own resources, which were now separated from the success of Zanzibar's clove plantations and industry and the prosperity it had once brought.[10] Sultan Thuwaini of Oman was compensated for this arrangement by the Canning Award, an annual grant of 40,000 Maria Theresa thalers (Rs. 86,400), paid from 1883 onward through the government of India (Bailey 1988, 3:318). Oman lost its navy and, no longer a part of the trading network with Zanzibar, saw a steady decline in trade with East Africa. With less than 5 percent of its land under agriculture, the region had little to export except dates, dried fish, pomegranates, and dried limes. Oman was increasingly dependent on the outside world for such staples as rice, sugar, tea, coffee, textiles, wood for boats, and kerosene. However, trade at this point was almost wholly facilitated by British subjects (resident Indian merchants who now had a virtual monopoly), transported on European steamers, and primarily conducted with the British Raj.[11] When Lieutenant Colonel S. B. Miles (1910, 176) visited Nizwa in 1885, the governor told him "the textile and embroidery industries, once so famous and extensive, had entirely disappeared." Within a few decades, even the cotton cloth worn by a tribesman in the interior was an import manufactured in Lancashire and brought in via steamships (Landen 1967, 80).

By the early twentieth century, the British dominions' trade with Muscat amounted to "about five-sixths of the country's entire trade" (Saldanha 1906, 59). Even the Arab traders of the interior were not considered true traders; they were buying and selling from the Banians and Khojas of Muscat and Matrah, who had full control of prices and supplies (Persian Gulf Political Residency 1873–1957, vol. 7, 62). The relationship of political ascendency, which brought the state of Muscat into the British sphere of influence, culminated in an 1891 agreement in which the sultan undertook "never to cede, to sell, to mortgage or otherwise give for occupation, save to the British Government, the dominions of Muscat and Oman or any of their dependencies" (Saldanha 1906, 59; see also Bailey 1988, 3:321).

The loss of local prosperity and ensuing stagnation, especially among the Arabs, led to a rapid decline in population in the port cities, many returning to home villages in the interior or migrating in increasing numbers to Zanzibar from the

1870s onward. Many Omanis turned to subsistence agriculture on date planta-tions or to fishing or engaged in illicit gunrunning and slave transport, which be-came a primary activity of the coastal economy. In a century, the Omani economy, once an imperial mercantile and shipbuilding enterprise at the heart of the In-dian Ocean trade networks, was increasingly agrarian and localized. The economic life of the interior still largely depended on the export of agricultural produce, as well as on the illegal but lucrative trade in slaves and arms.

To be processed for export, agricultural products, especially dates, had to make their way through Arab and Indian middlemen and dealers to the coastal ports. Such products were therefore subject to a number of taxes—a basic source of rev-enue for the sultanate. The leaders of the imamate revolt considered many of these new customs as "innovations," not in keeping with sharīʿa. These became stigmatized as marks of tyranny, especially when used as leverage to manipulate imamate affairs—as in 1920, when disputes with the sultan (with British support) led to a penalty that raised export taxes on produce from the interior from 5 percent to 25 percent on all dates and 50 percent for pomegranates (Bailey 1988, 3:17–18). As in Britain's dealings with the Ottoman Empire, including Egypt, for-eign loans and subsidies were key financial instruments in transforming Oman into "a progressive and self-supporting satellite bound to Britain by natural ties of finance and commerce" (Cain and Hopkins 1993, 404). The empire's control over customs revenues, through British Indian merchants, served as security for loans taken out by the sultan (Wingate 1959, 77).[12]

A primary subsidy was an annual sum of Rs. 86,400, representing the 40,000 payable by Zanzibar to Muscat under the Canning Award of 1861. The British government assumed responsibility for this payment in 1871 and, from 1883 on-ward, the British Raj used it to suppress the East African slave trade. Generated by evangelical and humanitarian fervor, the British drive to abolish the slave trade was borne out in a series of treaties (1822, 1839, and 1845), reluctantly signed by the ruler of the Omani Empire, limiting slavery in the Omani dominions. In 1873, Sir Bartle Frere, a leading abolitionist, persuaded Sultan Turkī (r. 1871–1888) to sign a treaty outlawing not only the lucrative slave trade (though not the owner-ship of slaves) but also public and private sales of slaves.[13] In 1873, the Muscati and Zanzibari states both issued proclamations making the slave trade (import and export) illegal. This intervention was outrageous to the Ibadi opposition, since slavery was conceived as integral to tribal society and in accordance with sharīʿa. From the 1860s, British naval cruisers along the Omani coast choked off the slave trade, although small boats could still slip through (Lorimer 1915, 2:2475–516).

Sultan Turkī signed the antislavery proclamation out of a combination of finan-cial need and a need to strengthen his crumbling rule; the loss of customs revenues and private income had increased his financial reliance on Britain.[14] In 1873, as an inducement to give up the lucrative slave trade, Sir Bartle Frere was empowered to offer the Canning Award, to be paid in perpetuity to the lawful sultan of Muscat, provided he continued "faithfully to fulfil his treaty engagements and manifest his friendship towards the British Government" (Lorimer 1915, 2:2475–516; see also British Foreign Office 1987, 2:186). The Canning Award formed a vital part of the sultan's annual revenues, ultimately becoming a means for the British to maintain control over his actions.

Another annual subsidy from the British government, beginning in 1912, amounted to Rs. 1 lakh (100,000). The "arms traffic subsidy" was made in compensation for the sultan's losses from suppression of the arms traffic in the Gulf.[15] In the late nineteenth and early twentieth centuries, Muscat had become a major entrepôt for a lucrative traffic in arms (Bailey 1992, 10:318; Landen 1967, 388–429; Lorimer 2015, 2:2556–88; J. Peterson 1978). Modern rifles and other munitions were imported from Europe into Muscat via steamers, 95 percent of which were "reexported" (smuggled) into other parts of the Gulf and South Asia (Gwadur, Oman/British Baluchistan, and Bandar Abbas in southern Iran), where they were reaching the Afghan troops at Herat who were at war with the British. Rifles made in Birmingham were being smuggled from Oman for use against the British in the northwest frontier. Beginning in 1897, tribal uprisings on the Indo-Afghan frontier brought the Gulf arms trade suddenly into the foreground (British Foreign Office 1987, 2:307–8; Lorimer 1915, 2:2560). Accordingly, measures were taken to restrict smuggling from Muscat to all neighboring countries, including India, Persia, and Turkish dominions in the Gulf, not to mention Trucial Oman (now the UAE), Kuwait, Bahrain, and British and Italian Somaliland. Arms trafficking bolstered the economy during a time of uncertainty, accounting for one-quarter of Muscat's import income in the 1890s and early 1900s (Landen 1967, 152–53). These profits declined precipitously when the British imposed a naval blockade in 1910 and 1911 and collapsed altogether when the British "induced" the sultan, via the arms traffic subsidy, to establish an arms warehouse in 1912. To make up for the massive losses incurred in import duties, the British increased the sultan's annual subsidy by Rs. 100,000 (£6,666).[16]

These forced changes to the flow of trade, perceived as direct strikes on the economic prosperity of the interior, were a primary reason for a series of rebellions from 1874 to 1915, fueled by anger about the perceived interdependency between the British and the sultan that was contributing to a collapsing economy while creating a paucity of ready arms and ammunition to maintain internal law and order (Persian Gulf Political Residency 1873–1957, vol. 7, 53). By this time, the loss of trade had reduced customs revenues to a trickle. The consequence was great poverty and active hostility among the tribes on the coast and the interior. Any alternative claimant to the throne or tribal incursions into the coastal regions was dealt with swiftly by the threat of the British naval gunships, a regular phenomenon from 1874 to 1920. In November 1895, during a rebellion in Muscat that attempted to usurp Sultan Turkī, the government of India authorized the sultan to issue a warning to the leading sheikhs of Oman that the government of India would not allow attacks on the port towns of Muscat and Matrah. This was a guarantee, the principle of which extended to the ports of the Batinah coast—stretching from Sohar, at the entrance to the Arab-Persian Gulf, to Sur, just above the southeastern tip of Arabia, which contained British subjects.

In sum, British colonial ideas concerning Omani "traditional" society, as characterized by a repetitive, ahistorical cycle of unity followed by tribal strife and unrest, were in fact a response to emerging circumstances. Members of mercantile and shipping communities, who had been pushed deeper into the interior or into emigration, were struggling to find viable livelihoods; they were not "traditional" tribespeople by choice. "Development" and "progress" of the Arab-Persian Gulf region, as a set of deployed actions, involved the configuration of political and economic arrangements that were both productive of British geostrategic aims and suppressive of a once prosperous Omani Empire, engendering a set of deeply hierarchical relationships that defined Oman vis-à-vis the West. The project of Western development of the Arab-Persian Gulf region was, therefore, one of generating difference, allocating Oman to the category of "backwardness" and "tradition" that must be undone and improved on. Oman became a subordinate region, wholly dependent on British largesse and military support, disempowered and conceived as a locale that needed constant propping up against anarchy. Although some British observers recognized the British role in these developments, particularly the repercussions of introducing steam power and halting the slave trade, many others took a more depoliticized view, seeing the region's "backwardness" as an integral characteristic of Arab-Islamic society (Lorimer 1915, 2:2475–516).[17] In this conception, British development of the coastal area was the region's best hope for enlightenment. In the pursuit of its economic, political, and strategic goals, Britain established the frontiers of progress in the Arab-Persian Gulf region through the submarine telegraph cable, the ships of the British and Indian Steam Navigation Company, and the Suez Canal, which enabled British dominance over commerce and shipping in the Gulf region. Piracy, slave trading, and arms trafficking were suppressed; by 1916, Sultan Taimur (r. 1913–1932) was presiding over a capital that, cut off from Arab tribes of the interior, primarily comprised British subjects, Baluchis, and those of African descent, with few leaders of Arab tribal importance (Persian Gulf Political Residency 1873–1957, vol. 7, 64).

The Ibadi Imamate as a Paradigm for Restoration

To subscribe the rise and fall of the Omani political economy and its subsequent subordination to British policy is one crucial means toward understanding the factors behind the rise of the Ibadi Imamate in 1913. However, doing so also circumscribes scholarship (Jones and Ridout 2015; Landen 1967; J. Peterson 1978; Wilkinson 1987) to the limited vocabulary of power struggles and desires as motivations for action. Such an approach moreover protects a secularized historical narrative, naturalizing the normativity of certain cultural and political categories and obscuring the ethico-religious dimension of Ibadi reasoning, underwritten by the role of God and the Prophet. There seems to be no place for a nonsecular logic of resistance and thus no way to make legible the nature of the Ibadi sense of loss and outrage. Little attention has been paid to how one might reflect on the specificity of the impact of British intervention and transformation of this life-world as it was being subordinated to the demands of global modernization and capital. What type of ethical, communicative, and political practices of the time would illuminate such a historical injury?

The specificity of the Ibadis as a *firqa* (sect) and a school of sharīʿa interpretation centered on a particular conception of history and time. Reading and listening practices, which I discuss in chapter 2, cultivated the past as an ethico-political stance out of which the present was lived and the future was anticipated. These ethical performances cultivated a capacity to appraise history through eliciting an affective receptiveness that habituated the listener and reader toward embodying an Ibadi ethical mode of being. Through the process of ingraining knowledge in the hearts of listeners and readers, a certain way of relating to and interpreting the past bound itself to the appropriate object, aligning them toward a more pious comportment in accordance with the Ibadi school.[18] These disciplinary practices, which structured a way of "seeing" and "inhabiting" the world, coalesced around a seminal Ibadi historical work of the twentieth century—a work that lies at the heart of the 1913 revolt—*Tuhfat al-ʿAyān fi sirat ahl ʿUmān* (first published in 1911), by Abdullah bin Humaid al-Salimi (1869–1914), who is also known by his honorific, Nur al Din al-Salimi.[19]

There are a number of ways to illustrate the temporal-ethical dimension in modern Ibadi thought, but a close reading of this text is paramount for two key reasons. First, al-Salimi was instrumental in and considered to be the intellect behind the revival of the twentieth-century imamate. Second, his textual narrative is not merely a chronological history but also a political and moral treatise that brought past actions, characters, and events under an analytic lens through which to designate the realizable goals toward which the true Muslim community in Oman needed to strive toward in order to restore the imamate.

Al-Salimi was considered part of the Ibadi Islamic revival movement, or the nahda, characterized as a great resurgence in Ibadi scholarship beginning in the nineteenth century due to increasing British intervention in Omani affairs, the military and ideological clash with the Wahabi movement in the region, and the decisive impact of the North African and Zanzibar revival among Ibadi scholars. This movement fostered open dialogue and correspondence. Major works—such as the *Kitāb al-Nīl*, by 'Abd al-'Aziz al-Thamini (1718–1808), the Maghrabi scholar of the Mzab Valley, and extensive commentaries by his student Muhammad bin Yusuf Atafayyish—were as well known in Oman as *Qāmūs al-Sharīʿa* (written by the Omani scholar Jumayyil b. Khamis Yal Saʿdi) was in North Africa. The printing press founded by Sultan Burghash bin Said of Zanzibar (1837–1888) facilitated the spread of Maghrabi and Mashriqi Ibadi works (Ghazal 2010; Hoffman 2012, 52–53; Wilkinson 1987, 230–45). Al-Salimi was in regular communication with North African scholars, including the Algerian Ibadi scholar Muhammad bin Yusuf Atafayyish, who admired al-Salimi's works and taught them to his students (M. al-Salimi 1998, 92). On his Hajj pilgrimage, al-Salimi met scholars of different sects from Turkey, India, North Africa, and Iraq and conversed with them in majālis (M. al-Salimi 1998, 92–94; Ghazal 2010, 33–34). He expresses his opinion of the British succinctly:

> The Christians war with us with cunning
> While every one of us is inattentive and confused
> They take our domain through treachery
> Which is stronger than the force of cannons (M. al-Salimi 1998, 91).

Experiences with the imperial powers had opened up common ground with the rest of the Muslim world, enabling al-Salimi and other scholars to neutralize sectarian differences with non-Ibadi Muslims to facilitate pan-Islamism and join the ranks of such reformers as Jamal al-Din al-Afghani and Muhammad 'Abduh. In 1908 and 1909, the Ibadi scholar and pan-Islamist Sulayman bin 'Abd Allah al-Bāruni published a series of questions and answers in his newspaper, *al-Asad al-Islami*, asking al-Salimi whether he agreed that the greatest reason for the differences among Muslims was the schisms brought about by multiple sects and their different perspectives. What were the primary reasons behind this dissension? Would it ever be possible for Muslims to unite and overcome their plurality? In his reply, al-Salimi agrees that sectarian differences were the cause underlying fragmentation and divergence of opinion, leading to a bid for supremacy and despotism—the basis for the first divisions between the companions of the Prophet, dating to the days of Ali ibn Abi Talib and Mu'awiya. Unity might be possible in theory but was impossible in the day to day. At the same time, the person inclined to unite Muslims was a reformer. The most efficient means to achieve harmony was to call on people to leave sectarian labels behind and call themselves "Muslims," a sentiment that might sediment gradually, until they could start thinking of themselves as brothers and leave off factionalism altogether (M. al-Salimi 1998, 93).[20]

Meanwhile, al-Salimi's reforms aimed toward a more localized and sectarian resolution, in his conviction that positive change could come about only through restoring the idealized past of the Ibadi tradition (ibid., 91). As far as he was concerned, the chaos and unrest that prevailed over the Omani region had come about due to ambition for worldly gain among the ruling elite, which had percolated downward, resulting in endemic corruption among the populace as a direct result of deviating from religious teachings rather than adhering to the Quran and prophetic sunna as an integral part of daily living. We glimpse his perspective on the Omani people before the rise of the imamate in 1913 in the following verse:

> To God Almighty, I complain about the people of my time
> Way of the Blind among them is their path of righteousness
> People see impotence as more fruitful and
> A clearer path when they are asked to fulfil their promises
> They have cut relationships between themselves
> Their aspirations have become trivial and rancor has spread
> Their strength is weakness and their grandeur is degradation
> As for their religion, it is criticism
> They do not respect the ties of kinship or covenant
> Nor do they respect the promises that they make to anyone
> (M. al-Hashimi n.d., 51)

Purging factionalism and tribalism, forging unity, and launching reform translated into a program for restoring the golden age of the first imamate (749–886 CE), when imams were chosen through *shura* (consultation) by a council of community scholars and elders and perceived as modeling their behavior on the ascetic conduct and humble deportment of the first two caliphs of the *rāshidun* (rightly guided)—Abu Bakr and 'Umar ibn al Khattab, who led the Muslim community after the Prophet's death. Only then could the Ibadis unite, rallying around one leader and fully realizing their covenant with God to build the just social order on earth, in accordance with sharī'a and through the divinely ordained institution of the imamate (M. al-Salimi 1998, 90; Saleh Nasser 2003, 321–39). In his writings, al-Salimi's son Muhammad mentions the many times one could see his father lifting up his hands to God in his *majlis* or on the road, entreating, "Here I am at your service, Oh Allah! Unite us! Reconcile people with each other!" (M. al-Salimi 1998, 91). These ideas stirred him to seek an audience with Sultan Turkī (1871–1888) on his way to hajj and, on his return, to beseech the sultan to steer clear of the British and restore Ibadi sharī'a rule. When that failed, al-Salimi undertook a tour of the Omani interior to rally the elders to his cause, succeeding in having Sheikh Salim ibn Rashid bin Sulaiman al Kharusi (r. 1913–1920) elected imam in the shura council in the Tanuf region. This act established the first and only Ibadi Imamate of the twentieth century.

A towering intellect, al-Salimi was renowned for his substantive scholarly output, manifested in works on *fiqh* (jurisprudence), doctrine, hadith studies, juridical and moral treatises, and compendiums—many written in poetic form to facilitate memorization—and compilations of his fatwa (juridical opinions). He was also a dynamic judge, teacher, and speaker and a formidable participant in the politics of his day. The traces of his influence are not restricted to his scholarly works, extemporaneous sermons, letters, and fatwa but embodied in the lives of his students, who numbered among the most famous tribal leaders, jurists, and 'ulamā' of the twentieth century, including the two imams who presided over the last imamate (M. al-Salimi 1998, 90).

His work on an Ibadi history, the *Tuhfat al- 'ayān*, is one of the few historical texts available for a sect that is more renowned for its legal literature.[21] Al-Salimi was participating in a larger Arabic-Islamic historiographical tradition that developed ethical and moral anecdotes about the Prophet and his companions in order to emphasize the ideals of ethical behavior and the basis for legitimate rule over the Muslim community. To such historians as Tabari (839–923) and al-Maqrizi (1364–1442), the question of who had the right to succeed the Prophet, the nature of just governance, and the criteria for leadership (grounded in tribal ties or religious and ethical merit) were central to Islamic historical narrations. Like his intellectual progenitors, al-Salimi was engaged in a political and ethical fight, and, like them, events and personalities were downplayed or emphasized within a specific frame, which cast religious moral and political allusions that resonated and mattered to the communities where they were written (Al-Hibri 2010; T. Khalidi 1994; Robinson 2002).

His work is generally considered to have been written with a view to reviving the Ibadi Imamate, in light of the chaos and tribal wars he witnessed and the growing debility of the sultan in the wake of British control.[22] His paramount aim is reflected in his overall works; his explanations, criticisms, and compilations are part of a general bid to reform society and implement justice through confronting *ẓulm* (tyranny). His aims in writing a history of the Omani people are elucidated in the introduction:

> It is well known to the discerning that a knowledge of history inclines
> [one] toward the emulation of the virtuous and guides [one] on the path
> of truth [*ṭariqa al-mutqīn*] inasmuch as it recollects [*dhkara*] past acts
> of devoutness and depravity. For when the judicious hears about such
> wickedness, he becomes wary of such a course and it may see him instead,

following the tracks/impressions [athār] of the piety minded and keep away from evil circumstances [ahwal min ṭalḥ] in order to exert [yujāhid] himself to fulfill his rightful obligations towards jihad. I desire to explore what I can of the athār of the righteous imams in order to acquaint the ignorant with their lives so that the seeker may follow their exemplary ways [iqtidāʿ bil athār] (N. al-Salimi 1961, 1:4).

In al-Salimi's opinion, the act of ingesting the past to be judged as good or bad, through reading or listening, is a mode of moral training in which history was conceived as a reservoir of multiple experiences that oriented its audience— through providing modes of guidance and exemplary behavior of the virtuous— toward acts of piety and virtue for the future. Undergirded by the Quran and the sunna, the past is perceived as one of experiential continuity that allows authoritative histories to be appraised as exemplars for life's teachings as a guide for the present and future. An assumption of a continuity of circumstances assures the relevance of past experiences to bind expectations. In other words, the past holds sway over the present and future by providing a temporal coherence, authority, and instruction that determines future action. Part of the daily pedagogy of the self is to follow the tracks (iqtidāʿ bil athār) of virtuous forbears (ahl al-faḍl) and attune oneself to the advice and admonitions deduced from their lives (N. al-Salimi 1961, 1:4). This form of spiritual progress is in contrast to Western imperial temporal logic, in which the future, premised on continuous advancement and innovation, is no longer related to the next world. Sharīʿa time was thus markedly different from the British understanding of temporality, in which past phenomena were conceived as unique events, distinct from the future. This future was perceived as holding the possibility of unfolding in new and unexpected ways consonant with imperial ideals and values.[23]

For al-Salimi, laying out the foundations of justice, sincerity (istiqāma), and virtue by way of a chronicle that ethically delineated the important events and personalities of a region's past was a fundamental means toward political and religious reform (M. al-Salimi 1998, 90–92; Saleh Nasser 2003). Drawing on a greater Ibadi and Islamic textual tradition, al-Salimi navigated a variety of local sources, written with different aims, in different periods, and with clashing opinions. He weighed their validity, critiquing their accounts of circumstances and personalities, with a view toward burnishing the believer and directing his reader or listener toward emulation of virtuous predecessors and avoiding what he considered to be their egregious abuses of sharīʿa, which had come about through factionalism and ignorance.

As a chronicle in two volumes, each stage of al-Salimi's history is demarcated by a new chapter (bāb). He makes it clear that Oman, as a single entity, is much older than the two political entities that emerged during his lifetime. Historical antecedents to the imagined unity of Oman are invoked through a brief introduction to rivers, mountains, towns, and ports—descriptions given by such luminaries of history and travel writing of the medieval Muslim world as Ibn Khaldun and Mas'udi. The first chapter focuses on the virtues of the people, as extolled by the companions of the Prophet when the first delegation was sent to Oman and as embodied in the lives and acts of contemporary and later leaders, commanders, and scholars. For example, early pages declaim hadiths from the compilations of Al-Rabi' bin Habib al Farahidi, such as one that observes that the Prophet's wife, Aisha, had heard her husband say, "The people of Oman, more than any other, would be allowed to drink from the Pool of the Prophet in heaven," since they were among the most praiseworthy of Muslims (N. al-Salimi 1961, 1:10).

Each subsequent chapter describes pivotal events and personalities as a chronological chain of events, from the migration of the Azdi Arab tribal confederation from Yemen to Oman in the pre-Islamic period, to the expulsion of Persians from the region and the subsequent inroads of Islam among the inhabitants, and the ensuing developments that shaped the course of the Umayyad and Abbasid Empires and determined, over centuries, the oppositional doctrinal and political bases of the Ibadi Imamate—the specificities of its doctrine, its rulers and leaders, and their noble actions and misdeeds that characterized the virtuous and ignoble lives of the intellectual and political forbears that made Ibadism the predominant Islamic tradition and school of law that most of the region's inhabitants embraced, definitively defining Oman.

Throughout the two volumes, there is a continuous entity called Oman, a region defined largely by its geographical frontiers, historical experiences in the domination of Arab tribes over the Persians, and the de facto emergence and prevalence of the Ibadi Islamic tradition. This is characterized by the region's governance—for the most part, a succession of Ibadi imams with the support of notable 'ulama' and tribal elders. Grounded in Ibadi doctrine, these rulers are noted for their vices and their virtues. The golden age of the first imamate (749–886 CE), characterized by imams renowned for their virtue and scholarship, ends with the end of the imamate of Salt bin Malik (851–886), as envisioned by al-Salimi, and the beginnings of a civil war that produces two factions, the Nizwani and Rustaqi schools of Ibadi thought, whose rift centers on whether it was possible to remove an imam from his position and the criteria for doing so. This division fell along tribal fault lines, resulting in a series of bloody conflicts (N. al-Salimi 1961, 1:158–59).

When narrating these events, al-Salimi delivers an admonitory warning that with the emergence of factions and civil strife, God had given over the Omanis' domain to the crueler (sayyi' 'adāb) hands of outsiders, led by the Abbasid governor in Bahrain, Muhammad b. Būr, who invaded Oman (892 CE). For the next century and a half,

Oman was ruled by a series of outsiders, including the ruling Abbasid dynasty in Baghdad and the Qarmatians. Fragmentation of the imamate was followed by rival imamates and rulers (*muluk*). By the eleventh and twelfth centuries, the possibility of an imamate died as Oman passed into the hands of the Bani Nabhan,

> because when God wanted to have his will carried out by the people of Oman, they fought among themselves instead and divided into two factions. God, in punishment, took their land and enabled a despotic group from among themselves, who became a byword for cruelty and ruthlessness [*sau' 'adhab*] (ibid., vol. 1, 354).

This dynasty of religiously illegitimate rulers governed for five hundred years that were, according to al-Salimi, Oman's "Dark Ages" (ibid., vol. 1, 357).

In relating subsequent events, al-Salimi describes the first imams of the Ya'ariba dynasty (1624–1743) in terms of their piety, modesty, and asceticism, their legitimate succession to the imamate through shura, and their efforts and successes in uniting the region by defeating the Portuguese in the seventeenth century. Their willingness to rule in accordance with shari'a, subsuming their worldly desires, united Omanis to overcome an invader. Subsequent imams of this house, however, were hereditary rulers who treated the region as a dominion (*milkīya*) to be fought over. Al-Salimi (1961, 2:168) laments their weaknesses, which led to tribal fragmentation and domination by the Persians, and delivers a stern warning that their acts caused God to turn away and bestow his favors elsewhere.

For al-Salimi, history as an ethical performance is inseparable from the act of worshipping God, whose will is an active agent, working through shari'a to ensure those who submit walk the "right path" (*jāddat al-mustaqīm*) in accord with Ibadi doctrinal interpretation of legitimate succession and rule. This is a recurring paradigmatic structure in his text, in which rulers who deviate from that which has been authorized by the Quran and prophetic sunna through their arbitrary hold on power—inasmuch as they immerse themselves in worldly ambitions through their struggles for domination and the exploitation of their subjects—are no longer religiously legitimate. Their bid to power encourages factionalism and leads to God's turning from the Omanis, in this case shifting dominion from Ya'ariba hands into Persia's.

This fragmentation, for al-Salimi, recurs once more as a major cause of the downfall of the Ya'ariba Imamate and entrenchment of the Al Bu Said dynasty, from the mid-eighteenth century, as ambitious hereditary rulers rather than elected imams. Oman is united once more under a new imam, Ahmed ibn Said Albu Saidi (1744–1778), who ousts Persian occupiers and is legitimately elected. Subsequent rulers of this house promote hereditary succession and are therefore illegitimate, inevitably resulting in fragmentation and foreign (British) intervention and control, weakening and dividing the Omani people.

Al-Salimi's chronicle ends in 1910 with this turn of events and a broad foreshadowing of the downfall of the Al Bu Said dynasty, ordained by God through the revival of the imamate and the final ousting of the British. John Wilkinson (1972, 78) recognizes this phenomenon, noting that Ibadi politico-religious ideology develops an automated natural cycle that encompasses its own downfall. When the region grows prosperous, religious ideals weaken, and retaining temporal power (*sulṭana*) becomes the key prerogative of a single group, to the detriment of anything else. For al-Salimi, however, God's will—his active agency—is the locomotive powering the historical narrative and the cyclical reality it is forging. The British are thus transformed into a paradigmatic, ever-repeating invader—much like the Umayyad and Abbasid armies, the Qarmatians, the Portuguese, and the Persians—who not only feed on the weaknesses brought about by power struggles between rulers in Oman but also are the basis for uniting and strengthening Oman against the invaders by reviving the idea of the imamate and bringing about a common uprising. Simultaneously, this paradigmatic narrative structure, made up of a repeating sequence of events, acts as a stable, authoritative basis for addressing change and determining the nature and significance of the British presence in Oman, while paving the way for action against them.

In a letter dated 5 Shaban 1333 (June 19, 1915), Sheikh Abdullah bin Rashid al Hashim, a qadi of the imam, writes to the British Political Agency and Consulate:

> Sheikh Humaid bin Sa'id al Falaiti brought a message [to us] from you [the British] . . . that you desire to negotiate for peace . . . and do good for all men and in reply I inform you that a Mussalman will never agree to be led astray from the Path of the Prophet. If the message which Humaid brought us is correct, then it behooves us to ask you for certain conditions both of a religious and a worldly nature. You Christians are well aware that the Islamic religion allows certain things and forbids others—
>
> I.   You Christians have stopped us from dealing in slaves. This is injurious to us Muslims. Owing to lack of harmony among Muslims you have gained strength. Were this not so, the benefits derived from our slaves would not have been lost.
>
> II.   You have taken possession of the sea and pretend that it belongs to you. The sea is common to all.
>
> III. You interfere in the affairs of the Sultans of Oman and support them in matters which are unlawful and contrary to their own religion and they have acted against their religion.

IV. The prices of foodstuffs and cloth has been increasing. Food is necessary to live and cloth is necessary to clothe the body which God bids us to cover.

V. You have also stopped the trade in arms and ammunition. Arms are very necessary to maintain peace. And you allow wine to be drunk and tobacco to be used, while both these are contrary to our Shari'a. Whenever a slave comes to you, you free him, although he belongs to his master. You allow things which are forbidden by God and disallow things which are allowed by God. You must give up doing injustice. You must allow lawful things and put a stop to unlawful things. (Bailey 1988, 3:11–12).

This letter construes the 1913 uprising against the sultan and his (British) supporters not merely as a struggle between colonizers and colonized but between justice and injustice, where one side strives to implement God's law against another's immersion in worldly military and financial ambitions. In the words of al-Salimi's son, "the sultanate loves power and tyranny while the Imamate imbibes from the system of shariʿa, by which the Imams are guided. This is a government based on shura and the election of a just Imam who works within shariʿa" (M. al-Salimi 1998, 114).

God as Agent in the Ibadi Imamate

In al-Salimi's narrative, ecological, economic, and political factors are forces that bring about a cascade of consequential events. Water loss, visible for the first time, is conceived as the material result of prolonged drought with the chain implications of low agricultural productivity, famine, rising prices, and malnutrition (N. al-Salimi 1961, 1:123–24). But these are symptoms, not the underlying cause: God has set this state of affairs in motion to show his displeasure. Like other historians in the Islamic tradition, such as ibn Athir, al-Salimi conceives the world as part of an integrated series of relationships, all subject to God's sovereignty. Compartmentalization is impossible. Politics, military, law, religion, and the economy are inextricably bound, grounded in shariʿa time—a God-centered history. When an imam or ruler is unjust, corruption and injustice prevail as God turns his back on the people; factionalism and ignorance become the order of the day, pervading every sphere of life.

For example, in narrating the overthrow of the imamate of Azzan bin Qays (1868–1871), a time of justice, peace, and prosperity, by the ambition of the exiled Turkī bin Said, he chronicles the ways God made his wrath felt (N. al-Salimi

1961, 2:300–307). He proclaims that God struck down the "hypocrites" who accepted Sultan Turkī's bribes and declared their hostility toward the imam. God further sowed discord among the tribes that had cooperated with Sultan Turkī by facilitating the spread of death through disease, fear, and rancor, resulting in bloodshed and war into the twentieth century.

For al-Salimi, neither economy nor society are separate categories of practices from religion. The way the community is ordered is in accordance with God's design, as elaborated first by the Prophet's small polity in Medina and then by those designated as his rightful successors, in accordance with the Ibadi understanding of sharī'a jurisprudence and administration. Daily economic, social, and political life is organized and grounded on the basis of divine justice and injustice. Raising taxes, regulating market transactions, settling disputes, and launching wars all fall under sharī'a, as administered by the imam and the judges and governors he appoints in each province of his domain. An ideal imam ensures his officials are incorruptible and knows what justice is, enabling peace and prosperity to spread over the land through the judges and governors he appoints. To underline these virtues, al-Salimi writes, "the governors that the Imam appointed were reliable and faithful [ṣādiqin]" (1961, 1:148).

Through the referential content of his narrative and the overall structure of his chronicle, al-Salimi uses history to draw out and animate a moral responsiveness integral to the experiences of knowing history. This use of history is tethered to an Ibadi interpretation of sharī'a, even while its mode of knowledge is rooted in the lived realities of its readers. Through orienting his readers' (and listeners') ethical sensibilities, al-Salimi (M. al-Salimi 1998, 91) aims to instill in people the cause of reviving the imamate, while addressing the dangers of factionalism. An Ibadi who has attained the proper ethical and affective mode of active awareness, through being made conscious of his history, is also aware of the consequences of his actions and the fear that came from knowledge of an impending day of judgment. Such a reader/listener would, in al-Salimi's view, become the core unit for generating a decisive confrontation (jihād) with the corruption, arbitrary will, and tribal factionalism that characterized the sultanate. Armed with a historically honed understanding of the politics of the day, he would have the moral wherewithal to subsume tribal interests, thereby laying the foundation to reunite the region under the banner of the imam. The anchoring of this knowledge would generate the basis for replacing poisonous circumstances with righteousness, paving the way for a revival of the imamate and the spread of learning. The people would be guided once more to salvation by the right leaders, who would direct them to live in accord with sharī'a. The overriding aims of writing Tuhfat al-'ayan was not simply to facilitate but to transform the reader's (listener's) perception of reality through binding an understanding of history to the very real object of reform.

By way of example, al-Salimi spends many pages on the civil war that marked the end of the imamate of al-Salt bin Malik (851–886) and raised centuries of divisive debates as to the ethico-moral conditions under which an imam could be deposed. Toward the end of his long reign, a frail and aged al-Salt bin Malik—considered to be among the virtuous imams—still had all his faculties. But, according to al-Salimi (1961, 1:181–200), citing the *sirat* of *A. Qahtan bin Khalid b. Qahtan* (tenth century), a new generation had emerged, one that displayed humility without piety, who "show[ed] a love of religion but hid a love of the world"; "God sought to test [*yakhtabar*] the people of Oman through worldly and ambitious men who have found a leader among the *'ulamā*'". With an eloquent tongue, Musa bin Musa seeks to discredit the imam and his officials, his qadis (judges), and walis (governors) in the majlis without specifying any error the imam had committed or providing any evidence that al-Salt had broken his covenant to implement God's rule. This continues until *fitna* (strife against a legitimately sanctioned sharī'a government) broke out and those gathered around Musa bin Musa are inclined toward him to fulfill their worldly ambitions for power and position. They do not call al-Salt bin Malik for an accounting of his actions or ask for repentance, as should have been the case; in al-Salimi's narration, al-Salt is simply deposed. Rather than risk bloodshed, al-Salt leaves Nizwa.

Musa bin Musa is considered one of the most powerful *'ulamā*' of the age. However, he incited discord in the guise of calling for the return of righteousness, seizing the imamate by force and coercion (*bal ghalaba wal jabarīya*), appointing his ally Rashid bin Azzan as imam (N. al-Salimi 1961 1:201–3), and making himself chief qadi. Rashid bin Azzan is made imam (886–890) without consultation with or consensus among the elders (*'ala ghayr mashūra*). The *bayt al māl* (state treasury) that was used to pay state officials, specifically the walis and the qadis, and the poor and destitute is looted and eliminated. Under Imam Rashid, Musa bin Musa gathers corrupt officials and other "riffraff" (*ra'ā'*) around him who cannot tell the difference between truth and hypocrisy. Their sins include seizing grain the wali of Izki had gathered for *zakat* (alms tax for the poor) to feed their armies, waging war on Muslims while under truce, slaughtering the weak and helpless, dragging prisoners of war to their deaths, imprisoning dissenting *'ulamā*, taking monies by force from the traders of the maritime city of Sohar, and controlling the prices and distribution of goods to maximize profits (N. al-Salimi 1961, 1:205–22).

In sharp contrast to these transgressive acts, Imam Ghassan bin 'Abdallah (807–822), for example, is known to all for his sense of justice, excellent moral character, sincerity, piety, and asceticism. His officials never fail to distribute zakat in accordance with the law; nor do they fail to protect and defend the people in accordance with the Quranic prescription "these are settled allotments ordained by Allah and Allah is All-knowing, All-Wise" (4:11). The judges and governors who ruled over the provinces are trustworthy, pious, and learned. They do not embroil themselves in quarrels with the populace, slander one another, or show rancor or envy toward other elders of the community (N. al-Salimi 1961, 1:86–87). Imam Ghassan is noted for his dedication even to the minutiae of daily life, insisting on lighting the archways in Nizwa after a woman passing through them is harassed by a profligate (ibid., 125).

Humility versus arrogance, consultation versus tyranny (*jababaira*), justice versus arbitrariness (*ahwā*), piety versus hypocrisy, sharīʿa versus force—these are some of the constitutive categories of morality by which al-Salimi's Ibadi historical narrative is conceptually structured and navigated. Far from seeing characters as historically contingent outcomes of specific life events or circumstances, as in a Euro-American influenced biography or history, for example, al-Salimi conceives of his in terms of how they tested the boundaries of sharīʿa, how they lived their lives, and the consequences of their actions through creating archetypical character patterns. Rather than elucidating the formative experiences of childhood or the development of relationships between family, teachers, and friends—the collective interactions, relationships, and experiences that define a person's uniqueness and way of being—al-Salimi portrays his historical characters in terms of their conformity to prototypes: the ideal ruler or scholar who has fulfilled God's rule on earth or the one who has been led astray.[24] These accounts are not meant to explain human actions so much as to elucidate how people and their actions fall within the continuum of the Islamic doctrine of human perfection through a recall of words and deeds.

In the *Tuhfat al-ʿayān*, fundamental principles of right and wrong, the basis of human morality, and the foundation of a just social order are undergirded by the Quran and the moral perfection of the Prophet, embodied in the sunna. The discursive figures of moral and political archetypes that serve to categorize and theorize ethico-political and moral experiences are sufficient for interpretations to be drawn for the future from past exemplary acts—in this case, the nature of the threat and consequences of British domination. To the reader (listener), the *Tuhfat al-ʿayān* contained the prescription of how to live.

Grounded in this paradigmatic framework, the actions of just and virtuous imams and those rulers, imams or otherwise, who were considered to have assumed authority through subjugation (*malak bil qahr*) in the Ibadi tradition provided exemplary models in the processes of anchoring and institutionalizing the criteria of morality, justice, and learning that sanctioned the imamate. These criteria, in turn, navigated the paradigms—those to be idealized or avoided—of the Ibadi imams, scholars, governors, and judges to finally coalesce in the histories of the *Tuhfat al-ʿayān*. These periods become a type of evaluative category whose interpretation, image, and knowledge establishes an exemplary view of history, the foundation that generated and institutionalized the Ibadi school of sharīʿa. By way of example, the qadi Abu Abd ʿAllah Muhammad bin ʿIsa al-Sirī calls on Imam Rashid bin Ali (1079–1119 CE) and his officials to repent for their sins in the Nizwa-Rustaq civil war, including murder, burning and looting, unlawful taxation and punishment, and breaking of covenants (N. al-Salimi 1961, 1:332):

> That God sent down his book, his Prophets and made his religion evident . . . he presented [from among Muslims], successors [khulafāʿ], judges, Imams and governors who are renowned and whose lives [siyar] are well known. Follow their path and be guided by them and he who deviates from them [khālafhum] will be led astray. For it is said: Follow and do not contrive or invent [tabdaʿū].[25] . . . repent to God for all your sins and fear his illustrious glory through your work in both public and private, in obedience to God, fulfilling all his religious precepts and avoid all that is forbidden by him and emulate [iqtidāʿ] the righteous predecessors among Muslims with faithful piety . . . and do not follow your own opinions (ibid., 324–25).

Association (walāya) and disassociation (barāʾa) from the authority of an Ibadi imam was often directly linked to the actions of the Prophet and the rāshidun, based on whether they fulfilled the criteria for piety (waraʿ), asceticism (zuhd), and justice (ʿadl) that adhere to God's decree in commanding the right and forbidding the wrong (amr bal-maʿrūf wa nahy ʾan al-mūnkar). Unjust (ẓālim) rulers were comparable to the actions of ʾUthman and ʾAli, the last two caliphs of the rāshidun, who become the prototypes of the sinning imams whose actions—tainted by political dissent, disputed behavior, and disorderly governance—justified their removal. This sharp division between the perfect rule and a phase of debility becomes the lynchpin for traditional Ibadi doctrinal thinking about the nature of the imamate and the just ruler (N. al-Salimi 1961, 1:76–80). This historical perception generated the idea that the imam's authority and duties are grounded in the Quran, the prophetic sunna, and, for the Ibadis, the notion of shura. For the past to project such an exemplary force, it must be considered to be in continuum with the present.

As exemplary models, historical figures and their actions were available for interpretation and were the mediums for reasoned evaluation that considered their past actions of piety, valor, asceticism, or rapaciousness constant, producing identical moral and ethical consequences on those around them. And yet the process of reading (or listening to) stories about their lives and actions was not merely communicative but involves practices of assimilation and absorption through which the Ibadi subject could cultivate an ethical disposition. Experiences and expectations take up the same authoritative character types, since past and present are considered in continuity with each other.

Thus, the lives of the Prophet and his companions and the imams do not end with their deaths but extended to "futures past," events and acts that are still unfolding in the future but already lie in the past for interpreters. The prophetic, early Medinan caliphate eras are not only acknowledged as Ibadi predecessors; the figures of the Prophet, Abu Bakr, 'Umar, the early Kharijite personalities, and the first Ibadi Imamate (749–886 CE)[26] are those from whom the Ibadi inherited the "true religion," becoming the objects of assimilative attachments (N. al-Salimi 1961, 1:77–78). The golden age of the Muslim community as an ideal type became the critical basis for debate and argumentation, even conflict, to rationalize practices and justify differing points of view on what it meant to live in accordance with sharī'a and approximate the ideals of the golden age, as embodied in the prophetic sunna. These athār, or traces, could set standards for an ethico-social everyday life or provoke political reforms and conflicts (ibid., 1:82–83).

For al-Salimi, the actions of the Al Bu Said sultan and his dependency on the British from the mid-nineteenth century are interpreted within Ibadi politico-religious historical categories as marking the presence of vice over morality, sin over virtue. Inasmuch as the sultan's actions are assimilated into an archetypical framework, only one course of action is possible for al-Salimi—a revolt to overthrow the sultan. For the Ibadi community in the interior, the sultan's words and actions are the latest manifestation of a battle between tyranny and piety, darkness and light—a repeated battle that structurally defines Ibadi history in al-Salimi's eyes. And it was a battle the sultan, as tyrant, was prefigured to lose when Oman united once more under a single banner, aided by God's will. This perspective by no means exhausts the many motivations behind the Ibadi uprising against the sultan, but it does critically destabilize the underlying epistemological assumptions that inscribe the history of the rise of the twentieth-century Ibadi Imamate into a secular narration of cause and effect (J. Peterson 1978; Wilkinson 1987). This perspective makes way for a theologically grounded understanding, specific to the lifeworld of the Ibadi Imamate, in which God is an active agent.

Modern State Building in the Sultanate

In private correspondence with the British Raj in 1917, Major L. B. H. Haworth mulled over an increasingly untenable situation. With British military and financial support, the sultan held the coastal strip, with Muscat at its center, while the interior was coalescing around a firmly established imamate, whose presence was a constant threat. As Haworth saw it, this was the "natural order of things for uncivilized or semi-civilized countries where weak dynasties of this nature [the sultanate] would be overcome by a line more virile" and could be stopped only by "British active intervention against a virile but uncivilized and fanatical Government [the imamate] which we cannot support" (Haworth Correspondence, 1918, India Office Record Files, British Library, R/15/6/48). Meanwhile, respect for the sultan and his family weakened as he resorted to subterfuge to pay his household expenses.

Muscat was too important to set aside, given its position on the main route to Baghdad, Basra, and the Persian Gulf. Rather than transforming her into a protectorate, an idea that was bandied in official circles, the British ultimately established an "improved and good government" to maintain stable and peaceful conditions (Haworth Correspondence, India Office Record Files, British Library, R/15/6/48). Haworth writes, "The Sultan is now so absolutely dependent upon us that an unvarnished exposition of the situation to him would leave him no alternative but to reform were that made a condition of our continued support of him" (Persian Gulf Political Residency 1873–1957, vol. 7, 42). This would involve employing certain British-trained officials to "reorganize" the judiciary, customs, and a standing army. Their reconfiguration and regulation of these key institutions would become the conditions for any further British support of the sultan (Haworth Correspondence, India Office Records Files, British Library R/15/6/48; Persian Gulf Political Residency 1873–1957, vol. 7, 42, 56). At the end of 1918, the government of India sanctioned a loan of five and a half lakhs of rupees to the sultan for the repayment of his debts conditional on the reform of his administration and to be secured on the Muscat customs. These conditions were the appointment of trained customs officials (primarily Indian) nominated by the British who would reorganize the financial system into the state, proper courts for the administration of justice, and the enrolling and training of a levy corps for the sultan's protection (Persian Gulf Political Residency 1873–1957, vol. 7, 56).

"Civilizing" Oman in this case, as part of a temporal process, required an overhaul of governance to secure the linear path toward modernization and cut through corruption and bring about systemic order. It would be divorced from its emotive and social particulars, guaranteeing stability and security through entrenched institutions of law and order and sources of finance that could stand apart from its rulers, thus existing as a distinct and enduring entity, not subject to the "arbitrary" actions of any one individual or group.[27] This involved the transformation of a state whose subjects were related to the sovereign through social and material obligations and rights, historic alliances, and tribal ties of support and protection to that of an increasingly abstract governing entity that set itself apart from both rulers and ruled, thereby enduring beyond allegiance toward any one ruler while subjecting all to the power of the state. At the same time, to climb to such a rung, a state's attainment of "self-determination" could only be possible through "a period of tutelage under more advanced nations."[28] Self-determination as a political vision could come about only through the reform of an archaic past to make it conform to a more universal modernity. Pursuance of such a goal in Oman, Haworth writes, "would make it impossible for us to leave the Sultan to his own devices since the result would not be in the interests of progress or civilization."[29] Britain's policy and actions in Oman were thus caught in a paradox: even as they took steps toward assuring administrative "self-regulation" as part of a new civilizing mission against institutional inefficiency and corruption, their continuing support and active military engagements toward entrenching that rule also had the consequence of generating a persistent revolutionary challenge.

The first necessity, for Haworth, was to cede the sultan's dependence on Arab tribal allies, whose loyalties were considered fickle, for a standing army under the control of British officers and to place financial administration, especially customs, under trained officials from the British Empire.[30] This standing army would maintain his position in Muscat and supply detachments at his *wilayat* (provinces). From this position of strength, the assumption was that many would come over to the sultan's side, as his strength increased at the expense of the imam's (Haworth Correspondence, India Office Record Files, British Library, R/15/6/46). This was in flat contradiction with the imamate understanding, that beyond a small garrison of *'askaris* for the imam and his walis, for the key fortresses, military forces would be raised from local tribes who were duty bound to help the imam in his time of need, by virtue of the *baï'a* (divinely sanctioned oath of allegiance). Introducing a standing army beholden to whoever held the reins of the British-supported state broke this system, which was ideally meant to prevent the creation of a centralized, autocratic government. In 1918, it was suggested that it be a Baluchi force with British-trained officers since most of them knew Hindustani and could be easily trained. Moreover, Baluchi levies had been used in Muscat for many generations, and the forts guarding the harbors of the coastal areas were, at the time, manned by Baluchis already.[31]

In addition, the sultan was informed he would need to put his financial system in order before receiving any more loans. The sultan and his family were using the customs as a bank, borrowing from merchants on the security of the customs. The merchants were recouping their principal and interest by short payment of customs dues, opening up the possibility of fraud (Persian Gulf Political Residency 1873–1957, vol. 7, 56). Three Egyptian customs officials were hired to reorganize the entire financial order, and the end of 1919 saw the sultan's debts paid off by a loan of six and a half lakhs of rupees (an additional one lakh was sanctioned by the British Raj to the original 1918 loan), a fixing of the monthly state expenditure of the sultan's privy purse brought about by a radical change in the customs administration. This relieved the British of "heavy expenditure and disproportionate responsibilities" including the withdrawal of the Indian troops from Muscat and Matrah (Persian Gulf Political Residency 1873–1957, vol. 7, 56; India Office Records, British Library, L/P&S/18/B400). Captain McCollumn, the British advisor and former political agent of Kuwait, undertook a complete overhaul of salaries and administration. Civil lists were prepared, surplus administration was removed, dubious contracts were replaced by more efficient arrangements, and a primary school was opened. New sources of income were discovered through quarantine and landing arrangements, and a council of ministers was created.

The result was an independent sultanate whose self-regulation was closely defined and controlled by a "progressive" British telos that had brought about the new administration—a reconfigured customs system brought under the management of officials recommended by the British Raj, a European advisor recommended and selected by the government of India, a British officered army. In 1919, Oman remained a hostile hinterland, in contrast to the two hundred miles of thickly populated Muscat coast, now the center of British-spearheaded "progress." As far as the British were concerned, "the coast will develop and the interior may look after itself. Today interior Oman is united, tomorrow it may split into a thousand fragments. To strengthen the sultan's hand is to enable him to rule the coast-line efficiently and to stand by himself" (Persian Gulf Political Residency 1873–1957, vol. 7, 55).

The Ibadi Revolt through British Eyes

For the British, the rise of the imamate generated a conflict, conceived in a secular language pulsating with myriad archetypes—one that resonates with political struggles today, especially those pertaining to religious violence.

> *Undiluted* Muhammadanism has not anywhere in the world shown itself capable of efficient rule. The end all and be all of the Imam, the support which he receives is due to his religious position. Extreme orthodoxy flourishes on ignorance especially in Muhammadanism and to promote the role of bigots is to condemn the country to a point of uncivilization commensurate with the bigotry of its priests. It raises the savages to a fixed point and then condemns all further advance as infidelity until it comes into enforced contact with advanced nations (Haworth Correspondence, March 5, 1919, India Office Records, British Library R/15/6/204).

These descriptions are set in terms of a dichotomy—religious fanaticism, bigotry, and an uncivilized way of life versus tolerance, knowledge, civilization, and progress (India Office Records, British Library, R/15/6/245; Notes on the Tribes of the Sultanate of Oman, 1951).[32] This perspective was underwritten by a set of rather problematic evaluations, premised on normative conceptions of religion, time, politics, and the subject. The underlying force behind these evaluations was a prior understanding of the proper role of religion, particularly in relation to politics, in a modernizing world. This notion of religion was rooted in a world forged by an alternative sense of temporality and of history that was transcultural and univocal, constructed as part of a teleological development oriented toward Europe and modernity. It was on the basis of such a universal understanding of history that the European medieval past could be directly compared to Oman's contemporary as signifying an "earlier" stage of development, with Oman in need of maturation, along the lines of universal progressivism, in the words of one British official, "Oman . . . has been passing through the same stages of evolution as took place in the kingdoms of the Eastern and Western Franks during the Middle Ages. The history of Clovis could have been written about a modern Arab potentate" (Fowle 1932; India Office Records, British Library, /R/15/6/52). A local European history had become a global category of time. In this scenario, the world was moving in unison along the same teleological matrix. Other histories were subordinated and absorbed into this universal history. Oman's alignment with the Middle Ages, according to British officials of the early twentieth century, placed it into the "not yet" category. It had not quite reached—or rather, pushed into—modernity.

Meanwhile, defined by its "backwardness," the imamate was castigated in its immutable alterity as a region that had not followed historically sanctioned guidance through a forceful decoupling of religion and politics. Nor was it guided by its Sunni counterparts in espousing a more diluted Islam, accepting the de facto power and administration of a temporal ruler, with the *'ulamā'* as intermediaries between rulers and the ruled. Instead, British imperial bureaucrats overtly assumed that the *undiluted* Ibadi practice of Islam, embodied in a theocracy, was a major threat to the principle of toleration, a requirement of liberal governance. For Haworth and his cohort, there was an easy secular equation between intolerance and religion: "The rule of pure religion is short. It is personal and selfish and based on no consideration of public policy. And in Muslim countries at least the more powerful the religious leaders become, the more intolerant does their rule become and the more they alienate the people who suffer from their unyielding attitude" (Hayworth Correspondence, March 5, 1919, India Office Record Files, British Library, R/15/6/204). This equation draws attention to the ways in which religion and its "proper place" in modernity have been underwritten and solidified by the master narrative of progress in secular liberal thinking. This has entailed the articulation of two primary principles—(1) the separation of religion and politics and (2) the privatization of religion as part of rendering it nonpolitical—that were intrinsically tied to the notion of liberty. Paradoxically, this was a "liberty" to be won only as part of Western tutelage of those colonized lands still in their "infancy" (Van der Veer 2001, 16–21). Allocating a place for religion in society thus entailed active regulating and reconfiguring of doctrines, practices, and beliefs to fit them into the preassigned category of normative religion (Asad 2003, 205–56). Remarks on the "pure" strain of Islam practiced by the imamate were premised on assessing and calculating their measure from the vantage of this liberal-minded yardstick, and the imamate was found sadly wanting; religion and politics were too intermeshed, leading to tyranny, irrationality, and domination. This was not simply from lack of education, as far as the British were concerned, but because of civilizational deficiencies that could be ameliorated only through contact with "advanced nations." This rationale was used to license increasingly interventionist policies, especially after the discovery of oil in the interior in the 1950s.

From the Ibadi point of view, Britain's role in Oman had led to radical transformations in the religiopolitical domain, as embodied in the revival of the imamate, with its avowed adherence to sharī'a in the pursuit of "true" justice. British informal rule of the region was the basis for the formulation and confrontation of two very different epistemological foundations, each conceptually and practically grounded in a temporal logic. Both approaches fashioned different forms of critique that underwrote their conceptual understanding of "religion," paving the way for a series of actions that culminated with the sultan's (British-backed) capture of the administrative capital of Nizwa, marking the official demise of the imamate, on December 15, 1955. The prospect of oil on imamate lands resulted in a series of brief, violent conflicts in the mid- to late 1950s, ending the imamate period and giving way to a British-backed sultanate that united the region under a single polity. The Jabal al-Akhdar War (1957–1959) witnessed the final expulsion of imamate forces, their eventual exile, and the sultan's suzerainty over the interior, uniting the region as the Sultanate of Muscat and Oman, simplified after 1970 to the Sultanate of Oman.

The concept of athār captures the very different ways Oman was in the grip of the past during the Ibadi Imamate, compared to the current "heritage crusade" of the contemporary era (Lowenthal 1996). As I discuss in the following chapters, the idea of athār—as the impressions or traces left by virtuous forbears, with actions their spiritual descendants could emulate—was primarily moral, grounded in the foundations of Islamic religious authority. This relationship of similitude was undergirded by a horizon of recurrence, where an unfolding future could be deduced from past authoritative and exemplary forms of justice and morality. Underlying this exemplary view was the assumption that the past took up a space of experience that was *continuous* with the present and future. The interpretation of what was ethical was grounded in Ibadi doctrine and practice, embodied in past acts and deeds and assumed to be constant and valid across time. It was the aim of engaging and approximating the virtues and pious accounts of the exemplarity of the Prophet and his companions that suspended temporal difference. The past was simultaneously dead and living, evocative and didactic for the present and future.

In post-1970 Oman, as will be explained in chapters 3 and 4, the notion of athār has achieved a particular salience as turāth (heritage) with the emergence of nation-state building, civic morality, and their consequent politics. In other words, time has acquired a new quality in assuming a secular logic. Athār has come to be construed as a memorialized past, grounded in the physical, as material traces of buildings and objects that stand as testimonies to the glories of Oman, paving the way for restoration programs that require specific features to be recognized and deemed worthy of preservation in the face of a changing future. I dedicate the next few chapters to the forts, watchtowers, *sabl* (council/meeting halls), and such objects as the coffeepot (dalla). These were no doubt constantly maintained and restored during the Ibadi Imamate, but not due so much to an understanding of their being testimonies to the past as to their embeddedness in a religiopolitical world where they were part and parcel of daily life. This distinct shift in the significance of athār also reflects a transformation in temporality as part of the modern state experience, one that embraces the notion of change over time. It presupposes the idea that the past is radically different from the present in qualitative ways and thus deserves to be preserved for the future in the face of "the implicit threat of time itself—forgetting, decaying, eroding" (R. Harrison 2013, 7). But it is only since 1970 that the view of the past as a foreign country has become institutionally established in Oman.

NIZWA FORT AND THE *DALLA* DURING THE IMAMATE

Nizwa is often deemed emblematic of the golden age of the Ibadi Imamate from the eighth to the twelfth centuries, from which it gains its title, *baydat al-Islam* (seat of Islam).[1] Sheikh Abdullah al-Saifi, an elderly scholar of the area, explained that *baydat* in this context means the "field" or "realm" of Islam; as the early capital of the imamate, Nizwa saw "the gathering of a great number of scholars, renowned for their virtue and learning." Even when the imamate moved to Rustaq, Bahla, and Muscat, Nizwa continued as a primary center of Ibadi learning and scholarship and produced generations of scholars, jurists, historians, and teachers. That importance was further raised in the twentieth century, when Nizwa became the capital of the Ibadi Imamate once more.

Wadi Kalbu divides the large, unwalled town into Nizwa ʿAlāya (Upper Nizwa) and Nizwa Safāla (Lower Nizwa), intersecting with Wadi al-Abyad at the market area. The city center, located in Nizwa Safāla, boasts a series of walled quarters with the remnants of arched entranceways behind an elongated modern facade of adobe-colored cement buildings with arcaded shop fronts. Through a small gateway, one can step beyond the post-1970s commercial developments and walk through these old quarters, with their unadorned mosques, guard towers, and the crumbling mudbrick walls of flat-roofed two-story houses. The close-set structures border a series of narrow lanes, interspersed by banana groves, apricot orchards, fields of melons, and groves of date palms, once the key cash crop of the region. Walking along these streets, one comes to the *aflāj* (water channels), many of which still irrigate the gardens throughout the day, much as they did during the imamate.[2] Even into the 1960s, the journey from Muscat to Nizwa was several days' journey by camel caravan. Today, a modern two-lane road passes through the city center, fronted on either side by a long line of bakeries, small supermarkets, banks, restaurants for tourists and migrant workers, electronics shops, and gold jewelers. Still, the hulking presence of the circular artillery tower of the fort (*qal'a*), with its Omani flag fluttering high on a flagpole, dominates the modern cityscape of Nizwa.

Situated in the center of the old city, in the al-'Aqr quarter, Nizwa Fort lies adjacent to the souq and the congregational mosque. During my fieldwork in Nizwa, my interest in the daily life of the twentieth-century Ibadi Imamate often took me to the fort. I spent many hours talking with custodians and tour guides, some of whose families had been in Nizwa for centuries. I often sat with one or more of them in a small room behind the ticket desk (the fort became a tourist site in the 1990s), drinking coffee from a plastic thermos and eating the dates that were always ready for those inclined to conversation. During one of my early visits, I met Saif, a custodian who had been a guard when the fort was still the courthouse and administrative center, housing the offices of the wali and the qadi until the mid-1980s.

Saif was a bent, wizened old man whose wrinkled mien often held a kindly smile. He was brought up in the vicinity of the fort, where his father had worked as a sentry and guard of the imam. He remembered childhood days when the imam would pat him on the head after prayer; the imam loved children, often stopping to talk to them, and his touch was considered a blessing. As a youth after the fall of the imamate in 1955, Saif traveled to Bahrain, Kuwait, Pakistan, and Qatar, looking for work.[3] In the early 1970s, he was working on an Abu Dhabi farm belonging to Sheikh Khalifa bin Said when he heard Sultan Qaboos's call for all Omanis to return to rebuild their homeland. He came home to become a chief guard at the fort, like his father. He defined his job as follows: "If, by the orders of the wali or the qadi, someone was requested to come in and he refused [*mumtani'*], I would need to bring them in. For example, if your presence is requested, I would bring you a letter requesting your required presence in a meeting with them. This was our work. In the nights we would go out on night patrols."

Much of daily life during Saif's time—and his father's—was spent in the sabla, where male neighbors and kin would meet in the mornings after *fajr* (dawn prayer). They met over coffee and dates after which they would go to their work in trade or agriculture. In the evenings after *'asr* (late afternoon prayers), they would partake once more in the ritual of coffee and dates (*taqahwa*) in the sabla. "We would talk, we would read out loud, and the *rashīd* [head] of the sabla would mediate and resolve quarrels in a peaceful manner, covering both sides. . . . A lot of robberies were addressed and security was assured through the sabla." As Saif explained, the sabla was where men from the *hara* (old residential quarter;

pl. *hārāt*) would meet with local elders (*ʿayān*): "It was the primary mover [*muhar-rik*] of the community, which interceded to resolve disputes among people, en-sured the security of the neighborhood, provided models of *adab* [the entangled set of dispositions, knowledge, and modes of behavior] through knowledge to the young, received guests into the hara, allocated water rights of the falaj system, and practiced social governance over coffee and dates."

Chapter 1 explored the modality of relationships between past, present, and future that undergirded the rise of the twentieth-century Ibadi Imamate. Yet this temporal consciousness still would not explain how an appeal to past exemplary authorities would translate into everyday administrative practice and governance. This chapter examines how the daily functional use of such material forms as Nizwa Fort and the dalla (coffeepot) in the imamate were socially, politically, and ethically significant. During the imamate, the role of Nizwa Fort shifted; by turns it was an administrative center, a school for the training of senior official, judges, and scholars, a high court and prison, and a defensive stronghold. The constant motion of the dalla in its role as a coffee server was considered as a necessary com-ponent of the workings of the sabla. This was a term that was popularly trans-lated as both a locale for the exchange of news and a social forum for arbitrating neighborhood disputes, administrating neighborhood affairs, schooling the young in adab (social decorum), and cultivating religious and tribal knowledge and eth-ical mores. It was the exchange of coffee and dates that was deemed to enable and lubricate the works of the daily sabla. As this chapter elucidates, these two key institutions—Nizwa Fort and the sabla—anchored the authoritative founda-tions of the imamate as a mode of governance. Daily use of the fort and the dalla were attuned to and in turn charged with a history made up of exemplary fig-ures whose words and deeds were guideposts for the present and the future by orienting everyday behavior toward divine salvation. Centered on God and di-rected toward cultivating the Ibadi Muslim, these histories were packed with the words and deeds of the Prophet and his companions, as well as subsequent gen-erations of imams, offering models, or exempla, to guide readers and listeners. Based on lessons drawn from the course of debate and discussion under circum-stances ranging from a juridical case presided over by the imam and his notaries at the fort to an informal reading at a sabla session, Nizwanis discovered the suc-cesses and failures of past authorities that informed their own assessments of what their duties were and how to fulfill them.

Thus, one former ʿulamāʾ of the city, now a government bureaucrat at the wali's office, told me, "It was necessary then to know the history of the imams, of the Prophet and his companions during the imamate, in order to know goodness [*khayr*] and evil [*shar*]." He then recited from the Quran—"It is possible that ye dislike a thing that is good for you. And that ye love a thing which is bad for you (2:216)"—and interpreted the passage for me:

> Any man who denies good and evil in history is ignorant and does not know. He would put good in the place of evil and evil in the place of good. He is ignorant and needs knowledge. If a man does not implement the knowledge of history, he is ignorant. If he is said to smoke, drink, acquire profit, take money from others, and is corrupt in consciousness, this man is *sayyi'* [evil] even though he is a judge and reads. If he does implement the history of the virtuous, he is a good man. When a man reads a book on the lives of the imams, prophets, judges or the 'ulamā' of the umma, he must get something from their lives and works in order to adapt it into his own life.

In this elderly scholar's understanding, historical knowledge had deeply moral undertones. Practices of reading and listening to history were a gradual process of sedimentation and absorption. Its active cultivation was a moral prerequisite for the acquisition of a particular set of dispositions and practices that, in turn, enabled the embodiment of the assessment criteria by which the Ibadi evaluated any action and its consequence, judging it good or bad. The honing of this mode of historical consciousness was part of the daily workings of Nizwa Fort and the sabla during the last Ibadi Imamate (1913–1957).

The Fort during the Twentieth-Century Imamate

Although Nizwa Fort is one of hundreds of fortified castles that characterize the Omani landscape, it is considered exceptional for having been the seat of the Ibadi Imamate from the eighth to the twelfth centuries, and once more in the twentieth century (1913–1955).The fortified citadel that still towers over Nizwa's city center lies within a quadrangular walled enclosure (*ḥuṣn*) and is linked to the tower through several substantial doors and zig-zag passageways. This enclosure formed the residential and administrative compartments of the castle where the imam resided and received guests and where he and his advisors adjudicated cases in the court and kept prisoners. This part of the fort complex, constructed during the first Imamate by Imam Al Salt bin Malik (851–886), predates the stone-and-mudbrick artillery tower, which was built during the rule of the Yā'ariba imam Sultan b. Saif (1649–1680), after his defeat of the Portuguese. Deeply influenced by the defensive architecture of the Portuguese forts of coastal Muscat, the Nizwa qal'a provided a circular gunnery platform, surrounded by a high, thick wall with viewing openings and musketry positions that shielded twenty-five cannons.[4] Linking walkways, high crenellated curtain walls, and connecting corridors provided quick access to all parts of the complex in a siege (figure 2.1). The fort complex is also well known for its ingenious traps, integral to its design, including false doors and "murder holes."[5]

The fort's physical features include the gunnery tower, curtain walls, arrow slits, and guard rooms and a layout that broadly divided its many chambers into the imam's personal quarters, the barza (audience hall and courthouse), student dorms, reception areas, and prayer room. These spatial divisions generated a series of practices, ranging from defense against sieges to daily administration, scholarly learning, and the adjudication of scholarly acts. The three key features of the imamate—administration, military, and justice—were cemented to each other by a past directed toward evaluating the virtuous life as part of a world view centered on fulfilling God's design. It might be argued that the fort, with its military features and administrative space, had little to do with ethical or moral order. However, neither the conceptual vocabulary nor the practices of the military, the administration, or the law could be distinguished from each other, since they were anchored to building a just social order in fulfillment of the Ibadi covenant with God through the divinely ordained institution of the imamate.[6] Regulatory activities, from tax collection to waging a war, all boiled down to the application of precepts of Ibadi shari'a, which was requisite for their practical deployment as part of daily living. These activities were generated, organized, and administered through the fort. For example, I was informed that the firing of the fort's canons summoned ordinary tribesmen from their daily work to rally to the imam's cause if a territory was being threatened.

As a juridical and administrative center, the activities of shari'a law and administration that took place within the confines of Nizwa Fort were grounded in three sources: (1) the Quran, (2) the sunna of the Prophet and his companions, and (3) the formative experiences, words, and deeds of a succession of imams reaching back to the early Madinan caliphate of Abu Bakr and 'Umar ibn al Khattāb, as well as jurists, scholars, and judges.[7] The fort's authority, in its embodiment of the twentieth-century imamate, was premised on weaving together these three primary tiers of interpretation to scaffold the idealized "just" Ibadi community. Shari'a structured everyday practices and morally shaped the social norms that governed how community members related to themselves and others. Sheikh Muhanna, once a student of Imam Khalili Madrasa in Nizwa, explained the fort as a basis for "uniting the sword with the pen. With the sword, you preserved shari'a . . . but the imamate could not exist without learning and learning is not possible without the pen."

Nizwa Fort Plans

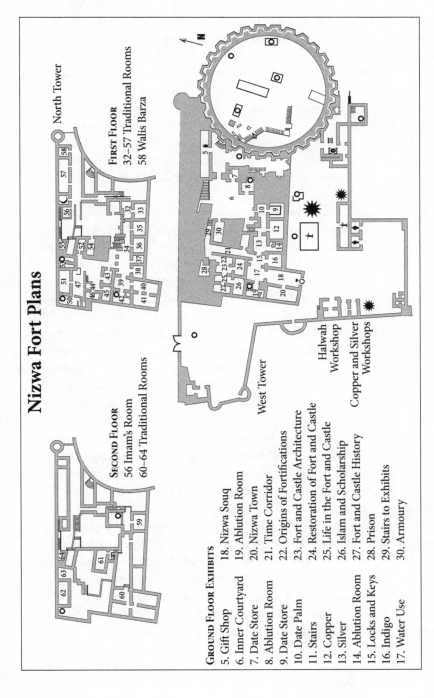

North Tower

FIRST FLOOR
32–57 Traditional Rooms
58 Walis Barza

SECOND FLOOR
56 Imam's Room
60–64 Traditional Rooms

West Tower

Halwah
Workshop

Copper and Silver
Workshops

GROUND FLOOR EXHIBITS
5. Gift Shop
6. Inner Courtyard
7. Date Store
8. Ablution Room
9. Date Store
10. Date Palm
11. Stairs
12. Copper
13. Silver
14. Ablution Room
15. Locks and Keys
16. Indigo
17. Water Use
18. Nizwa Souq
19. Ablution Room
20. Nizwa Town
21. Time Corridor
22. Origins of Fortifications
23. Fort and Castle Architecture
24. Restoration of Fort and Castle
25. Life in the Fort and Castle
26. Islam and Scholarship
27. Fort and Castle History
28. Prison
29. Stairs to Exhibits
30. Armoury

FIGURE 2.1. Ground plan of the Nizwa Fort

Courtesy of the Ministry of Tourism

As mentioned in chapter 1, this God-centered history was oriented toward evaluating the virtuous life as a way of fulfilling God's design. It was founded on the idea of the exemplar and emerged from the collection of hadiths (words and deeds of the Prophet) that, along with the Quran, formed the fundamental sources of shari'a. However, these sources were interpreted and reinterpreted in light of a specific understanding of a past that centered on the question of criteria for legitimate rule after the Prophet's death. A conception of history grounded in an understanding of events following the Prophet's demise was instrumental to subsequent political, doctrinal, and judicial debates pertaining to the faith. In its authoritative and institutionalized form, this history formed the center of debates that structured the Islamic world in terms of determining authority, legitimacy, and the body politic.

Contemporary Omani scholars often question why historical chronicles have never become a more pervasive genre in Oman, compared to the rest of the Muslim world.[8] One common explanation is that the Islamic past was recorded, analyzed, and represented in Oman but was done so as the basis for establishing and strengthening the foundations of Ibadi jurisprudence and sectarian thought rather than for developing and spreading history. This distinguishes Omani histories from those of such famed scholars as Ibn Isḥāq, al-Madā'ini, al-Ṭabarī, and Ibn 'Asākir or Ibn al-'Adīm.[9] When al-Salimi wrote his Omani history, he drew from a corpus of textual genres that were fundamental to law and doctrine. These included hadith collections, *siyar* literature (words and deeds of the "*ulamā* " and imams), multivolume encyclopedias on doctrine and fiqh, and older histories, such as Ibn Athīr's *al-Kāmal fi at-Tarīkh* (late twelfth and early thirteenth centuries), al-Iskawi's *Kashf al-Ghumma* (eighteenth century), and Ibn Ruzayq's *Fath al-Mubīn* (nineteenth century).[10] In short, an understanding of the past was fundamental to the practice of law and doctrine taking place in Nizwa Fort.

Siyar is a genre of biographies, edicts, fatwas, and *ṣaḥāba* (correspondence between the Prophet and his companions and, later, between Ibadi "*ulamā* ", delineating their perspectives on an unfolding set of socioeconomic and political circumstances). In following this interchange, one can see how changing contexts shaped the opinions of Ibadi scholars on such events as those that followed the death of the Prophet—the assassination of the Rāshidun caliph 'Uthmān, the arbitration between 'Ali and Mu'āwiya in the aftermath of the Battle of Siffin,[11] the rise of the Ibadi movement, its transfer from Basra to Oman in the eighth century, the clash in reasoning of scholars and jurists on criteria for accession to the imamate (which resulted in a series of civil wars), and the impact of outside invaders, including the Abbasids (893–922), the Saljuqs (eleventh century), and the Portuguese (sixteenth and seventeenth centuries). These documents are the contingent product of a specific set of historical circumstances, including internal and external threats and important community debates, which substantiated the parameters of Ibadi fiqh, doctrine, and conceptions of just and legitimate governance.[12]

One example of siyār is a letter written by the Prophet to his envoy, or wali, for Bahrain, al-ʿAlāʾ bin al-Haḍrami about the spread of Islam in southeast Arabia in 625 (al-Salimi 2010, 124). Another is the documented debates and opinions conveyed through correspondence by the companions of the Prophet, including ʿAlī bin Abī Tālib on the first civil war among the general Muslim populace that had come about as the result of the assassination of ʿUthmān bin ʿAffān (656–665). Sectarian and political divisions that defined Ibadi thought are delineated in a *sīra* (letter) from ʿAbd Allah bin Ibāḍ to the ʿUmayyad caliph, ʿAbd al-Malik bin Marwān. And the civil wars that ended the first Ibadi Imamate, revolving around the controversial removal of the aged imam, al-Ṣalt bin Mālik (851–886), led to a furious exchange of letters, edicts, and opinions between scholars over the centuries; these were later collected to clarify and sediment two schools of thought and learning, the Nizwani and the Rustaqi, whose primary conflict was the criteria for selection and removal of the imam.

The collection and preservation of these documents assumed even greater importance when they became the basis for mobilizing doctrinal opposition to the ascendance of the Nabhān dynastic rulers who seized power by force in the sixteenth and seventeenth centuries. During the time of Imam Muhammad bin Ismail (1500–1518), the jurist Ahmed bin Madād and his associates renounced the imam and issued a fatwa calling for his removal, declaring that the imam had deviated from the path of Ibadi sharīʿa by raising unlawful taxes to fill his coffers. Abd Allah bin Khalfan bin Qaysar chronicled the life of Imam Nāṣir bin Murshid al Yāʾrubī (1636–1649) in the first sīra (1640), still extant today, which documented the life of an individual as a volume unto itself. It was considered a model to emulate in the midst of the civil wars that later pitted rival Yāʿariba rulers and their supporters against each other (al-Jāludi 2003).

The cultivation of a historical orientation based on siyār generated a set of values and practices that distinguished the Ibadis from the Shiʿa and Sunnis. The twentieth-century Ibadi revival was roused by a utopian vision of the golden age of the imamate (eighth and ninth centuries), when Nizwa was the capital and its imams were considered paradigmatic, elected on the basis of merit and unencumbered by foreign interference or arbitrary seizures of power. The *sirat al-nabawi* (biography of the Prophet), accounts of his companions (*ṣahāba*), and important aspects of the lives, words, and actions (athār) of the Ibadi imams were another integral part of the multivolume fiqh compendiums. Laden with ethical import, they were constituted as normative deeds capable of transmitting attitudes and instigating imitation. As Chase Robinson (2003, 131) notes, "the task for Muslim historians was not to explain human actions as it was to exemplify known truths and to teach lessons." Several of the older 'ulamā' who had attended the Imam Khalili madrasa at the congregational mosque in Nizwa in the 1940s and 1950s often referred to these pivotal, multivolume texts—such as the *Bayān ash-Sharh* (eleventh century), *Muṣannaf* (twelfth century), and *Qāmus al-Sharīʿa* (eighteenth century)—as relevant references to life during the imamate. The works consisted of prophetic hadiths, accounts of the lives of the Prophet's companions, and histories and correspondence of Ibadi judges, jurists, scholars, and imams that articulate the nature of the imamate, the conditions for selecting or deposing an imam, the duties and obligations of his judges and governors, the criteria behind waging jihad, and the judgments delivered by Ibadi jurists in a variety of situations, from drinking wine to murder. They explain the reasoning that defined Ibadi legal scholarship and sanctioned its ethico-political rubric.

The impressions left by virtuous (and not so virtuous) forbears are what al-Salimi means in his reference to *iqtidā ʾbil athār* (following the traces of predecessors). This conception was fundamental to infusing the past authoritatively into the present as a mode of reasoning for implementing sharīʿa. The "traces" were continually reenacted as part of the daily workings of Nizwa Fort in adjudicating cases and administering the interior.

When I inquired about the relationship between history and Ibadi jurisprudence, an aged former qadi replied that history was once part of the development of fiqh and an inextricable part of documenting the lives of imams through the ages.[13] The exemplary words and actions of former imams established a tangible record of their lives (athār) that, in turn, was a primary basis for fiqh, instrumental in the exegetical elaboration of the foundational sources. Thus, the past became an institutional storehouse of orientations, embodied in the deeds of the celebrated ṣalihīn (righteous) and made accessible to future generations through their transformation into oral and written records. These figures and their deeds became ethical models that guided later generations in determining the right action in any given situation or evaluating the attitudes and behaviors of others by following their virtues and avoiding their vices. The aim of these histories was to cultivate "the perfect Muslim" by instilling the attitudes, dispositions, and skills that enabled justice through piety.

Through a process of recollecting impressions of virtuous and not-so-virtuous forbears, precepts were extracted through analogical reasoning to address contemporary situations through a process of juxtaposition and comparison. These core precepts presupposed an authoritative model that emulated the attitudes, actions, and beliefs of the Prophet and his successors, the imams. The authoritative past was part of an infrastructure of institutional power and disciplinary practices that institutionalized merit in the form of piety in commanding right and forbidding wrong and struggling in the path of God ("amr bal ma'ruf wal nahy 'an al-munkar wal jihad fi sabil allah").[14] In securing the authority of the imamate, the fort was the site of a historical consciousness that organized law, administration, and ethics in ways that defined or defied Ibadi religiosity. Normative ethical principles guided the interpretation and deployment of fiqh and everyday administration. Underlying the "exemplary" view was the assumption that history was continuous—the past blended seamlessly with the present and future. This sense of continuity and constancy aimed at engaging, ingesting, and approximating the virtues and pious accounts of the exemplarity of the Prophet, his companions, and the imams, while avoiding their shortcomings. Thus, the past occupied a space of experience homologous with the present.

After one studied the Quran in madrasas, these texts became the objects of more advanced study as a part of exegetical literature (*tafsīr*) and fiqh in the higher realms of learning. One former student of the Imam Khalili madrasa in the congregational mosque of Nizwa (the Great Mosque of 'Aqr) mused over the schooling he had received in Nizwa. During the twentieth-century imamate, after attending the madrasa to study the Quran, he joined study circles at the congregational mosque, where he studied Arabic grammar, memorized prophetic hadiths, and acquired a "firm hold" (*maska wa qabḍa*) on fiqh, doctrine, and siyār literature, including the sīra (biography) of the Prophet. He told me, "The school at the mosque was not merely interested in having us use these works as references; nor were we supposed to merely read from them. In fact, the teacher was interested in explaining [*muṭāla'at*] these books and was intent on delivering them [*yulqa 'la*] to his students orally. The students would take them in [*yākhudūhu*] through listening." The daily techniques of recitation and memorization of past exemplary accounts was a key means of internalizing narratives and events. These techniques became part of the process of domestication and incorporation in working on one's body and soul (Carruthers 1990, chaps. 5–6). In training Ibadi *ulama* through intensive study and discussion, such disciplinary practice honed ethico-political and legal forms of judgment that structured a certain style of reasoning, in which specific legal and doctrinal issues could be debated and resolved.

Fort custodians, religious scholars, and ordinary Nizwanis who had lived through the 1940s and 1950s often recounted scenes from the barza (judgment hall) at the fort.[15] In the mornings and evenings, disputes were resolved and petitions presented in the public presence of the imam, with his coterie of advisors, judges, and students of fiqh in attendance. In the evenings, when students were not attending lessons at the congregational mosque and there were no cases to settle, the barza became a *majlis al-'ilm* (learning council). After ṣalāt al-'asr and into the night, legal texts and histories were read aloud, discussed, and debated in *halqāt al-'ilm* (study circles) on a daily basis as part of the process of translating them into the practical desire to implement everyday justice. These accounts were perused through a corpus of shared historical texts, including the multivolume fiqh compendiums, hadith compilations, biographies of the Prophet such as the *Maulid al nabī* by Hasan al-Barzanjī (eighteenth century), chronicled histories such as al-Salimi's *Tuhfat al-ʿayān* (early twentieth century), al-Izkawi's *Kashf al-Ghumma* (eighteenth century), al-ʿAwtabi's *al-Ansāb* (eleventh century), and siyār literature.

The past as a source of law and regulation and an object of contemplation conditioned the basis by which the morality of any act could be assessed as leading to or impeding the path of salvation. This created a legal and moral classification of obligations and rights that informed social relationships and ethical mores. This perspective is elaborated in a series of letters from Imam Muhammad bin Abdullah al-Khalili to his officials in the imamate provinces. In one such letter, dated to 1945, the imam appointed Sheikh Saud bin Khamis al-Maliki as qadi of Bidiya in the Ash-Sharqiyah region of Oman. He advises his new appointee to help the people

> distinguish the signs of their religion through reviving within them the sunna of their Prophet and to dispense justice by way of the Quran, as you understand it, and if that is not possible, then the sunna of the Prophet. And if the answer you seek cannot be found in either the Quran or the sunna, then seek it through consensus among Muslims. And if consensus cannot be found, then look to the athār of righteous predecessors [*ahl al-istiqāma*], who were intent on seeking a similar justice, and implement what appears to be closest to the right thing. And do not make a judgment until it can be ascertained [*yatayaqun*] that it is right (al-Shukaili 2013, 79; see also Al-Saifi 2008, 3:163).

In another letter, he advises Sheikh Abdullah bin Saif bin Abdullah,[16] "If you see your companions among the *ahl al-bāghi* [unjust or oppressors], stand up to them and advise them to remain steadfast and look towards the companions of Muhammad as examples to follow. Do you not see that tyranny and oppression grows and proliferates when it is not stopped?" (O.M.NRAA.A.3.2.2) Centered in the forts of the region, the imam's qadis and walis, who ruled over the imamate provinces, were considered extensions of his rule; a good imam would spread justice and prosperity by ensuring the officials he chose adhered to sharīʿa in meting out justice and ruling over the land in his name. An official or ruler was judged by how closely he fulfilled this Islamic doctrine of human perfection, as embodied by virtuous predecessors. The past was simultaneously dead and living, evocative and didactic for the present and future.

The Dalla, the Sabla, and the Imamate

When I started asking Nizwanis about the importance of the dalla as part of their daily routines before 1970, their explanations usually included mention of the sabla, a daily institution pervasive before the nahda. And when I asked whether its importance was similar, Nasser (the elderly proprietor of Nizwa Fort's gift shop) explained:

> Neighbors and kin . . . would sit and chat in the afternoons and evenings [*yasmūrun*], exchanging news on the latest events in the area, mediating quarrels and complaints between groups or effecting consultations about a bad crop or a political meeting to reform the outlying region [*balad*], assisting those in need in the residential quarter [hara] or sharing in the expenses of buying meat for celebratory occasions such as 'Id al-adha [Feast of Immolation]. In translation, the term *sabla* means both the place where friends, kin, and neighbors gathered for the exchange of news, resolving differences and the act of talking.

Before the nahda, Nasser told me, men gathered at the sabla to break their fast with coffee and dates, returning after work to stay from salat al-'asr (late afternoon prayers) until 'ashā (late evening prayers). The sabla was open to all men; a man could come in at any time to discuss the issues of the day and help resolve quarrels. Men would bring books to read or a craft to work on, such as *khiwāsa* (plaiting of palm leaves for mats, baskets, or rope), thus socializing while earning their income. They would exchange water, coffee, and *rutab* (ripe dates).[17] If an emergency arose in the community, those passing time in the sabla could readily respond.

I asked other Nizwa elders about the role the sabla had played in their lives and the lives of their fathers. These were scholars, teachers, and administrators, members of tribes and families who had resided in the city for centuries, were renowned for their scholarship and learning, and had led famous sabl. Their ancestors were governors, scholars, jurists, poets, writers, and judges during the twentieth-century imamate, and their descendants have been co-opted into business or government, occupying administrative positions in a number of ministries and the University of Nizwa. They formed a tightly woven network, known to everyone, it seemed, even in a city of more than seventy thousand.

Sheikh Khalfan was one such man. Wearing the white *masar* (turban) and disdasha (long robe) that identified an '*alam* (scholar) on sight in Oman, Sheikh Khalfan received me in a spartan living room with three low tables and three armchairs. He was considered among the last generation of students to have been educated by the imam and his advisors at the Great Mosque in Nizwa and at Nizwa

Fort. With the advent of the nahda, he had worked with the new Ministry of Justice; in retirement, he had a reputation as a scholar and author of a number of works interpreting Quranic verses, the names of God, and commentaries on old manuscripts by *'ulamā*. As his secretary poured coffee and placed a dish of dates on the center table, the sheikh asked about my background and interest in the imamate in Nizwa and then, rather unusually, asked me to scribble my questions on a piece of paper. After looking them over, he recalled that in the old days, the sabl of the hara had been a daily affair headed by the *"ab" al sabla* ("father" of the sabla). Seating in the sabla enacted and reflected a broader world of overlapping hierarchical categories founded on learning, tribal descent, and occupation. As the most senior man, the *ab* sat at the *ṣadr* (place of honor), with important guests at his sides. Next to them sat other men of learning and scholarship, those of distinguished tribal lineage, wealth, and standing, the elderly, youths, and finally children. The sabla's rectangular configuration meant these groups faced each other, facilitating both conversation and the passing of food and coffee.

Each daily session was divided into periods devoted to different activities. First, participants would ask about each other and their news: *Shai'ulūm* (what's new)? *Shai akhbār* (what's the news)? *Hal shai jadīd fil balad* (anything new in the area)? Are there any new governors or imams? Any travelers from abroad or from the coast? Then the group would take turns discussing affairs in need of discussion and resolution—hearing complaints about neighbors or men who were reticent about attending Friday prayers, discussing assistance to the poor, resolving quarrels among youth or divisions (*faṣal*) about prices or quotas from the aflāj, writing marriage contracts, and settling divorce matters. If a matter involved a grave crime, the group would inform the rashīd (sheikh of the hara) or refer it to the qadi. For all other matters, the *ab sabla* would intercede, listening to those present and finding a solution to the problem between them.

The third period was allocated to reading books considered important by the scholars of the age. Some of the books Sheikh Khalfan mentioned were the same as those Saif and others had named: *Dalā'il ila al-lawāzem wal wasā'il* and books on the hadith and the *sirat al nabawīya* (life of the Prophet) and his companions (ṣahaba).[18] These were read aloud so all could hear. The judge, jurist, teacher, or other educated members of the sabla would interpret the passages and give their opinions, interposed (*yatakhalal*) with discussion and debate, a desire (*irād*) for historical accounts, and a setting forth of daily events. Thus, according to the sheikh, more than one topic might be addressed in a general way so all could understand: "Someone might not know how to read or write, but he could learn by heart a great deal of it by listening to the reading. Even if someone was illiterate, that did not mean that he was not learned and he could not understand. . . . These were the modes of knowledge that were in circulation [*mutadāwala*]."

The ab sabla—the foundation of the sabla—were the notables or prominent elders (*ashraf*) of the quarter. When prominent scholars, teachers, jurists, qadis, or sheikhs (a title earned through learning or tribal affiliation) attended the sabla, Sheikh Khalfan said,

> They attracted [*yastiqṭabun*] people who came to talk, get news, and resolve issues. But the 'ayan of the sabl could be anyone whose word was respected. For example, I have a violent quarrel with you. Who is going to judge or resolve it? It would be resolved by someone who was an elder or a sheikh, someone who by talking could resolve difference between two conflicting parties. But this person was the master of the good, respected word [sahib li kalima ṭayyiba muhtarama] to which all people turned [*yaltafatu ilaih*]. I will tell you why the sabla was so important in the old days. It was because it resolved [*yafṣil*] the problems of the people of the hara. It brought a lot of peace and security [*amāna*]. And people would choose only the most virtuous among them [*afḍal al nās*].

I heard this account of the daily proceedings of the sabla, with little variation, from men of all walks of life—shopkeepers and government administrators, teachers and merchants.

The old sabl could be found near aflāj and mosques among the crumbling mudbrick houses of the hara, which today are largely abandoned or inhabited by Indian, Pakistani, or Bangladeshi guest workers. However, walking through the oldest and largest walled and gated quarter of the city, the *hārāt al-'aqr* adjacent to Nizwa Fort still shed light on how daily life obscured the lines between public and private for men and women. Individual houses cleaved together, creating continuous mudbrick walls facing each other across a series of narrow lanes. A merchant of silver and handcrafts, whose family had long resided in the quarter, reminisced about how such living arrangements generated *ta'āluf ijtima'ī* (social intimacy). There was essentially no boundary between one house and the next: "We felt as if we lived in the same house. We were forty families; even if one was in the house, we were moving from house to house by way of the roof." In these small houses—scarcely more than fifty square meters—the ground floor was for keeping the animals and storing dates, while the one- or two-room upper floor was reserved for the kitchen and living areas. The ground floor had a small vestibule, the *dahliz*, that could receive one or two visitors. Each day, the men of al-'aqr would gather in the sabla, returning home only at night.[19]

Amjad, a journalist and ardent activist for the preservation of the harat al-'aqr took me to the sabla his father and their kin and neighbors had once frequented in al-'aqr, close to one of the old mosques.[20] It was completely abandoned and had partially collapsed because of the rains. Through its single entrance and within the large mudbrick chamber, dirt and rubble were strewn across one corner. One could still admire the ceiling, constructed from the trunks of date palms, and find traces of simple painted motifs on the walls—geometric patterns and roundels in faded reds, blues, and greens. All four walls held the *rowāzan* (recessed niches; figure 2.2) where, Amjad informed me, books would have been placed as men gathered to read and discuss jurisprudence, the Quran, and history. Along the

FIGURE 2.2.   Recessed niches of the sabla

Photo by the author

walls still hung the pegs that had once held ceramic water jugs and woven palm baskets for dates and other fruit. People of varied social classes, from '*ulamā*' to agricultural workers, frequented this place daily, right into the mid-1980s.

A constant theme of recall and contemplation was the sabla's constitutive role in forging interactive relationships. Concepts such as *takātuf* (mutual solidarity), *tafāhum* (mutual understanding), and *takāluf* (mutual guarantee) were the substance of relationships and feelings that were, from many Nizwani perspectives, generated primarily through the sabla. But could the sabla truly subsist on mutual understanding and solidarity? Wasn't it possible to rouse factionalism through gossip? I posed this question to several elderly Nizwanis, and Sheikh Khattab's response encapsulated their thoughts—this might have been possible in more tribal hārāt, but most quarters of Nizwa housed a mélange of families. "Of course, there were quarrels and problems," he told me, "[but] the sabla would return to these differences, treat it, and resolve it the next day. They would not leave someone upset or angry because of a quarrel. This is what the sabla was for."

Although these descriptions are obviously rather idealized, the sabla was understood as an institution with an integral role in daily life. Even as Nizwanis had direct access to the imam and his officials in the barza, it was the neighborhood sabl always accompanied by the dalla that led local governance and public welfare. It was the quarter's elders, chosen for their scholarly acumen, intellect, and virtue, to whom people turned to resolve disputes, settle personal, economic, and social affairs, and write land deeds and marriage contracts, and for celebrations and guidance on how to live a virtuous life.

Coffee as Part of Sabla Socialization

Mandar was the son of a leading scholarly family in Nizwa who had once lived in the harat al-'aqr. Guiding me through the old quarter, he took me to a sabla once led by a famous '*alam* who had been a *faqīh* (jurist) and judge under Imam Khalili. This sabla had been in use into the early 1980s. When we arrived, we found a low, rectangular mudbrick building, in a rather derelict state, that had become a residence for Indian guest workers. Amid the mattresses, posters of Pantene shampoo models, hanging clothes, and a makeshift kitchen, we could see the familiar rowāzan. Mandar, reminiscing about his childhood, told me this sabla had always been filled with the smell of coffee. He pointed to a place near the door, explaining that this was the *mawqid* (hearth) where coffee berries had been roasted, pounded, and boiled.

Coffee featured prominently in descriptions of the sabla, where it was an indispensable part of forging relationships in a hara and prepared daily, for every gathering. As I was often told, "the neighbors brought coffee to the sabla in the mornings," "there was always a dalla warming in the corner of the sabla," "we just brought a little coffee and some dates with us to the sabla," or "in the evenings, we would make the rounds of coffee." It was compulsory for each house, represented by its senior member, to take turns providing a daily portion of coffee and dates. This affirms the view shared by Limbert (2010, 68–70), who notes that coffee and dates have had specific assumptions embedded in their use in Oman and have formed an intimate role in shaping interpersonal relationships. Those who did not do taqahwa (the social act of "doing coffee") by offering their guests dates and coffee were seen as dishonoring them, even if they offered an otherwise sumptuous repast. As Mandar elucidates, the mixture was a way of safeguarding health, "a way of balancing the sweetness and hotness of the dates with the slight bitterness of the coffee, lightening the taste overall so it would not be overwhelmingly sweet even while extinguishing the heat [*yutfi'al-harāra*]."[21]

Hierarchical relationships grounded in learning, wealth, occupation, and tribal lineage were reflected and sedimented in how the youngest of the group—youths and older children (and slaves, if present)—distributed the coffee and dates.[22] Service was divided along the left and right parts of the sabla. According to Sheikh Khalfan, dates were first passed to the ab sabla, the most senior person there, then to the right, serving guests, men of learning and scholarship, and the elderly. Service then moved to the left, ending with the younger men and children. Those descended from enslaved people were usually near the doorway at the end. However, an increase in stature was possible (and would entail moving up the sabla ranking toward the ṣadr position) through learning and scholarship, as well as occupation and standing. As one member of a scholarly family mentioned, during his father's time, one scholar of slave descent, renowned for his learning, was always invited to sit at the ṣadr in place of his father. Literary descriptions from Western residents, such as Paul Wilberforce Harrison (1940, 34), speak of being a guest at sabl in the interior that were presided over by a slave: "The master of the plantation was absent and the entire place was administered in his absence by his chief slave." The service of washing hands and serving coffee followed a similar hierarchical pattern, serving those in accordance with social stature, means, and age. Children were considered an undifferentiated mass. They carried water and served dates and coffee and, as Sheikh Khalfan explained, "whether they were the children of a faqih [jurist], *sheikh* or a farmer, all of them were equal and all of them undertook these works. If there were no children present, then the least senior person would serve the coffee."

Recalling his childhood days in the sabla of his ancestors, Mandar ruminated over the complex habits and knowledge (adab) instilled in the young through, for example, greeting people by shaking hands with the right hand, pouring coffee for elders, and learning when to eat and drink and when to listen in silence. When he was young, his father allowed him to enter the sabla and serve coffee to guests. Over time, he learned how to pour from the dalla—with the right hand, not the left, and only a quarter of a cup at a time. At times, people would look into the cup of coffee he had poured and say, "Ma' Shallāh [by the grace of God], this boy is an expert in pouring coffee." The boys had to be *muntabih* (alert); the slightest movement of a hand indicated that someone wanted more, but a slight back-and-forth shake of the cup signaled they were done.

The dalla was a vessel that garnered attention not for its decoration—although it was incised and embossed with designs—but for its movement around the sabla, which delineated the social hierarchy and conditioned the modes by which social interaction and discussion took place. As a serving vessel, it was in constant motion in the hands of the young, always pregnant with the implications of pouring coffee properly or committing a faux pas. Its mobility and durability as a vessel that retained the heat of the coffee gave it significance. Mandar recalled that his father would consider a dalla *nau aṣlī* (authentic) based on how long it could retain heat. His family was unusual for keeping their copper dalla into the 1990s, when most had thrown theirs away in the 1980s. After that, like everyone else in Nizwa, they used a plastic thermos.

During the imamate, the very form of the dalla—a spouted and handled vessel—invited the act of pouring coffee, an action that remains necessary to cement ties of obligation and reciprocity today. In its form and function, the dalla was embedded in people's social interactions. In a Maussian sense, it was an extension of the giver's personality and the lubricant that forged socioethical relationships. These relationships were articulated by, and thus inseparable from, the material exchange of dates and coffee, yet the exchange also facilitated the acts of obligation and reciprocity that defined guest status, friendship, and communal ties.

Narrating History as Part of Sabla Socialization and Ethical Formation

During sabl gatherings in the late afternoons and evenings, an 'alam from the neighborhood often brought a book to recite. The most popular works were poetry and accounts of the prophets, imams, and *ṣālihīn* (the righteous). Many of these works were the same ones perused by students and scholars, ranging from multivolume encyclopedic works on fiqh to more conventional histories and prophetic hadith. Ali, one of the fort custodians, recalled that when people celebrated the Prophet's birthday, one of the more learned among them would bring a book on the *sirat al-nabī* (the life of the Prophet), and coffee would be prepared for the sabla. He would read the most important passages on the Prophet and the events of his life before reciting a *du'a* (supplication) prayer. This ritual infused history with religious and moral understanding.

Sheikh Khalfan had a rather matter-of-fact perspective on the role of learning in the Nizwani sabla. According to him, it was the desire of the jurist to spread his knowledge among the populace that led to the foundational educational role of the sabla. Thus, it was the qadi, teacher, or *faqih*—after teaching or presiding over juridical matters at study circles in the mosque or the barza of the fort—who would gather the people of the hara in the sabla in the late afternoons and evenings to discuss what had been read so it might benefit them. Young boys would accompany their fathers to become acquainted with their neighbors and kin and learn how to work with them and to acquire the community's ethical mores and the adab (rules of conduct). The sheikh told me:

> The sabla was about creating a model [*qudwa*] that the young will emulate. You observe your father, and you are guided by those who are older. They warn [*tuhadhiru*] you against lying, cheating, but also how to receive people, how to offer respect, when to be silent, how to present coffee to those older. These are all the practices of attendance. But it was also about receiving wisdom [*hikma*] and cultivating elevated morals [*akhlaq al-faḍila*] through learning. When they wanted to censure [*yu'ib*] a person who had no sense of moral obligation, people would say, "He never sat at a gathering nor entered a school" or "He was not brought up [*mutarabi*] in an Arab sabla." For example, when they learn that when one person meets another, they would receive them with the words, *Shai 'ulum?* [What's the news?] This is something that is part of prophetic sunna [ways]. When the Prophet would meet other people, he would ask them where they were from? From which tribe? About the water or if there were rains. These are morals that have come down from the Prophet. And the children were learning them as they grew up in the sabla. . . . Even craftsmen and farmers would know their histories through the sabla.

Books were thus not solely for the scholarly. Nizwa men from different walks of life—shopkeepers, government administrators, and schoolteachers—all recalled that even though many people were illiterate, even after 1970, they were well aware of such historical works as al-Salimi's *Tuhfat-al-A'yan* (1961) and al-Izkawi's *Kashf al-Ghumma* (2006).

I asked Sheikh Khattab about the importance of reading histories in the sabla. He replied, "It is necessary to know history in order to know goodness [khayr] or evil [shar]. It is necessary for man to know his history to make it possible for him to implement the history he learns. A man would be considered ignorant because he does not adapt this knowledge." He then recited some poetry I could not follow and continued,

> If a man wants to live in any age, he must live *sirat al mustaqīm* [the right path]. If you do, you will be beloved by God, and he will safeguard you and help to remove you from *fisq* [moral depravity]. When a scholar is reading a book to all on the lives of imams, prophets, kings, judges, *'ulama'* of the umma, they must be getting something from their lives and works in order to adapt them to their own lives. But if they don't take anything, and are not listening, they will live lives of ignorance and dissipation. There is no use to their knowledge. Whereas the use of knowledge is virtuous works [*'amal al-sāleh*].

A younger scholar from one of the leading scholarly families in Nizwa, who was now a teacher and writer, also tried to impart the importance of the sabla during the imamate: "Of course, most people couldn't read or write at that time. But learning was so diffuse that an onion seller or someone in trade was an 'alam."

Al-Salimi's *Tuhfat-al-A'yan* and al-Izkawi's *Kashf al-Ghumma* explicitly mention their readers as an audience of listeners. In the introduction to *Kashf al-Ghumma* (eighteenth century), which many recalled as a popular work often read aloud, al-Izkawi explains why he writes:

> I had noticed that most of the people of our time have forgotten the origin of their honorable doctrine and they have become uninterested in reading books written by former generations. In including information on the Ibadi Imams and their doctrine, I have given it a superficial disguise as stories and historical accounts, whilst inwardly it relates to the chosen sect because people will not listen to the actual historical tradition but are more desirous of hearing legendary stories. So I have bent myself to please them so that they may listen and concentrate their attention in reading it with a pure heart so that they may know the fundamentals of the sect and acknowledge the people of truth in a true manner (translation from al-Askari 1984, 6–10).

Through recasting the listeners' thought into the structural mode of authoritative exemplary accounts, al-Izkawi is preaching and guiding in line with the criteria for fulfilling God's will, as understood by an Ibadi interpretation of the Quran and the prophetic sunna. Such acts of recollection were not merely edifying tales but authoritative ethical guidelines counseling the listeners toward correct courses of action. Public reading as an integral part of the sabla contributed to a heightened awareness, in which the self became an object of scrutiny and assessment. History was an integral part of the pedagogic process—inspiring pious fear, revulsion, passion, or myriad other emotions—generating an inclination toward a pious disposition in everyday life. In other words, such relations to the past were not merely referential or communicative but provided guidance on how to inhabit the world.[23] The moral past, in the form of the authoritative accounts of the Prophet, his companions, and the imams after them, loomed larger than life. The process of recitation and memorization of past exemplary accounts was a key means toward internalizing these narratives, which became part of the process of domestication and incorporation in working on one's very body and soul (Carruthers 1990, 210). Meditating on past acts of piety of the virtuous and the good, as well as those of sin, through these oral and aural techniques became keys toward embodying and cultivating a habitual familiarity that sedimented the practical conditions of knowledge formation and an ethical form of being (Hirschkind 2006).

The sabla, therefore, had a fundamental ethical dimension and played an important role in cultivating habits of moral health and virtue through a certain mode of tradition, with its own specific way of conceptualizing the relationship between past, present, and future. It was one where exemplary modes of memory and the authoritative figures of the Prophet, his companions, and the imams were histories that could be summoned up, becoming the very basis by which the present could be assessed and the future anticipated.

As a set of practices, the sabla continued long after the end of the imamate. Amjad, the young journalist, remembered attending the sabla with his father in the early 1980s. By that time, the plastic thermos was in full requisition for coffee service, having supplanted the dalla. Today, for the everyday household in Nizwa and across Oman, thanks to new consumer habits, the plastic thermos imported from China is considered more efficient in keeping coffee warm and so has effectively replaced the dalla, which has been relegated into the category of artifact and antique.

By the 1980s, the sabla was no longer a daily occurrence, taking place perhaps once a week, when Amjad's father would gather with other kin and neighbors in the evenings, just to talk. There was also no longer a central locale for the neighborhood to gather. By the time of my fieldwork in 2010 and 2011, all that remained were crumbled ruins of sabl in the old quarters. When I asked where the communal sabla was, people indicated a cement building with a large doorway, fronted by a grandiose *pishtaq* (a rectangular frame with an arched opening) off the main roads. Built in the 1990s as part of the new suburban development on the opposite side of the old *harāt*, it was called the *majlis al-'ama* (public majlis), as were many others throughout Oman. These new sabl, or *majālis al'amma*, are primarily for weddings and funerals, lectures on health, hajj guidelines or other religious matters, and classrooms for combating illiteracy, among other subjects, for the general populace.

People recalled the sabla as still at work among a few families but having mostly given way since the 1970s to a growing tendency toward privacy. This was a result of social transformations brought about by the services rendered by an increasingly bureaucratized centralized state, satiated by commercial oil and driving fundamental changes in people's lifestyles. In the 1970s, the government began distributing plots of land and subsidized building loans for a minimal fee. With increased family incomes resulting from a rush of government jobs and business opportunities, the houses of the old hara were considered too *muqayyada* (stifling), leading to mass migration out of the old quarters. Amjad remembered that in 1980, most inhabitants of *harat al-ʿaqr* had been Omanis, and Mandar recalled that people once knew that his family, their *ʿulamāʾ*, sheikhs, and jurists all lived in the hara: "But then we moved, because the family became bigger. . . . The present generation of young people do not like to live in their mudbrick houses. They consider them too cramped [*ḍayyiqa*], and they don't have proper bathrooms, kitchens." Omanis began renting their houses in the hara to Asian workers.

Strongly echoing Farah Al-Nakib's (2016, 186) analysis of Kuwait's urban transformations from the pre-oil *firjan* (neighborhoods) to the detached suburban villas, in Oman, a massive shift from the old harāt, with their closely bundled homes, to self-contained modern family villas was occurring "at the expense of communal relationships." Each family could now boast of having a private sabla for entertaining guests, and coffee had been internalized in the home, though it remained a constitutive part of hospitality rituals in occasional gatherings of family and friends. Meanwhile, with longer working hours, Omani men no longer had time for daily sabla gatherings. On Fridays, the family I resided with did gather with extended kin on their family farm, but as my landlord informed me, sighing, "It is just talk, and we sit and drink coffee! These are discussions and conversations which do not have any practical implications. . . . We are no longer people of the sabla. Institutions have taken over, for justice, arbitration, schools, and universities. The sabla in the past would have undertaken all these things. When there were differences between man and his wife, he would go to the sabla. Nowadays, he goes to court."

"The age of institutions!" I often heard this phrase in Nizwa and elsewhere in Oman. My landlord was referring to the fact that since the oil era, an increasingly centralized and intrusive state has extended its jurisdiction over the education and well-being of the populace to ensure the efficient running of an emergent civic domain, with mass schooling and local disputes resolved through Councils for Reconciliation and Settlement (an extension of the Ministry of Justice). Welfare benefits now flow from government coffers, not the tribal and religious elders of the sabla. As a result, the sabla's multifaceted role has become redundant. And, I was repeatedly informed, longer working hours meant Omani men no longer had time for daily sabla gatherings; they wanted to return home to relax with their families and watch television.[24] Incorporated into heritage discourse, *sabla* has become a term rich in connotations of the value of social interactions, strong ties, and mutual guarantee, but it no longer wields the force it once did as a powerful intercessor in sociopolitical life.

Conclusion

Ibadi Islam was constitutive of a distinctive Islamic sectarian ethical and political system, whose last manifestation arose and ended as the direct consequence of British military and economic colonial intervention in the twentieth century. The Ibadi sectarian tradition that predominated for more than a thousand years is still evidenced by the material presence of the fortresses, citadels, watchtowers, council chambers, mosques, and walled residential quarters that dot the landscape, as well as the everyday objects, such as the dalla, whose form and function facilitated the socioethical practices that embodied Ibadi sharīʿa law and ethical ways of living, defining a community grounded in a messianic sense of time. These sites and objects, lived in the styles of reason and practice, fashioning a distinctive, theologically defined space of a community marked by difference rather than by the homogeneity of the nation-state. Even as the notion of the umma (the theologically grounded Muslim community that belies national boundaries) assumed an idealized egalitarian order, the sharīʿa community of the imamate recognized and worked within a sociopolitical order structured around hierarchies grounded in scholarship and learning, descent, tribal lineage, occupation, and wealth.

The ways in which such material forms as the dalla and the forts and castles of the imamate were related to by the inhabitants of the twentieth-century imamate cultivated a modality of history that directed a specific form of administration, sociality, and ethical sensibilities that permeated daily living. An ineluctable connection was drawn between the past (the sunna of the Prophet and his companions) and virtuous norms (reciprocity), such that history assumed the necessary means through which normative virtues were cultivated (and vices warded off) and expressed. As exemplary models, the acts and deeds of these historical figures provided the standards for evaluating the acts and obligations that guided followers of the day. History was an evaluative category whose interpretation established an exemplary view that generated and institutionalized the juridical and doctrinal foundations of the Ibadi school of sharīʿa. Experiences and expectations took up the same authoritative character types, inasmuch as the past and the present were not sharply distinguished but considered in continuity with each other. In other words, there was a stable, authoritative basis for not only addressing change but also determining its significance.

MUSEUM EFFECTS

National Day on November 18, 1974, celebrating the fourth year of Sultan Qaboos's accession to the throne, turned into a several-day extravaganza. In prepa-
ration, triumphant plywood arches were erected over roads and painted with
patriotic slogans and designs, such as the dalla, the dhow (traditional ship), and
the khanjar (ceremonial dagger), and frantic arrangements were made for the
opening of infrastructure projects.[1] The event reached its climax with military
pageants featuring guns and armored cars, an air force flyby, presentations by
schoolchildren, and fireworks. The pivotal moment was the sultan's annual speech.
As had become customary, the speech was a catalog of the achievements of the
nahda period, inaugurated by his ascent to power in 1970, which brought dra-
matic transformations in socioeconomic modernization by way of an influx of
oil revenues. This included investing in large-scale infrastructure—hospitals,
roads, schools, and communication and information networks. This year, his
speech mentioned the inauguration of the Omani Museum, Oman's first.

Under the auspices of the Ministry of Information and Culture, the sultan had
officially opened the museum the previous day, claiming, "In the Omani Museum,
the citizen will see the heritage of his forefathers, and the civilization they achieved"
(Ministry of Information 2005a, 29). To commemorate this history was "to re-
gain the glories of the ancient past by asserting that it is not the time factor that
counts, but the achievements themselves on the path of civilized progress, the all-
out development of the country . . . the effect of such events on the course of its
progress" (ibid., 23). The sultan's words made clear that the presentation of the
material past was not merely about preservation but was fundamental to directing

contemporary affairs. Thus, the pivotal question is, *What kind of past is considered consonant with Oman's modernization? And why?*

In this chapter, I argue that in Oman, establishing the modern nation-state entailed a three-part operation in which particular material forms that were once part of daily living—including Nizwa Fort and the dalla—were co-opted by the state in a process of "purification" (Latour 1991). Firstly, this process involved stripping these objects from the concrete relationships that embedded them in the shari'a society of the imamate that gave them their significance as delineated in chapter 2. Second, these material forms underwent heritage operations of collection, documentation, preservation, and display to be consequently transformed into artifacts, architectures, monuments, exhibitions, and museums. Third, this construction resulted in a new social relationship with the past, simultaneously generating novel modes of inhabiting the present and future. The work of heritage processes acted as a temporal force that generated a new set of conceptual categories—culture and civilization—that now anchor the past in ways that engage directly with local and regional political and religious struggles the sultanate has been confronting for the past forty years. In the process, a new form of tradition becomes public. With a distinctive new conjunction that connects past, present, and future, it governs the sultanate and becomes integral to being modern in post-1970 Oman. Acting as a reference point, this past becomes the grounds for a program of social organization in religion, ethics, and history, displacing the imamate while anchoring the sultanate in the public domain.

The Omani Museum

Located in the hilly district of Qurm, the original Omani Museum was part of the Ministry of Information complex, called *Madinat al-i'lām* ("Information City"), along with new television and radio stations. The original floorplan remained in place until 2004, when the Ministry of Heritage and Culture transformed the museum, later closing it and transferring the collections to the new National Museum, which opened its doors on July 30, 2016.[2] Through conversations with retired museum directors and tour guides and by perusing photographs, booklets, and old documents, I acquired some understanding of the historical narrative and tense patterns of the text panels in the original exhibition.

The arrangement of objects was carefully orchestrated to engender interwoven conceptions of the past as an evolutionary chronicle that culminated in an array of traditions that are considered part of a living present. Following a chronological sequence around the main reception area, the ground-floor exhibits began with *Lands and People*. Large, walled photographs elucidated the variety of terrains with a textual panel, "from regions affected by the monsoons to mountains over 3,000 m high, sandy deserts and fertile plains," that define Oman's territory, which "ensures a wide variety of products and an abundant surplus for export." Through a variety of photographic depictions of "traditional livelihoods," each region was portrayed in terms of the particularities of its famous products or prevailing livelihoods. Agriculture as "tradition" was encapsulated by large color photographs displaying terraced farming in the Jebel Akhdar region in the interior, date harvesting in the Batinah coastal region, irrigation methods such as the *zaygra* and the aflāj system in the interior, and mineral mining in the mountain regions.[3] The texts surrounding the photographs used present tense, emphasizing that these livelihoods still defined the present day. For the Ad-Dhahirah region, for example, the text read, "In this region, we find vegetables, fruits. . . . Irrigation in the Dhahirah is mainly based on wells and falajs."

The longevity of such modes of habitation was on display in *Early History*, the next chamber, where large panels displayed text and photographs of early rock art, models of archaeological sites (such as beehive tombs from 3000 BCE), and early Omani settlers, one "drilling a stone bead with a flint tipped hand drill"—a technique thought to date to the New Stone Age. The chamber centered on large glass cases housing stone tools, rock carvings, copper wares, and pottery, all evidence of early human settlement and civilization in Oman. In an inner section, the emphasis was on Oman's strategic location, along ancient trade routes and the later Indian Ocean trade network, as a rich source of copper, diorite, and frankincense.

On the upper floor, in the *Islamic Period* section, wall panels emphasized Oman's voluntary submission to Islam. One panel noted that Oman's conversion moved the Prophet to declare, "God bless the people of Ghubaira (Oman). They have believed in me without seeing me." Emphasizing "how Islam enriched Oman's ancient culture and opened up new horizons for its people," a series of glass cases displayed old manuscripts of jurisprudence and doctrine, such as the *Kashf wal Bayān* (AD 1692), and sections of the legal encyclopedias *al-Musannaf* (557 AH / AD 1162) and *Bayān Ash-Sharh* (551 AH / AD 1156). These manuscripts were on display as material indexes for the paneled text sentiment, "Islam became the basis for opening up new horizons of knowledge and enlightenment as well as the flourishing of new trade networks and routes, the foundations for a spiritual life, based on the holy doctrines revealed by God through Muhammad, His Messenger." A series of photographic panels depicted the development of Oman's trading entrepôts, Sohar and Qalhat, from the ninth century until the coming of the Portuguese in the 1400s. There were examples of excavated ceramics from these sites, displays of weights, dried lemons, cardamom and other spices traded over time, and maritime instruments such as compasses and astrolabes.

An antechamber was dedicated to seafaring and ships. Surrounded by textual and visual panels set in blue, this display centered on models of traditional ships. The displays emphasized seafaring as a major national activity that continues to the present day. In this narrative, the Omani sailor is the protagonist of heroic enterprises, including the "longest sea-route in the medieval world." Advances in shipbuilding were assimilated into a narrative of progress: after the defeat of the Portuguese in 1650, wooden ships gave way to modern European techniques and new types of boats still in use today. In 1650, according to the text panels, the Ya'ariba Imamate (1624–1743) not only achieved a historic victory, but "drove the Portuguese from strongholds in the Gulf, Western India and East Africa." Then, during the reign of Sayyid Said bin Sultan (1807–1856) of the Al Bu Said dynasty (1744–present), the "sea trade reached its greatest extent," while creating an East African empire centered in Zanzibar and Pemba. The fruits of their rule were displayed in the chamber *Omani Architecture*, where large photographs and models of, for example, Jabrin and Nizwa Forts illuminate the fortresses as "great architectural treasures of Oman." The architectural legacy was further documented in the photographic and text panels showcasing the "fine large houses" of Ibra and Muscat in the eighteenth and nineteenth centuries and highlighting details of their wood carvings and stucco decorations.

Much of the original museum exhibition was devoted to an evolutionary chronicle, beginning with Paleolithic people's stone toolmaking enterprise and culminating in flourishing trade networks and a mighty navy that led to the development of the Omani empire in the eighteenth and nineteenth centuries. However, the final displays echoed its first, exploring Oman's varied terrain, which "has enabled the adaptation of subsistence operations that have continued for five thousand years into the twentieth century including pottery, copper work, and silver and gold work." In this final chamber, *Omani Arts and Crafts*, open exhibits displayed the products of these activities. An array of pottery was encapsulated with the words: "A wide variety of potting techniques are used in Oman. In Dhofar items are sun-dried, not fired, while Bahla, the largest range of pottery wheel thrown and kiln-fired is produced." The dalla and other metal objects were presented in a text panel that explained: "Copperware comes particularly from Nizwa, where the techniques used in silver work are used for making lidded containers, spoons, rose water sprinklers and coffee pots." And the label for craft industries added: "The art of transforming raw materials into useful tools and equipment in daily life was an indispensable pre-requisite that enabled the people of Oman to rise to the challenges posed by their harsh environment." Even though the labels were set in the past, the descriptions of techniques and regional distribution of material examples on display used the present tense.

The Museum Narration within a Larger Context

If a Western historical museum works through a process of cataloging, separating, and displacing customs and traditions thought to stand in the way of modernization by transforming them into historical representations of themselves (Bennett 2006; Chakrabarty 1992), the Omani Museum took up an oppositional stance. Even preserved as "historical evidence," an object's contemporaneous use was not denied. Past livelihoods—boatbuilding, maritime trade, date cultivation, pottery, and copper- and silverwork—were never assigned a specified stage in calendrical time, the "traditional/historical" never completely severed from the "modern." The activities of the past were in a fluid continuance with the present and future; they reinforced each other. Thus, Oman's past comes to be read as inextricably linked to a national present that assumes a niche in a longer history of the stages of "progress" and "civilization" (Chakrabarty 1992).

The museum narrative appears grounded in indelible links to the land. Omani culture, in this context, becomes a process whereby taming the land and surrounding seas and harnessing their many resources becomes part of a dynamism of purposive becoming. Time, in this evolutionary schema, is modeled on that of natural history. It echoes Johannes Fabian's (2014, 22–25) understanding of "typological time," where time is assessed not in terms of abstract units on a linear scale but in terms of socioculturally significant events placed within a specific territorial schema. The mastery of each stage of development through rational endeavor (agriculture, mining, shipbuilding, and arts and crafts) or warfare (defeat of the Portuguese and Persians) in this paradigmatic process forms the foundation for transforming the self toward full maturity. It engenders a people through development of their capabilities, culminating in distinctive and continuing Omani ways of life, represented by the exhibits on livelihoods and crafts.

However, the specificity of the narration—the evolutionary-cum-environmental-tradition interpretive frame—strongly resonates with one of the most prominent narrative frameworks that once reflected and facilitated fundamental transformations in European relations with the rest of the world from the mid-nineteenth century. For Timothy Mitchell (1988; 1989), the process of objectification, in which an object is estranged from its material context, distantiated, and put on display to be investigated and experienced, is an epistemology closely intertwined with Western power and the proliferation of a material and moral order that is integral to the global project of modernity. Mitchell's "World as Exhibition" (1989) develops the argument that representation as a mode of knowing and experiencing reality becomes a form of intervention and transformation of the colonized world, in accordance with how Europeans saw their history as part of the universalism of a "narrative of modernity" (Keane 2007, 9–13). It became an efficacious basis for organizing, consolidating, and differentiating multiple histories and disparate geographic spaces within the singular historical time of modernity (Betts and Ross 2015; Breckenridge 1989; Kirschenblatt-Gimblett 1998). Distance from the West resulted in the Other being placed backward in time, leading to the rejection of coevalness (Fabian 2014).

In Tony Bennett's (2006, 51–57) writings on the Western history museum, this narrative was articulated through distancing effects and became closely linked to a form of liberation through which new forms of individuality were forged. As part of this process, representational practices were conceived as enabling one to extricate oneself from blind immersion to custom, tradition, and habit, instigating a process of self-critique and self-development through standing apart, forming the basis for cultivating new forms of being as a matter of choice rather than through enforcement or unconscious habit. In this rationale, semiotic forms following the logic of representation are concomitant with liberal notions of individual autonomy and choice (W. Brown 2006, 166–71). For the colonized world, Mitchell (1988) goes to another extreme, seeing this process as a source of oppression and alienation. Facilitating the construction and governance of global empires and nations, this conceptual format of managing difference soon spread to world fairs, expositions, and museums during the nineteenth and twentieth centuries as part of a global flow of ideas and expertise.

Regarding the space accorded Asian material culture in colonial interpretive grids, these works were construed as the products of once dynamic and innovative cultures and civilizations that had ossified, becoming static societies of ritual habits rather than historical change (Prakash 2002). Conceived as closer to natural history than social history, this paradigm of evolution-cum-tradition was deployed even in the late twentieth century in the *Hall of Asian Peoples* at the American Museum of Natural History in New York, where such a framework structures an exhibit hall that opened in 1980 and tracks the peoples of Asia across time and space. At one entrance, the museum narration begins with prehistoric humans and the hunter-gatherer lifestyle, ending with a series of ethnological tableaus frozen in an intermediate position. Cultural/national groups across Asia are categorized as neither primitive nor industrial-modern but as enacting micronarratives dating to a period before Western contact, envisaged by way of text panels as embodying the present day (Sachedina 2011, 145–46).

In the wake of Said's *Orientalism* (1978), scholarship in museum studies has emphatically overridden the segregation of curatorial methods from broader structures of power and intellectual life that condition their deployment.[4] Today, museum methodologies are generally understood as paradigms of inclusion, exclusion, and transformation. Ethnographic museums have often been problematized by the very logic with which the art and material culture of the exotic Other is made legible through matrixes of knowledge and discourse to the West (Barringer and Flynn 1988; Karp and Lavine 1991; Karp et al. 2006; Kreps 2003). Given that the evolutionary-cum-tradition paradigm is often lambasted for portraying the non-Western Other in terms of ahistoricism, essentialism, and absence of change, it is puzzling that a non-Western state would borrow this paradigm— despite its being one of the most common frameworks—for its first national museum. Authoritative practices of representation in Oman make it possible to see the modern nation-state through an alternative set of relationships between the modalities of knowing the past, object creation, and ethical formation, problematizing the perspective of liberation versus oppression.

One simple explanation for the choice is that, as in other Gulf countries, a network of Western consultants and experts were used, and at the behest of the Ministry of Information and Sultan Qaboos, the museum was constructed as another conduit for disseminating national education and information, like the television and radio stations with which it shared a complex. There is some indication that the Historical Association of Oman worked with the government to establish the nucleus of the museum. This nongovernmental organization was established in 1972 for those who were interested in the preservation, documentation, and collection of Omani history and heritage.[5] According to one former secretary (and old membership lists and reports of meetings), members of the association were primarily Dutch, American, and British oil executives and financiers, including the sultan's economic advisor, John Townsend; embassy officials; and officers of the Omani armed forces, who (judging from their names) were also British. Documents indicate they were responsible for nascent activities to collect swords, guns, manuscripts, jewelry, carpets, and clothes meant for a new government collection. Only a few Omanis were members in the early 1970s, although there were efforts to recruit more. According to membership lists from 1972, Omani members included Ministry of Information officials, schoolteachers, and other government officials.

Unfortunately, my attempts to learn who was responsible for the practical tasks of organizing the exhibition, writing the text panels, and arranging the objects were unsuccessful. The Ministry of Heritage and Culture informed me that those files were probably lost when responsibility for the museum was transferred. Most people who would have been involved in construction of the museum were no longer living. All that remained were old museum booklets, some documents with text labels, and directors and museum guides from the 1980s.

Nonetheless, when one peruses the writings of scholars and policy makers of the Arabian Peninsula, an alternative explanation for the narrative structure of the museum appears. One notices that the notion of "heritage" is generally not so much about a static past as it is an assertion of a mode of governance. The standard argument is generally that the political impact of the concrete material practices involved in engendering a public historical consciousness in the Gulf region contributes toward the articulation of a collective notion of the people in ways that overcome partisan sectarian and tribal lines and affiliations, where none existed before. The pragmatic construction of museums, textbooks, popular publications, heritage villages, festivals, and sports is considered generative of an affective sense of collective belonging. The appeal is considered along the lines of Eric Hobsbawm and Terence Ranger's (1983) argument on the "invention of tradition," in which public history projects are an investment toward authenticating novel practices and such concepts as the nation-state, the people, and a ruling family (Carapico 2004; Chatty 2009; Cooke 2014; Exell 2016; Fromherz 2012; Kanna 2011; Khalaf 2000, 2002, 2008). The creation of a state-sponsored museum narration is generally construed as another example of nation-state building; the appeal of heritage practices lies in elevated ideals as once daily objects and major sites are extracted and lifted from the quagmire of local ties, histories, and politics to become a guiding beacon toward the newly minted notion of nationhood in the region. The pacifying potency of heritage derives from the fact that its institutional and semantic networks seem to transcend power struggles; it shepherds political action while remaining untainted by it.

Certainly, Oman fits within the broad brushstrokes of this scenario, wherein a distinctive relationship between space and territory is delineated through the authorized museum narrative. Scattered settlements across varied terrain were removed from their particular histories and placed within the parameters of a unitary set of assumptions: an organic conception of culture and history tied to mastering of the land and surrounding seas defines Omani nationhood, while territorializing it.

In Oman, like other Gulf countries—notably Qatar, UAE, and Bahrain—it could be argued that the histories authorized by state actors play a constitutive role in establishing the foundations of nation building as part of state pedagogy. The problem with this vision of heritage practice is that every country in the Gulf becomes interchangeable under the weight of a monolithic logic, which asserts that the functional use of heritage operations in the rentier states of the Arabian Peninsula is the legitimization of state-society relationships and the shaping of modern citizenry. This singular rationale obscures the specificity of historical circumstances and the unfolding power relations that determine the nature of heritage discourse and practices that characterize each locale and have led to divergent postnational politics.

After all, Oman's historical narrative and value judgments did not spring forth fully formed and self-evident. The marks of political conflict and struggle may be discerned in the strategic operation of selectivity and forcible elimination involved in the making of Omani history in the public domain. If we consider Barbara Kirshenblatt-Gimblett's (2000) thoughts of the museum as performative theater, with "objects selected as props to support a story," then we need to realize that although its evolutionary paradigmatic framework is one that has been repeatedly appropriated across the museum world, the purpose and content of any particular reenactment is determined by its historically contingent circumstances. To understand this process, I interrogate this rendering of history and work backward to understand the sociopolitical conditions that surrounded museum construction.

Politics Enabling Museum Construction

Although the imamate infrastructure was destroyed in the Jabal al-Akhdar War in 1958, it became a movement in exile with Imam Ghalib, leading a government from Dammam, Saudi Arabia, with offices in Cairo. Supported by the Arab League, headed by Egypt's Jamal Abdel Nasser in the late 1950s and 1960s, the Imamate Movement called for the end of British foreign intervention and colonial policies in the region, which necessarily entailed the overthrow of the sultanate. In an era of global postindependence nationalist movements against Western empires that characterized the aftermath of World War II, imamate followers regularly proclaimed in radio broadcasts on Ṣaut al-'Arab,[6] "the true situation in Oman was the greedy imperial ambitions of Britain and its brutal aggression against the people of Oman who are fighting for national liberation."[7] An Omani intellectual and informant of Dale Eickelman (1987, 38) recalled that in the 1950s, "the common Arab priority was to get the British out. Because the [sultan] was so heavily involved with the British, some saw support for the Imamate as the only way. . . . For this reason, even non-Ibadis became associated with the Imamate movement. By the 1960s, most Omanis had ceased to think of it in religious terms."[8]

A number of the imamate's followers later became members of more leftist-oriented guerilla movements and organizations in the region. In the South, Dhufar Province had similar aims of overthrowing the sultanic regime, part of the wider pan-Arab nationalist movement that grew into a socialist armed struggle in 1965 and 1975. A number of groups emerged at this time, including the Popular Front for the Liberation of the Occupied Arabian Gulf (PFLOAG)—trained and funded by China, the Soviet Union, and South Yemen—and the National Democratic Front for the Liberation of Oman and the Arab Gulf (NDFLOAG), formed by young Omani activists and intellectuals as part of a greater Gulfwide Marxist anti-imperialist movement that emerged in Dubai in 1968 (Allen and

Rigsbee 2000; Graz 1982; J. Peterson 1978; Skeet 1992; Takriti 2013, 164–71).[9] These groups launched plans ranging from assassinations to laying mines on roads, armed incursions into military camps, and ambushes of the Sultan's Armed Forces units across northern, central, and southern Oman. As Ian Skeet (1992, 48) succinctly puts it, "if the first phase of the civil war had been primarily aimed towards the survival of the Sultanate, the second phase was concerned with revolutionary social and political aspirations."

However, these events were conditioned by and reflected in the phenomenon of thousands of Omanis in exile, who were discontented and eager for the socio-economic and political changes common to the late 1960s and early 1970s that were too slow in coming to a sultanate increasingly perceived as an isolated enclave in the midst of the region's rapid modernization. While abroad, these Omanis were also subject to the ongoing ideological currents of Arab nationalism, the Ibadi Imamate, communism, and such movements as the Muslim Brotherhood (Rabi 2006; Takriti 2013). In 1970, with a sense of impending threat from "young Omanis," officials at the British Foreign Office concluded that "the Sultan's rule cannot go on since it will lead to a take-over after what might prove to be a bitter period of fighting by the young Omanis, encouraged by their Communist supporters"[10]. On July 23, in a British-sponsored coup, Sultan Qaboos ousted his father and ascended the throne amid civil war in the region. These struggles were quelled in the early 1970s with the heavy intervention of Anglo-sultanic, Jordanian, and Iranian armed forces. By 1975, the leftist revolts against the sultan had been defeated and the Sultanate of Muscat and Oman became the Sultanate of Oman.[11]

Despite this outer turmoil, the evolutionary-cum-tradition narrative that enframes the museum would have seemed to the ordinary visitor no more than the story of Oman's distinctive beginnings. There was nothing to suggest anything contentious or political, even though, as a senior official of the Ministry of Heritage and Culture informed me, Oman in the early 1970s was in a state of disunity. In a contemplative tone, he spoke of the importance of the museum:

> Capitalizing on the past was a very important tool to bring people together in order to educate them. . . . When the Sultan came to power, he had to depend on something specific to unite people. One of these things was a shared history [tarikh al-mushtarak]. He had to look for a past that was not connected to tribal or religious wars and conflicts. Educating the people through heritage established a foundation where we can all belong to one main stream, where we are all tied by love of the country and the cultivation of proper citizenship.

His words were a reminder: when placed in historical context, the arrangement of objects and the chronological path through the exhibit halls appear as anything but the same tired iteration of the evolutionary paradigm. Instead, the material practices of museum narration in Oman transcend politics, becoming a crucial volley in the struggle to create the cornerstones of a modern-day sultanate. By creating explicit relationships between people and things, the museum story line bears the marks of political stratagem: to reconfigure Oman's relationship to its history by displacing the Ibadi Imamate and its temporal assumptions and anchor a new nation-state, the Sultanate of Oman, to its accompanying sense of history, religion, and ethical norms.

Reinterpreting the Museum Exhibits

I asked a retired director who had worked in the museum in the 1980s about the rationale behind the museum narrative framework. In 1974, Oman was already undergoing massive modernizing changes. Old ways of daily living were being forsaken, and men and women were flocking to join the armed forces, such new industries as fisheries or oil, and a burgeoning government bureaucracy. Meanwhile, consumer demand for plastic imports was displacing traditional wares. Why would the museum narrative emphasize an ongoing vibrancy of traditional livelihoods that were becoming moribund? He explained, "Omani history is made up of a series of successive pages [*ṣafḥāt mutatāliya*], each of which gave rise to important events and accomplishments. Each of these are fundamentally rooted [*rāsikhan*] to a long continuing civilization that never ended [*bighayr tuqaf*]. It is from this civilizational foundation itself that contemporary Oman emerges on her path to create the nahda epoch under Sultan Qaboos in order to bring back to the people the glories of their past to place her in the ranks of modern, progressive nations." This response elucidates an apparent contradiction in the museum's conceptualization. Even as contemporary Oman was moving along a linear stream of "progressive" time, in the sense that each successive epoch was distinctive, including nahda Oman, it was also clear that the past, witnessed as a panoply of achievements, was considered an immanent force that laid claim to the present and future of the national community. The question remains, however, as to what kind of past is required to fit the imperatives of a rule along progressive lines for planning a future that was conceived as irrevocably changing.

Through the process of collection, preservation, documentation, and presentation, the significance of such objects as the dalla and Nizwa Fort (visual portrayal) transformed from one tied to day-to-day use to a state of suspended animation. They became still-life forms whose significance was honed through artfully crafted scenarios and proximity to other objects, maps, text panels, and large photographic cutouts. Heritage practices have cultivated a mode of perception by transforming these sites and objects into texts that assume importance as tangible forms of evidence to a different kind of past and future than those which oiled the workings of the Ibadi sharī'a community. Nizwa Fort and the dalla, whose social and political uses lay in sedimenting the exemplary life and conduct of the Prophet and the imams among the populace as part of a divinely willed future, were now experienced as a history centered on the development of humankind through ecology and the environment, refiguring the place of Ibadi Islam in the process.

In the museum, these objects and sites become significant through order and display as the evidentiary terrain that substantiated the reality of the sultanate as a linear-cum-tradition chronicle.[12] Simultaneously, through curatorial methods, the hurly-burly of political schisms, power struggles, and violence that conditioned the lives of objects were filtered out, effectively depoliticizing Omani history, including the twentieth-century Ibadi Imamate, its doctrine, the turbulent nature of its final overthrow with the pivotal support of a colonizing power, and its bitter aftermath, which resulted in the imprisonment of senior 'ulamā' and judges who were once the representatives of the community. The outcome appears to be a landscape increasingly denuded of tribal networks, differential kinship relations, and genealogy. In the process, a new mode of perception is developed, in which the physical qualities and architectural features of daily objects and sites, once important for their utilitarian role, become the iconic bearers of a new mode of Omani history and its concomitant values in order to render them perceptible and interpretable. In such a role, Nizwa Fort and the dalla organized a common political ground that defined territorial nationhood at the expense of the imamate or tribal forms of authority and polity.

Time itself had shifted from a calendar grounded in the events of the Prophet's life to retreat further into the history of humankind, allowing a temporal expanse for complex interactions between the land and human development. The creation of an evolutionary historicism transformed the relationship between history and religion, remapping the terrain of the Ibadi Imamate into a modern-day sultanate in ways conducive to creating a homogenous citizenry. As heritage, time's fundamental premise was defined not by attempts to achieve human perfection and divine salvation in accordance with Ibadi sharī'a but by the agency of a person who develops the distinctive attributes that define the Omani: through the ability to successfully exploit the resources of the lands and seas that mark out the nation's territorial domain.

Islam has not disappeared. Fiqh manuscripts once read to acquire historical, legal, and ethical acumen, now placed in vitrines, become integral to a new temporal rationale in which Islam defines one epoch in the greater narrative of Oman's progressive story. Islam becomes a concept equated to the abstracted understanding that "embracing Islam enriched Oman's ancient culture." Ships, forts, and trade items are untethered from their local histories and consolidated as the fruits of religion. Islam emerges as a category undergirded by the new conceptual vocabulary of civilization and culture.

Even conversion to Islam in the seventh century was culturalized, inasmuch as it was the distinctive attributes of the people of Oman that, according to one text panel, enabled the Prophet to proclaim, "God bless the people of Ghubaira (Oman)." In Ibadi doctrine, the Ya'āriba imamate are part of the umma, a theologically defined space centered on God, in which they stand as exemplars of virtue or sinful conduct that each Muslim seeks to emulate and avoid to achieve salvation. Under the rubric of culture and civilization, the Ya'āriba imams were categorized as national heroes who defeated a foreign occupier, united Oman, and created an overseas empire in East Africa and western India.

In contemplating the tours he gave to school groups during the 1980s and early 1990s, Ahmed, an elderly museum guide, reflected on how he had emphasized that Oman's long history and strategic location have culminated in the "lively spirit which allowed Omanis to face dangers in the exploration of new lands." The aflāj system became one example of hard work and an innovative spirit. Trade and sailing became attributes of entrepreneurship. Ahmed ended by observing, "I was trying to instill the vibrant energy that our forefathers once held so that they might understand that their future will be the result of their work in that past and in the present." Simultaneously, objects and sites on display or as visual backdrops became the embodiment of cumulative sets of values and principles that are suprahistorical, insofar as they transcend temporal circumscribing to become constitutive of the idealized Omani national character.

One museum pamphlet shares this sentiment, asserting, "the geographical, historical and economic circumstances which encompass Omani society since the early beginnings of its history have inculcated [ḥatamat] it with a love for noble work and effort in the inclination behind acquiring a worthy source of livelihood to become in turn one of the basic components [muqawwamat] of the Omani character" (Ministry of Heritage and Culture 2002). In imagining history at the museum, the visitor was involved in something of a double recognition. On the one hand, the museum was fostering a linear narrative whose "positive facets" have been culled to inculcate an idealized ethos amenable to a national imaginary. On the other hand, the Omani was proclaimed to be no stranger to the required qualities. The languages of innovation, toleration, hard work, and exploration became the basis by which the past is read as "tradition," a contemporary force for the guidance and cultivation of a progressive citizenry (Bennett 1995).

This perspective of history as turāth did not remain in the confines of the museum. In the 1970s, growing numbers of literate men and women were reading the two national newspapers, ʿUmān[13] and al-Waṭan, published under the super-vision of the Ministry of Information. As I perused copies of ʿUmān from the 1970s and early 1980s at the newspaper offices in Muscat, the recurring theme of Oman's history and heritage at times took up an entire page. As presented in the newspapers, there were two paradigmatic approaches to this topic. The first fo-cused on the museum's interpretive framework and transformed it into a widely disseminated standard narrative of Oman's history for public consumption. From the mid-1970s, at least once a month, the back pages of newspapers were filled by such headings as "Heritage of Omani History," with a series of articles titled "The Omani Man Has a Deep-Rooted Civilizational Authenticity" or "Origins of an Ancient Civilization and Heritage."[14] The articles explore archaeological dis-coveries and surveys by foreign research expeditions, contextualizing them as evo-lutionary tales of the first Omanis as agriculturalists, seamen, and traders whose success in civilizational development was linked to the construction of ancient settlements, trade in frankincense, intrepid sailing, and the building of coastal empires.

The iteration of this history generated the basis of the second paradigm: a tour-istic exploration of a particular city, region, or landmark. These articles describe sites in terms of their topographic features, agricultural crops, architectural and historical landmarks, and the people who emerged from such a habitat and his-tory. One article describes the reason for such a focus on history in the nahda era: "Heritage is the brilliance of light which gives our present an example [ʿibra] for the future. And with this we will return to the majesty of our forefathers. Our con-templation of the past will be a blaze of energy [shuʿlat al-ṭaqat] which propels us to the future, through providing us with guidance in building and developing the nation."[15] A new historical paradigm was being forged, habituating Omanis to gaze at even regularly traversed locales and sites in an entirely different way. The presence of preservation projects, handicraft workshops, and museums alluded to another geography of history, one that marginalized allusions to the divine and proudly proclaimed the abilities of Omani men.

In the ensuing decades, this focus on heritage has continued. Yusuf, a journal-ist from the Nizwa area who worked for the newspaper for twenty-eight years, said heritage was featured at least once a month: "We have a page called ahlan wa sahlan [welcome]. . . . Every week, I would visit a region and shed light on the particular cultural aspect of the region, especially architecture, forts, old mosques. . . . As an Omani, life today is based on the idea of heritage. I do not see the past as museum pieces that must be seen behind glass. No! I live the past, in order to be guided in my future. We are preserving the heritage of previous generations in order to make life meaningful." When I asked more pointedly about the dearth of information on Ibadi Islam and the twentieth-century imamate in the public domain, he gently reminded me that religious education had been organized and managed by the state since the 1970s through the school curriculum, mosque building, mass media, and the creation of the post of mufti in 1973, the first in the Gulf region. State efforts also led to the rise of a bureaucratic class of religious scholars and judges (Eickelman 1989). Its aim was to bring religion into the jurisdiction of an expanding, modern state. In the midst of cascading regional events—such as the Iranian Revolution (1979),[16] the Islamic piety movement (early 1980s onward), the Iran-Iraq War (1980–1989)—the subsequent impact of Bin Ladin and Islamist thinkers, the occupation of Afghanistan and Iraq that followed 9/11, and the growing sense of Sunni-Shi'a conflict led to growing concern that association with any one sect would create the possibility of a violent upheaval or cast suspicion on the state following a particular political agenda.[17]

A senior undersecretary from the Ministry of Heritage and Culture summed up the museum's framework: "It is very important that we focused on elements that bring people together by means of histories. Our history is built on the basis of inclusion. We believe the Ibadis are fewer now.[18] There are more Sunnis in Oman. There are Shi'a. The important goal . . . was to find histories and values that bring all Muslims together rather than create the big differences that we see in sectarianism today in Iraq, Yemen, Syria." According to such officials, despite changing contexts, the strategy is always the same. The official religious tradition is still Ibadism, but Ibadi Islam has been restructured by depoliticizing the historical and political specificity of its governing doctrines and jurisprudence through (1) an emphasis on the basic principles of Islam, a common ground that creates a desectarian mode of religious propagation in the public domain,[19] and (2) in terms of heritage practices, neutralizing the political barbs of the imamate by placing Ibadi Islam within the rubric of culture and civilization. In short, the doctrinal specificity of Ibadism has been made and remade at the expense of subordinating alternative forms of life and authority.[20]

The National Museum Narrative

In July 2016, a new national museum opened amid much media fanfare, supplanting the original Omani Museum. In the words of the former chair of the museum project, Sheikh Salem al-Maskri, during an interview, "The goals of the museum are not merely to preserve and document the heritage and culture of Oman, but to educate future generations about the history of their country, both their minds and their senses; to strengthen their links [*intima'*] to their inheritance through knowing the work of their forefathers, their originality in all fields. . . . They will not look at history with a sense of nostalgia but with open eyes, seeking inspiration for a better future, a way of thinking, and thus contribute positively to the future." A number of scholars have considered the construction of national museums in other Gulf countries as means to delineate ethnonationalist zones that separated the citizen from the noncitizen among populations overwhelmingly comprising noncitizen expatriate workers (Exell 2016; Fromherz 2012). This does not appear to have been a strong priority in Oman. Unlike other Gulf countries, Oman's population of foreign workers is not a majority. In the last census (2018), 44 percent of residents are expatriate workers.[21] What worried Omani state officials during my fieldwork in 2011, which occurred just before, during, and after the Arab Spring protests, was Omani youth. At the time of the protests, at least one-quarter of people aged eighteen to twenty-four years were unemployed, and 70 percent of Omanis working in the private sector were earning less than the official monthly minimum wage of $520, or 200 Omani rials (National Center for Statistics and Information 2011[22]; Valeri 2015, 7). Popular demonstrations broke out in Muscat and regional city centers, such as Sohar and Salalah, in protest of rising unemployment, stagnating salaries, unequal distribution of state resources, corruption, and nepotism in government.

The construction of the museum and its overall aims have been deeply influenced by two events of the recent past. In 1994 and in 2005, many Omani citizens were arrested, accused of being part of religiopolitical movements seeking to overthrow the government. The 1994 case involved about four hundred Omanis in their midtwenties and early thirties accused of having financial and organizational connections with the Muslim Brotherhood (Owtram 2004, 180–81); Jones and Ridout 2015, 218–21). The 2005 case involved senior governmental officials, religious scholars, and university academics and was deemed by the state to be an Ibadi plot to overthrow the sultan. In the decades since it opened the Omani Museum, the government had become increasingly conscious of the need to educate youth. Although both museums declared the need to preserve the material past, unlike the first museum, whose aims were primarily to articulate and substantiate the historical framework for nationhood, the new National Museum shifted its priorities toward reenforcing national civic values and ethical norms among its citizens.

Members of the all-Omani museum council often informed me that some key differences of the new museum project were its use of audiovisual technologies and its learning center, a collaboration with the Ministry of Education to provide education and community outreach to Omani children of all ages, and teacher-training workshops to maintain coherence between the national curriculum and the museum; it also includes facilities for people with special needs, such as braille.[23] Its strongest similarities to the 1974 museum are in its overall conceptual framework and spatial organization, which follows the process of depoliticizing while rearranging history, religion, and ethics in the public domain by way of replicating the evolutionary-cum-tradition chronicle. The political emergence of the Sultanate of Oman is naturalized through a display that insists it came about as a result of interactions with the environment, culminating in distinctive ways of life. Likewise, the new museum espouses a desectarian mode of Islam forged through the conceptual matrix of culture and civilization, divested of power and history and emphasizing a living past that historicizes the present and future as a means to cultivate the ethical citizen-subject.

The National Museum

The main entrance to the National Museum is a projecting bay leading to a gleaming white exhibition floor, part of a larger spatial narrative as the visitor enters the central courtyard at the heart of the museum. Here, tradition is writ large, embodied in the theme of the hall, *The Land and the People*. In this central space, the visitor is introduced to Oman's contemporary geographical and ethnographic setting through traditional crafts. Set in elongated glass showcases, an array of objects meets the eye: copper and silver dalla, earthen jars, wooden storage chests, textiles, frankincense burners, and jewelry (figure 3.1). Part of a dhow protrudes from one wall. On the opposite wall is a reconstruction of one of the richly carved balconies of the sur al-Lawatiya, the vernacular architecture of a prominent merchant community who settled the Matrah/Muscat area from the Indian subcontinent in the eighteenth and nineteenth centuries. What ties these myriad crafts together, according to the wall narrative that enframes the hall, is "a visual representation of the nation, its past and present—giving form to patterns of life in the Sultanate and expressing the cultural qualities for which it is renowned, including the shared faith of Islam, hospitality, generosity and community."

A changing screen near the ceiling displays a pastiche of images from each province, emphasizing how geography and resources in a range of habitats (mountains, coast, desert) have adapted livelihoods over the course of centuries, culminating in objects that are not only useful but still carry "personal and communal priorities such as adornment, identity, ceremony and religious expression." An object such as the dalla, once animated through its function, is now a still life that achieves significance through the following label on the glass casing: "The virtue of hospitality is a key attribute of the Omani people, historically stemming from the struggle to survive in a challenging environment with scarce resources. In the past, human contact was paramount, the traveler was almost the sole source of news. . . . Today, Omani hospitality continues to be associated with the compassionate treatment of visitors and is symbolized by the ritual serving of coffee and

FIGURE 3.1. Central courtyard exhibit space of the National Museum

Photo by the author

dates." Baskets in the case "have been manufactured for a specific purpose since the time of the first craftsmen on the basis of perceived human needs—food, water, shelter and safety—and are coupled with an innate requirement for self-expression through artistry and personal adornment." Accompanying a row of incense burners and boxes, a label explains, "The very mention of Oman connotes fragrance. Everyday life is infused with the mingled scents of flowers, woods and resins . . . with the passing of a fragrant incense burner at the start of a visit."

The label for a Quran stand, accompanied by large earthen water vessels, reminds the visitor, "underlying every aspect of Omani society is the devotion to

Islam, and the rhythm of daily life is aligned with the timing of prayers. Linked to this unbroken cycle of prayer is a constant striving for balance between the material and the spiritual and a constant search for wisdom and tolerance in an ever-changing world." The great metal serving trays and giant cauldrons are linked to the words "Generosity and a strong spirit are deeply held values in Omani society." Traditional dress is highlighted in its functional uses, ranging from modesty and warmth to religious belief, identity, and protection.

As I walked through the exhibits, it became clear that the objects embodied not so much discrete meanings but complex chains of significations. However, unlike the linguistic sign of Saussure, where, as symbols, their relationship is based entirely on social convention and arbitrarily relate to their referent, these conveyed a sense of being "witness," indexical, inasmuch as their material forms stood in as evidentiary testimonials to this story line. The abstract values they now signify can only be grasped through their concrete presence and sensuous qualities.

As in the first Omani museum, the use of present tense is striking. The texts do not acknowledge dynamics of social change; nor is a specific historical context given. Instead, despite being labeled "traditional," the past is clearly linked to the present in a logic of continuity through a textual insistence on their continued relevance. This perspective was confirmed by a series of conversations with curators of the museum. On my first visit, standing in front of the case for "Traditional Costume of Eastern Oman," I asked a curator whether this type of dress had not been effectively marginalized by store-bought imports or radically transformed by global fashions, since it was worn only by women born before 1970 or on celebratory occasions. She acknowledged these facts but argued that women's traditional dress is still essential to Omani identity, being "not so much clothing as much as cultural values. There have been changes, but these clothes are foundational to the Omani way of life." When I asked the museum director about the lack of representation of the dalla's transformation to the plastic thermos, rendering it virtually obsolete, he replied, "Perhaps the dalla in its past form and material is being used less and less from a utilitarian point of view. However, it has acquired new value as a cultural symbol that brings together a set of values around it. These values are enduring. The dalla is still being used in the countryside and still being made by local craftsmen."

What was continually reaffirmed about these objects and the practices and ideas they conveyed was that they represent an essential core that needs to be lifted out of the upheavals of history and reenvisioned as more enduring and universal than the narrow confines of historically specific social and economic changes. The multiple local particulars through which these objects have passed becomes commensurable with each other through a notion of a continuity in spirit that has come about through their production and use and remained constant despite political, technological, and economic transformations. In the process, a unified narrative is created that links the nation with an ethos of authenticity. Despite the variety of livelihoods adapted to different habitats, their underlying essence is assumed to have generated similar processes transforming the self; the Omani is distilled from the same underlying substance, despite major disruptions to the physical and social settings of these objects.

In interacting with the museum's linear narrative thus far, the visitor is interpolated by the construction of an ethical self, defined as "Omani" and part of an imaginary community that, despite changes across time and space, stands as an enduring substratum that outlasts finite biological life. Man's ability to master the environment generates the ability to shape his natural self and his external conditions, an ability that is metaphorically resonant with "tilling the soil" for the ethical and intellectual development of mind or soul. The mastery of different ways of life, which have moved from utility to artistry in this linear paradigm, forms the foundation for transforming the self toward full maturity, through the development of inner capabilities that have left the Omani generous, communal, hospitable, and creative. In this imagery, there is an underlying assumption of Oman as a unitary entity that defines territorial boundaries and maps them onto a historical reenactment of uninterrupted presence and historical "essence" through material signs. The organization, documentation, and display of these objects materialize and entrench a set of historical "facts" onto the landscape, substantiating Oman's identity and simultaneously cultivating a territorial and moral ethos. Acts of God (as part of the Islamic eschatological domain) become increasingly remote in shaping the conception of history and an ethical way of life. This is an Omani character, moreover, not enabled by a theologically defined umma that morally binds each Muslim toward the divine but a nation of people who have directed their energies to master nature, adapting themselves to varied environments. In the process, the pillars of civilization they have developed as part of their everyday lives forge the roots of spiritual values, practices, and dispositions that span the finitude of the ages of history. The museum director described this central hall as "an orientation space, in the sense that the first thing we do is . . . introduce the visitors to the values that unite us as Omani across time and space."

The museum's fifteen exhibition halls radiate out of this central plaza, amplifying the story of adaptation that has culminated in tangible markers of Omani civilization. The result is a spatial narrative that is, in the director's words, "chronological as well as thematic," producing a multilayered experience of continuity and change through the organization of objects and the words accompanying them. The ground floor roughly focuses on the cumulative hallmarks of Omani history—maritime trading ships, weaponry, forts, and castles. In such a textual narrative context, the architectural distinctiveness of Bahla, Jabrin, Nizwa, and other imamate forts is modeled with their engineering and defensive system in the *Civilisation in the Making* gallery. Imamate forts become props to convey an inspirational message that summons a different kind of history and values to conscious and collective recollection, denuded of their imamate and tribal working pasts. Instead, this exhibit chamber lauds the "aesthetics of traditional architecture . . . and its historic uniqueness" as one of the hallmarks of Omani civilizational achievement. An illuminated series of wall panels at one end of the chamber home in on distinctive features, such as the use of local building materials, carved wooden doors, palm paneling, inscribed ceilings, and decorative stucco.

The upper floor consists of a series of chambers that outline Oman's chronicle from prehistoric times, the age of Islam, and interactions with other lands and peoples across the ages in the *Oman and the World* gallery. It ends with the *Renaissance* (nahda) gallery, which presents Oman's modernization from 1970 onward, centered on the person of Sultan Qaboos and the rule of the Al Said dynasty. The visitor moves through six broad epochs of Omani prehistory and history, each showcasing objects that evoke the accomplishments of the Omani. Each epoch is rendered distinct and cumulative; events and circumstances in one gallery lead to the next along a rough developmental logic. In the *Iron Age* gallery, bronze and stone vessels, daggers, bracelets, and beads "shed new light on the egalitarian foundations of tribal society in Oman." Adaptations to the varied terrain, from coastal plains to mountains and desert, are imprinted by activities, ranging from hunting and fishing to copper mining and the flourishing of sea trade networks, which led to the development of villages and large urban settlements. In this official story line, periods and the artifacts produced within them are allocated their own time and place in a processual story line, where each stage is superseded by the next, moving continually to a higher and more complex order of "culture" and "civilization." This processual framing fosters an understanding of a fundamental experiential difference between past and present.

Simultaneously, other galleries within this progressive chronicle emphasize temporal continuity between the past and present through their juxtaposition of objects from different times. In the *Land of Frankincense*, the boundaries between time periods are more ambiguous, with the local desire for frankincense presented as a continuous thread connecting past and present. The wall panel at the entrance draws the visitor's attention to Dhofar, "one of the few places on earth where the frankincense trees thrives." Old south Arabian inscriptions dating to the first century BCE and incense burners dating to 1300 BCE establish an evidentiary terrain for long-distance trade in frankincense that linked Oman to Mesopotamia, Indus, and Egypt. Texts from ancient and medieval manuscripts scroll across a screen, emphasizing the importance of frankincense across the ages. Meanwhile, rows of twentieth-century incense burners, a highlight of the gallery, emphasize its importance as a tradition that feeds Oman's "spiritual" core. This sense of the past achieves a transcendental status as integral to the present and future.

In the *Splendors of Islam* gallery, the visitor sees the dalla in a very different context, as part of a longer linear narrative anchored to the Omani landscape and its history. The labels accompanying these displays highlight the decorative elements, the dotted circle and palm motifs, emphasizing the longevity of the designs and their popularity from prehistory into the contemporary period. Through an organization of displays that insists on a logic of continuity, the material culture of Islam is presented through its integration with the larger category of Omani civilization.

Along with these primary signifiers of continuity and adaptation, *Splendors of Islam* emphasizes the transformations brought about by Oman's conversion to Islam. Manuscripts such as *an-Nafs Ar-Rahmani*, *Kashf al-Ghumma*, *Diwan As-Sītalī*, and *Bayan Ash-Sharh*—whose contents once entrenched the foundations for the practices of law, history, ethics, and poetry—are translated into works whose mere physical presence conveys the "importance of the ninety-nine names of God in Islamic tradition" and the "production of doctrine, law, and learning over the courses of centuries." Coins from the eighth through the fourteenth centuries signify the importance of the *shahada* as "the most basic requirement of being a Muslim." A nineteenth-century sword is placed next to a twentieth-century necklace with a *hirz* (Quran case) to illuminate the custom of anonymity among Omani artisans, which "reflects the central belief of Ibadi Muslims that work is done for the glory of God and not for the self." The Quran itself, in the museum context, becomes an art object to be admired for its geometric decoration of interlocking circles, a pattern that, the label states, may grace doors, windows, musical instruments, and jewelry.

Finally, the dalla comes to signify the celebration of the two Eid festivals marked by "prayers, charity, sacrifice, visiting family and friends, making traditional dishes, using perfume, giving money to the children." Under the rubrics of the term *Islam*, the value of these variegated objects is equated with a way of life depicted as spanning the wide range of histories, rendering Islam as something timeless, even as the representative objects are tied to the linear chronological history and geography of Oman. Islam assumes a temporally frozen aesthetic and set of values and beliefs, binding a geography to a religious identifier that spans the ages through to the present day.

The visitor is left with a sense of an Islam in which the aesthetics of objects and architecture were left unchanged, scholarship flourished, and Eid celebrations were observed in the same way. A series of display cases hold fragments of bowls and coins, with a timeline of ruling dynasties and Ibadi Imamates but without context and an occlusion of any sense of the structures of power that brought about these transformations in governance. There is no mention of what Ibadism is or its doctrinal or ritual distinctiveness from other sects of Islam. The kind of Islam on display in the gallery is conceived as a series of overarching principles or ongoing practices that become rather abstracted in the process of being elevated from the concrete contexts and material relationships that would articulate a mode of living Ibadi Islam. What is left is a neutralized Islam, wherein Ibadism is diluted and incorporated in terms of its contribution to Islam as a global ecumene. Inequality, subordination, and social conflict—the space of the political as an integral part of Islamic rule—are not merely marginalized but actively naturalized. An ontological naturalness sets in, in the universal propagation of a depoliticized authoritative discourse that espouses a moral ethos, tethering its warranty to a tolerance of difference and peaceful coexistence.[24]

The gallery's arrangements subvert the devotional and ritualistic usage of the Quran and other religious objects, transforming them into objects whose physical attributes are admired for their artistic appeal and the information they impart, which is vouchsafed by their presence. Stripped of the emotional and embodied practices by which Muslims would have come to relate to these material forms, these objects have exchanged such value for the equivalent of becoming the secular means toward learning about the nation-state, a polity whose claim to legitimacy entails a past that stretches beyond the beginnings of Islam and is entrenched by exploiting the resources of the land itself.

Eschewing the linear narration of the museum, the temporal-spatial framing of the Islamic gallery emphasizes how the advent of Islam in Oman enabled the emergence of a vast and powerful metaphysical system. This system becomes ingrained into the social fabric of a community and the psychological habitus of its individual members, especially craftsmen, forming the backbone of its ethos. In envisioning such a conception, a certain presumption is bolstered that this thing called "religion" still holds. It is marked by an essential nature inimical to sociopolitical and economic transformations. One consequence of this analytic and taxonomic discourse is the transformation of these museum objects into spiritual practices, displayed as expressions of something that transcends the confines of time and place to be incorporated into a nonsectarian, nonpolitical version of universal Islam.

The foundational text of Islam, the Quran, now offers itself to reflection within a space defined and regulated by the modern nation-state. In other words, religion has entered a space already built on secular assumptions erected on the foundation of "Omani civilization"—naturalized and culturalized as part of a linear chronological history rather than the theologically defined premise of being oriented toward God and daily life assessed on the basis of following the *sirat al mustaqim* (the right path). The nahda has thus become part of a past where man in his purposive activity dominates nature, generating a temporal order subject to natural laws—laws of evolutionary development that define a lifeworld whose embodiment in signifying practices becomes a source of moral and political anxiety, demanding active intervention. Religion, too, becomes part of the natural order and is given the same status as a number of social components foundational in the construction of a distinctive Omani culture and heritage.

At the same time, these objects and architectural pieces are considered the outward form of rather abstract significances: the values and principles of Islam as a way of life, scholarship, artistry, creativity, women's equality, toleration. In their embodiment of idealized attributes of civilization and culture, the object forms escape political and social consequences by inhabiting a transcendent terrain that connects past, present, and future as an abstract plane of unchanging values lifted out of the narrow confines of historically specific social, political, and religious practices that might have the effects of tribal, doctrinal, or sectarian tensions and conflicts in the present day. At the museum, culture and civilization, as categories of organization, are insulated from power structures, becoming effectively domesticated as depoliticized realms in Omani official thought and practice. Simultaneously, even as abstract values, these suprahistorical ideals do have political consequences in their material embodiment—as coffeepots, architectural elements of mosques, manuscripts, jewelry—since they lend themselves to a depoliticization that naturalizes the national narrative and its accompanying values these objects now embody. As material forms whose wide dissemination animates, directs, and unifies the nation-state, they bring into sharp focus the pedagogical practices of knowing this national past as integral to Oman's modernity—a new grammatical foundation laid down by the categories of culture and civilization. Religion itself becomes a category forged on such a terrain.

One of the most striking features of the final gallery, the *Renaissance*, is a wall mosaic of lighted panels that portray "the unifying vision of His Majesty Sultan Qaboos" through his role in establishing modern infrastructure for education, health care, tourism, heritage, and culture. This brings us back to the question of why a living relationship with the past is so crucial to the present and future. To help me understand the precise role of such a past, the museum director explained,

> The national museum addresses the Omani character, made up of Omani values across themes, ages, and times throughout the displays. This is not specific to the land and people hall, but we start there as we celebrate the land of Oman and all its diversity. We focus on all sorts of values, including our openness to the world, the ability to be inspired and to inspire others, the spirit that took Omanis all across the world. . . . This

is something that can be followed and makes up the Omani character. Its earliest roots can be found in the *Pre-History and Ancient History* gallery and reaches its peak in the *Oman and the World* gallery. Other values we celebrate are religious coexistence and toleration, which may be found in the *Splendors of Islam* gallery. This also includes contributions made by Omani women and the status of women in Islam.

History and human experience are part of a single continuum. One generation builds upon the experiences of others. And Oman has a deep-rooted civilization and statehood that dates at least to two thousand years. And this is an experience that should be ongoing in terms of the values it imparts through the ages into the present and future. For example, one of the values we cherish is that of the cultural diversity in Oman and how it has evolved with the settlement of new peoples and new communities. We can see that today, from the oil era onward, with the rapid expansion of the expatriate community and so forth. This is an example of a modern context for something that has deep roots in Oman and has been recorded for the past five thousand years.

In other words, objects whose physical presence as heritage indexes material practices and values become simultaneously spiritualized. In this state, they come to indicate such abstract values as toleration, equality, religious diversity, and innovation. On the basis of this transcendent mode, they can slip between past, present, and future, becoming something that is beyond historical contingency. It is on the basis of their material forms and their systemic, institutional dissemination that these abstract values reenter a social and political dimension. Through their embodiment in material objects and sites, such values can visibly exert their productive force as constitutive of heritage and as mediators of ethical conduct and moral action. Viewed through this transcendental spiritual realm, culture, civilization, and Islam come into being as ideologically depoliticized categories, even as their organization and display, via these material forms, have very real political consequences through establishing the fabric of the nation-state and fostering a national ethos.

The heritage museums in Oman show distinct differences from the authoritarian structures of temporality that emerged in other Gulf countries. In Qatar, a linear chronological periodization enframes the exhibit displays of the National Museum, drawing a sharp boundary between tradition and national modernity through sequentializing the past into a bygone era that gives way to contemporary Qatar (Exell 2016, 30–31). Modernity is displayed through a focus on the triad of modernization infrastructure, the ruling family, and the oil industry.[25] The national museum narratives in the UAE and Bahrain are similarly structured by a periodization that explicates "a transition from poverty to wealth as a result of the exploitation of oil and gas" that has come about through the guidance of the ruling families (Exell 2016, 12; Jeong 2016; Maclean 2016). In these museum narrations, modernity is rendered distinct from traditional ways of life through an emphasis on disjuncture and difference forged through oppositions: tradition versus modernity, poverty versus plentitude.

Oman's heritage museums are distinctive in the very fact that there is no mention of the transformations wrought by oil discoveries; the defining triad is conspicuously absent. In Oman, through much of the twentieth century, oil exploitation and the fortunes of the Al Said ruling family were taken up by an understanding best elucidated by such ṣaut al-'arab broadcasts as the following: "The period we live in is marked by a gigantic struggle against the imperialist tyranny. The people of Oman are pursuing the imperialists over the mountains and across the deserts and are defying their aircrafts and tanks . . . but imperialism is depriving them of their resources and draining their blood"[26] In short, the legitimacy of the Al Said family and oil prospecting were conceived as sources of political dissension and civil war. Both were construed as the ongoing political effects of Britain's informal governance of the region, its pivotal role in the rise and fall of the Ibadi Imamate (1913–1958), and the civil wars of twentieth-century Oman. The Al Said dynasty's role in constructing a nineteenth-century maritime empire was mentioned briefly in the Omani Museum as part of an ongoing saga of progress. In the new National Museum, although the *Renaissance* gallery on the upper floor is dedicated to the nahda and the achievements of modernization under Sultan Qaboos and the Al Said dynasty, it is not the focal point of the museum. Both museums' spatial arrangements, though forty years apart, pivot around a central axis of a pre-oil past—the distinct ways that life evolved over millennia and its ongoing power in shaping contemporary Oman. The Al Said dynasty is recognized but continues to be conceived as a niche in a much longer and richer history that defines Oman.

Unlike Kuwait, Qatar, and UAE, whose national days mark their independence from British rule, Oman's national day (November 18) is the sultan's birthday.[27] Moreover, Oman never officially acknowledged being part of the British Empire. The British-sponsored coup that brought Sultan Qaboos to power in 1970 would have made it rather discomfiting to announce a national day marking independence, especially as the British continued their rather conspicuous presence as advisors, administrators, and military offices in the post-1970 era (Clements 1980; Owtram 2004; Skeet 1992).

In his exploration of the relationship between Emirati nationhood and ruling lineages, Nadav Samin (2016) argues that state attempts to create a genealogical family tree that includes (nonruling) Emirati lineages fails. This weakens the national fabric by directing attention to the state's unacknowledged ethnic hetero-geneity, made up of Emiratis of South Asian and Iranian origin (Samin 2016). In Karen Exell's (2016) analysis of state museums in Bahrain, Qatar, and UAE, trade and other long-standing relationships between the Gulf countries, South Asia and Africa, and Iran are obscured and elided. In their stead, a unique Bedouin or tribal heritage is emphasized. In the Oman heritage museums, diversity and trade are acknowledged and celebrated as the fruits of the working man. However, inter-regional relationships between Oman and the Indian subcontinent or East Africa are set within the framework of history that is naturalized through its anchor—the act of becoming Omani through harnessing regional resources through the ages. Varieties of frankincense, metalwares, inscriptions, old manuscripts, and tradi-tional ships are explicitly linked with discoveries at archaeological excavations, testifying to Oman's contact with East Arabia, the Gulf region, India, and the Mediterranean. Roman amphorae, ceramic shards from China, items from In-dia, and model shops of Omani workmanship become representations that move Oman beyond a national narrative toward one set within a supraregional account of trade routes and diverse societies. Translated into heritage, these objects are brought forth to testify that the role of maritime navigation, trade, and empire in Oman dates from the Neolithic period, into the Islamic era, and up to the late nineteenth century and was a matter of mutual influence in the Indian Ocean world. In short, intercultural connections are celebrated. Through this framework, however, a common history underwrites all groups, Arab and non-Arab alike, even as it purifies the conflictual sociopolitical differences that emerged among communities from South Asia, Persia, and East Africa in their roles as merchants, soldiers, and administrators during the sultanate versus imamate eras. The his-tories and lifeways of ethnic groups such as the Baluchis, Zadjalis, al-Lawati, and Baharna, among other non-Arab communities, go unrecognized, even as their contributions are acknowledged through being absorbed into the all-encompassing parameters of a national historical narration and reconfigured accordingly. The framework serves to transform the historical heterogeneity of the Indian Ocean cosmopolitan settler into the purposive labor-driven Omani everyman.

Culturalizing history in such a manner has vanquished politics from history. There is an occlusion of any sense of determining forces including colonial rule, the imamate, global economy, and geopolitical interests (W. Brown 2006). The material effects of such history practices summon a notion of culture that sediments a new place for Ibadi Islam and new modes of punctuating time and defining the ethical actions necessary to become an Omani modern citizen through the frame-work of tradition. Through these changes, a hereditary sultanate is able to take root while displacing the foundational tenet of an elected imam and a sharī'a society from the public realm.

When I asked a senior member of the museum council about the lack of mention of colonialism or the imamate in public history, not just at the museum but also in official publications, textbooks, and audiovisual media, his reply was abrupt:

> The important goal is that this historical dimension should have useful and beneficial values extracted [*yatakhalus minhu*] from it in order to develop the present and renew it based on integration [*takamul*], harmony [*ta'aluf*], and to live cooperatively ['*aish mushtaraq*] without big differences. We see what sectarianism has done now in Iraq, Yemen, and Syria. Therefore, it is very important that Oman makes this history continue to be suitable for the future and to take values and ideas from it in order to take points of view, ideas, and results and incorporate [*nudmijuha*] to our present situations which have come about in the modern era but only after we have cleansed [*nunqī*] it of all that is unsuitable in contributing toward a better way of life or mode [*namaṭ*] of behavior or intellect, actions, or our treatment of each other.

Through museum practices, a history is being created that transcends politics, but the region itself is also being conceptualized in ways amenable toward domesticating discord. For museum organizers and public officials, a new conceptual vocabulary—of culture and civilization—has created a transcendental (moving between past, present, and future without being tied to a concrete history), modular past made up of state-sanctioned practices, values, and principles. This past is an ongoing presence that is meant to survive its time through a visual and discursive material language, rooted in and resonant with a territorially grounded history.

Conclusion

Scholarship generally places the countries of the Gulf Cooperation Council, which includes Oman, within a single framework where the many heritage activities they seek to sponsor and cultivate are ascribed to two roles: (1) seeking to consolidate a normative social and political claim to national authority and meaning and (2) assuaging the effects of an overwhelming global culture and the alienating effects of modernization. Following the lines of such an argument, the case of Oman would hardly be distinctive, especially given that the national historical narrative follows a common museum interpretive framework that has been used in colonial and national contexts since the nineteenth century. However, little attention has been paid to the centrality of difference in the institutional construction of the national museums (Sandell 2007, 1–5).

My aim in this chapter is to draw attention to the historical sensibilities being cultivated through laying the foundations of a new authoritative grammar, sanctioning a sultanate in the place of an imamate in the Omani region. If the language and practices of heritage discourse are rehistoricized and examined in context, they may be read against the grain to reveal the more fragile and contingent performative process of nation-state building. Rather than assuming material forms—forts or coffeepots—are moving toward greater abstraction as they are co-opted into the language of nation-state building and citizenship, I explore how the ways in which they are experienced is intimately tied to the manner in which they are materially organized around rationales of history and time as the result of much state labor.

In so doing, the staging of Omani history, through the arrangement and display of objects and sites, does more than transcend the political conflicts at work within the sultanate. Conflict itself is tamed through transformation into a contending historical framework. In other words, heritage practices go beyond legitimizing the nation-state, becoming a colonizing force in their own right through restructuring the relationships between history, ethics, and religion. This national history is a powerful force that addresses and ameliorates the contextual vicissitudes that may menace the ongoing performance of nation-building in Oman. The successful performance of the pedagogical history enacted by the museum is dependent on contextual conditions, which are not always under its control.

The effects of this operation on history are as follows: When cleaving through the temporal assumptions of sharīʻa time, conservation practices of the modern state substantiated a secular national imaginary and actively intervened to restructure authoritative time. In the process, the imamate conception of history was lost. The imamate and the sultanate both laid claim to a past assumed to be immanent to the present and future. However, since 1970, the logic of time has fundamentally changed due to a reversal in the valuation of the past and future (Carvounas 2002, 21). The productive powers of heritage practices are revealed by their decisive elimination of alternative modes of history to set up a past that has established the bases of a modern hereditary sultanate and homogenized it in a top-down operation. In the process, Nizwa Fort and the dalla, once embedded in daily modes of sharīʻa governance, become tethered to a new mode of tradition (a new configuration of past, present, and future). New ways of thinking have historically transfigured the place of Islam, ethics, and history by adopting a temporal engagement with a past grounded in the expectation of a changing and unknown future rather than one continuous with the exemplary deeds of the past.

ETHICS OF HISTORY MAKING

In the depths of the new fruit-and-vegetable souq in Nizwa's city center is a series of underground storage areas I visited frequently during my fieldwork. The facilities were usually shut, their metal gates fastened. It was a glad sight when the one closest to the basement steps was open, because it meant Said was in his workshop. Among the clutter of tools, old metal cooking vessels, ceramic dishes, and plastic receptacles of all sorts, I knew I would find him sitting near the entrance, hammering a piece of copper into shape. There was always a bowl of water filled with small coffee cups, a plastic thermos, and a covered dish of fresh dates—the necessary accoutrements for receiving visitors. We talked about the transformations he had witnessed and been a part of since the advent of the nahda in 1970. Said was ninety-two, he proudly informed me, and his work was part of a family tradition that went back two and a half centuries. He was one of the last craftsmen of the region who made the dalla in the old way. When I asked him what changes the dalla had undergone since the nahda, he gestured toward cans of silver and gold spray paint:

> My grandfather, my father, and then after me, for ninety years we have been making the dalla with no changes. . . . These types of colors—gold, silver, red—never sold before the nahda. These are new demands. But now ordinary people want it for decoration and not for cooking or anything. In the old days, they would use a big dalla for cooking the coffee and leave it there. When guests or people entered the majlis or sabla, they would transfer the coffee to a small dalla and bring cups to pour the coffee. . . . The dalla that I now make for decoration can never be used for cooking.

I asked him to clarify, and he explained that during the imamate, the *'ulamā'* considered silver to be *makruh* (disliked or offensive). The imams were known to be abstemious (*zāhid*) in their dress and lifestyle. Silver was not used for the dalla because of Islam. Said told me, "The dalla that I now make for decoration can never be used for cooking. If you want to use a dalla for cooking or serving, the inside has to be white." Extremely confused, I asked for further explanation. He put his hand inside one of his newly made coffeepots and withdrew it, showing me a hand covered with black streaky dirt:

> Drinking coffee from it would not be good for the stomach. You need white [*abyaḍ*] for it. . . . To prevent dirt and rust [*ṣada'*] from adhering to copper vessels, you need to put a coating of lead [*raṣaṣ*] on the inside surface. Otherwise, it becomes a poison and is very bad for the stomach. But because this is for decor, you don't need to cook with it or serve with it. So there is no need for anything white inside. Only if you want to use it for cooking or serving hot coffee, you must put lead inside.

Since the late 1970s, the introduction of the plastic thermos as a coffee server has meant the dalla is increasingly encountered only as a display piece—behind museum glass, on a drawing-room shelf, in a street sculpture in Muscat, or as an illustration in a textbook. Physical changes during the nahda have transformed it from a utilitarian vessel to a decorative canvas to contemplate. What once was formed with thick layers of metalwork is now lighter and thinner, and color is a priority, but these decorative changes make it unsuitable for daily use. Instead, it now belongs to what Susan Stewart (1993, 37) terms "the world of surfaces . . . whose physical aspects give way to abstraction and a nexus of new temporalities." The dalla, along with silver jewelry, trading dhows, the khanjar, incense burners, and water jugs, has spilled out of the museum setting to become part of the quotidian landscape of Omani national life. The hulking outlines of forts and watchtowers have become interchangeable as they are distilled into a series of prominent features—crenellated towers, arched windows—creating a generic, portable form. The great highways of Muscat and Oman's regional capitals are punctuated by visible copies of these objects and sites as montages on street roundabouts, bridges (figures 4.1 and 4.2), architectural facades, and park landscapes (figure 4.3). These ubiquitous icons in educational, print, and audiovisual media become a national heritage vocabulary through the systemic mechanical circulation of currency or postage stamps, dress codes, textbooks, and heritage festivals and in popular design motifs for keychains, refrigerator magnets, and other kitsch items (figure 4.4). In the process of extending museological values and methods (collection, documentation, preservation, presentation, evaluation, and interpretation) to objects,

FIGURE 4.1. Coffeepot sculpture in front of the Muscat Municipality

Photo by the author

FIGURE 4.2. Dhow roundabout on a street in Muscat

Photo by the author

FIGURE 4.3. Incense burner as part of the Muscat streetscape

Photo by the author

FIGURE 4.4. Heritage items as home ornaments in the domestic sphere

Photo by the author

knowledge, and practices, heritage practices have produced artifacts, landscapes, architectures, historical vistas, and living spaces.[1]

If imamate authority was established through the physical and geographical concentration of knowledge as embodied by the fort, a shared corpus of legal-historical texts, and the personal mediating efforts of a group of religious scholars, teachers, and administrators, then the imagery circulated in audiovisual and print media has engendered a very different order of pedagogical learning—one grounded in the need to systemically disseminate, ritually repeat, and thereby standardize. Continual reproduction has made these once-daily objects and sites into a national visual language. The structuring of the public arena in such a manner is the result of the concerted efforts of several state ministries with overlapping concerns, including the Ministry of Heritage and Culture, different municipalities, the Ministry of Information, the Diwan of the Royal Court, the Ministry of Education, and the Public Authority for Craft Industries. The state has also created a heritage-saturated focus through its control of television, radio, and newspapers.

This chapter explores the underlying reasoning behind the sheer ubiquity of heritage imagery and the social reality it creates. Ethnographic investigation into this question led me through a statewide bureaucratic network and a hierarchy of cultural advisors, undersecretaries, architects, urban planners, preservationists, heritage managers, and curriculum designers. Their offices became interchangeable as they all assumed a certain type—expansive rooms with a large desk and chair at one end; glass cabinets displaying state awards, heritage objects, and iconic symbols of Oman; walled photographs of the sultan; and, usually, a set of dark, plush sofas around a small coffee table where officials could talk with their guests over—of course—coffee. At first, the official language I heard was repetitive, a standardized authoritative discourse that appeared predictable and could be argued away as mere officialese. However, it became increasingly clear that the mandate of heritage was being placed within a bureaucratic structure and was deployed to cultivate a certain set of dispositions toward the past that was constitutive of Omani public life. Their talk also yielded insights into how heritage discursive imagery was seriously considered as a prophylactic against the twin anxieties of Westernization on the one hand and Islamist revivalism on the other.

In her analysis of UAE, Bahrain, Qatar, and Kuwait, Miriam Cooke (2010, 11) follows a long line of scholarly thinking in considering the deployment of dress, heritage symbols, spectacles, and cultural programs as a basis for Gulf youth to "comprehend the dignified poverty and the restlessness of their ancestors" as part of strengthening of ethnonational identity over noncitizens and non-Arabs.[2] In this scenario, the past is cast as a reservoir of objects and practices that are either included or excluded by a sociopolitical elite to consolidate an ethnonational, territorial imaginary and forge a mass citizenry out of differences. They differ only in the finer details of the type of heritage they pursue: Kuwait pays more attention to pearl diving (Khalaf 2008, 40–71), while Qatar and UAE pursue falconry (Koch 2015).

A second scholarly orientation elaborates on the first, even as its focus differs. In this model, the specific articulations of heritage structures and material practices are attended to in their productive potential to structure the citizen-subject and one's way of life.[3] It homes in on the idea that heritage is about the erasure of certain kinds of past. But in this approach, heritage is also examined as a context-driven normative understanding of the past that is being pursued and aspired to as the grid of intelligibility by which good citizenship is being questioned and sanctioned. This necessarily entails examining the distinctive styles of reasoning and overall goals embedded in the civil and administrative governance of a people who need to be incorporated into the nation-state. For Exell (2016), Qatar's investment in iconic cultural projects at home, from architectural extravaganzas to the opening of the Museum of Islamic Art, is rendered consonant with the cultivation of Western modes of cosmopolitanism, on the one hand, and the increased support of such groups as the Muslim Brotherhood, on the other. Calvert Jones (2017, 113–15), in her study on citizenship building in the UAE, elucidates how the state encouraged Emirati youth to immerse themselves in their history and heritage through partaking in the food and visiting historic houses as part of becoming "aware of the suffering of their ancestors" to provide them with the disposition to fulfil the country's neoliberal citizenship ideal. A turn toward a neoliberal-oriented future has resulted in the state's attempts to cultivate the citizen's ethical capacities of reflection and action through a conceived difference between the Emirati past and future. Even as the past continues to be a force in the present, it does so by being discontinuous with contemporary life. Heritage, in this scenario, becomes more than a technique for delineating a collective people or a territorial imaginary. It goes beyond alleviating the destabilizing effects of modernization toward engendering a new constructive mode of living and being, one that accords with a new set of idealized virtues aiming to cultivate a "pro-globalization and pro-market citizenship building" in UAE (ibid., 15–16).

In both approaches, there is an explicit focus on the state's structuring and engineering of the public sphere and its notion of citizenship. Oman is no exception to this trend, but it propagates an understanding of history and heritage with very different ends in mind. Both a visual and political practice, the ubiquity of representations of the past in Oman articulates space and time in the public domain. Not merely arbitrary signifiers, imagery of once-daily objects is ascribed an organic connection with their museumified referents and the new mode of history they invoke. Simultaneously, as public aesthetics, they center on what can be seen and said about history, while creating the boundaries of the social community, what Jacques Ranciere (2004) calls the "distribution of the sensible," through active intervention and organization of a bounded public space. For Ranciere (2004, 12), aesthetics creates the grid through which the constructed nature of the social domain becomes intelligible, in terms of making visible what is shared and excluded; it opens the possibility of understanding the terms that determine "those who have a part in the community of citizens" and a right to share in its governance. This understanding of the force behind the visual moves beyond reducing it to a matter of interpretation toward possibilities for mapping the relationship that binds image to spectator.

I embrace a similar approach, interrogating the ways in which Omani state officials attempt to naturalize the productive possibilities of a living connection with heritage imagery through (1) their mode of rationalizing the connection between past, present, and future and (2) how this temporal logic becomes the ground upon which ethical values, dispositions, and practices forge the basis of the idealized relationship between the Omani citizen and heritage imagery. Thanks to state initiatives, the pragmatics of daily activities among the citizenry are now enshrined as heritage, creating a sense of self-consciously repeating the habits and traditions of forbears. These activities slice through modern distinctions of public and private, state and society, acquiring a new significance as the basis for forging the "Omani personality." These include daily household chores, such as serving coffee, sprinkling rose water over guests on leave taking, weekly burning of incense throughout the home, wearing the disdasha to the office, or making traditional bread for breakfast. Omani intellectuals and state officials proclaim, "It does not behoove us as Omanis to turn our backs on the past without consideration for civilization. The roots of the present and future stretch out into the past. Those nations who feel compelled to look toward their history are the ones who succeed in keeping different aspects of the past still alive. They are the ones who are able to create a harmony [tanāgum] between contemporary living and the authentic past, creating a constant source of inspiration and pride" (al-Maʿmari 2016, 36).

With such an end in view, the post-1970 state has lavished considerable care to establish the grammar of a new mode of history, discussed in chapter 3, and deployed a network of institutions to sustain it. As a form of governance, the principles, values, and practices extracted from knowledge about the national past come to the fore as part of a range of organizational practices. These may coalesce around new (post-1970) kinds of activities—memorizing social studies texts, frequenting heritage festivals, watching documentaries on historical sites in Nizwa or Salalah, buying a little khanjar for one's son for Eid, having a dalla as a decorative piece in the drawing room, or habituating one's vision to the sight of heritage

FIGURE 4.5.   Architectural facade of a fort framing a highway in Muscat

Photo by the author

sculptures, mosaics, and castle-esque architecture in the urban landscape (figure 4.5). With these activities, according to state officials, citizens' relations with the past changes. The cultivation and soundness of their dispositions, thoughts, and actions depend on how they engage with these exemplary values and principles of the past. If Western modernity is conceived as enabling the individual to extricate himself or herself from blind immersion to custom, tradition, and habit, instigating a process of self-critique and self-development, then heritage practices brought about by the Omani nahda are about the disciplinary power of history in the public domain and the ways the state strives to provide citizenry with the necessary skills and ethos to navigate modernity in Oman in the "proper" way (W. Brown 2006, 166–71; Mahmood 2005).

Aesthetics of Heritage

For Sultan Hamdoon al-Harthy, chairman of Muscat municipality and former undersecretary of the Ministry of Heritage and Culture, creation of the modern sultanate involved the preservation of "the best aspects of the past" that were both enlarged or miniaturized to become a grammatical foundation for generating a modernist infrastructure and way of life. In a bid to reconcile the traditional with the modern, the forts, castles, and watchtowers in Muscat and elsewhere were preserved, as were the renowned nineteenth-century houses of Muscat and Matrah. In other cities (Doha, Dubai, or Abu Dhabi), historic buildings and open-air museums create enclaves, apart from the skyscrapers and high-rise towers that embody the modernist cityscape (Amrousi and Biln 2010, 256). However, in Oman, past architectural forms are not only considered as exempla in heritage museums but "evolved into a cultural filter to create a contemporary architecture in a way that was environmentally sound while being locally relevant." As al-Harthy elaborated during the interview, since the late 1970s, the vernacular architecture of the capital area has created an aesthetic language in sharp contrast to the hypermodern architectural fantasies of Kuwait, Qatar, or UAE, which emerged from the demand for rapid urban expansion. It is the distilled essence of the fortified and vernacular architecture of the region, with its mass and scale, its delicately crenelated rooftops, its recessed windows, its round or pointed arches, and its teak doors, ceilings, and screens.[4]

This aesthetic vocabulary is evident in a number of contemporary state buildings—the police headquarters in Qurm, ministries in al-Azaiba and al-Khuwayr, the conference building near Seeb airport, the Parliament, the Royal Opera House, the High Court, and a number of others in Old Muscat, where the national museum is found. Situated opposite al-Alam Palace, the official residence of the sultan, the national museum is a two-story, free-standing block articulated by squat square towers at each corner. Its architecture communicates a subtle defensive quality, reminiscent of the older fortified architecture of the region. Its white stone cladding is punctuated by narrow-slitted windows at the top, while the ground floor contains a series of arched openings. This look is entirely in keeping with the general aesthetics of Old Muscat, now a government and administrative center.

Unlike Kuwait, where urban development in the 1950s and 1960s yielded a mélange of residential and commercial architectural norms (al-Nakib 2016, 122–47), Oman's nahda architectural aesthetic extended to residential and commercial buildings throughout Muscat and Matrah, including low-income housing sponsored by the Ministry of Social Affairs. The growth of a contemporary urban architecture rooted in heritage forms the basis of a series of guidelines to, in al-Harthy's words, "avoid the sense of a downtown or a formal cityscape of skyscrapers."[5] At the same time, building codes were attempting to implement traditional archetypes of Arab/Omani/Islamic architectural features onto modernist buildings to homogenize the city's urban fabric of the city (Damluji 1998; Hegazy 2015).[6] The result is a set of guidelines that regulate construction—restrictions on materials, building height and color (including a ban on glass facades), door and window size, and visibility of modern installations, to name but a few (Damluji 1998; Scholz 2014).

A Muscat municipal official reminded me to look to the roundabout street sculptures, which were, in his words, "terms of reference [*marja'iya mushtaraka*] that bring everyone together within a common history, its high values and laudable traits [*sajāyā ḥamīda*]." One of the most-cited monuments is the Burj al-

Sahwa (Renaissance) clock tower, built in 1985 to mark the fifteenth anniversary of the nahda. It stands at a major crossroads that leads travelers to and from the regional capitals of Nizwa, Sur, and Salalah. Its towering columns are the city's most recognizable icons, rising against the skyline of one of Muscat's most important traffic roundabouts and surmounted by the crenellated outlines of Oman's traditional defensive architecture—the forts and castles of old that dot the landscape. Surrounding its base turreted, modelesque watchtowers and walls set with colorful mosaics arrest the eye. Here, one sees an intimate juxtaposition of once-everyday objects and scenes (the dalla, khanjar, halqat al-'ilm [religious study circles], dhows, silver jewelry, and incense burners) with those associated with Omani contemporary life (heavy construction machinery, factory assembly lines, and oil refineries). This fast-developing urban space was not forged merely for nostalgia or to differentiate Omanis from the growing number of expatriate workers flooding into the region to develop Oman's infrastructure. The past as a mode of conduct becomes the very foundation through which modernity is inhabited as part of daily living in Oman.

This curiously intimate portrayal of old and new, which defines the urban landscape, is something that state officials often considered in contemplating heritage in my presence. Terms they used to convey the importance of reconciling this paradox included *insijām* (harmony), *mulā'ama* (concord), and *muwā'ama* (unity). They used these words to convey ways of reconciling the past with the present, historical authenticity with the contemporary, as a mode of inhabiting modernity. And this juxtaposition was echoed in the crafts industry, institutionalized by the government in 2003 with the Public Authority for Craft Industries (PACI) and marketed throughout the country through their outlets and annual heritage festivals. In Katarzyna Pieprzak's (2010, 7–8) analysis of Moroccan crafts, officials were "establishing a canon of prototypes for authentic cultural practice that reined in contemporary creativity to create the authentic Moroccan experience, while maintaining the urban economy." For Omani administrators, a new generation of craftsmen were being trained to "modernize and develop the Omani craft sector; in addition to raising the level of creativity" (Public Authority for Craft Industries 2009, 1). As I was told by respondents from several departments (training, marketing, design) at a group session at PACI, the diversity and plurality of Omani crafts and monumental architecture through the ages was broken down to the basic components of decorative motifs, designs, techniques, or raw materials that the Omani craftsman has mastered since antiquity, constituting a cultural and civilizational stock. This basic vocabulary defines an Omani identity and history that is being used to create products that accord with (*tatanāsab ma'*) contemporary needs. Another official added, "The metalwork or woodwork we do is similar to other countries in the world. But what makes it Omani is . . . what is added to it, on the side of the vocabulary/components of her form or the decoration. . . . The reality of the product is its appearance [*maẓhar*]." In other words, its value is now its surface material and appearance.

A distinctive overall aesthetic vocabulary is thus abstracted from the outward forms of objects and buildings to serve as the lexicon of decoration for Omani crafts-manship. These may be used to beautify and decorate a ceramic item, a khanjar belt, or a button, taking a variety of forms and a wide array of uses to adapt to modern-day consumers' needs and tastes, in accordance with global markets. They serve as truncated and standardized material traces to the past, evoking its experiences even while being rearranged to address the desires of modern life. The phenomenon of state-organized handicraft and souvenir production has effectively blurred the boundaries between public and private, establishing a new life for heritage forms in the private domains of market consumption, the home, and life histories. The rise of tourism in the late 1990s—accompanied by increased state investment in handicraft production, training, and marketing—has generated a new matrix of consumerist and sentimental practices. Traditional textile motifs are now set in silver to become earrings, ceramic vases are decorated with the design motifs of silver jewelry, old water jars become flowerpots, *khanājar* are incised with designs from the painted panels of Jabrin Fort, and forts become model centerpieces.

In answer to my inquiry about the prevalence of heritage throughout the Omani landscape, a PACI official replied, "We want to take from history positive things and adapt them to the present, to continue into the future. This is the general idea." Another elaborated,

> Look at our five-star hotels. When you are on the outside, you feel they assume the architectural outlines of an old building, one of heritage. But when you enter the building, you are dazzled by its furnishings, lights, and cities . . . everything contemporary with the modern age. There is a great deal of innovation [*ibtikār*] involved. . . . This summoning [*nidā'*] of history is about directing its positive elements toward strengthening our society, evoking [*nastiḥḍar*] it always in the midst of uncertainty. The future is different, but the fundamentals [*asāsiyāt*] remain the same. We know there were tribal wars and slavery, but there were also positive things. . . . The lifestyle of the Omani family will be global in orientation, but the values will continue to be present as long as the family lives in ac-cordance with the core of their history and its values.

Such an understanding is echoed in the discursive sentiments of daily Arabic newspapers:

Civilizational heritage is still the epitome of that authenticity in which Omani Man has witnessed the importance of the past which creates strong ties with the present insuring the strength of a linkage between them for a present without a past does not have any real value that would qualify his sons to build the nation by preserving its primacy; These embody the strength of belonging and the strength of feeling in ourselves and become part of blending the spirit of authenticity with the character of the contemporary. They become part of a call [da'wa] for Omani youth to summon [istihḍār] this inheritance and work towards using it [taskhīr] to serve the present and construct the future.

Among the components of heritage are those forts and castles which seem to occupy almost every inch of the land and are not simply examples of architectural and engineering arts but express the desire of people struggling to preserve them. They embody determination, forbearance and strength. When we want to take in the majesty of these forts and castles, we must not merely absorb the lofty buildings and the impregnable walls but we must also account for the thoughts of Omani Man hundreds of years ago in his creative ability, his artistic style and the needs which led to his establishing these forts and castles. . . . This would include the aflāj which deserve study and which are unique to Oman and reflect the genius ['abqarīya] of Omanis. (al-Yahmadi 2011)

The forts and castles (among other sites and objects)—once essential to the workings of law, history, and ethics during the imamate—are transformed into a new form of standardized iteration that is working through new urban spaces and technologies. Through this continual performance, it instills the ethical and affective groundwork of the sultanate by propagating a certain understanding of history and cultivating it as an aesthetic experience for the making of a proper Omani citizen. It is precisely because of post-1970 media technologies that the citizen can access the historical and aesthetic experience of the Omani past as part of daily life. Heritage imagery is not merely the signs of identity to be decoded into immaterial meanings. The material forms—a traffic roundabout, a disdasha, a textbook—demand and anticipate the values, sensibilities, and behavior anchored to Oman's national historical chronicle that defines citizenship or the "Omani man" as a way of life. The wide dissemination of these forms as part of daily interactions among Omanis is understood as visual cues, habituating the eye and body. These agents mobilize the practices, passional attachments, and ethical qualities that they have become synonymous with in order to sink them into people's experiences as a habit-forming force. Through modern state efforts to domesticate the material past into a specific logic and moral ethos, heritage as an aesthetic and discursive experience becomes integral to the process of continually attuning to a selective mode of history as an integral basis of inhabiting modern citizenship.

Creating a Heritage Ethos in the Midst of Globalization and Terrorism

At the heart of this continual attempt to reconcile the past with the contemporary was a fear for Omani youth and the contemporary challenges they faced. As an undersecretary of the Ministry of Heritage and Culture put it:

> Oman is full of young people [who] find themselves open to the world through its material civilization. . . . Can they comprehend the great heritage values they possess while seeing others disassociating [*yataḥalalu min*] from these things, considering them old, out of date, reactionary [*rajʿiya*]? . . . The young man sees how, in American programs, the Arab is put in the position of riding a camel, a symbol of backwardness. So the same feelings happen to the youth here in Oman. There is a sense that I must be a modern man among them. In order to be that, I must disassociate myself from all these matters. Instead of sitting in a sabla, I should be sitting in a Costa Coffee or Starbucks, modern places.

There was a recognition that Oman, like other Gulf countries, was living in the midst of overwhelmingly globalized cultural trends emanating from the West that acted as temporal sifters, propounding certain practices as "modern" while relegating others, of local importance, as backward or "traditional." Another Ministry of Education official told me, "Globalization is a process of domination [*haimana*]: all societies must be democratic, must be capitalist; all must speak English. But the domination and power to spread these tools make peoples of smaller communities vulnerable."

This was in clear contrast to the Omani state, whose representatives clearly promoted that being modern meant a return to or a renewal of past glories and the values they imparted. At the same time, such officials as Salem al-Maskri, former chairman of the museum council, emphasized that the state accepted carefully calibrated change:

> We are inhabiting everything—telephones, the use of modern technologies, such as computers—but we don't forget our core values, which include mutual respect and mutual understanding. We don't reject modern

ideas. We accept that change is inevitable, but it has to be approached very carefully. We preserve and live a past that survives with us as we are changing. For example, nowadays we have the influence of Western culture penetrating our system.... [Young people] see it everywhere. But there has been a countereffort being encouraged by the government, elderly people, and parents. They are saying, "OK, you are modernizing your life, but look to your heritage, keep it with you, practice it, learn from the past and don't forget it." But there must be a balance.

Another Ministry of Heritage and Culture official said, "If you are saturated [mushabba'] with heritage and history . . . you would not be a terrorist. This is very important. You are tolerant. In Oman, we don't have sectarian and ethnic conflicts between Sunni, Ibadi, and Shi'a. It is like one family. It is not like Saudi, Syria, or Iraq. And this is because of the orientation of the government. This is the importance of preserving heritage." This continual refrain of a balance among past, present, and future led ministry officials to clarify to me the difference between their valorization of the past and that espoused by Islamist groups such as Da'esh (ISIS). This involved a subtle shift in temporal rationale. As Salem al-Maskri explained, "Da'esh does not want the present.... Da'esh wants to return the region to fourteen hundred years ago, and they do not want to confront modern life. You can't keep yourself busy by going to mosque all your life or staying at home and reading the Quran. There must be a mutual way of living safely [ta'ayush salman] between past, present, and future. You take a little from the past as guidelines on how to live the present." This emphasis on balance was further elaborated on by an advisor of the Diwan of the Royal Court in charge of cultural policy, who, while offering dates and pouring small cups of coffee in his office, explained,

> Heritage [turāth] in Oman is one of the basic factors in the development of a nation and its progress. It's a term that indicates the deep rootedness ['arāqa] of the past, the authenticity [aṣāla] of the present, and a view [naẓra] of the future. The human experience of the past becomes the new experience in the present and continues into the future. This is one of the most important elements of development [taṭawwur]. . . . This isn't a process of copying [taqlid] the past or going back but renewing consciousness with heritage and its authenticity as a useful recourse for the development of the present and its renewal.

When I requested an elaboration as to why, he chuckled and replied, "Amal, the Arab-Muslim world, whether in the Arab-Persian Gulf or in other Arab countries, is facing a culture invasion after sustaining other kinds of military invasion. Renewing heritage is the foundation [asās] of our activities in the modern age. Its loss means the disavowal [*ankar*] of self, the lack of acknowledgment of our existence and weakening ['*ajz*] the creativity of works which involve preparing heritage for the coming generations and adapting to the needs of the age accordingly." This perspective on heritage became clearer in light of an article (one of many) published in the government Arabic daily newspaper, ʿ*Umān*, which echoes the official state discourse. The article delves into the issues at stake for youth in modern Oman in the midst of global consumer culture and national heritage:

> Youth are moving in the direction of the future in different fields and diversifying in different social ways. They are the strength on which society is based, the basis by which security is maintained, as well as advanced. At the same time, they also have the ability to weaken society and render it helpless, one which cannot answer for itself even on the simplest matter that might threaten it.
>
> There is therefore a great fear of Oman becoming a completely consumerist [*mustahalik*] society rather than a productive one, dependent on copying the innovations of those other than itself. In copying the west, there will be a loss in innovative energy. This could have a negative rather than a positive mark on them (youth) and lead to their transformation from innovators and exemplars to that of being the oppressed of the powers of occupation. Secondly, they could lose innovative energy—the aim is to generate a creative and innovative youth. In general, it is the weakness of the umma and their location in the claws of occupation which shakes self-esteem. The youth are therefore affected by it. If some sense of pride returns to them, then a sense of pride can achieve a victory.
>
> There have usually been two responses to the fall of a civilization, meaning that there have been two approaches to colonialism and occupation: reject the west and assume a model of the past of our ancestors or copy the west blindly in terms of their material emphasis vs. spiritual values and religious morals. The first would lead to a withdrawal into oneself [*taqauqaʿa*] and a hardening [*iltazamat*]. The second would not lead to a true civilization but would be a copy instead. This in turn would lead to a state of chaos in society and there would be no place for the different spiritual values inherited from our forefathers.
>
> The solution is to preserve the past as a means of guidance for future generations. The past is not the end of everything but bears witness. By urging our youth to preserve our Arab-Islamic character, we create a future not in terms of blind imitation, but a future that is harmonious [*yulāʾim*] to this past and the forging of a character built on history. (K. al-Belushi 2011)

The official press and government officials emphasize the dangers of a future that is now conceived as highly contingent. Unlike the imamate period, where present and future were assessed on the basis of continuity with a ubiquitous and exemplary past, this is a future fraught with the unknown, even as it is conditioned by the perilous forces of Western globalization on the one hand and the ideologies of Islamist groups on the other. It is no longer defined by a way of life that is teleological in the manner of development, common concepts in official discourse of the 1970s and 1980s.

Instead, it is on the basis of this unknown future that the past is being considered and a new temporal logic (relations between past and future) is being calibrated. For Reinhart Koselleck (2004), modern temporal experience in the West is defined by a growing disjuncture between the past, present, and future. The past is no longer able to inform an increasingly unpredictable future, and chance plays an increasingly prominent role. Today in Oman, according to official voices, rejecting the past altogether would result in Oman's becoming a completely consumerist (mustahalik) society rather than a productive one, dependent on copying the innovations of those more powerful than itself. To reject the West and assume the model of an ancestral past, on the other hand, is considered to lead to a state of isolation and a "hardening" (iltazamāt). A focus centered wholly on a glorious history, with no acknowledgment of historical changes or the lasting effects of modernity, would leave Oman to an Islamist way of thinking. The changes being brought about by an unknown future must be accepted, but the past cannot be altogether abandoned, since it defines the specificity of Oman in terms of history and way of life. The solution vaunted by the state is to cultivate the particular virtues and desires necessary to maintain a certain kind of past that acts (1) as a guiding beam, facilitating youth who are navigating the unchartered waters of a national future; and (2) while forging an "innovative" basis for reconciling the specificity of an Omani history and culture with changes structured by powerful but contingent geopolitical, social, and economic forces.

In the other Gulf states, such as UAE, Qatar, or Kuwait, scholars such as Sulayman Khalaf (2008, 64) have examined how a heritage infrastructure, ranging from television programs and heritage villages to banknotes and stamps, has aimed toward consolidating the rootedness of a nation's "sense of *authenticity* while safeguarding against the global culture, which is regarded by many as a generalized threat to the local cultural identity." Oman may certainly be considered among that number. Unlike Oman, as elucidated in chapter 3, the heritage projects with which residents of these nations engage fit into the "rags to riches" narrative: the poor and simple life gives way to the discovery of oil, and its impact produces prosperity and modernization under the careful tutelage of a ruling family. Even as heritage is incorporated into the ongoing process of nation-state building, it does so on the basis of a perceived sharp disrupture between the past and the present, then and now.

In Oman, the past was often considered as an ongoing structuring presence of both present and future. In the words of one articulate official, as the exceptional country:

> The region called Oman dates back to three millennia. The UAE was only born in 1971. Oman has a history whose productivity goes back to ancient civilizations. Even in the beginnings of Islam, Oman was a kingdom. Islam entered Oman without war. They embraced it voluntarily. Omanis are tolerant and quiet since days of old. These things are inherited and still present today. It has a rich landscape of mountains, oases, wadis, a long coastline that became the natural setting for thousands of traditional settlements that have developed into different ways of life . . . and have created a rich cultural fabric. These characteristics are inherited from heritage to become citizenship today.

Such a perspective of history in Oman has led to its being transformed into a storehouse of exemplary wisdom to be documented, plumbed, and repeatedly deployed to address the fraught nature of present and future circumstances. The state officials' emphasis on ethical guidelines, values, and principles is the result of a tightly organized communicative regime created through the transformation of material objects and sites into signs conveyed by architecture, media, education, and festivals. This communicative mode continually enacts an ethical sense of history, made up of habits, values, and principles being applied to domesticate and filter the sensorial and habitual experience of modernity in ways amenable to the Omani nation-state.

Indeed, the systemic cultivation of a national historical consciousness in Oman appears to go far beyond fostering an inner sense of belonging that is identity or the alleviation of an alienation brought about by the ravages of modernization (Smith 2006, 48). Instead, its aims to shape citizens' desires and actions as part of daily practice bear strong resonances with Bourdieu's notion of habitus. As one senior administrator of the Ministry of Education informed me, "As citizens we would not accept everything if it does not agree [*lā tatawāfaq maʿ*] with the values of our tradition and history which is our country." A historically grounded code of conduct is being instilled as part of citizenship, one that is structurally capable of adapting to society's changing conditions while retaining its fundamental ethical virtues and principles.

Textbooks

This more abstracted way of being was accomplished systemically. One method was by training new generations of Omanis through social studies, a compulsory course from grades 1 through 12. Part of a systemic network of civic technologies directed toward youth, the introduction of each textbook explicitly states, "In the face of a society in rapid development, the ministry has developed a curriculum that reconciles/harmonizes [*yatalā'um*] these developments with deference to the specificity of society and its cultural identity." During a conversation with members of the curriculum board of social studies, one clarified the overall goals:

> I believe that what students need from history is that which is appropriate to understanding reality and taking pride in oneself through Oman's accomplishments. But if we give the students just wars, wars, and more wars, where is the success? A student of thirteen years of age needs to consider that his ancestors lived in a time that was also great and had noted accomplishments rather than just wars and being on the battlefront. . . . We are trying to create a generation that is conscious [*ya'ī*] of the requirements of the age in which they are in, which adheres to their religion, their civilization, and its reality. They need to acquire knowledge and skills for contemporary life from history.

Reiterating the overall framework of official publications and museums, the texts focus on the links between the land and human development in a chronological history that encompasses more than one class.[7] By the end of the eleventh year, I was informed, the student "will acquire an overall deep sense of the history of Oman and its development." Oman is distinctive in these texts for its strategic location—open to the outside world, a transit point for world trade since ancient times—which has given it a specific geographical/civilizational character. The texts explain that despite an extreme climate and variable terrain, the number of settlements indicates Omanis' adaptability. These assumptions become pivotal in defining the categories of culture and civilization. In defining civilization, the seventh-grade textbook begins:

> God honored man and distinguished him from his remaining creations, in a number of ways, one of the most important being his potential to think and use his hands. Man exploited his abilities to satisfy his basic needs for food, clothing and living from the environment around him. He obtained his nutrition from the fruits of trees and wore the skins of animals and lived in caves and caverns. Man advanced by degrees in social

> life which was organized by clan. He hunted animals and made tools
> and after he was able to till the soil, raise animals and invent writing,
> moving from the life of a nomad to a sedentary one. (Ministry of Edu-
> cation 2007, part 1, 12)

This becomes the basis for human development through stages; the Omani is
assimilated into a universal teleological narrative through the Stone Age, the
Bronze Age, and the growing impetus of sedentary civilization and trade networks
with ancient Egypt, the Gulf, and Yemen. Imagery of cave paintings, stone tools,
and frankincense complements the text or elucidates the material differences between modern Oman and ancient times. Illustrations of copper smelting, the honing of stone tools, or the making of fire become signifying practices, vehicles of
meaning, and objectified accounts of history and geography with moral and political consequences. Images of archaeological sites and artifacts become testimonials to this abstract history, affirming that Oman has "deep roots into human
civilization" (ibid., 23).

These texts emphasize that the human experience has involved understanding the environment and adapting accordingly, learning by degrees. Rather than
a mechanistic understanding of civilization's role as constraining humans, these
textbooks conceive of human and Omani civilization as tools of cultivation by
which man adapts to the land, thereby acquiring the institutions and skills by
which to progress. Oman's topography, geology, and climate are the basis for the
adaptive capabilities that have created the Omani man as a purposive actor who
can shape nature to his needs. In the seventh- and eleventh-grade textbooks, this
autonomous effort transforms him and improves his nature through rationalis-
tic efforts to exploit and adapt to the environment, creating a specific personality that is uniquely Omani across the ages: "Omanis are known across their long
history for a spirit of adventure and for bearing hardship. They have embarked
in small groups across the Indian Ocean to transport commodities and products
to far-away places and to export goods to regions which need them as well. All
these developments have contributed in the formation of the identity of this society [which] is the biggest spur for the Omani towards his continuing to undertake
his civilizational role in different aspects of life" (Ministry of Education 2007,
part 1, 23).[8] This character (*shakhṣīya*) becomes the foundation for a number of
textual units, in the chapter titled "Authenticity and the Social Contemporary,"
that aim to expand the parameters of the Omani man to "the nature of Omani
society and its formation" and explaining "the factors which have changed
Omani society and . . . defined it" (Ministry of Education 2006, 64–86). These
units enumerate the factors that define the uniqueness of Omani society and its
istiqrār (consolidation) over time, while transcending temporal-spatial dimensions,

as (1) Islam; (2) Arabic language; (3) a civilizational inheritance; (4) one nation in which all cooperate under the rubric of equality, entrenching national unity, which contributes to preserving Omani society; and (5) customs and traditions ('adāt wa taqālid) and authentic values (ibid., 66). These are considered the essence of Oman, differentiating it from the rest of the world. The eleventh-grade textbook further states that despite varied regional habitats and livelihoods, Omanis share fundamentals of social behavior and culture—a common denominator character- ized by specific material and spiritual geographical, historical, and civilizational dimensions.

Such texts herald the Omanis' past accomplishments as imprinted in the ideal forms of everyday social habits involving food, clothing, and work. These assume temporal continuity manifested in flint instruments, rock paintings, and weap- onry from the ancient past and extending to the values and morals of Islam and everyday customs and traditions. The resulting imagery intersperses date cultiva- tion, national dress, folk dances, towering forts, and two images of a sabla, the first a group of old men sitting among palm trees and the second showing men in na- tional dress in a carpeted chamber amid books and hanging weaponry. A dalla and an array of cups stands to the side. No contextual specifics are given, and the para- graph concludes that "all these ways of life have contributed across the ages in transferring a version [ṣūra] of the Omani personality" (ibid., 67). Depictions of the sabla/majlis are juxtaposed with a narrative that emphasizes that the majlis is one of the most prominent social forms of "hospitality, neighborliness, coopera- tion, harmony, counseling and education imparted across generations" (Ministry of Education 2006, 71). In this narrative, the sabla becomes metonymic of Oman as an "institution that . . . guarantees the relations between individual members and society, to become a modular school in cultivating the virtues [faḍāʾil], the social expertise of the community as well as practicing traditions such as hospital- ity to the guest, thereby transferring a life world to the next generation" (ibid.).

The imagery and accompanying text portray a typical pre-nahda past, but the portrayal is too ambiguous to assign to a specific historical context. This very am- biguity delineates a realm for the past's continuing role in the present. Culture and civilization in pedagogical practice designate a realm where these material forms and images are objectified as part of a reality independent of the histori- cally contingent circumstances of their production and use. The sabla and its links with the dalla are fetishized, achieving power by being tethered to immaterial sen- sibilities and moral evaluations that undergird the cultivation of the national citizen. The eleventh-grade textbook states this clearly:

> Omani society is strengthened by its customs and traditions in the au- thentic values inherited from various aspects of life. Benefitting from

national heritage enables the entrenchment of the correct foundations of values through following these customs and traditions and taking what is useful of the accomplishments of the age. On this basis, there would be a blending [*mazj*] of the authentic with the contemporary. These [traits] are tied to the past and strengthen the consciousness of the nature of the challenges which it has faced and the obstacles in growth that it has overcome, in its bent toward accomplishing the goals of the nahda (Ministry of Education 2007, 71).

These ideal principles become objectified as customs and traditions and embodied in material semiotic forms and imagery. Their ubiquity as part of pedagogical strategies transforms them into portals, admitting the individual subject into a reality where the concepts of civilization and culture form an integral part of creating the citizen-subject. At the same time, entering these domains involves a process of transcending finitude as the inherited accomplishments and works of previous generations endure beyond concrete historical contexts, becoming part of a process of spiritualization, moving between past, present, and future to become timeless. The province of the spirit, in the form of values and principles, is objectified through discourse, images, and objects, forging the normative modes of the "proper" citizen.

As a standardized genre whose reach through mass education makes it required study for every child in the sultanate, social studies textbooks are authoring a history that defines the parameters of citizenship. One effect of such a history is that its abstracted and homogenous form becomes the referential basis against which the emotional capacity and ethical guidelines of the citizen are imparted and honed. In the process, the very different temporal grounds of the history of an Ibadi sharīʿa community—once tethered to the notion of divine salvation and the exemplary lives of the virtuous—are excised from memory.

Indeed, there are biographies of major Muslim personalities in these textbooks. For example, grades 3 and 4 include short tales of those who played a decisive role in developing Ibadi doctrine and practice. Imam Jabir bin Zaid's biography emphasizes his studies in Basra, where he became renowned for his knowledge and learning. The narrative emphasizes his contribution to Islamic civilization as one of the first to write down prophetic hadiths. Imam Rabīʿa bin Habib is also educated in Oman and travels to Basra, where he acquires instruction in the Islamic branches of knowledge of hadith, tafsir, and fiqh in the hands of senior ʿulamāʾ. He is emphasized in the textual narrative as a scholar of prophetic hadiths, who wrote famous books and trained a generation of noted scholars. Imam al-Julanda bin Masʿud is also noted for his learning and piety. His imamate is distinguished for its zeal in spreading Islam and his rule characterized by justice and amity. But in the Omani national context, the Ibadi sect flows seamlessly into these historical accounts as its specificity is diluted and accounts of its imams are elucidated in terms of their contributions to Islam as a global ecumene.

As in the museums (chapter 3), the nahda ushers in a shift in common assumptions about religion that becomes internal to the discursive formations of culture and civilization. These values are the foundation of a new culture, which calls for contemplation and reflection and has produced intellectual and spiritual works. For example, in a fifth-grade lesson titled "Social Work," Islam is considered a foundation for cohesion (*tamāsuk*) and solidarity (*takāful*), which in a community setting are the sources for doing good and disavowing evil (Ministry of Education, 2003 part 2, 89–106). This principle is sanctioned by Quranic verses and explained as the basis for social practices heralded as part of Omani heritage, such as date harvesting, wedding celebrations, and regular visitation in the sabla/majlis, where men congregate on a daily basis and for celebratory occasions.

The second volume of the eleventh-grade textbook explains Islamic culture and civilization as forged on a foundation (*uṣūl*) derived from the Arabic language and Islam. This foundation is established on a series of principles by which the Arabs launched their conquests. Islam refused tribal conflict (*taʿaṣṣub*) through embodying the spirit of toleration, justice, and equality, the premise by which people enter Islam and which have enabled Arabs to forge an Arab-Islamic civilization. The book emphasizes that these principles of Islam become a political and social system, organizing relations between peoples in an Islamic society and instigating them toward communication and cooperation.

The Omani people's role in the spread of Islamic civilization into Southeast Asia and East Africa, through trade and missionary work, is also emphasized. For example, merchants, who often assumed the role of *ʿulamaʾ* by propagating Islam and mosque construction, are characterized as models of equality and toleration, embodying the principles of Islam as part of their working worlds and influencing those around them to convert to Islam. The religious past is reorganized and set in place within a longer national teleological framework. Simultaneously, this new religion is conceived in terms of a series of principles that have become abstracted in the process of being lifted away from the concrete contexts and material relationships that formulate Ibadi Islam. The result is that Islamic history is distilled into a series of moral principles and ethical habits that provide the raw material necessary for the proper forms of deportment that determine the citizen-subject.

I asked the curriculum board about the omission of certain crucial parts of Omani history, such as the British Empire. They replied, interrupting each other:

> First writer: The curriculum in social studies has a focus on subjects that will inspire study and will not form problems in other directions whether it is for the country or other individuals.

Second writer, a former teacher (interrupting): There is a kind of balancing act in not mentioning things that may cause problems. It is a balance of neutrality or pacifism in not mentioning that Omanis attacked or did this or that. What is there in these textbooks are mentioned in a manner that is a neutral [*hayādiya*]. Since Oman is an Arab Islamic country, most if not all of its values are Islamic. And thus they are extracted from this history: the love of *watan*, love of the sultan, loyal attachment, sincerity, fidelity, respect for women, et cetera. We are trying to entrench [*tarsikh*] the values of these practices and provide opportunities to transfer these dispositions [*sulukiyāt*] to new generations. This becomes a way of balancing [*tawāzun*] repetition with innovation or the need to copy past impressions [athār] with freedom of thought and initiative.

The increasing disjuncture experienced between the past and an anxiety-filled present and future demands a new calibration of the past that maintains continuity with the present and future in order to assuage and manage this anxiety. With history distilled and standardized, the ultimate goal is made possible: the Omani state can distance itself from the accusation of seeking to return to the past in a material sense, an approach to history ascribed to backwardness, isolation, and Islamist ideologies. Simultaneously, with a dematerialized past in hand, the state reformulates the ethical habits of its citizenry through what I call a "mobile foundation"' that allows the possibility of adapting to the dynamic demands of a changing future through the cultivation of a core but abstracted set of ethical dispositions and practices. These guidelines are extracted from a national history and work toward structuring patterns of perception and moral orientation that guide the citizen-subject in the pragmatics of daily living. They act as the generative principles by which the ideal citizen-subject should formulate a propensity toward thought and action while living in contemporary Oman. In other words, history becomes the basis for regulating the improvisations worked out by the citizen-subject when confronted by the challenges of globalization and modern living.

Heritage in Ethical Formation

As in other Gulf countries, the Omani disdasha and its distinctive form have been part of a process for differentiating and distancing Omani men, especially from the substantive presence of resident foreign nationals and other Gulf Arabs. Laws issued by the Ministry of Commerce and Industry have determined the minutiae of its form, neckline, stitching, and length to give it a distinctive Omani look. Although the white disdasha and the *masar* (turban) are obligatory only for government jobs, Omanis of different age groups spoke of the embarrassment of wearing anything else in the public domain or at formal occasions.[9] Anh Nga Longva (1997) and Farah al-Nakib (2016, 180–81) both elaborate on the effects of donning the disdasha in Kuwait, rousing reactions that immediately confirm the Kuwaiti's place in an ethnic hierarchy of social privilege and power. This was only part of the effect, however, as far as the Omani state was concerned. Omani officials were more likely to see the disdasha in terms of its more positive implications—guaranteeing a homogeneity in public sociability, irrespective of tribal or ethnic differences. One official declared, "What the disdasha does is orient [*yatajaho ilā*] the citizen toward a single template [*qālab*] that directs attention to how he acts and behaves as a citizen and how well he is incorporated into society." Another elaborated that wearing the Omani disdasha is

> like the continuity of a heritage that a man may carry inside him. It may be stitched by an Indian, and the cloth may come from elsewhere, but the style and design is Omani. It makes possible feelings of continuity, of belonging with this country. And when you feel this continuity, you carry feelings of citizenship and act accordingly. You may use new methods in making a disdasha, but the traditional form [*al shakl al-turāthi*] must be preserved in order to render it contemporary [*ta'āsur ma'a*] with the new generations, to teach them about their culture.

These views bore those of Saba Mahmood's (2005, 134–36) sentiments in her arguments that the exterior form of the hijab in Cairo, through continual wear, may become a fundamental means toward developing the requisite ethical norms and attentiveness toward the nation-state and all it entails. This was certainly an understanding espoused by Saif al-Ma'mari, professor of education and citizenship at Sultan Qaboos University and special advisor to the government. For him, the inescapable sight or use of Omani coffee, the khanjar, or the disdasha instigates the general notion of *dhauq*:

> The proper protocol of behavior [*ādāb al-suluk*] which demands a sensitivity [*hasa*] toward knowing what is suitable or in accordance with any given social situation. In Oman, it means the proper ways in which to interact and behave with each other within a single community. It is these interactions that determine how a society is characterized, whether it is hospitable, good or moderate [*ghayr muta'assib*]. . . . It is not enough to think of this concept merely in terms of the English word "etiquette," to open the door for someone or to receive women in certain places. We must place it within a wider framework that focuses on how the arrangement of values create the human character and determine the

standards [ma'ayīr] of mutual interaction. In the case of Oman, such values as good conduct toward others, humility, modesty, toleration, strong decisiveness ['azīma] and respect express authentic Omani dhauq which not only created Omani history but influences the formulation of Omani life today.

Al-Ma'mari gave the example of the specific rituals involved in receiving guests and the service of coffee: "For most houses in Oman, it will always be coffee and dates that are used to receive guests rather than tea or juice. We don't even ask if you want tea or coffee. This is the way we show hospitality, and if I go to any house, I anticipate they would offer me coffee and dates. You could say that I don't want to drink it, but she [the hostess] is still obliged to offer it to you." He continued, saying that these practices of hospitality oblige him "as an Omani, to receive a business colleague from abroad at home at the first meeting. I could not take him, as a guest, out to a restaurant for dinner. It is considered a lack of ikrām [generosity]. After that, it is possible for me to take him out."

When I asked him to clarify the relationship between past and present behavior and action, he explained, with a book in his hand,

> This is the Quran al-Karim [Holy Quran]. I could tell you that this is the past and that it came down during the time of the Prophet, fourteen hundred years ago. So why read it now since it is no longer relevant? We live in a different time now. So why don't you read a more contemporary book instead, something from the modern age? We are tied to the Quran despite it having come down to us fourteen centuries ago. Why? Because it talks and lays out a path of life [masār al-ḥayāt] for us to follow.

One of the more contemplative intellectuals at the Ministry of Heritage and Culture elaborated on al-Ma'mari's understanding of heritage values in building a self-scrutinizing citizen, through examples from her life experience:

> Heritage values guide the ways in which a woman might enter modernity. At one point, covering the woman's face was compulsory in the Sharqiyah region. Today, we might consider this something extraneous as long as it does not infringe [lā tamass] on something foundational that lies at the core of our values. If I uncover my face, that should not violate something more fundamental. When we work to enter into modernity, we allow ourselves to do things that do not infringe on the foundation of things, in terms of being active in society, traveling alone. This was never part of our customs and traditions. But now it is fine for us to travel by ourselves. We relinquished [takhalaīna] something in order to acquire something from modernity. At the same time, we did not

violate any religious or cultural foundation in doing so. This has now become the norm. I travel by myself, attend conferences. This has now become the process of being incorporated into an acceptable modernity [hadātha maqbula]. This is a modernity that we embrace but one which still preserves the foundation of our culture.

In these examples, the past becomes the very stuff through which change can be brought. In such scenarios, tradition becomes part of an embodied capacity, a filter through which innovations may be measured and sifted to discriminate the indispensable from the reprehensible in the construction of the modern yet authentic Omani self. State officials from different branches of government explained the institutional ubiquity of heritage imagery and discourse as a bid to strengthen a mode of reasoning and conduct grounded in an Omani past and the values it bore. This ethical foundation was ideally meant to be internalized to inform the varied opinions people formulated in deciding such daily minutiae as clothing, greetings, education, behavior, and social interactions.

The efficacy of heritage discourse for the undertaking of ethical reform was never more demonstrable than the steps the state took in the aftermath of the Arab Spring protests in 2011. A number of scholars have enumerated both the causes that drove hundreds to street protests and company strikes and the measures taken by the sultan to address their concerns (e.g., Jones and Ridout 2015; Valeri 2015; Worrall 2012), such as the dismissal of cabinet ministers, the creation of thousands of new public-sector jobs, a monthly unemployment allowance, and trials for a number of senior government officials and business heads, based primarily on charges of bribery on major infrastructure projects. These measures, positively received, were followed by the arrests of hundreds of protestors, journalists, and human rights activists charged with illegal gathering and destruction of public and private property, as well as the destruction of the Globe Roundabout, one of the most prominent gathering places for protesters in Sohar, which led to violent clashes with police.[10] A lesser-known consequence of the protests was a series of state-sponsored symposia among government circles and state intellectuals that were trumpeted in the national press. Their aim was to "raise the level of consciousness of Omani morality." Their titles, to name but a few, convey some sense of their focus: Debates on the Concepts of Freedom, Citizenship, Mediation;[11] Strengthening Citizenship Values in Growing Minds;[12] Omani Values and the Role of the Citizen in Growth;[13] Youth Aspirations in a Changing World;[14] Youth and Their Concept of Citizenship and Human Rights.[15] These symposia typically resulted in the distribution of large hard-bound volumes through educational and governmental channels, national press coverage, and suggestions for new policies to "strengthen the values and morals of citizenship." They were even accompanied by the introduction of new television programs, such as Hiwār Ash-Shabāb (Youth dialogue) on Omani state television, which attempted to create a dialogue between the state and the younger generation. These efforts coalesced around the fact that many in government circles were more disturbed by the behavior of "youth" during the protests than the fundamental problems of growing unemployment, the high cost of living, or government corruption. As one senior administrator informed me, "Change shakes [taza'za'a] a lot of the foundations [thawābit], principles, and values around us especially in spreading negative behavior among youth, in weakening their ability to accept the social roles required of them by members of society and the societal and moral standards of Omani society." A senior official noted,

> When young men and women appear with these heavy ways of thinking [tafkir al-thaqil], it leads to what happened in Syria and Libya. What is the reason why youth picked up guns and killed people like this? They did not walk on the middle path [tariq al wasatiya], one of balance. You even saw this in the demonstrations in Sohar. What did the youth do there? They undertook to cut off the streets and the roundabouts, and they tried to cut off some of the areas which lead to petrol stations.[16]

Other officials expressed a similar sense of anger: "If you feel you are being wronged, you do not break cars or house windows or beat an official or revile and abuse. This is not moral. You can tell us what you need without frustration, without becoming an extremist."

Although the nurturing of citizenship values through heritage discourse and imagery had been a cornerstone of nation-state building in Oman since the late 1970s, the protests led to renewed efforts to counter "extremist" behavior ascribed to the effects of social media.[17] The overdependency on social media was ascribed to the inundating effects of globalization, on the one hand, and the failure of the educational system, as well as the family, to entrench the proper morals and values among youth, on the other. Heritage institutions and practices were considered one means of mediating the shift from dangerous supranational linkages to those anchored to the national public domain through recalibrating the dispositions and loyalties of citizen-subjects. One such national institution was the sabla, whose traditional role was recollected amid calls for better communication with and education for young people, with its accompanying exchange of coffee and dates. In April 2014, the Majlis ad-Dawla (State Council) organized the Best Omani Social Practices symposium, in coordination with the sultan's cabinet and the Majlis ash-Shura (Consultative Council).[18] The symposium's president, Saif al-Ma'mari, later informed me, "Globalization has left a youth fascinated [maftun] with everything that is fast and technological. Society today has lost that intimacy of communication which helped in the transfer of proper conduct." His wife, who had accompanied him to our meeting, said, "Even if a young person is in the family majlis [in the home] or in an official majlis, they are on the phone. . . . Today each one of us is on the phone, and we rarely even ask each other, as family members, how we are."

The symposium's answer to behavioral reform was, in al-Ma'mari's words, "to continually adhere to the time represented by Oman's great history" to produce the ethical conditions for a historically anchored public life. He cited a twentieth-century incident involving Wendall Philips (1921–1975), the American archaeologist, oilman, and former advisor to Sultan Said bin Taimur. When Philips visited the port of Sohar, he found people of varied nationalities, including Omanis, working at the port. Al-Ma'mari alluded to this incident to point out the admiration laced in Philips' observation that "the Omani workers in the port of Sohar closely adhere to work and do not talk. They do not enter into conversation. They were concentrating on their work." Al-Ma'mari ended this account by emphasizing, "These are one of the Omani values that heralded [qādat] empire. They built an empire not only on military strength but the values which they embodied which included tolerance to others, acceptances of others, and benefitting from others' wisdom." These were the values now under threat. The utility of heritage discourse and the striking visual images it roused generated a certain kind of ethical receptivity attuned to the guidelines laid out by a national past. A knowledge of history and heritage was ideally understood to create the disciplinary conditions in which differences in opinion could be carefully regulated and mitigated within the territorial boundaries of national citizenship and its sense of ethical responsibility. The sabla, now defined and deployed within the temporal framework of the nation-state, was construed as the channel for domesticating the more aggressive tendencies of youth.

The homogenous space created by heritage discourse was now sharply disrupted with the emergence of a hierarchy anchored to ascribed differences between wise elders and riotous youth. One of the more prominent results of the symposium was a report, *The Public Majlis and Its Role in Strengthening Values* (al-Masruri 2014), presented and written by Muhammad bin Hamad bin Ali al-Masruri, a former member of the Majlis ad-Dawla. The report was distributed through government channels and education networks. As al-Masruri notes, the Ministry of Social Development is supporting planned public majlises in newer residential suburbs around the country to cultivate such modes of interaction through lectures and weekly sessions between older and younger generations. When we discussed the role of these majlises, al-Masruri urged me to consider how—like modern infrastructural development in other Gulf countries—the new residential districts throughout Oman were no longer based on tribal or kinship settlement patterns. Neighbors were virtually strangers. The new majlises are intended as a forum for social interaction where problems with government and commercial services, assistance, alleviation of illiteracy, unemployment, and other matters could be resolved; the head of the majlis could talk to the municipality or the wali on the district's behalf.

For al-Masruri, this new type of sabla needed to be a place where the young would once again sit and talk with their elders, learning how to debate with each other and how to acquire *fada'il* (moral virtues). He elaborated, "Youth . . . are in a hurry, so when they sit with their elders and listen to them, debate with them, there are issues present that are producing differences of opinion. That is not a problem. Instead of going to court, demonstrating, or burning buildings, they can sit with the elders and analyze and think through the solution." The importance of the sabla for the state was the constellation of habitual techniques of daily interaction and the expected forms of public conduct that necessarily accompanied the practice of sabla. In one senior official's words,

> Youth did not understand or comprehend how to express their ideas. This was the reason for the chaos [*fauda*] that happened. The truth is that people should have understood that you can express your opinion and different points of view, but at the same time from within the limits of a series of specific principles [*min thawābit al muayyana*'] that do not oblige people to destroy public property or private property, as is attested to by a prophetic hadith "*la darar wala dirar*," or "Let there be no harm or the reciprocation of harm."

For al-Masruri (2014, 16), and for most government officials, the sabla becomes a space for cultivating what was perceived as habitual modalities of conversation, debate, and critique, a forum "where children learn the value of silence and how to listen when an elder talks, . . . in the customary ways recognized by society." These forms of interaction would regulate and mitigate the impetuousness (*nazaq*) of youth, enabling even the most contested ideas to become a matter of civic debate, perhaps even general opinion, as long as they worked in accordance with the ethical parameters of the sabla, as set out by the state. Community elders would continue to discipline future generations in the work of ethical self-improvement through honing modes of public conduct, language, and styles of social interaction to engender mutual respect, forbearance, toleration, and firm resolution of virtues set within the greater project of building a "properly" moral national domain. Instead of cultivating an ethos oriented toward divine salvation and the exemplary life of the Prophet and his companions, the sabla in modern state discourse and policy becomes an ethical space oriented toward the cultivation of public practices of debate and critique, harnessed to the goal of creating the correct kind of speaking and listening citizen-subjects.

These symposia and conferences (which numbered in the hundreds, according to one state intellectual) roused a great deal of animosity among the former demonstrators, especially human rights activists. One of the most vociferous, Muhammad, wrote a blog post decrying the introductory address by the minister of endowments and religious affairs at the Best Omani Social Practices symposium, published in the *'Umān* daily newspaper. In the opinion of Muhammad, a slender but wiry scholar and teacher from Sohar, it was the very idea of the minister's words—"the country is responsible for directing the general interests of society in terms of formulating social consciousness [al-'aql al-jam'ī] which propels it towards the positive and efficacy"—that had generated his anger and fear. These words implied that state institutions were demarcating what was suitable to be absorbed by society in terms of ideas, principles, values, orientations, and conduct in order to arrive at that notion of "positivity" or "efficacy." In short, he feared the state was aiming to cultivate and entrench a behavioral uniformity to the detriment of individuality, which was later disparaged in the same speech by the minister and equated with "dissoluteness" (shahwāni) and anarchism (fauḍawiya). As another activist explained, "With these acts, there is a marginalization of my personal beliefs, decisions, and internal spirit. For example, it is my decision as to whether I want to keep the spirit of hospitality alive or not. Why are you [the government] interfering in my life?"

When I explained such a point of view to one of the senior advisors at the Ministry of Heritage and Culture, it rather startled him. To his thinking, the state was not instilling a standardized mode of behavior so much as "establishing a foundation where Omanis acquire their distinctive historical and cultural characteristics." His colleague elaborated earnestly, "These are merely the supports [rakā'iz] that allow forms of faith, learning, and work to be pursued in order to allow Omanis to be creative, advance, and develop without forsaking their foundation. You are preserving your roots in a way which will survive while embracing change." From Muhammad's (the activist's) perspective, the state's renewed efforts to cultivate a heritage consciousness echoes a liberal tendency to view the autonomous individual's right to choose as inevitably in conflict with community institutions and their techniques of collective education and discipline. For the state, however, heritage discourse and imagery are a force of knowledge the citizen needs to be attuned to in order to attain moral and intellectual autonomy. The citizen needs to cultivate a historical consciousness to possess the proper attitudes and moral disposition to ward off conditions that make citizenship impossible: the overwhelming supranational forces of globalization (Westernization) and Islamist ideologies. Tooled with the right techniques of ethical discipline (education, mass media, museums), the citizen is now conceived as containing the capacity to fashion himself into the modern Omani, fully equipped to navigate the changing tides of modernization through maintaining his rootedness to the land and its resources. For the state, history ceases to be merely a matter of abstract cognition. Instead, the past becomes constitutive of the ethical capacities deemed necessary for the citizen to continually immerse himself or herself in through daily acts of modern living.

Conclusion

If, as Laurajane Smith (2006, 54) postulates, heritage is a "mentality, a way of knowing and seeing," the heritage project in Oman ceases to be a simple matter of establishing the boundaries of the nation-state and its symbols. Instead, heritage discourse and imagery are cultivating habitual forms of attention that rationalizes a certain understanding of the national past and its relationship to the present and future to continually reform citizenship as automated habit. Tradition versus modernity, in the context of Omani nation-state building, ceases to work in terms of an opposition. Rather, the past is distilled into a portable series of ethical principles and practices that the citizen may carry as a habit-forming force, which is the generative basis for thought and action. Some virtues cultivated in this form were not familiar during the imamate period. Virtues I often heard about from state officials, such as innovation, entrepreneurship, and creativity, would not have been sought as the basis for seeking divine salvation or fulfilling the will of God, but they are on the list of desirable values the good Omani citizen should acquire, especially the ability to reconcile the known past with an unknown future. It is this "portable foundation" that the idealized citizen carries into a calamitous present and an uncertain future. Rich with possibilities in such a form, the past becomes a pragmatic filter whose fundamental disposition weeds out the undesirable in modernizing trends, leaving the desirable.

However, the very act of incorporating once daily objects and sites into a homogenous history of a national people, grounded in such categories as land and people and a generic Islam, is an exercise in selectivity—a contingent process that has carved out new social and political spaces through state institutions. I asked a senior official at the Ministry of Heritage and Culture how successful the heritage project had been in weakening old loyalties and tribal and religiopolitical schisms. In reply, he informed me,

> I just lost my nephew a few weeks ago in an accident, and we were surprised at the network of friends that he had from all segments of soci-

ety. I would never have guessed it. When I was growing up [he was in his sixties], I was very selective about choosing friends from among my own tribe, and not looking beyond. But the new generation goes beyond this because of their education; they are traveling abroad, they have access everywhere. And in a sense, this has political implications. Those sets of values and principles established by heritage have been helpful in creating the harmony we have, and I think it is important that those values continue.

Another Omani friend replied rather drily to my question about human rights activists and bloggers having been arrested in 2011 during the Arab Spring protests: "It wasn't tribal leaders who agitated for their release but a huge mobilization from people across Oman. In fact, their tribal leaders refused to speak on their behalf, worried that they be would be considered anti-regime. It was fellow journalists and professional ties that spoke up for them."

The sultanate has made use of its massive bureaucratic resources to deploy a regime of knowledge about the past that has become increasingly standardized and predictable. This has become the foundation for not merely consolidating a national identity but constructing the ethical society it envisions through that history. However, the successful performance of heritage as a national pedagogy is susceptible to its contextual re-presentations among the populace. As a selective process, the enactment of a national past involves gaps, disjunctures, and diversity at the core of what passes as a unifying history of a sovereign nation. This issue begs consideration of the many ways Omani citizens inhabit the sultanate's understanding of the past and the values it entails, a subject that is the focus of the next three chapters. In so doing, we will also get a sense of how, like Althusser's policeman, the authoritative presence of heritage forces Omanis to acknowledge the past in myriad ways, some of which may fall outside the boundaries of state expectations.

NIZWA, CITY OF MEMORIES

On one of my first visits to the fort at Nizwa, I noticed a picture I had not seen before. An old black-and-white photograph, tucked under the glass cover of the ticket desk, showed large holes in the upper portions of the fort's great tower; in the foreground, a group of soldiers stood beside a jeep (figure 5.1). When I asked the young custodian about it, his answer was terse: "The Jabal al-Akhdar," he said, covering the image with a newspaper. Perhaps he was not in the mood for queries, or perhaps he was concealing his ignorance of local history. Still, his silence was potent. Today in Oman, the Jabal al-Akhdar War of 1957–1959, in which the British-backed sultan overthrew the Ibadi Imamate, is conspicuous for the official silence about it.

Such a photograph evokes what has been purged from official memory, becoming an overt index of British military presence and informal governance that is at odds with the public conception of Oman as a sovereign and self-authored nation-state. More importantly, it evokes the alliances and conflicts that formed the larger backdrop of regional clashes between the sultanate, with its British overseers, and the Ibadi Imamate, with Saudi and Egyptian support—each side scrabbling for territory and oil concessions. It also alludes to the memories many Nizwanis spoke of when I asked them how the old city had changed in the forty years since the nahda began. These descendants of scholars, merchants, and farmers—young people who had never known the imamate, as well as elders in their seventies and eighties—recalled when Imam al-Khalīlī had patted them on the head or spoke a kind word, spoke of lively discussions and readings in the sabl, and described the strange, unexplained perfume emanating from the body of the imam as he was buried. They spoke of Nizwa Fort, miraculously unscathed after

FIGURE 5.1.   Bombed facade of the Nizwa Fort in the late 1950s

Photo by the author

bombardment by the British Special Air Service, the imprisonment and deaths of leading *ʿulamāʾ* in the fort of al-Jalali, and the wretchedness of self-imposed exile undertaken by thousands during the civil war era of the late 1950s through the early 1970s. The operations of national heritage had cleaved through these life histories and memories, leaving remainders, "survivals" that problematized and discreetly upset the proper order of the system of historical interpretation, which the Omani state had systematically striven to cultivate.

A number of Western scholars have considered the 2005 arrests of a "secret" Ibadi network, which I allude to in chapter 3, as the return of these repressed memories. The network of military, judicial, intellectual, and state officials, which the government accused of a plot to overthrow it and "reinstate the Imamate,"[1] was considered to be a reanimation of these memory fragments and their propulsion to the fore among Omani Ibadis (Jones and Ridout 2015; Valeri 2015). Espousing a return to an imamate way of life, these remainders figure in these writings as a return of what had been unthinkable since 1970—the reassertion of an ethical and historical imamate tradition.

The Omani scholars Khalid al-Azri (2013) and Said Sultan al-Hashimi (2015) argue, however, that their many interviews with organizers of this movement reveal that it started among government circles, as a result of perceived threats to the Omani ethos and way of life from the Wahabis—a trend recognized by Eickelman (1989) in his analysis of the widely televised debate between Oman's grand mufti, Sheikh Ahmad bin Hamad al-Khalīlī, and a Saudi senior scholar, 'Abd al-Aziz ibn 'Abd Allah ibn Bāz. Far from attempting to overthrow the government, the organizers felt cultivating an understanding of Ibadism among youth—through symposia, conferences, and summer institutes and camps—would strengthen Omani national identity in the face of an overwhelming Saudi hegemony on the Arabian Peninsula. From the many published confessions, some members acknowledged that although there had been much debate on the idea of implementing the imamate, the notion was "dangerous. . . . The Imamate had come and gone. The very different circumstances defining contemporary life in Oman would no longer permit it" (*al-Shabība* newspaper, April 20, 2005, as cited by S. al-Hashimi 2015, 147).

Irrespective of the sincerity of these remarks, this understanding was widely prevalent among my interlocutors in Nizwa, that institutional transformations brought about by the nahda era preempted the possibility of a return of the imamate. One noted young scholar of Ibadi history (and scion of a learned Nizwa family) informed me trenchantly, "Sharī'a Islam is no longer prevalent because of modern-day institutionalization. Even if they [Ibadis] established an imamate, they wouldn't have the necessary *'ulamā'* and sheikhs for organizing political administration, military training, and economic matters. The Ministry of Endowments and Religious Affairs was set up by the sultanate and does not have the capacity or the capability of establishing an imamate." My interlocutor was emphasizing that Ibadi Islam had been itself refigured to become consonant with the requirements of a modern sultanate. Its reformulation no longer includes a domain made up of military, political, or economic matters, all of which once fell under the administrative aegis of the imamate. The very institutional fabric of the imamate has been displaced.

Memories of life during the imamate and the violence that followed were managed and contained by the sultanic state through the concrete practices of heritage discursive practices, tourism, and historic preservation acts that made the last physical traces of the imamate and tribal histories—the fort, the watchtowers, the *ḥārat al-'aqr*, the oldest of Nizwa's residential quarters and the souq—meaningful through a national-modernist temporality. But this new sense of time, the history and imagery it conveys, assumes a performative dimension. To borrow a phrase from Veena Das (2007), it "descends into the ordinary" to mediate people's mundane daily experiences. People's memories of the imamate during my fieldwork (2010–2016) were often generated in relation to antagonism with the large-scale, modernizing sociopolitical transformations brought about by the nahda, including heritage practices. The memories of the imamate or the pre-1970 era that Nizwanis pondered over were less about a general resistance to the sultanate that looked for a return of the repressed, instead unfolding as a historically and culturally specific type of embodied historical knowledge (Das 2015, 54). Their distinctive form emerged from the deep disjunctures between heritage material practices, the values these heralded as embodying the good life and the personal, social, and religious interactions and relationships that now defined such spaces as the fort, the old residential quarters, and the souq as part of the routinized habits of daily living. These tangible remains acted as "ethical affordances" (Keane 2015), instigating an evaluative stance among Nizwanis through the memories these material remains produced on being experienced. Memory thus incorporated a critique of modern practices of governing and acted as a moral spur toward attempts to rework the fractures in ethical life and conduct that had come about through migration, modern living, and capitalist consumption.

William Bissell (2005) delves into the emergence of colonial nostalgia among young Zanzibaris as a result of the neoliberal economic restructuring of the region. Nizwa appeared to witness a similar phenomenon. Memories of the imamate were often voiced by people born during the nahda period—underemployed shopkeepers, taxi drivers, teachers, government administrators, and small-time business owners between twenty and fifty years of age, who had heard these memories from their fathers and grandfathers. For them, the imamate (the days before modernization) was an era that embodied the virtues of cooperation, solidarity, justice, consultation, and entrepreneurship—in fact, the same values espoused by heritage discourse that defined the national ethos.

Even as all Nizwanis were subjugated to this understanding of national popular history, many considered it a formal language with no significant context to give these values substantive significance, as socioeconomic and political ties and relations had been obliterated in the wake of the changes to their city over the course of forty years. Instead, Nizwanis were harnessing the imamate history and its still-tangible signs through fragmented memories that held an alternative understanding of the past from that of the nation-state. Ironically, even as an imamate past was once more becoming intelligible as an ethical intervention among people, it did so as the grounds of a critique generated by the transformations inaugurated by the modern state.

Transformations in the Old Urban Center of Nizwa

After 1970, the imamate social and political order toppled as the state reworked the old urban fabric through a series of ventures. Although still a prominent landmark of the urban landscape, Nizwa Fort was emptied of its administrative and judicial functions. One of the fort custodians told me, "When His Majesty came, he ordered that new offices were to be built outside the castle, and so the qadi moved to the new courts, and the administrators worked in new offices." These were near the new regional highways between Muscat and Nizwa. The guards still had official shifts and sentry duty, but no one was allowed entry without written permission from the Ministry of the Interior or the wali's office. Under the rubric of development and modernization, this new urban infrastructure was further strengthened by bureaucratic expansion in social affairs, the housing industry, a water and electricity grid, and a network of schools and roads that forged the institutional presence of the modern state in Nizwa. The city shifted from a primarily agricultural base to one whose residents were primarily involved in small-scale retail, building and construction, and government bureaucracy.

Free health and education were established as a major consequence of these developments, even as the sabla—once the local forum for education and dispute resolution in the residential quarter—was effaced. Another consequence was the demolishing of the imam's mosque, the congregational mosque, adjacent to the fort in 1970–1971. Many considered this, in the words of one shopkeeper, the result of "the congregational mosque [being] too old, and its surface area was not very big." This could have been the case. But at the time, Nizwa was still considered a focal point for armed resistance. The British-backed sultan Qaboos was still an unknown force who might replicate the actions and policies of his father.[2] Thousands were still in exile, the population was small, and the imamate way of life was still very much in place of daily life.

The current congregational mosque, now called the Sultan Qaboos Mosque, was built on the same site in the 1970s, and today is as much an icon of Nizwa as the fort; they are often portrayed together in postcards. Some Nizwanis, especially members of the old scholarly families, did consider the obliteration of the imam's mosque as an intentional act that emphasized the displacement of the imamate by a hereditary sultanate. One official from the Ministry of Endowments spoke of the importance of this act of erasure:

> During the time of the imamate, ṣalāt al-jum'a [congregational Friday prayer] could only take place in the presence of the imam or one of his representatives, who would deliver the khutba [sermon]. Friday prayers were conducted in just one mosque. . . . Everyone in the surrounding region would gather there. Now,

in Nizwa, there are more than twenty mosques. . . . The preacher who delivered the sermon was generally appointed or approved by the Ministry of Endowments and Religious Affairs. The authoritative figure of the Imam had given way to the bureaucratic ranks of the modern Sultanate.

By the time I arrived in Nizwa in 2009, fears about depleted oil reserves had resulted in the state's increased emphasis on diversifying Oman's economy. Tourism discourse and historical preservation practices had incorporated the landmarks of the old city, transforming the fort, the hārat al-ʿaqr, and the old souqs into tourist and heritage enclaves, with varied consequences. The old city now framed an ambiguous pre-nahda medieval past and was transformed into a living urban museum rendered distinct from its newer environs. By 2010, the Ministry of Tourism had transformed twenty-three of Oman's hundreds of forts, castles, and citadels into heritage sites. Many of these were large complexes, like Nizwa, and were the administrative, judicial, and military centers of a region once ruled by the imam and his retinue. The Ministry of Heritage and Culture restored Nizwa Fort between 1985 and 1995, placing Chinese ceramic dishes, weaponry, bedding, books, and palm ornaments—objects that had been collected from all over the country and stored at the ministry—in various chambers to re-create a "living" space. By 2010, the ministry had fully equipped the fort with visitor's facilities, such as restrooms, a gift shop, a coffee shop, and an exhibit in the old prison quarters.

Meanwhile, the adjoining tenements that lined the streets of old residential quarters were abandoned (chapter 2). One journalist and social activist, whose family still owned two of the old houses, told me, "After 1970, changes happened in a very big way. The Omani family got salaries, and the husband, and sometimes the wife, worked in the government. So the income was good. And the government started distributing land. . . . There were loans from the Ministry of Housing, and the government also built free housing for the poor." With larger salaries, new positions in the armed forces, government, or retail, and expectations of a higher standard of living, people began migrating to the new suburbs in the early 1980s onward. For a minimal fee, the government allocated plots to men and women for building houses, thereby enlarging urban residential neighborhoods at the expense of the old quarters.

The date and fruit orchards that had once covered a large part of the quarters adjacent to al-ʾaqr, such as *al-ghantaq*, were reduced to make way for residential villas. There were no more than five or six Omani families living in the old quarter, which consisted of some three hundred houses, each with one or two wells. The hārat al-ʿaqr and its environs were reoccupied by migrant workers, primarily from India, Pakistan, and Bangladesh, who labored as maintenance workers for civic infrastructure and building, in agriculture, as craftsmen of mass-produced silverwork and other goods, as cleaners, and shop-front and supermarket sales assistants. Meanwhile, a more professional class of trading company managers, teachers, doctors, nurses, and engineers swelled the growing numbers of expatriates residing in the suburbs outside the historic center.

Lying behind the fort and thus just a few steps away, the hara was now characterized by rubbish-strewn doorways, disused aflāj water channels, old zaygra wells, and disintegrating mudbrick structures with cracked and broken wooden doors and window frames, interspersed with modern cement blocks and metal grills (figure 5.2). The state had set down conditions for the preservation of historically significant old quarters, such as hārat al-ʿaqr, which was deemed important not only for being the noted residence for prominent ʿulamāʾ (historians and poets) over the centuries but for its proximity to the heart of the old city—the fort, the congregational mosque, and the old souqs. In Nizwa, I heard plenty of accounts from relatives of former residents about how the state was the primary author of the old quarter's dilapidation, having prohibited residents from undertaking any kind of building connected to the old houses, let alone permitting their demolishment to build anew.

A local jewelry shop owner was vehement in his account: "The house my brother was born in fell because of the rains. No one was living inside, since it

FIGURE 5.2.   The Harat al-ʿAqr today

Photo by the author

was already in ruins. And the government today doesn't even allow the rubble to be removed." If a house was falling down, restoration was governed by strict guidelines from the Ministry of Heritage and Culture, with formal permits that could only be obtained through lengthy bureaucratic procedures. Former residents told me the last renovations in the quarter had taken place two decades earlier, before the year 2000. One angry local journalist and blogger informed me, "The ministry has sought to prevent people from doing any restoration work while, at the same time, hasn't undertaken it itself. The result is this catastrophe [*kāritha*]. Even the ruins are being destroyed by neglect."

It was cheaper to build in the new suburbs than to undertake the extremely expensive process of restoring a family home using ministry-sanctioned materials (mudbrick and certain types of wood) and traditional construction techniques required to retain a certain heritage aesthetic. There were stories of families who found a way around the heritage laws and built small modern houses in the orchards behind their main domiciles and then waited for the original building to collapse before rebuilding according to their needs. Others were unofficially accused of destroying their houses under the cover of night in order to rebuild them for modern convenience. In the meantime, new construction near these historic sites was required to use the color of mudbrick to blend into the urban heritage core. The outer frames of windows and doors were to be wooden, and building height could not exceed two floors to preserve the overall heritage landscape. No buildings could be taller than the fort or the mosque, the iconic emblems of the city.

Many of the building projects and consumer retail chains not only catered to Omanis but also adapted to the needs and tastes of a growing expatriate population. From 1974, the old souq areas and the silver and copper workshops became the center of a rapidly expanding shopping district. The outer defensive walls of the fort and the hārat al-ʿaqr were now fronted by a major retail phenomenon, made up of two-story storerooms and shops for textiles, ready-made clothes, cosmetics, groceries, supermarkets, banks, and pharmacies, flanking the newly tarmacked main road from Muscat to Nizwa. In the early 1980s, as a result of rising standards of living, gold jewelry (primarily from India) was in greater demand for the *mahr* (bride's dowry) than silver jewelry, and a number of shops established themselves in the area. The large old souq quarters, souq al *gharbi* (western) and souq al- *sharqī* (eastern), with their open shop stalls, were being made redundant. By 2015, the outskirts of the city center were lined with lavish shopping malls and hypermarkets.

In the early twenty-first century, the Ministry of Heritage and Culture began its conservation of the hārat al-ʿaqr by restoring part of the high wall enclosing the hārat al-ʿaqr and six other residential quarters with Nizwa Fort. The walled enclosure was interspersed with twenty-two watchtowers and four gates, one of which had been restored. The ministry's heritage management plans in 2010 and 2011 included the restoration of about sixty old houses in the old quarter, focusing on the city's historic core. These houses were considered distinctive for their architectural and historic importance and were fairly easy to restore and maintain. Plans were afoot to rent them out, denude them of their South Asian worker residents, and transform six of them into a museum focused on the area's history and architecture. The rest were to become restaurants, cafés, craft houses, and boutique hotels. As one of the key personnel of the heritage management plan informed me, when we perused the ministry's Nizwa plans,

> here there is a beautiful house, and a blind man live in it, and his family lives there. There is a *tanur* there.[3] They [the ministry] want to transform the house into a traditional coffeehouse there. There is still a family there, and we are going to undertake restoration, and they will be left to live and work in the house, offering coffee to guests. We will ask them to open their house to guests in exchange for restoring it.

The residents themselves would become part of these exhibits, and their actions would further exemplify the notion of living heritage. However, the drop in oil prices between 2011 and 2014 led to a decrease in public spending, hampering state efforts to continue the project. Instead, the state encouraged an overall neoliberal policy of privatizing efforts to conserve. The Ministry of Tourism urged prominent merchants in Nizwa to salvage and recuperate the historic sector of the city, investing in them as primary economic assets and attracting foreign investment by marketing the city and its heritage.

Simultaneously, unemployment was high, due to a growing population and stagnant salaries that could not keep pace with the rising cost of living. In such circumstances, the forms and expressions that people's memories of the imamate have assumed might be plausibly examined through the shifts in how Nizwanis were reworking their historic relationships with the fort, the hārat al-ʿaqr, and the old souqs. These major sites, which defined the historic city, became nodes in the clash between a heritage utopia—bounded to the notion of the perpetuation of durable values and principles as a way of life—and a capitalist vision, unleashed by the modernizing state, of historical conservation, touristic enterprise, and profitable investments. In the process, these two rationales of thought and action forged the conditions for the recall of an imamate past as a political and ethical intervention and critique among Nizwanis, in the name of resolving the contradictions and paradoxes of two different sets of values and toward imagining the "good life" as the basis for conciliating themselves to the transformations brought about by the nahda.

Transforming Nizwa Fort into a Mode of Heritage Governance

These days, the guns and cannons at Nizwa Fort are silent, and no guards patrol its crenelated contours (figure 5.3), but the castle and gunnery tower stand as an imposing seventeenth-century edifice, with the Omani flag flying high. Restored in the late 1980s, its stone and earthworks tower over a line of tourist shops, bookstores, cafés, and a large parking lot for visitors. Two cannons flank the entryway, which leads to a large desk on a platform. Two of the custodians and guides I often found there had family members who had been ʿaskariyīn (guards) during the imamate period (1913–1957). These men now greet visitors and handle ticket sales.

In other words, Nizwa Fort—once a center of military, political, and administrative power—is now a museum. Palm fans, textiles, swords, khanājar, and handicrafts decorate its walls. The former prison, with its maze of corridors, is an exhibit hall, each cell taking up a theme in Nizwa's history, and text panels stand alongside dioramas reconstructing the fort's history. The overall effect is a perceptual and sensorial experience of the past. Such contemporary practices of

FIGURE 5.3. The front entrance of the Nizwa Fort

Photo by the author

public memorialization propagate forms of history, culture, religion, and time even as they (re)organize them.

One room invites visitors to watch a film (in Arabic and English) on the fort's importance. Through images juxtaposing men's dances with crowded souq areas, handicrafts, cattle auctions, and decorative historical mosques, the narrative places Nizwa and its fort in a contiguous relationship to a more comprehensive but absent whole: Oman. Objects and sites become evidence to a past that, despite a brief note dating the fort to the seventeenth century, is rather ambiguous; the images and buildings are never assigned a time line. Instead, the fort is transposed upon and linked to seventh-century mosques and late twentieth-century souqs, generating a sense that the past is not entirely distinct from the present but is in continuity with it. Like the national museums' exhibit framework, this amorphous sense of time is strengthened by vacillations between past and present tense in the narration.

In another strand of the film's narrative, Nizwa's physical past is inextricable from a sense of nationhood and tied to the processes of working the land, which transforms the laborer into an Omani. This sense of rootedness or national belonging becomes tethered to a longer teleological history of "progress" and "civilization" that triumphs over the Other. The film extols the naval significance of the Ibadi Ya'āriba Imamate (1624–1743), which built the fort, freed Oman from the Portuguese in 1650, and established an empire in East Africa. The depiction of the Ya'āriba Imamate as Omanis who harnessed local resources to defeat European imperialists and establish their own empire reverses the classic theological view. In Ibadi doctrine, the Ya'āriba are part of the umma and stand as exemplars of Muslim virtue (something to emulate) and sinful conduct (something to avoid). In the film, Ya'āriba imams are heroes who embody fortitude, bravery, and entrepreneurship—national values that endure as lasting traits of the Omani people.

As a monument, the fort's engineering and defensive system becomes a signifier that can summon a history and its values to conscious and collective recollection. In their immediate associations with each other, architectural landmarks and material objects become tokens of "authenticity" and "tradition" as integral parts of Oman's modernity. Elements of the cityscape are "live testimonials [*shawahid hayya*] to Nizwa as a center of culture, spiritual enlightenment, and learning . . . since the very beginning of the Islamic era." Without specifying the fort's historical and cultural past, the film casts its structure as a convergence point for political, social, and religious interaction and a center of learning and administration. The concrete practices of Ibadi politics, law, and administration that once anchored an exemplary history are now alienated from the fort's function, paving the way for an alternative framework.

Once the foundation for the workings of the Ibadi sharīʿa polity, the fort has been purged of intimate associations with imamate politics, religiosity, and tribal conflict and revaluated into a reservoir of abstract values, moving between past, present, and future to embody the nation-state and its normative standards. The past becomes a force that is immanent to the present rather than disassociated from it. At the same time, the fort's material form and its new role as an iconic symbol are tethered to a different way of organizing and experiencing the past, facilitating another means of reflecting on history. Echoing the national heritage discursive practices explored in chapters 3 and 4, this new world of abstract values involves man, not God, as the central actor in the story, with the Omani citizen rather than divine salvation as the telos.

History Production through the Nizwa Fort Complex

On my first visit in 2010, I had the pleasure of being guided by Yusuf, one of the fort's custodians. Yusuf repeatedly drew my attention to the cunning defense layout as "living witness" to the depth of Oman's civilization and its innovations in architecture, craftsmanship, and engineering. Although few textual labels existed to explain the fort's historical and cultural specifics, some effort had been made to suggest each room's function with a variety of furnishings, not the originals, that conveyed a generic understanding of "tradition." Old matchlocks and swords were mounted on the walls; palm mats, carpets, and embroidered cushions lay on the floors. Wall niches held metalwork, ceramics, woven handicrafts, and books, indicating the imam's residential, administrative, and judicial quarters. However, the objects used to evoke this past were also present throughout Nizwa's streets, markets, and shops outside the fort complex; they failed to convey a sense of entering another time-space. A diorama of a "traditional" souq was even stocked with contemporary consumer goods—canisters of food, jam, milk powder, and ghee.

This temporal ambiguity was further instantiated in the exhibit hall. The former prison, with its maze of cells, is arranged along two temporal axes, forming a spatial itinerary for the visitor and a progressive trail of evolution and traditional life. Geological, archaeological, and historical periods are connected to create one national time, linking ancient periods and recent times and creating a narrative of development and increasing complexity. The corridor comprises a series of colorful, elongated panels that follow Oman chronologically, beginning with Paleolithic cave dwellers and culminating in traditional practices that remain part of the present. Settlements throughout the region are summarized as adaptations to desert, mountain, and coastal terrain, although clearly affected by man's spiritual and rational activities, from the construction of the aflāj canal system for agriculture and copper mining to the gradual flourishing of sea-trade networks that led to the development of city, state, and empire. Socioeconomic activities are assimilated into a story of ecological adaptation. This linear teleological narrative peaks with ethnographic exhibits of traditional life, depicting the harnessing of natural resources for indigo dyeing, silverwork, date cultivation, and fortification. Oman's oldest towers, the beehive tombs that date to the early third millennium BCE, are placed in a direct line of progressive development leading to the forts and castles of Oman's Islamic period, including Nizwa Fort. Through signs of an ancient and supposedly uninterrupted occupation, these artifacts and buildings bring Oman as national homeland continuously into view. No longer working toward the Islamic doctrine of human perfection, the new Omani citizen-subject develops and grows through harnessing the land and its resources in distinctive ways.

Alongside these depictions, wall panels and labels are written in the present tense. Large-scale color photographs that form the backdrop to exhibits of basketwork or silver jewelry remain temporally ambiguous, insofar as they are not contextualized. This ambiguity bridges the spatial and temporal gap between yesteryear and today. The glass cases for each activity display the tools and their products, with labels that ignore changing circumstance. The text panel next to one display describes silverwork as "capturing the spirit of Nizwa's artisanry. It can be forged, drawn, cast and wrought extensively. As the metal of the Prophet, silver also carries the connotation of purity, and is often engraved with verses from the Holy Qur'an."

Extracted from the material ties that once anchored it to a sociality grounded in the Quran and prophetic sunna, the fort is monumentalized as a national spectacle. Islam and its practices are thus transformed into spiritual values that embody national cultural traits. Livelihoods and material forms that emerged at different times are abstracted from their contexts, only to be retethered through this national teleological timeline to fundamental values of entrepreneurship, creativity, hard work, and family ties that define the ethical actions necessary to become an ideal Omani citizen. Moving beyond representation, heritage practices regulate the relationship between politics and history by rendering the perception and practice of Ibadi Islam and the imamate more amenable to state regulation through transforming it into another mode of tradition, one undergirded by the modern nation-state.

The Imamate as a Part of Fort History

A more explicit understanding of Ibadi Islam in concordance with the fort's over-all historical representation can be found in a small chamber in the exhibit hall, which features a series of colorful panels creating two themes: Ibadi Islam and Omani imams. The first series emphasizes Oman's voluntary, early embrace of Islam before the death of the Prophet, emphasizing age-old affinities with the message of the Prophet. Ibadism, still the sect of a slight majority of Omanis, is defined as one of the oldest Islamic sects, founded on "the true principles of Islam" through embracing the principles of elected leadership.

This rather dangerous note, especially to a dynastic rule that nonetheless espouses Ibadi Islam as the country's predominant sect, is mitigated in several ways.[4] First, a chronological list of imams on a large wall panel includes the last three who ruled the interior in the twentieth century, but without sociopolitical or historical details. According to the exhibit designer, this was an intentional act: "[The Ministry of Tourism] just wanted a list of imams without referring to what the imamate meant in terms of authority or dominion." The list is structured within a framework that encapsulates almost thirteen hundred years and characterizes the imam, according to one text panel in the *Ibadi Islam* exhibit, as a prototypical figure—"always a spiritual leader . . . and the final judge of appeal on all religious matters. To the extent that he could impose his will he also administered the secular government and imposed taxation."

The imamate is thus positioned as part of a long-gone past, creating a sharp divide with the present. Simultaneously, the imam is linked to an understanding of religion indebted to modernist secular principles through emphasizing clear dichotomies—public and private, material and spiritual, the state and religion. This set of binary assumptions naturalizes the modern state's understanding of religion as confined to the sphere of privatized belief, the boundaries of which are regulated by law, even as it generates a set of modern ethics concomitant with state religiosity and civic virtue.[5] This history repositions Ibadi Islam within a Western modernist framework.

However, it is clear that religion was a constitutive part of the state during the imamate period, and thus it is difficult to claim the imam was a spiritual leader who might or might not have influenced politics, law, or taxation. The museum panel intimates that by influencing politics or taxation, the imam would be reaching beyond his "natural" domain. Religion and its relationship to politics during the imamate period, which ended in 1955, reflect a fundamentally different understanding that made it the basis for the everyday sociality and functioning of the imamate as a polity, including *zakat* (alms tax) for the *bait al-māl* (state treasury), guarding boundaries, and the dispensation of sharī'a as part of mediating the vicissitudes and tensions of daily living. It is misguided to discuss religion as an autonomous domain that influenced politics and the economy during the imamate period. Rather, Ibadi doctrine, as constitutive of the imamate, enabled and regulated its existence. Nizwa Fort and its intimate link with the twentieth-century imamate are thus mainstreamed into the public realm through immersion in a depoliticized formulation of history.

Translated into the mode of heritage, the fort comes to represent a past grounded in the human subject, armed with knowledge rooted in working the land and seas. Framed by a developmental narration of history and cast in its new historic garb, the fort is elevated above the quagmire of religious politics to steer its own ideals of moral practice and political authority without being contaminated. In answer to my query on the depoliticization of the narrative, the designer of the narrative informed me, "The Ministry of Tourism emphatically told me not to refer to any type of civil wars or conflicts. However, they did not stop me from referring to foreign threats or invaders, such as the Persians or Portuguese. I was asked to use Nizwa as a platform to talk about Oman's history, almost like a case study." Nizwa's immediate history as the administrative capital of the Ibadi Imamate (1913–1957) is thus excluded. Its existence in the twentieth century is assimilated into official accounts through the observation that "before 1970, Nizwa—as was the case in the rest of Oman—was steeped in a life of ignorance, poverty and illness which prevailed over all parts of the country" (Literary Symposium in Nizwa 2001, 93). The twentieth-century imamate is co-opted into a narrative of "lack" in material development and progressive modernization, effectively depoliticizing the existential presence of the imamate as a once-legitimate alternative to the sultanate and its British supporters.

As part of Oman's interpretation of its past, Islam is cast as a series of generative values and principles rather than as ritual practice (Asad 1993, 27–54). This resonates with Talal Asad's claim that the universal understanding of religion as part of the ideology of modernity shifts focus from power and material practices to inner beliefs and sets of propositions. In Oman, the process of socioeconomic modernization and nation building, the nahda, also witnesses a shift in common assumptions about religion. This kind of religion is conceived in terms of principles and values extracted from the concrete contexts and material relationships that once defined the Ibadi imamate, to be reanchored toward a religion more amenable to a distinctively national way of being.

The discursive practices of heritage are a resource by which to tame the potential for violence in the transition from imamate to sultanate in the latter 1900s. The very notion of "imam" is recalibrated in the public domain. The Ibadi sectarian tradition, which elected the imam by consensus (shura), has given way to a hereditary sultanate, undergirded by a nationalist framework within an evolutionary history of man's ability to work the land.[6] The foundational texts of Islam, the Quran and sunna, are reflected on within a space defined and regulated by the modern nation-state. In other words, religion is entering a space already built on secular assumptions and erected on the foundation of the "Omani personality."[7] In the context of national space, the physical features of the fort are co-opted into a chronicled, linear history oriented toward human progress rather than a premise of divine salvation.

The nahda embraces a sense of historical time in which man dominates nature, generating a temporal order that realigns agency away from the divine (Chakrabarty 1997, 35–60). History is secularized and proscribed to natural laws of evolutionary development. Nizwa Fort, like other museums in Oman (chapter 2), becomes integral to a disenchanted time of human history, transforming the relationship between religion and politics in public spaces. This rubric of national culture and civilization excises Ibadi historicity, religious and political schisms, British colonialism, and violent conflict. The restructuring of institutional history in the latter part of the twentieth century purifies it of the administration, law, and ethics of the imamate, producing, in the process of disassociation from these fields of power, a new form of Ibadi Islam, one that facilitates a history grounded in the nation-state and the modern, secular political order of a public-private divide.

The reconstruction of the past in old imamate forts has resulted in a new mode of governance in nahda Oman. But in Nizwa, to those brought up in the nahda era, the fort becomes an integral component of another widespread phenomenon—the circulation and collection of photographs of old Nizwa from the late 1960s and early/mid-1970s, before its material transformation into heritage and tourism projects. These photographs circulated in offices and homes and were collected and transmitted through mobile phones and laptops, especially among those in their thirties and forties, who had grown up in the nahda period. I obtained many such photographs, as aids to facilitate personal reminiscences, from the main photography studio in town, where framed prints of old Nizwa could be seen on the walls. The ubiquity of these old photographs did not strike me as greatly relevant until people brought them forward to illustrate their relationship with the fort, the old quarters, and the souq and illuminate their accounts of contrast—how Nizwa was socially and economically better off, as a whole, before the nahda.

During my early fieldwork in Nizwa, I often sat in Abdullah's stationery and bookstore, adjacent to the fort. He was a rather interesting man to talk to; his family had lived in Nizwa for generations and were renowned for their scholarship. They had been judges, governors, and jurists for the twentieth-century imamate and still held a private library of important treatises, personal documents, letters, and books that enticed a steady stream of tourists in the spring and summer months who would often interrupt our early-morning conversations. Other shopkeepers would also gather at his shop during the late-morning lulls.

I asked one such group about their relationship to Nizwa Fort, now that it was a site of heritage and tourism. In response, they showed me photographs of the fort, the old quarters, the souqs, and the surrounding date and fruit orchards on their mobile phones, lamenting the days before the nahda and into the 1970s and 1980s as "a time when men and women helped each other and life was simpler, cheaper, and clearer [*sāṭī*]." The past, in official discourse and practice, was considered in terms of revival, continuity, and unleashed potentiality for navigating an uncertain future, but for many Nizwanis, it was an experience of loss, irretrievable in the face of inflation, rising costs and standards of living, and growing unemployment. A regular complaint was how much harder they found the "demands on life" as houses had become more expensive to build: "In former years, they were considered more economical since the materials, primarily mudbrick and the palm tree, were local." Building and repair work, among other tasks, had been a communal effort, and life was characterized by the group in general as one of mutual solidarity (takāful) and connection (*tarābuṭ*).

One shopkeeper went on to elucidate the shift in family life: "In marriage, a man would usually live with his father and grandfather in the same house, in contrast to nowadays, when each man, on getting married, feels compelled to build or rent a house or apartment of his own, resulting in dispersion." Back then, I was told, a few silver bangles and a ring were enough for the mahr (bride price), especially as one was more than likely to marry a family member (usually a first cousin) or a girl from the hara.

The average mahr cost 50–60 qursh (OR 100–200), and one's morals and character were more important than salary or job expectations.[8] While I was in Nizwa, I heard constant complaints from the younger men that marriage had become one of the biggest economic obstacles—becoming, as Samuli Schielke (2015, 112) points out in the context of middle-class existence in Egypt, "a nodal point of consumption and a key occasion to go into debt." The mahr now averaged OR 5,000–7,000 ($12,987–$18,100), given the increasing demand for gold and precious stones over silver, in addition to another OR 2,000 ($5,194) for the wedding and engagement celebrations.

Beyond this group, the general sentiment among Nizwanis was that men could not marry until they could afford a car, a house, and furnishings. This has resulted in increased expenses, especially if there are parents or other dependents, and a massive increase in the workload to meet the rising standard of living, especially for young and middle-aged men. An Omani friend whose family still lived near the fort summarized the contrast between then and now: "If a neighbor was not there in the mosque for prayer, people would go to his house to ensure his well-being. Now, if he prays in the mosque for a year and then he doesn't come for a month, his return would pass unnoticed and unobserved."

Tariq, another Nizwani, often took me on my research trips to Muscat, giving us a chance to chat. Like many others, Tariq worked at the Nizwa branch of the Ministry of Defense. Evenings and weekends, however, he roamed the streets in his taxi, looking for customers. He had steady work and a subsidized loan from the government to buy a plot in one of the new suburbs, but his mother and sisters depended on him for living expenses, and he was trying to earn enough money to build a house for his future family. His story is representative; most taxi drivers I traveled with during my sixteen months of fieldwork had two jobs—one day job in government administration, a factory, or a private company and another driving taxis in the evenings, seeing their families on the weekends, if they could.

Older Nizwanis, many of whom were returned exiles, often spoke of the civil war of the 1950s and 1960s as a time of chronic political instability, mass arrests, unemployment, and lack of socioeconomic possibilities. One former member of the Majlis ash-Shura (Consultative Council) commented, "As a result of politics, people in their livelihoods were wretched [ba'isa]. When Sultan Qaboos came, all this wretchedness ended. For families, grandfathers and fathers, now whenever we compare our wretched life before . . . we would have no desire to conjure it back." When I asked about the old days, members of the older generation often said, in the words of one succinct commentator, "Praise be to God, because today, you can live a wonderful life, where you can eat, live in stability and security, when you can work."

Simultaneously, many like Tariq, who grew up during the nahda period, used the photographs of old Nizwa on their mobile phones and laptops as evidence of the material changes they had witnessed during their lifetimes and the material consequences for their lives. These images did not merely inspire a selective understanding of history but became part of a travelogue into the history of Nizwa, authorizing a romanticized ideal that became equated with life during the twentieth-century Ibadi Imamate. The images appeared to saturate the present with the past, but the critique they vocalized was not couched in the language of history espoused by the imamate (the need to fulfill the exemplary acts and words of the Prophet, his companions, or the imams); nor was it oriented toward a submission to divine will as part of daily living. Instead, the sight of old landmarks was engendering a form of nostalgia. the imamate past was conceded as one that could no long exist. Yet it was also becoming legible as an exercise of critique, operating with reference to the growing contradiction between the sultanate's utopian vision of a living heritage and disillusionment with contemporary socioeconomic forces unleashed by state modernization, including growing economic disparities resulting from unbridled capitalism, social discontent with the number of foreign workers, unemployment, and political corruption. These had resulted, as far as residents were concerned, in the fracturing of the moral community.

Memories of the imamate were being deployed through imagery that had little to do with the return of the imam and his mode of governance. Rather, this imagery stood for a simpler but energetic community-oriented way of life, when neighbors and kin personally guaranteed social provisions of economic welfare, work security, long-term stability, and moral upbringing. As one prominent young scholar heatedly replied during our conversation in the fort,

> When a European woman comes and she wears something up to here [gesturing toward his thigh], that's one thing. But when they are entering the fort, which was considered the seat of Ibadi Islam, frequented by *'ulamā'* and imams . . . how is that preserving our habits and traditions when a youth who is not married sees her? When you enter Carrfour and Lulu [hypermarkets], you would see that there are no values or morals. Even the *shisha* [hookah] is sold, as well as some things that are not permitted by sharī'a. Wine is being sold in hotels. This was not known in the age of the imams, and it was not considered to be part of Omani values.

For this scholar, the contradiction between an espousal of heritage values and modernization/Westernization was evidence of a split (*infiṣām*) in thinking. "They [the state] think they are reforming [*yuṣliḥūn*], but they are in fact corrupting [*yufsidūn*]. They say that they are preserving habits, traditions, values, but when you see the city, . . . you will find that they reform the lives of foreigners and demolish intimate ties and relations [*yuhadimu 'ushará'*] between locals."

According to a number of Nizwani journalists, merchants, and residents, one consequence of the circulating images of the old city was that it became the basis for a new, communally oriented ethical future through repeated calls for the sanitization, conservation, and restoration of old sections of the city that were generally considered to have been ravaged as an unintended consequence of modernization. Many Nizwa residents had embraced the state's top-down, heritage-filled visions, but in recent years, the lack of state funds for preservation had resulted in local initiatives among local entrepreneurs. Their rationale for "saving" the old quarter was not merely the possibility of a profitable investment; nor was it a matter of salvaging an enclave of tradition. The impulse to transform the ḥārat al-'aqr and the old souqs was largely due to the residents' daily experiences in these spaces.

Transformations in an Old Residential Quarter

In one of my conversations with Nur, a tour guide at the fort whose family had once resided in the ḥārat al-ʿaqr, she asked if I had visited al-Shawādhinah Mosque, one of the oldest mosques of the quarter and once the center of intellectual and social life. I told her it had always been closed when I was in the area. She wasn't surprised and asked if I knew why. After hearing my haphazard guess—that perhaps there were treasures inside—she laughed and said, "It is better that I inform you that the foreign workers have a desire to bathe inside the masjid." When I asked why, she replied, "I told you before that ʾaqr is now prohibited/forbidden [maḥjūr]. Foreigners have overwhelmed it. Indians want to bathe there, and that is why it is locked." She went on to share stories of kidnapping and wine drinking, concluding with an account of how she and her mother had gone to look in on her mother's old family home in the quarter. They thought of knocking but were too afraid.

This was one of many stories making the rounds among Nizwanis about life in the ḥara. A teacher with family ties to the quarter shrugged when I asked about his relationship with the quarter and then lamented, "These workers have become heavy burdens [awqār] for things that are . . . not suitable for Islamic religion and not suitable for our habits and traditions as Omanis. For example, wine or drugs might be considered something very different for them."

Knowing my great interest in this quarter, my landlady periodically warned me not to walk in the area in the evenings on my own. She explained that there were hunud (Indians) about and it was no longer safe. Their presence as bachelors and foreigners—dislodged and isolated from familial ties and relations—in the quarter had, in effect, transformed the spatial boundaries of the quarter and its significance into a space of moral ambiguity. Being within its thick walls and its watchtowers and gates had once been synonymous with safety and security. Today, these neighborhoods, with their moribund physical boundaries and now-fluid borders, are increasingly encased within a set of generalizing stereotypes that equates daily life there with immoral conduct, the antithesis of sharīʿa governance and the "Omani way of life." In the words of another interlocutor, "It is an area full of the presence of foreigners, the spread of alcohol, drugs, and fornication [zināʾ]." Venturing into the area was now an act fraught with moral jeopardy, not to mention possible physical danger.

Everyday tensions and annoyances culminate in castigating the foreign unmarried worker as the polluter of sacrosanct spaces. In the words of one wakil (guardian) of one of the quarter's old mosques, "Foreigners bathe here [in the mosque], and at times they are not Muslims. They enter here and then bathe and sleep inside the mosque. If they were Muslims, it would be fine. . . . They take over this and other mosques with alcohol and make it their place. They become intoxicated [*yasakaran*]. At times they lose consciousness and, without thinking, become drunk and urinate in the mosque." Other stories revolved around the presence of foreign workers in local households. One Nizwani bureaucrat told me, "The Omani man inside the house does not care that there is a Bengali with his wife and daughters. So they cause problems between family members." He concluded with a sigh: "At one time, if a man saw even his brother entering without permission, he would have fought with him. Now there is nothing."

Other Nizwanis complained of lapses in general decorum (*adab ʿamma*). Objections ranged from "I saw with my eyes the rubbish heap [*qumāma*] they transferred from one house to the one next door" to "They come out in shorts" to "They drink and smoke and raise the volume of their video recordings." Such assessments were no doubt racist, inasmuch as they were delineating boundaries that sharply differentiated Omanis from the Pakistani, Bangladeshi, and Indian men who lived in groups and made up the majority of the inhabitants of the quarter. However, the general conclusion, in the words of a local Nizwani teacher, was that "all these people are bachelors, and so this kind of behavior emerges from them." There was an understanding that unmarried men—unfettered by acknowledged social ties and lacking vested interests in the area as strangers—were more likely to behave unethically and immorally.

Ibrahim, an elderly gentleman, was one of the last Omani residents who refused to leave the old quarter. His memories of long-departed neighbors, displaced by incoming workers, had led him to buy the traditional mudbrick house next door. He had no plans to use it: "I will leave it as it is, but I will not rent it out to anybody. . . . This house was inhabited by one of the ʿulamāʾ. I don't want to see immigrant workers in this place." Such stereotypical notions fueled the local circulation of images of old Nizwa among locals, while igniting longings for the orderly and ethical ideals of the imamate. But they also lent an impetus to restore an old quarter and sanitize its residences with the only resource at hand—a tourism venture. Houses and old communal structures, such as the sabl, tanur, and aflāj system, could only be saved through investing in them, displacing the foreign workers, and transforming these once everyday spaces into hotels, eateries, craft houses, and other capital assets.

In 2016, a Nizwa company, Sharikat al-Bawāraq (Bawaraq Company), took over plans to restore ḥārat al-ʿaqr. Headed by the area's leading businessmen and retailers, the company aimed to invest in a number of lucrative ventures, including transforming the quarter into a tourist enclave. When I met with members of the board of governors, they had already bought four houses near the fort and old souqs and were negotiating the sale and rentals of other properties.

By 2017, the company directors were beginning to clear rubbish, tree debris, and rubble from prime locations and negotiating house prices with owners, who happily apprehended that their houses, once worth no more than 4,000 OR ($10,000), could now garner 20,000 OR ($52,000) due to the demand driven by both the state and, more recently, private companies. Legal frameworks were being discussed on how to remove the workers residing in the quarter, including offering building owners more rent than they could get from the workers. As one tourist retailer and member of the company board told me, "When women come to al-ʿaqr, [the workers'] houses cannot be too near the tourist areas. If a European comes to live here with his family, he would not want to be next door to a group of foreign workers living there without a family." Couched in the language of a profit-driven venture with moral overtones, the company was aiming to refigure the social and moral topography of the old quarter through spatializing new ethnonational boundaries between different groups hierarchically organized in accordance with their citizen status, privileges, and wealth.

A Curious Incident in the Old Quarter

As we passed the communal tanur through the old quarter, Sulayman—one of the Bawaraq Company's investors—pointed out a house that had just been purchased. The house, like so many others, exuded a general air of neglect and deterioration, but the house next door had its front door wide open, and an older Nizwani woman emerged, calling to us. Sulayman knew her well, and we both accepted when she insisted we be her guests. Her elderly husband, who walked with difficultly, was in the receiving chamber by the front door. During our conversation over coffee and dates, our hostess asked about the company's plans and talked of her sorrow at losing her neighbors and witnessing the transformation of ʿaqr into a place for foreigners. After Sulayman explained the company's buying the house next door and their plans to remake the quarter as a tourist destination, he asked her to become the embodiment of Omani hospitality by allowing the planned hotel's guests to come in and share coffee and dates with her family, for a daily fee of five to ten rials ($15–25). She asked whether they would, in turn, help her transform a space below the stairs into another bathroom, which would help her husband. Sulayman promised to get back to her after talking to the other shareholders.

Afterward, Sulayman said, "If it is possible for craftspeople, even girls who do henna designs, to offer a service, we should definitely utilize it." Plans were afoot not only to transform old houses into hotels, cafes, and restaurants for tourists and to reestablish the quarter as an all-Omani enclave, but to have Omanis staffing the establishments, thereby increasing employment opportunities: "Anyone with a hobby or expertise, even retired people who can cook, can take advantage. We won't deny them."

Muhammad, one of the leading directors, spoke enthusiastically of emulating the success of other tourist destinations in the region, such as Bait As-Safah in the town of al-Hamra near Nizwa, a living craft museum where local people repetitively enact tableaus such as baking bread and roasting coffee beans—activities considered metonymic of traditional Oman—in a restored mudbrick house. The hotel would be a series of contiguous mudbrick houses that, in the words of another board member, "will be a residence by way of old heritage as will be the popular common areas [jalsāt ash-shāʿbiya]. These will assume a traditional style, under the date palms with traditional seating on the ground and low tables and traditional Omani food on offer. There will be no television or Wi-Fi. It will be like living in the old days, the way people lived five hundred years ago." The board also talked of transforming the entire space of the quarter into a pedestrian zone, with no cars allowed to enter the narrow lanes. Donkey cart rides would be introduced to give tourists "a sense of how Nizwanis were living in the city fifty years ago."

Nizwani conservators and venture capitalists involved in the project were fleshing out a past whose rationale was grounded in the fulfilment of a Western fantastical utopia. Their plans to transform the houses were, in effect, a materialization of many of the Orientalist tropes that were on hand for representing the historic towns and cities of the Dākhilīya region in popular domestic and international media. Oman was often described as "ancient" and "steeped in heritage and tradition." For Western tourists, its uniqueness among the Gulf countries was evoked with effusive descriptions: Oman was a place where "palms not high-rises, form the skyline" (Sherwood 2005) and "the atmospheric ruins of many forts that dot the landscape"; its old quarters and souqs were "a complex maze of tiny alleyways" whose air was "thick with the mixed fragrances of frankincense and myrrh" (Humble 2015). A sense of timelessness and romanticized voyeurism wove themselves into descriptions of Nizwa through such vivid vignettes as "dunking a date into a glistening pot of sesame paste, chewing its toffee like flesh and washing it down with a shot of cardamom-laced coffee" (Healy 2018) or "walking through tawny mudbrick houses with carved wooden doors . . . amongst the aflāj irrigation system through verdant terraces of pomegranates, figs, almonds, grapes, apples and roses" (Simmons 2011).

For company personnel, and for many Nizwanis, including my landlady, the prospect of a sanitized and orderly heritage quarter dovetailed perfectly with the possibility of evoking the Nizwa of old—the administrative capital of the imamate and a city renowned for its scholarship and jurisprudence. Locals would be able to walk safely once more and visit places that were part of family history. In fulfillment of state heritage values, one board member declared,

> There are Omanis who are less than forty years of age, who have never gone through this experience—they have never lived in a mudbrick house, without electricity. They have always found themselves in cement houses with big rooms, central air-conditioning, and running water. They would come to stay for two or three days and know how people slept, how they used the wells. They will try old foods that people ate two hundred years ago. Self-dependence . . . is a new experience for them, and they need to experience it.

Staying in the old quarter would be a way of immersing younger Omanis in a history that was intimately associated with the imamate, but a history carefully calibrated to the popular vision endorsed by the state and its demarcated private sector and now embodied by the fort. In the process, this romanticized past would exorcise any mention of the sociopolitical and religious impact of colonialism on the governance of the region, which had been the cause of violence, war, and internal divisions for almost two centuries.

For other Nizwanis, however, privatized investment and restoration did not fit neatly into a purely profit-driven motive or the need to foster a national historical ethos through heritage revival. Instead, it brought out a series of disjunctures. Some considered the profit-seeking tourism venture as a heavy-handed mode of top-down intervention that would restructure their social relationships with the quarter. For others, it was an outrageous intervention that would result in an invasion of privacy: "These people would no longer be strangers who would come here for a specific reason, but visitors who would go around and take pictures." Others, I was told, were extremely reluctant to sell their houses: "This is my grandfather's, so I don't want to sell it."

Khalil was another elderly man who had brought up his family in the quarter and refused to move. An Omani friend of mine, a preacher from a local mosque, took me to meet him and his wife. (His sons and daughters had married and moved away.) Khalil had been a student of Imam al-Khalili and later, during the nahda era, had worked as a custodian at the Ministry of Social Affairs. One reason he refused to move was a lack of funds to build outside the quarter. Even if the government offered him a plot of land for a minimal fee, it was always in unsuitable areas. Building alone would cost 60,000–70,000 OR ($150,000–$188,000). It was possible, he contemplated, to get enough money from the company to build elsewhere, but he loved the quarter too much. He refused to talk any further with me, since he assumed I had been sent by the government to spy on him and persuade him to move. The lives of these last few older Omani residents retained strong emotional stakes to an imamate Nizwa, grounded in embodied memories. Like the younger generations, Khalil saw changes to the quarter in terms of displacement, but it was a displacement of decisive finality, inasmuch as the quarter could never be revived in the same way. For Khalil, the planned changes spoke of the lasting implications of the changes to sociopolitical belonging and political governance.

The Old Souqs

Historically, women were not generally allowed in the souqs, because of the large numbers of men who tended to congregate there. Shopping was, and still is, usually done by men. As an alternative, I was told, a number of women (especially widows) set themselves up as merchants, selling clothes, cloth, and jewelry to other women through neighborly visits and social networks. This was a normative state of affairs into the 1980s; today, women can visit the souq as they please, although a general reluctance to visit the main souqs or the open-air Friday market has continued. Many Nizwani women, including my landlady, were reluctant to walk or shop in the area because of many men in the city center—not only foreign laborers but also Omanis from all over the interior, who came to work in government, retail, or as taxi drivers. Muscat, with its anonymity, was often preferred as a shopping destination, especially to avoid gossip.

Nizwa women would typically travel by car to a favorite shop in Nizwa's city center, returning to the vehicle almost immediately afterward, or send one of their children to do so. When I asked my landlady about these shopping practices, she replied that she preferred the supermarkets because they were quieter and, being on the city outskirts, there were fewer men about than in the city center. She explained that most teenage girls felt too embarrassed or awkward (*tastahī*), partly because of the crowds of men milling around. The old city center had increasingly become construed as an area of precarious exposure.

The social and economic changes that transformed other monuments to the imamate past have also rendered the two centuries-old souqs of Nizwa, gharbi (western) and sharqī (eastern), into vestigial entities made superfluous by the new department stores and supermarkets. However, as fabled old markets, they became, simultaneously, the object of restoration and planning for the Ministry of Heritage and Culture's "revival" (*in'āsh wa al-nuhuḍ*) project, as monuments for the selling of "traditional" crafts to tourists. Through the 1990s and into the 2000s, this project was considered a way to save the souqs at a time when the government was increasing emphasizing tourism as a means of reducing dependence on oil revenues.

Both old souqs were incorporated into a large walled and gated complex that was designed and built in 1993. A series of walkways, arches, and small parking lots lead directly to the fort and the old residential quarters within the walled enclave. The idea, according to its architect, Ole B. Larsen of Larsen, A&CE, was undergirded by general principles that were assumed to operate in the layout and organization of the "Arab souq," where each product has its own place. Thus, instead of being a multisectional complex, each part of the "traditional bazaar" becomes a small building in its own right, facilitating sanitation and a greater sense of order and creating a cluster effect around a large open plaza, characterized by intricate wooden balconies and arched doorways (figure 5.4). Each building is dedicated to a particular product—fruits and vegetables (including a section for dates), fish, meat, handicrafts and tourism products (including weighty silver- and copperwork, pottery, and old rifles), and an open area for cattle auctions on Friday mornings. It has won international recognition including first prize for the Architecture of the Souq by the Arab Town Organization (in Doha); in 1995 it was nominated for the Aga Khan Award for Architecture.

The *souq ash-sharqī* stands at the northern end of the new complex, opposite the *souq al-gharbi*, the fort, and the road that leads to the *hārat al-ʿaqr*. It once

FIGURE 5.4. The handicraft section of the new souq complex, Nizwa

Photo by the author

was the primary market in the region for meat, fish, and grains. Flanked by wooden doors, its mudbrick walls and wide arches show cracks and fissures. On either side of a narrow corridor are the seventy-four raised stalls that once characterized the souq. Most are shuttered, in disrepair, and used for storage. I visited at different times of day, morning and evening, when they should have been open, but they remained closed. Only a few stalls at the end were in business, selling nuts, Arab and Indian spices, herbs, teas, Arab coffee, local honey, and other products not easily found in a more Western-oriented supermarket.

The souq al-gharbi stands in the shadow of the fort, opposite the congregational mosque and beyond the residential quarters. Similarly surrounded by thick mudbrick walls, with two large wooden doors on either end, its interior space comprises a series of narrow corridors and high archways, with large stalls on either side. Unlike the souq al-sharqī, however, the souq al-gharbi saw a major renovation (*tarmīm*) and restoration (*iʿādat bināʾ*) in the 1990s (the same time as the building of the new souq complex), although the few local tradespeople who still worked there preferred to think of it as more of a demolition and reconstruction project. When I visited Nizwa in 2006, it was a bustling and crowded market, primarily selling jewelry, weaponry, hair accessories, perfumes, and women's and children's clothing. By 2010, it was virtually deserted, and most stalls were shuttered. A few older stall owners still waited listlessly for customers; most sat on their stall steps and chatted with each other over coffee and dates.

The busiest person in the souq was the sheikh of the district, who kept a cramped office, full of books and files, and was one of the area's public notaries, as well as an official advisor for anyone who cared to drop in. The sheikh took time between clients to explain to me that the reason for the general state of desolation in this souq was that the renovation, in implementing the model of an "authentic" Arab souq, with its narrow alleys and cave-like shops, had reconfigured the stalls. Before, the shops had been roomier, with space to move around. "Now," he told me, "all activity has been cut, and a great deal has been lost."

State development strategies had once more germinated a series of contradictions. The state's self-proclaimed role as custodian of a living national heritage and its values was being undercut by other top-down initiatives, including preservation and tourism. And again, the un-sought-after consequence was the conjuring of memories of the twentieth-century imamate. The sheikh reminisced about a time when the souq al-gharbi had been the heart of all trading activity. Back then, he said, both souqs were simple affairs that sold fish, meat, and seeds. He ended on a sour note: "The increasing number of markets and shops that are open until midnight are what has finished off [*khalas*] this souq and left it lifeless [*mafi nīshāṭ*]."

When I asked about media reports linking the old souqs with the revival of handicraft production, he replied that with the new complex, "they have limited themselves. They've built redundant shops and markets that specialize in every-thing." Another shopkeeper affirmed that tradespeople were unsatisfied with the small spaces following the renovation and, despite government support to set up shops there, they had no place to put their goods; it was impractical, and many stalls have ended up as storage spaces for foreign workers. Those who tried open-ing stalls could not make enough profit from the straggling groups of tourists who managed to find their way to the old souqs. Instead, they rented spaces in the tourist plaza and along the road, within easy reach of parked cars and buses.

There were quite a few angry grumbles among shopkeepers as to the unwill-ingness of the Ministry of Heritage and Culture to transfigure the building's in-terior to make it more amenable to commerce. There were complaints about its quasi-darkness (*shubh maẓlūm*), the difficulty of moving goods into the build-ing, and the new doors, which could not fully open from the outside, so custom-ers were not always aware the souqs even existed. Apparently, the ministry had refused any additions, on the grounds that the souq was listed as a historic build-ing. They told me, with regret, that the souq—once the center and even busier than the souq al-sharqī—had failed because of the renovations and the ministry's control.

One shopkeeper from souq al-sharqī talked with me about the old days when goods would come right in by camel and donkey to be unloaded, spilling out of each stall. The souq was open from *salat al-ẓuhr* (around midday) to *salat al-ʿaṣr* (midafternoon). In those days, most shopkeepers were also farmers or build-ers, working from morning to afternoon at their main occupation before com-ing to the souq. Back then, he mused, the souqs were crowded and many of the goods would be sold within a few hours. Now he was losing customers and money, despite an increased population; the larger shops could undersell him. Most of his customers came specifically for Omani goods, such as red sugar (made from sug-arcane), spices (such as *zaʿatar* and fenugreek and local date syrup. As for the souq al-gharbi, in the words of one local journalist, "Its restoration was one that destroyed it rather than raise it to its former glory." The underlying critique in these accounts among Nizwanis was the sense of marginalization and exclusion that the state's modernization venture had spawned, displacing age-old institu-tions in the old city.

Circulating stories and photographs of life in the crowded market areas, in turn, fueled a narrative of how good life had once been among young and middle-aged Nizwanis. Bawāraq Company was planning to ask the state to hand over the souq al-gharbi to them, so they could revive it as part of plans to create a more robust tourism enclave. Plans ranged from enlarging the shop stalls to opening them directly to the outside. As one director informed me, "If the government plans to revive the old souqs again, it will 100 percent fail. It is better that the people themselves work on the organization and administration of these sites. The government can issue the general guidelines and provide the materials for restoration, as well as counsel. And the local citizens can undertake the process of restoration through specialized companies. If the local is a partner to this process, he is more likely to feel the responsibility and preserve the place properly."

Conclusion

Fragmented memories of the imamate past were continually brought to the fore by Nizwanis who had been born during the nahda era. But these memories, and the mode of nostalgia they gave rise to, were not the direct result of tensions created by the binary of lived memories versus the "official" narrative established by the sultanic state's restoration and heritage projects. The specificity of local relationships with the built remains of the imamate—the fort, old residential quarters, and the souq, now conceived as the old city—were enfolded within a greater context of social and economic transformations Nizwa has experienced since the Sultan Qaboos era. The kind of storied and visual memory that the imamate past had assumed formulated a critique that worked as a response to the daily sensibilities of socioeconomic and ethical dislocations that were part of experiencing the modernity unleashed by the nahda era in Nizwa.

Even as Nizwanis, like other Omanis, were subject to the overwhelming hegemony of heritage discourse and the recurring emphases of its durable values, they also confronted the abandonment of institutions that were an integral part of imamate social life, the rise of an interventionist modern state, its public services and bureaucracy, spectacular changes in urban infrastructure, and mass tourism and consumerism. The generative impact of these contradictions was the formulation of a domain of circulating memories of the imamate and its way of life in the recent past as part of the Nizwani urban experience. The form these memories assumed was not linked to a relationship with God or the need to seek out or embody a past made up of exemplary forbears. Instead, their temporal structure was fundamentally linear, reflecting a past that was deemed lost to the passage of time.

As romanticized imagery, these memories were a biting critique of modernization by way of being poignant commentaries on how good things had once been. But even as these nostalgic tendencies adopted a historical language that no longer corresponded with popular heritage discourse, it assumed political overtones in its link with organized ventures to "rescue" the old residential quarters and souqs in order to return them to their former glory. However, restoration has its limits, inasmuch as the only authoritative terms for refashioning these spaces would be negotiating with the modern state and its standardized sense of propriety as to what constitutes the idealized past and how it may take material form. Preservation and restoration practices of imamate monuments as part of modernization and the social and political specificities of the Nizwani urban experience have generated the conditions in which the material past has come to be conceived.

NIZWA'S LASTING LEGACY OF SLAVERY

> **The human (insān) in the Sultanate of Oman has his hierarchies and levels beginning with the terms, "sheikh," "pure" and "Arab" but not ending with the terms "subordinate" (tabaʿ), "servant/slave (ʾabd), "client" (mawlā), "servant" (khādim) since the establishment of the modern nation state in 1970.**
>
> —Salem Aal Tuwaiya, "An Entry into Racial Discrimination in Oman," 2007

On the upper floor of the National Museum in Muscat, the *Oman and the World* exhibit hall, aims to illuminate the cosmopolitan character of Omanis by displaying Oman's historic ties with the rest of the world since ancient times. Old coins, porcelain, gifts to the sultans, illustrated maps, letters, and travelogues all speak of intercultural interaction and friendships through trade, diplomacy, and political and commercial alliances. By way of example, a series of textual panels portray the strength of the intimacy between Britain and Oman (if not its nature): the first recorded British visit to Hormuz (1580), the first treaty of Friendship, Commerce, and Navigation (1839), and the opening of embassies in each country in the 1900s. Accompanying these milestones are a set of late nineteenth-century British ceramics found in Oman, the illustrated travel writings of naval lieutenant J. R. Wellsted, and an engraving of an Arabian horse bestowed by Sultan Said bin Sultan al-Busaidi (1807–1856) on Queen Victoria. Meanwhile, the determining force of colonial power and the paradoxical relationships between British and Omani groups through the nineteenth and twentieth centuries are occluded; the national heritage narrative (chapter 2) subsumes colonial violence through omitting the forcible encounters and asymmetrical entanglements between the British and the Omanis. We are left with a historic narration that levels historic difference and naturalizes a national community predicated on the principles of civil and political equality. Forging a homogenous entity by evoking the past also becomes a potent means for expelling those elements deemed too controversial for the public domain. These become a series of residues, sorely lacking in explanation.

One such residue, the focus of this chapter, is the legacy of the slave trade. As slavery remains officially unacknowledged, it has become a vanished history. I was told that the official excision of memories of the regional slave trade in the public domain was for fear of exacerbating tribal tensions and long-standing conflicts. Yet memories survive in the reconfigured experiences of modern living among Omanis. Slavery's tangible effects in the Omani interior today may be best understood as the product of contradictions produced by modern state endeavors to idealize a homogenous community through heritage practices, on the one hand, and the enduring significance of ancestral genealogy and hierarchical social standing on the other.

In sum, among Omanis, slavery's ongoing legacy has been conditioned by the clash between two different senses of time and historicity—the first being a supratribal national history solidified by heritage discourse and practice and, the second, a past anchored to ancestral lineage and genealogy. The tribal ethos pivots around an alternative understanding of history based on the notion of *walā'* (clientage) with its language of patrilineal descent (*naṣab*), lineage, and the stigma of slavery. Caught between two paradoxical histories, daily acts such as gossip, scandals, education, and marriage become the basis for negotiating the space between equality and a tribal mode of belonging. Through such practices, slavery continues to determine the finely grained social distinctions that establish the standards of social respectability in the interior, in ways rooted to the historical experience of slavery in Oman. To examine the ongoing legacy of ancestry, lineage, and slavery as an ongoing mode of historicity, I first describe the specific nature of slavery in the region and the social relationships it generated through the idea of clientage even after manumission. I then examine the social and political dimensions of being descended from slaves or being from the *khādim* (servant) class in the era of modern state building and homogenous citizenship. I analyze these aspects through the politics of lineage and naming, marital practices, and the impact of human rights, suggesting an answer as to why the history of slavery, although never officially acknowledged, remains a source of tension and debate in Oman.

Twentieth-Century Slave Sociality

Slavery in Oman was characterized as industrial (date plantation workers and pearl divers) or household (domestics, bodyguards, coffee makers). In the Gulf region, the industrial boom of the nineteenth and early twentieth centuries, ending around 1929, generated a high demand for labor, specifically slave labor, leading to a sharp rise in the number of enslaved people in the region. The Gulf's pearl and date industries were determined by global economic forces and the rise and fall of supply and demand (Hopper 2008). The Arabian date was increasingly shifting from domestic agricultural production to a cash crop for export, especially to India and the United States.[1] Date exports facilitated the import of rice, a daily staple to this day in Omani households.[2]

Despite an antislave treaty between the British and the sultan of Muscat, signed in 1873, intermittent traffic in slaves, predominantly from East Africa, continued despite British naval surveillance of the Indian Ocean waters.[3] Slavery continued in the Arab-Persian Gulf region for those who were born slaves. In the 1920s and 1930s, the traffic in slaves from East Africa ceased, but smuggling continued through the trafficking of young girls, women, babies, and boys from the coastal regions of Baluchistan.

Colonial reports note that domestic slavery in the Arabian Peninsula was not the "conventional *Uncle Tom's Cabin* picture from the Atlantic of keeping the slaves as prisoners or in gangs with overseers" (Express letter from the Political Resident, Bushire to HM Secretary of State for India, June 5, 1939, R/15/2/601). In contrast, enslaved people were often sent unattended to tend date gardens, fish, or dive for pearls,[4] which presented opportunities to reach the nearest manumission authority, either through the British sloops that frequented the coast or the political agent stationed in Muscat (and other Gulf ports); however, few did so (report by the British Political Resident, Bushire, Iran to the India Office, July 20, 1935, R/15/1/228,; report on "Domestic Slavery in the Persian Gulf" from the Honourable Lieutenant-Colonel H. V. Biscoe, Political Resident of the Persian Gulf to the Foreign Secretary to the government of India, New Delhi, March 18, 1930, R/15/1/230,; anonymous note, titled "Minute file xiii/3," July 23, 1948, R/15/1/234).[5] During times of financial stringency, such as a bad pearl market, an enslaved person was also noted as being frequently better off than the free Arab tribesman. His lot in the industrial sector was deemed considerably harder than working in a household, but no more than that of the free tribesman (report from the Residency, Bushire to the India Office, July 20, 1935, R/15/1/228). One reason the British gave for the dearth of applications for manumission among enslaved people in Oman was that, economically, the enslaved domestic was, in most cases, no worse off than the free person (report from the British Residency, Bushire, to the India Office, July 20, 1935).[6] Tied by economic necessity, the slaveholder was bound to feed and clothe his dependent sufficiently and provide him with a wife and a home. The free person, although able to keep his earnings, had to support himself and his household for the rest of the year beyond the pearling season[7] (a report on Domestic Slavery in the Persian Gulf [Honourable Lieutenant-Colonel H. V. Biscoe, Political Resident in the Persian Gulf to the Foreign Secretary of the Government of India, New Delhi], Bushire, March 18, 1930, IOR R/15/1/230).

Also noted was how the household slave was "often attached by ties of senti-ment to the family in which he serves and the possibility of freely mingling with the community" (ibid). In the Omani region, in slaves' roles as coffee makers and domestic servants, British colonial officers alluded to the status of slaves in terms of a relationship beyond that of bonded labor. They observed that servitude was often laced with intimacy and affection, complicating the slave/master power bi-nary as one that could not be reduced to economic exigency. Bertram Sidney Thomas, former finance minister and wazir of the sultan (1925–1932), recounted an incident in which he asked a slave why he did not apply for freedom. The man replied that his master, falling on bad times, could not afford to keep him and had turned him out to earn his own living. If, however, he was out of work, his master always fed him until he got work, and he expressed himself ready to re-turn to work for his master when his financial situation improved. Thomas writes that the majority of enslaved domestics in the Persian Gulf were more concerned about the practical issues by which they could obtain the necessities of life rather than abstract considerations such as freedom (Report by Bertram Thomas, wa-zir of the Muscat state, R/15/2/601).[8]

These reports by colonial officials may well have been prepared to counter the pressure from the League of Nations to end slavery in the 1920s and 1930s (Hop-per 2015). As chapter 1 mentions, British authorities had substantially reduced the slave trade in the Arab-Persian Gulf region but were reluctant to intervene politically in regions where they had vested social and economic interests. Al-though their reports might have exaggerated the degree of comfort afforded to slaves, they do take note of the nature of slave sociality in the pre-nahda era.

For example, enslaved people born into their slaveholders' families were re-garded as part of the household, attached to them through a hierarchical sense of intimacy and dependence. Social ties of belonging in the region were based on notions of extended family, along the lines of tribal networks and relationships, in strong contrast to the modern conception of the nuclear family forged through the conjugal bond. The pre-nahda period was characterized by a network of kin-ship ties, which included dependents, freed and enslaved. Constant voluntary emancipation did take place in Oman in the nineteenth and twentieth centuries (Barth 1983, 46–47; Jwaidah and Cox 1989, 50–54; Sheriff 2005, 115–16). Those emancipated were regularly co-opted into fictive kinship-creating family networks and tribal ties. Whether pearl divers, administrators, or family retainers, freed people and their descendants were adopted into their former slaveholders' tribes and became dependent clients (*mawāli*; sing. *mawlā*), assuming the name and descent line of the Arab tribe—the clan eponym—they had been adopted into and establishing patron-client bonds with their former masters.[9] They accom-modated themselves to lives conditioned by "patronage," forever bound to the family through hereditary bonds of kinship. As one informant explained, "This created a system of tribes that were free and not free. Those not free were clients [mawāli]." With the official abolishment of slavery in 1970, progeny of former slaves retained their tribal affiliations as surnames and were registered accordingly with the modern state bureaucracy.

However, these tribal names were embedded within a larger social world of complex status differentiation in accordance with legal status and its accompanying rights, honor, lineage, wealth, and occupation. As many of my informants in Nizwa and Muscat observed, a series of broader categories generated a hierarchy of aṣal (pure), the free tribal Arab, as opposed to the servant class (khādim; pl. *khuddām*) which included those mawāli who had been enslaved or descended from enslaved people and were relegated to the lower rungs, vis-à-vis other branches of the tribe. These oppositions emerged around the ability to trace patrilineal ancestry and conceptualizations of blood ties. Noble and leadership qualities were not acknowledged exclusively on the basis of demonstration but were also considered to manifest through tribal descent. The *sharaf* (nobility) of a tribe was judged according to the accumulated deeds of their ancestors.

Personal faults or defects of a tribal member could be attributed to the "taint" of slavery in ancestral pedigree, and the excellence of a line could be affected by marriage. Purity of one's descent was dictated by the tracing of the paternal tribal genealogy (and, to a lesser extent, the maternal line), which determined marriage choices, potential attributes, qualities, behavior, and resultant expectations in life. This partly accounted for more than half the current marriages in Nizwa, as I was informed, being between first cousins; underlying assumptions about descent encouraged agnatic endogamy of marriage with the father's brother's daughter. As one elderly sheikh informed me, "Those who could not trace their lineage back to the beginnings were not [free] Arabs." Thus, the relative supremacy of a tribe was assessed with reference to a patrilineal genealogy going back to the first Arab migrations of the Adnani and Qahtani tribal confederations to the Oman region in the pre-Islamic era.

The idea that "blood would tell" was strong in the much-discussed allusions that descent from enslaved people could be ascertained without specific knowledge of their lineage but by recognizing African somatic features. Although one could therefore call the category of khādim a racial category, it assumes a more complicated turn when one notes that there were those who were known to be khuddām and therefore slaves in origin who had come not from the African coast but from Persia, Baluchistan, or even the Ottoman lands. These are, therefore, not hard racial categories dividing Arabs from non-Arabs on the basis of ethnicity and color but flexible indications of wealth, stature, and power.

Simultaneously, the category of khādim was not solely one of social status or race but also mapped a whole series of social attributes and moral qualities onto an Omani based on the line of descent. In indexing ancestral origins and connections with the past, the category of khādim carried with it the constraints and possibilities that these genealogical histories enabled. Whose lineage one chose to join determined the prospects of one's descendants, as marriage entailed not only ties with one's spouse but with the person's tribal ancestors. In Nizwa, stories circulated about prominent tribes, including the Al Bu Said tribe (the tribe of the sultan), whose sheikhs were known to have refused all marriage offers from tribal outsiders, fearing that any progeny would inherit attributes not associated with the tribe. In consequence, their daughters languished unmarried into middle age, single women in a society that frowned on such a status. Marriage, in other words, was valuated in accordance with how "Arab" one's spouse was, a designation that moved beyond the confines of patrilineal descent and bloodlines to include a moral and ethical way of being.

Social mobility was an integral part of Ibadi sharīʿa sociality in Oman. Mawāli and khuddām did, in fact, acquire wealth, honor, or scholarship by becoming administrators, governors, judges, and scholars. Simultaneously, the polarity between the aṣali and khādim had broader connotations in the occupations generally pursued by enslaved people, former slaves, and their progeny before the nahda. Certain occupations—auctioneers/brokers, metalsmiths, butchers, shepherds, or cuppers (bloodletting)—were considered debased and synonymous with the mawāli.

S. B. Miles (1901, 471) and Bertrand Thomas (1931, 117–18) both note their ubiquity in the sabla, where khuddām often prepared and served the coffee and were an integral part of that community. One elderly teacher painted a picture for me, noting that before the 1970s, "when one entered the majlis, the chief [sayyid] would sit at the place of honor [ṣadr] and then the khādim or the mawlā would sit at the end [the bottom of the hierarchical seating arrangement in the sabla]."[10] A number of my interlocutors emphasized that even forty years ago, one could find land deeds and passports naming someone as fūlan mawlā fūlan (client of so-and-so tribe/clan), which designated their lower place in the community.

What It Means to Be Khādim in Today's Oman

One day, as I talked with the custodians of Nizwa Fort, an older gentleman joined us—a former guard at the fort and uncle to one of the custodians. His nephew, knowing my great interest in pre-nahda daily life, had invited him to sit with us. He had an old property deed of sale and offered to make me a photocopy. On looking over the copy, however, he noticed the word mawlā linked to the buyer and hurriedly asked his nephew to erase the name before handing it over to me.

A bottle of White-Out was produced, and when I, half amused and half curious, asked him why, he replied that he was making the erasure out of respect for the sultan and his efforts to promote equality after slavery.

In 2011, erasing the term *mawlā* from a copy of a forty-year-old deed of sale was a resonance of the nahda-era transformations that had altered politics, law, and education in Oman and challenged the old epistemologies of history by introducing new ethical modes of engaging the past. Nation-state building and citizenship created the foundations of equality and engendered free state education, health care, subsidized housing, and government jobs. As an Omani friend noted, "Many of those who were former slaves or descendants of slaves have changed their rank in society. They are engineers and teachers. At times, they are more learned and educated than pure Arabs." Another observed, "I may say that I am Arab and therefore better than this mawlā. But now he may be the boss and in a higher position; I must obey him."

However, modern state logic in Oman also testifies to how such "traditional" ways of life as the tribe have not been eradicated so much as become objects of centralized state management. When mentioning marriage practices, most people in Nizwa would caution that laws or sultanic decrees since 1970 proclaimed three things: (1) all Omanis are equal and should be treated accordingly; (2) slavery has been officially abolished; and (3) the word *khādim* was not to be used in public; nor was anyone's origin to be mentioned, on penalty of imprisonment or fines.[11] No official mention could use the term *mawlā* or *walā'*, which typically accompanied a person's written name pre-1970. If someone had been *al Saifi bal walā'* or *al-Sulaimani bal walā'* as clients of a tribe, after 1970 that person's surname was officially registered as that of the tribe only (i.e., al-Saifi or al-Sulaimani). The ideal implication was that since the name no longer alluded to ancestry or lineage, the result would be a sameness in social interaction, education, and job prospects.

Simultaneously, the modern state actively intervenes in tribal politics to render it more consonant with a secular-liberal form of governance, with its accompanying goals of social and political development. Tribal sheikhs and their lower ranks—often hereditary positions, endorsed by the Ministry of the Interior— become an integral aspect of the bureaucratic state by reporting to the local wali and assuming an intermediary role between community members and the government. The modern state grants local sheikhs yearly salaries, as well as such gifts as cars and houses. They are legal notaries, representatives of their districts, and official mediators for any problems that arise or are referred to the local police or government offices.

Their status as paid officials of the state facilitates a network of relationships that embodies the historical ties between each tribe and the pre-1970 sultanate, even as they are domesticated by it. Distinctions between tribes and their ancestral lineages thus become an object of political concern to the modern state.[12] Key government agencies—the Ministry of the Interior, the Ministry of Justice, the Omani Internal Security Service, the Majlis ash-Shura (National Consultative Council), the Royal Diwan, and the Ministry of Endowment and Religious Affairs—have a reputation for being under the purview of "free" (ahrār) tribal Arabs. The tribe has not been marginalized so much as reconfigured to become the organizing basis of modern state governance; its engagements with the past continue to inform the present. As one human rights activist informed me, "The political system still believes the tribe is a power and it is a referential source. So the sons of the tribes and the sheikhs facilitate distinctions on the basis of residence, employment positions, marriage partners, ways of living, and income." The consequence of this paradoxical situation was rather ambiguous. On the one hand, those categorized as being of mawāli background lived their lives as normal citizens, with good-paying jobs in government bureaucracy, mass media, and the private sector. However, one interlocutor observed, "You feel the discrimination socially [in daily life]."

During a lunchtime conversation in the first week of my fieldwork in Nizwa, my landlord mentioned people's ongoing interest in tribal aṣl (lineage/descent) as an open secret (sirrīya lākin maʿrūfa) in the community—knowing which families were mawāli in origin. This way of thinking, he told me, was widespread before the nahda but was no longer as visible, due to the new laws. However, local gossip and talk of reputation, work, and marriage scandals still shaped people's perceptions and relationships. He qualified this idea, noting that that the phenomenon was less prevalent, especially as the mawāli have earned a respectable place as intellectuals in society. He also observed that people engaged with mawāli on every level—as neighbors and friends, transacting business together and visiting each other—except through marriage. When it came to marriage practices, notions of sharaf (honor) and ʾayb (shame) played a pivotal role in refashioning the hierarchical divisions between asal and mawlā.

One night, in celebration of Oman's national day, I visited the handicraft festival at the woman's association (jamʿiya al-marʾa) with my landlady, Ruqayya, and her young daughters. Having visited the group previously for lectures and gatherings, I had gotten to know several of the women quite well. That night, many of them called me over to look at the crafts and weavings in their stalls and to try the local beauty products on sale as part of national heritage. On our way home, Ruqayya told me quietly that I should be careful in my relations with these women; many of them were khuddām, she said, as evident in their features, and might try to take advantage of me. She was emphatic that even if many of them were middle-class or even rich, pursuing their crafts as a hobby, the khuddām were more exploitative than others in the community. They had a reputation (sumʿa) of loving wealth and taking advantage.

At the time, the generalization rather startled me, but I came to realize that the men and women known as khūddām were considered to be at the margins of respectability in Nizwani society. Certain arenas, such as the Friday open market by Nizwa's fortified complex, were stigmatized as frequented by too many men from different regions of the interior, making it a place no respectable woman would frequent. Outside the haven of the domestic domicile, these public spaces were fraught with the unknown—they are areas of potential moral impropriety, where local ethical mores were uncertain. To visit them would be a source of shame ('ayb) and lead to embarrassment (*nastaḥi*)—hence the preference for the more enclosed and closely policed areas of supermarkets.

During a visit to a neighbor's house, I expressed interest in visiting the Friday market and inquired about the women who did attend. I was told that many were likely not to be from Nizwa (facilitating their anonymity) or likely to be khuddām or Bedouin women, who were frequently seen selling or buying things there. When I asked for details, the women elaborated that the khuddām were "ready to get into everything [*yadkhulna fi kul shaiˈ*];" what the Arab tribal women in the neighborhood would see as a source of shame—keeping them in their cars rather than enter such spaces—a khādim woman would see as an opportunity for commerce. As far as the women of the neighborhood were concerned, this type of behavior, whatever its truth, placed them outside the boundaries of respectability.

During my fieldwork, I learned that other characteristics considered as inherently part of being khādim included being prone to a certain unrestraint (*mubāḥa*) in violating (*naqḍ*) the protocols of respectability necessary for being a good Muslim, for example, playing music too loudly after the call to prayer has sounded, when a "respectable" person would have switched it off to shift into a more pious deportment. The men were more likely to wear disdasha in shades of purple, orange, or red—considered more effeminate than white—and the women were often deemed as wearing immodest clothing (*ghair mutaḥashima*) and makeup.

The modernist Omani state performatively defines the boundaries of public and private through forbidding mention of the term *khādim* as a discursive act in the public domain. Heritage pedagogy, among other civic acts, is systematically disseminated in the public realm to cultivate the liberal principles of equality that undergird citizenship. But these practices have effectively generated a more intimate sphere, in which the division between the khuddām and the Arabs are constituted through gossip and talk of reputations—oppositional forces that define the limits of acceptable behavior among men and women in the Nizwani community. Often characterized by a series of ahistorical traits, the khuddām, by virtue of their ancestry, are effectively relegated to the margins of respectability. In lineage lies the testament for noble origins and proper ethical normative behavior.[13]

Although people of slave ancestry seldom, if ever, spoke about their ancestral lineage, even in a town as large as Nizwa, residents usually knew the backgrounds of long-standing families, either by name or by where they lived. Many of my interlocutors warned me never to approach the topic directly with those who were known to be khuddām but only to allude to it in the most oblique manner I could manage. However, since the term *mawlā* had fallen into disuse as an indelible link to one's name, there were few ways of knowing a newer resident's paternal lineage. With growing migration to the larger cities and interactions in schools and places of work, there was increasing talk of how to recognize someone's lineage among Nizwanis, especially in matters of marriage. As one young college administrator noted, "Before 1970, this was not an issue since everyone was well known. Now, with the government implementing equality, there is no way of knowing the family origin in terms of name." Visits to my landlady Ruqayya's family and neighbors were often characterized by discussion of the doubts accompanying marriage, especially in ascertaining family background, especially of a potential husband. How was it possible to ensure a family's origin, especially as physical features were not a surety and the subject could only be pursued through discreet inquiries with the right people?

One rather exasperated informant, a legal consultant, gave me an overall picture of the importance of lineage in contemporary Oman:

> Whether you are at work or seeking a wife, people will try and compartmentalize you in terms of tribe. In the workplace, they will try and elicit information as to whether you are of sheikhly status, ordinary, or below ordinary. And they will deal with you accordingly. They will be very careful how they would joke about slaves and *bayāsir* in front of you. If you do come from a family of very good standing, they would take extra steps to be kind and courteous. If you are seeking their daughter's hand in marriage, they would be even worse making inquiries into your genealogy, wealth, relatives, and in-laws.

Although worth was definitely something an individual could demonstrate in Oman, it was often constitutively premised on tribalism. It was on this basis that a reputation developed within a social milieu.

Certain accounts I heard during neighborhood and family visits in Nizwa were possible only during the nahda. In forty years, through continuous engagement toward embodying its narration of equality, via free education and other rights, the state had produced a citizenry generating a new mode of ethical being that embodied the temporal framework of "development." In this framework, respectability as a citizen was conceived as moving upward through the national grammar of labor, knowledge, and conduct. With new resources available from the nation-state, those of mawāli ancestry were transforming the meaning of status and reputation, often through contestatory understandings of the past. One such case I heard about involved the weekly auction of water time for irrigating the local gardens from the aflāj. This was usually transacted by a *dallāl* (auctioneer/broker), who was invariably of khādim origin. These occupational practices had once drawn social distinctions between tribal Arabs and those who were mawāli. On the occasion in question, no auctioneer was available, yet somebody had to mediate the sales. Those of slave ancestry were of the younger generation, most were well educated, and with government positions; when asked, they angrily refused to broker the auction, rejecting its historical implications of hierarchical domination. The situation escalated into a major quarrel between the tribal Arabs and those of khādim origin until the local sheikh was brought in.

Many craftsmen I came to know in Nizwa, especially metalsmiths (another occupation associated with the mawāli), had sons who had decided to seek government positions, with their more secure status and better salary, leaving their fathers' crafts (with their negative implications) behind. I came to know the Said family through a series of unforeseen but fortunate events. I had gotten hold of a set of endowment documents from an old mosque. Having difficulty reading the scrawling handwriting, I inquired at the library of the great mosque, and one of the librarians put me in touch with Said's wife's family. This inquiry marked the beginning of a succession of visits with a warm and vibrant family whose hospitality put me very much at ease. The two eldest daughters were at university, studying computer science and English-language translation—skills in high demand in the job market. Their father often joined our conversations or walks in the small date grove and farm adjoining the house to talk about the impact of the nahda on his life and the possibilities it had created. An administrator at the army post in Nizwa, he had not received a promotion in almost twenty years. Like other Omanis, he supplemented his income with other work—buying and selling fruits, vegetables, and animal products from his small farm to keep his children in comfortable circumstances. As far as he was concerned, life before the nahda had been limited; education of any sort had been the privilege of a scholarly and tribal elite. Since 1970, new opportunities, especially in education, were intimately connected to the benevolent personhood of the sultan, who had ushered in a new era and ended inequities of access. Growing up in 1960s Nizwa, he could get only as far as the third grade before leaving school to work, before he was twelve. He was determined that his sons and daughters would take full advantage of the new opportunities.

Of course, other Omani fathers echoed this belief in the central importance of education. What struck me about the head of this household was that although his family was much worse off than his neighbors—evident in the simplicity of their dwelling and its poor furnishings—he was putting his daughters through private university in Nizwa, even going over the younger ones' lessons each evening. One of his elder daughters was being sent to Scotland for the summer to study English—an overwhelming expense, she told me privately, but he had insisted it was crucial to her future.

At the time, these facts did not really strike me as important. However, when I touched on the story while helping Ruqayya, my landlady, prepare breakfast, she was surprised a father would allow his daughter to go alone to Scotland. It was not until I mentioned their name and where they lived that she informed me that they were a khādim family. An Arab tribal family, she went on, would be much more reluctant to send their daughter away (although it did sometimes happen) and that gossip circulated in the neighborhood as to the consequences of such an undertaking. She then recalled a story about one of the most prominent scholarly tribes in Nizwa. A daughter from that tribe had studied in Egypt for eighteen months, married clandestinely, and become pregnant there. Her husband left her, and she came home to Nizwa crying and desperate. Her family took her back in, and her husband came to Oman, but only to divorce her and leave again. Her former husband had no interest in the child, who was being brought up by his mother's family.

She observed that there was a constant fear that young women would stray, losing their sense of 'adāt wa taqālid (customs and traditions). She told another story, recounted by her son, about a young woman who had gone to London to study. Her father, a religious scholar (mutawwa), had seen her off at the airport. Once on the plane, she removed her hijab and 'abāya and put on a shirt and jeans. To Ruqayya, this was tantamount to the young woman's abandoning the basis of her upbringing—the daily practices that conditioned her to become a proper Muslim and Omani that, ideally, should have enabled her to navigate the unknown (including studying abroad), while remaining within the confines of Islamic ethical norms. It was through the successful embodiment of tradition that one maintained respectability. In Ruqayya's stories, the two young women—both Omani and both tribal Arabs—had failed to fulfill the protocols of respectability when confronting an unpredictable outside and therefore failed to embody the necessary social virtues. This was either due to their youth or to "improper upbringing," as she phrased it.

Such stories animated the gossip channels of the neighborhood and continually defined the norms of respectability and moral status integral to social belonging. In considering my friend's trip to Scotland, Ruqayya's storied accounts pivoted on the socially charged ambiguities brought about by educational opportunities, enabled by the modern state but also involving forms of exposure beset with moral hazards and possible physical danger. Those who availed themselves of these opportunities were more likely to be from the lower rungs of Nizwani societies rather than "pure" Arab families. Families deemed khuddām were ostensibly welcomed everywhere, but their stature, reputation, and respect could only come about through walking the tightrope of the moral social order. Even that avenue had its limitations, as the following example shows.

Ashwaq's family were long-standing acquaintances and neighbors of my land-lady. Ashwaq, the mother, was an informative person to talk with, as her life had been a full and rich one. She had married in the late 1970s at age sixteen, like most Nizwani girls of the time, but took an unusual step, deciding to continue with her studies. Most young women of her age were raising children and setting up households. She endeavored to do this as well, while continuing to educate herself at home and sitting for the exams at an official center. She emphasized how much her family had encouraged her in these endeavors, through to university, which she had completed through correspondence classes with the University of Beirut. Later, Ashwaq began to work, taking important administrative posts in Nizwa. This was an unusual number of roles to balance in Nizwa, even thirty years later, when I heard her story.

Toward the end of my stay, I went to pay a long farewell visit. I learned that Ashwaq was a candidate for the Majlis ash-Shura seat representing Nizwa Dis-trict. She had just returned from a training session for women candidates, guid-ing them through the crucial exercises of how to deliver speeches and give media addresses. She was adamant that I ask Ruqayya to vote for her as part of the cause for women's rights in Oman and for better future prospects for her own daughters. When I conveyed the message, Ruqayya smiled and replied that, in the end, Ash-waq was a khādima and would never be able to build the necessary ties with local tribes that she would need to win the election. The successful candidate would be someone who already had a reputation for mediation between tribes and could facilitate access to the resources of Muscat and Nizwa. She informed me that Ash-waq had stood for elections the term before and received only a handful of votes. The obvious intimation was that only a tribal Arab of aṣal lineage could com-mand that type of respect; previous members of the Majlis ash-Shura had been scions of the old tribal mercantile and scholarly elite. It was assumed that a modern-day election campaign would merely reenact the old tribal hierarchy, along the lines of patrilineal descent and genealogical history.

Indeed, Ashwaq did not win.

What's in a Name?

If the Omani state has introduced the notions of labor, resourcefulness, and civic values as the generative basis for the future among its populace, the persistence of alternative styles of reasoning the past, such as the continued importance of genealogical histories in social and political life, is increasingly conceived as an anomaly. Omani human rights activists have demanded the elimination of certain 'adāt wa taqālid (customs and traditions) to bring the state closer to fulfilling its national historical framework, which is enshrined in civil and political equality. Tribal hierarchies, for example, are deemed unnecessary; there have been frequent calls to loosen their foothold in organizing peoples' lives. The debates accompanying these movements played out primarily online, as an alternative to the strictly regulated official media.[14] Such outlets provided a medium for forging an alternative language that cut through institutional logics to formulate its own mode of historical consciousness. In 2010 and 2011, during my fieldwork, a growing number of Omani activists, corresponding in digital space, argued that local social realities needed the idealized national imaginary in order to conform to the "spirit" of universal human rights and leave behind the legacy of slavery.

Instituting taboos on discrimination and insulting language based on tribal origin and social status was one means for the state to level differences as it sought to forge an ethos of sameness as a cornerstone of Omani national modernity. Its aim was to cultivate a didactic model of citizenship, abolishing differential ancestry through nullifying the use of the term mawlā and its social implications. However, to a number of those descended from mawāli, this practice also effectively erased their blood ancestry by linking their lineage with the patron Arab tribe, displacing their sense of an autonomous past and inheritance. Assimilated into a lifeworld that still articulated itself through bloodlines and tribal kinship, a number of my informants felt they had been denied any sense of lineage, robbed of kinship with their true ancestors, whose status as servants, dependents, or clients had made them a tabula rasa to be reworked into the history of the "larger" tribe. As descendants of enslaved people, they were fundamentally tied to the historical patron-client relations that had displaced their genealogy and continued to feel that shame through the social networks of neighborhoods and gossip circuits, marriage practices, and, most importantly, their surnames.

Some Omanis have changed their names and moved to the big cities and towns, where they are more anonymous. In Nizwa, some of khādim origin have changed their lineage (naṣab) to a known ancestor who was a mawlā. In time, this has become a family name, even as their tribe remains officially registered as that of the patron's (slaveholder's) tribe. Many of these families, I was told, have tried to efface the histories of the patron-client relationship by assuming such family names since the 1970s. This was deemed a part of the process of severing connections and a necessary means toward refashioning social ties and connections through the prism of equality and anonymity that the nation-state now embodied.

During my 2010–2011 fieldwork in Oman, the tense process of severing connections to historical tribal relationships had come to the fore, especially in online forums, which were buzzing with debates about a major case involving the Aal-Tuwaiya clan (comprising more than two hundred members) and their attempts to dissolve historical ties with the al-Harthi, one of the most powerful tribal confederations in Oman, by officially changing their naṣab.[15] A passionate essay by the primary defendant, Salem Aal-Tuwaiya (2007), notes that in 2006, the Ministry of the Interior set up a "Council to Rectify Tribal Designations, Titles and Names" as a measure to standardize citizens' identities according to genealogical criteria. Their proceedings resulted in a decision to cancel the names of two unofficial "tribes" from all official documentation (including passports and ID cards) on the basis of rectifying (*taṣḥih*) them. One was the Aal Tuwaiya. The reason (ibid., s4) was primarily due to a lack of historical evidence to sanction the official use of the surname (*laqab*) Aal (household of) Tuwaiya.[16] The council concluded that this eponym was not an established tribal name but that of a man; it was not known by the wali in the district of the family's origin (in the governorates of Al Qabil and Ibra, in the Sharqiyah region); and the clan were the mawāli of the al-Harthi tribal confederation. They recommended that the name be officially changed to Awlād Tuwaiya (sons of Tuwaiya), without the *Aal*, a designation assumed only by a few of the most powerful noble families in Oman including the royal family, the Aal Said. The second alternative was to change the clan's family name altogether to that of their former patron tribe, the al-Harthi.[17]

The main proponents of the case, brothers named Salem and Abdullah, who had been educated in the West and the Arab world, considered this an example of the tribal discrimination and racism that characterized everyday life in Oman. As Abdullah Aal Tuwaiya informed me during an interview, "You still get a sense of being a slave . . . the genealogy, the feeling. Everything is there." For them, this ministerial decision—its language and rationale—had rearticulated a society polarized by the designations of aṣal versus mawlā and entrenched a hierarchy with untenable sociopolitical consequences within a national community that officially professed equality for all citizens. As Salem Aal Tuwaiya notes in his blog posts (2007, 5), the ministry's recommendation was underwritten by assumptions about "lineage" and "origin," the results of which would have an impact on every piece of civil and legal documentation the family held, from bank statements to passports. For Salem Aal Tuwaiya, the *qabīla* tribe was defined, according to the *Lisān al-ʿarab* dictionary, as a specific kin-based grouping that claims descent from a single ancestor. From his perspective, this definition affirmed his argument that every human is fundamentally associated to his forefathers, not to a lineage that is not his by direct descent. On this basis, he argued, his clan had a right to designate their own naṣab. It was on this notion of a "natural right [*al-ḥaq al-ṭabīʿī*] to choose" and the right to "freedom of expression" (ibid., 5–6) that human rights groups took up the case.

In 2008 and 2009, the case began circulating among human rights organizations, including Amnesty International and the United Nations Human Rights Council, and was broadcast by al-Hurra satellite news channel. By 2011, an international lawyer was working toward a resolution with the Omani government, on the basis that "the right of any person to use the name of their family is a fundamental human right which is an integral element to the right of expression."[18] To the Aal Tuwaiya brothers, tribal ties and hierarchical relations seemed a backward legacy for an official history that was being calibrated on the basis of national citizenship and homogeneity anchored to the act of labor. And yet, in Salem Aal Tuwaiya's (2007, 6) words, the state was "clinging on to a past that was corrupt and racist, regarding it with distinction and pride through the very act of holding the Council to Rectify Tribal Designations, Titles and Names."

Enfolded within the claim to determine a family name based on the human rights principles of freedom of expression and freedom of choice was the assumption that naming one's own lineage was a repudiation of historical ties and past sociopolitical relationships. From this perspective, ancestry and its representation become matters of arbitrary choice, in which the act of assuming a family name is removed from any specifically grounded historical concerns. Naming becomes an act of individual human autonomy, independent of social and political institutions—a matter of choice. As such, the process is depoliticized. In my email correspondence and interviews with Abdullah Aal Tuwaiya, he emphatically stated that their desire to pursue the case was premised on "living the way we want and doing things according to our beliefs." Establishing equality, for the Aal Tuwaiya family, was a process of doing away with hierarchically arranged historical relationships and the power relations that structured them. He went on to explain, "Our insistence on keeping the *Aal* was because it is our name. And it is printed in all our official documents, and nobody has anything to do with it." For Abdullah, determining one's own naṣab meant no longer being placed within a historically determined sociopolitical niche and being "acknowledged as a people who have their own identity where we can recognize ourselves and our family on our own terms."

The Omani state and the Aal Tuwaiya family were both fully aware that the role of the citizen was also grounded in a very different understanding that an Omani's naṣab is fundamentally political, inasmuch as it is a tangible index to genealogical and historical relationships. The Ministry of the Interior did not have a problem with the family's changing their name but insisted on their doing so in ways that conformed to the state's understanding of tribal histories and past lineage networks. For Abdullah, this implied a tacit acknowledgment of their family's being continually relegated to a hierarchy, determined by former relationships of domination and subservience. For Salem, the act of naming went beyond the logic of a surname. Stating one's naṣab in modern Oman is a practice with wider consequences; it develops a sense of personhood that is irrevocably tied to the history and sociopolitical status of one's ancestors. Even as the Aal Tuwaiya brothers claimed the right to choose their surname on the basis of human rights, they did so to reclaim their family's history in ways that removed it from its status of subservience to a powerful tribe.

Although the modern state has materially and discursively cultivated an ethic of equality, an identity based on genealogy and kinship ties continues to delineate a social mode of belonging that structures a hierarchy as part of the Omani citizen's experience. The modern state continues to organize and regulate the tribal structure. And the continued emphasis on the normative claims of aṣal as an intrinsic acknowledgment of ancestry and its relations to the past—as part of the workings of modern statehood—renders the resulting biased connotations deeply problematic. These assumptions spurred Salem's call to fully realize the state's rhetoric of equality through pursuing his case in national and international juridical settings. However, the zealous pursuit of a resolution through the bureaucratic channels of the Ministry of the Interior was not conceived by the Aal Tuwaiya brothers to do away with tribal hierarchy altogether, as the humanism of human rights discourse suggests. As Abdullah explained, "The idea of replacing our name with the al-Harthi threatens our very existence, our freedom." Their bid to claiming the *Aal* as part of the family name was conditioned by the permeating sense of tribal hierarchical differences, even as this state of affairs generated the need to consciously emancipate themselves from the historic servitude embedded in the continual recall of their patron tribe. As Abdullah later informed me, "Our ancestors were able to live with it, but we could not."

The Aal Tuwaiya controversy and the debates it generated also produced the realization that the act of tribal naming in Oman is a constitutive force that necessarily entails sociopolitical relationship ties to the past. The legal act of naming categorically grounds the legacies of historical experiences in ways that saturate everyday life, conditioned as it is by the complex realities of lineage, origin, and history. Marriage practices, specifically the selection of a spouse, are another such example, as will be explained below.

Marriage as a Fractured Tradition of Interpretive Practices

Ashwaq, my neighbor and friend in Nizwa, invited me to have lunch with her son and daughter-in-law, who were coming from Muscat on one of their regular visits. Her daughter-in-law was a legal research consultant and fiery human rights activist who had taken part in Oman's Arab Spring sit-ins in Muscat the previous month. As we conversed after the meal, she mentioned a divorce case she was working on, one that had found its way to the High Court. A woman, married to a man whom she had liked, had requested a divorce after two years of marriage, upon discovering her husband had deceived her about his family background; she had learned he was of māwlā descent. The judge ruled in her favor, citing the lack of kafā'at az-zawāj (compatibility or equivalence in marriage) by way of lineage as grounds for divorce.

This was not the first time I had heard of the widespread phenomenon of marriage practices determined by criteria of lineal descent, but it was the first time I realized it had been institutionalized through the notion of kafā'a as part of sharī'a in the Sultanate of Oman.[19] Greatly shaped by Egypt's historical trajectory, nahda Oman's sharī'a has been reconfigured by the division of public and private, state and domestic, as part of modern governance, following the rubric of a now near-universal formula for secularization (Asad 2003; Mahmood 2012). Sharī'a is relegated to family or personal status law (versus the civil or criminal domains) and presides over the now privatized affairs of family, marriage, and gender. Within this normative categorization of sharī'a is the notion of 'urf (custom), which conjoins with family law to juridically delineate an autonomous space where the customs and traditions of the Omani community are recognized as overlapping with religion to create a single legal domain. The textually based criteria for marriage selection have been a frequent object of debate and critique among different Ibadi jurists and scholars over the centuries, including the twentieth-century Ibadi Imamate, and included extensive discussions on the conditions of kafā'a.[20] These ongoing debates were then codified in 1997 in an abstract and principled recognition that marriage is socially constitutive (in contrast to the domain of individualism, choice, and self-will). Article 20 of the Omani Personal Status Law recognizes the notion of kafā'a as part of the conditions for marriage.

Criteria such as "religion, profession, lineage that are absent from either party (of the marriage) and which would result in the lowering of a family's social status or daily living making them ashamed or embarrassed" (Al-Azri 2013, 57) would be grounds for annulment or divorce.[21] It was these assumptions that embittered Ashwaq's daughter-in-law as she spoke of her disappointment at the verdict. As a human rights activist and researcher, she took the notion of civil and political equality, enshrined in Oman's Basic Law (White Book, article 17), as a cornerstone of nationhood. From her perspective, the idea of the law's recognizing the validity of traditional and religious criteria, predicated on hierarchical differences rather than the language of equality, fundamentally contradicted Oman's commitment to equality and the nullification of discrimination.

Nonetheless, such a scenario seemed bound to repeat itself. I was told by many in Nizwa and Muscat—district sheikhs, scholars and teachers, craftspeople, shopkeepers, government officials, neighbors and relatives of the family I was living with—that the nahda had brought about new forms of interaction between those descended from mawāli and those of "pure" tribal Arab lineage, especially through work, school, and new forms of interaction generated by migration to cities and new residential suburbs. However, this has only exacerbated fears of marital "mismatch." In response, fathers ascertain a potential spouse's tribal origin, wealth, and occupation to establish the foundations of social respectability. "When it comes to marriage," one Nizwani friend informed me, "families will dig your root to the tenth grandfather to make sure." In short, the doctrine of kafā'a recognizes the intrinsic social base of a marriage as entailing not only the union of two individuals but also the forging of important ties between families and tribes.

These days, the story of a boy of slave descent falling in love with a girl of a "pure" tribal lineage is the stuff of tragic love stories. A journalist from Nizwa told me of a friend who had visited a young woman's home seven times, trying to convince her father to let them marry. Her father was emphatic, however; there were many reasons this was impossible, one being naṣab. The journalist told me that when his friend came to him, asking him why the father would not allow the marriage, he replied, "Here in Oman, we are Arabs. For us, you are my friend and dear to me and I respect you, but in the matter of lineage and marriage, we have a huge problem. We cannot mix lineages."

The repercussions of a mismatched marriage were severe: the larger family circle would consider it an unacceptable dishonor ('ār) and cause an uproar by refusing to acknowledge the union. A scholar and advisor at the Ministry of Higher Education in Nizwa explained that "the premise of kafā'a is to ensure that husband and wife are a match to each other [*mutamāthilīn*] in the basics of their lives and in their principles, in order that they may be able to live together." In this paradigm, a woman would not want to live with a man who was beneath her in naṣab, even though his morals were lofty. Even if she did, and her father and guardian accepted the marriage on the basis of the husband's having acquired status through education and wealth, the tribe or wider family would never accept it: "Our people would treat me with hostility and might even cut me off [*yuqāṭi'ūnī*] and no longer consider me as one among them." His wife added, "Mentally [*nafsīyan*], if we even contemplate the future and the children of such a marriage, how would the children be perceived, and how would they see themselves? How could they take pride [*yufakharū*] in themselves, as their lives would continue to be splintered [*mushatitīn*] by an in-between where they would never be accepted, socially, as children not begotten through a certain 'proper' order that would enable them to live life accordingly?" She noted that this was not so much a problem with the self or the family but an issue that concerned society as a whole. I was often told of love marriages—a woman's forsaking her family to marry a man of mawāli origin—whose children could not find spouses among the tribal Arabs after inquiries revealed their father's background.

The issue of marriage in the interior of Oman has nothing to do with the personal autonomy of the potential spouses, as human rights activists would have it. As one Omani explained it, "When a girl here reaches eighteen, she does possess freedom to choose for herself, but social relations here are very strong."[22] Community in Nizwa is a matter of how a finely grained social hierarchy contracts marriage alliances that determine the levels of respectability by which one can live and achieve status. Family sociality and the self merge, cultivated and instilled in the embodied self as part of developing a finely tuned disposition that can formulate such "social" questions as a potential spouse might ask: Will my marriage be a compatible one? Can I respect my husband, knowing what he is in the community? How will our children be treated in the neighborhood and by our families?

The objectives, I was repeatedly told, were not simply to preserve "harmony" (insijām) and stability (istiqrār) between the spouses but to develop the proper social relations to avoid community upheaval (fitna) and ensure commitment to customary practices. But these were customary ways grounded in and justified on the basis of authoritative sharīʿa sources that recognized the hierarchical nature of an asymmetrical sharīʿa community, the enslaved versus free, scholar versus commoner, elder versus youth—even as it endorsed an idealized understanding that all Muslims are equal before God. This contradictory perspective formed the basis for deliberations that Nizwanis and other Omanis were grappling with in the rather fraught issue of kafāʾa.

One evening, as I sat at the back table in the library of the Great Mosque in Nizwa, waiting to keep an appointment with a writer who had recently published on the topic of kafāʾa, I began talking to two middle-aged scholars of Islamic fiqh. Although both had written on topics related to the Ibadi school, like many others I had met, they also had more practical professions: Sulaiman was a schoolteacher, and his companion was an administrator at the University of Nizwa. When I explained my interest in naṣab and its relationship to kafāʾa, Sulaiman—a thin, bearded man with a rather measured way of speaking—quoted a prophetic hadith. When I expressed surprise at its words, he assured me it was sound: "All Muslims are equivalent [akfāʾ] except the mawlā, cupper/barber, grocer, and the weaver."[23] He explained that a marriage between an Arab tribal woman and those from lower occupational levels was not equitable, because it would not result in stability (istiqrār) for the family or, on a larger scale, in the community.

To elucidate the point, his companion recounted the marriage between Zaynab bint Jahsh, a first cousin of the Prophet, and his adopted son Zayd ibn

Haritha, a former slave and a much-beloved mawlā to the Prophet. Originally Arab, Zayd ibn Haritha had been kidnapped as a youth and sold into slavery, finally coming to the Prophet and his wife, Khadijah. Zaynab was against the marriage in the beginning, as she considered herself a member of the Quraysh tribe and a tribal Arab. She was, therefore, in a higher social position than Zayd ibn Haritha. Their two years of marriage were unhappy, and there was conflict between them, until a Quranic verse (22:18) came down that enabled her to divorce Zayd and marry the Prophet, placating her sense of honor. These hadiths and accounts were often repeated to me as legitimating grounds for marriage practices in an exemplary past, even as others emphatically noted alternative narratives, establishing Islam as equalizing all Muslims in the face of piety.

A sharīʿa judge from Nizwa District shared the same story of Zayd ibn Haritha and Zaynab, stressing that, regarding potential spouses, "the notion of equivalence among potential spouses was not compatible [takhaluf] with the egalitarian spirit of the law." He deemed it more important to emphasize that Zayd ibn Haritha, a mawlā of the Prophet, had married a woman from the Prophet's noble family. Further proof of equality in Islam, as espoused by the Prophet, was relayed by ordinary Nizwanis through authoritative stories, such as that of Usama bin Zayd, the son of Zayd, the Prophet's adopted son and a freed slave. Usama was therefore a khādim, who distinguished himself in battle from the time of the Prophet onward, becoming a military leader under Caliph Umar ibn al-Khattab (634–644). A number of activists talked of Bilal, another former slave, one of the earliest converts to Islam, and a companion of the Prophet; one close friend told me how the Prophet—in his assumption that all men were sons of Adam and thereby equal—became extremely angry when a Muslim called Bilal "O son of Black." The Prophet called him "a person of ignorance."

Alternative hadiths substantiated the notion of equality over stratification on the basis of lineage. One often-cited prophetic saying in Nizwa was, "There is no preference of the Arab or the ʿAjami [Persian] except in piety." Here, the emphasis on being Muslim lay in the fulfilment of the rights and duties tied to the act of worshipping God, which equalizes all Muslims even as it assesses them along a different kind of hierarchical plane, one based on belief and piety. Other contentious hadith included "Choose your seed carefully [natūf], for blood will tell [ʿirq dassās]." This one, a librarian's assistant of the congregational mosque in Nizwa informed me, emphasized the notion of choosing one's spouse with care based on any number of socially grounded criteria—moral character, lineage, wealth, occupation, piety—going beyond the stigma of slavery to achieve an "equivalent" marriage. One thoughtful friend from the area paused when I mentioned this hadith and considered that it might have very little to do with lineage but rather the need for caution in contracting oneself to a spouse of dubious origin (manbat as-

sayyi'); the hadith could be referring to an inherited disease or a family of bad character. To him, it resonated with the English adage "What's bred into the bone comes out in the flesh."

The authoritative reasoning deployed in marriage debates between people in Nizwa and elsewhere also emerged in the type of evidence used in controversial divorce cases. In al-Azri's (2010, 2013) analytic work on the resolutions of court verdicts, judges were torn between buttressing the endorsement of Oman's Basic Law that "all citizens are equal before the law" with Quranic verses (49:13)[24] and prophetic accounts against the force of kafa'a as a codified determinant to validating marriage. In the High Court case examined by al-Azri (2010, 132), the judge cited "the opinion of the majority of Muslim scholars" that kafa'a in marriage was defined as "equivalence in religion, lineage, freedom and profession." A number of divorce cases made their way to the High Court via this paradox (see Al Azri 2010; 2013, 48–63).

Increasing attacks on the establishment of kafa'a in family law—specifically, its tacit acknowledgment of stratification based on descent—could be considered a result of ongoing structural tensions in the modern state-building project. The assumption of the continued presence of a differential tribal hierarchy as part of a modern sociopolitical order contends sharply with the principle of equality, which sanctifies a unitary history and citizenship in the nation-state. This is the contradiction both sides of Nizwani society (and beyond) are deliberating through their debates on kafa'a and what constitutes correct Islamic thinking and practice in marriage. The forms these arguments take move beyond gender and generational lines and are structured around evidence derived from the Quran, the prophetic sunna, and accounts of the golden age of the Prophet and his companions. These exchanges coalesce in a common moral goal of establishing a proper ethical way of being yet formulate two different modes of argumentation. Each style of reasoning establishes its bearings through adopting a different interpretive reading of Islamic discursive tradition. The process weaves together fragmented story lines, quotations, and deeds, forging contending understandings of morality as part of cultivating "proper" Islamic practice in the modern world.

Many supporters of homogenous equality in Nizwa and beyond were inclined toward human rights as an intervention into removing what they considered the reaffirmation of a racist hierarchy within a national and legal framework. In their view, such practices go against the principles of equality that define Islam as it should be practiced by a modern Muslim state. This egalitarian ideal becomes the basis for engaging with the Islamic discursive tradition—Quran, prophetic sunna, and the authoritative past—to prove that Islam overlaps with human rights discourse in endorsing egalitarianism, independent of the lengthy debates by jurists and scholars that have produced so much legal literature on the subject of kafa'a.

Instead, the specificities of a centuries-old corpus of juridical exegesis, interpretation, and jurisprudence give way to an all-encompassing general principle, more consonant with a "universal" religious perspective, that centers on a history of universal humanity and the notion of equality (Masuzawa 2005).

This shift marks a changing conception of historicity as Oman's experiences of sociopolitical modernity and the role of the tribe are assessed against a Western progressive teleological yardstick, with its telos definitively marked as political and civil equality. On this scale, Oman's modern experiences are incomplete, necessitating reform and the purging of the tribe and its underlying asymmetrical grammar of lineage and blood ties. The "not yet modern" scenario becomes the lens for recalibrating the Quran and the prophetic past to conform to a future that bears such an aim. Human rights supporters are incorporating this modernization narrative into an ethical way of living through deep engagements with an inherited past, intimately tied to the Prophet and his companions, in order to reform the tribal landscape while retaining sharīʿa as integral to modern Oman's political and legal framework.

The result is noted in Abdul Hamid al-Jāmiʿī s work, *Kafāʾa and God's Plan in the World* (2003), and the Internet controversy it roused.[25] Hamid, a petroleum engineer and son of a High Court judge, published a book many consider one of the first to instigate recent debates on kafāʾa and its consequences in Arab tribal discrimination. It centers on transforming the terrain of kafāʾa through grounding thinking on the "unity that Islam calls for rather than division" (10) and in invoking the International Convention on the Elimination of All Forms of Racial Discrimination, which Oman ratified in 2003. On the basis of fundamental equality, Hamid's book filters Quranic verses and "correct" prophetic sunna to problematize certain Ibadi sources of kafāʾa and their use in legal reasoning during marriage cases. A number of key hadiths that continue to be cited in legal thinking as evidentiary criteria for the importance of tribal lineage in a compatible marriage are theologically analyzed and found weak. In talking with Hamid in person, it was clear that he still considered kafāʾa legitimate in laying out the conditions of "equivalence" in marriage; however, this was to be on the basis of a family's status in morality, education, and culture, not tribal ancestry.

Hamid claimed he was trying to sift what was truly Islamic about kafāʾa from Omani customary ways, which he felt had deeply shaped jurists' and scholars' prevailing opinions about marriage. Their interpretations would have been informed more by historically and culturally specific circumstances and were, therefore, no longer pertinent to changing times. There was an understanding implicit in his thinking—and that of other human rights supporters—that any form of hierarchical discrimination was antithetical to Islam. If it did exist in the centuries-long textual traditions of sharīʿa exegesis and jurisprudence, it was, in the words of one activist, "because some habits and traditions are stronger than religion. And there was a lack of understanding between what religion is and what were originally customary ways [*'urf al-ijtimā'i*] of doing things."

One scholar of Omani history and a strong advocate for equality further qualified, "There is a difference between the sharī'a as represented by the Quran and the interpretations of jurists, which could be right or wrong since they are subservient to the cultures of society. . . . The books of fiqh [jurisprudence] are not the Quran."[26] He was clearly separating what he considered "true" Islam from that adapted by tribal ways of life. "True" Islam, as embodied by the Quran or the unadulterated life of the Prophet, thus became an entity that stood apart from and beyond the reach of historically or culturally informed practices of living Muslims. To my question as to whether he would be willing to have his daughter marry a man descended from slaves, the scholar replied, "I would be afraid for my daughter and not because Islam doesn't allow it. Of course, she can marry him, but I am afraid that after a time, people would reproach and condemn her and look at her with contemptuous eyes."

For human rights supporters, separating Islam from the "customary ways" of a tribal society also facilitated categorizing those who claimed religious authority to advocate marriage based on differential lineage as "backward" (Aal-Tuwaiya 2007, 20). The idea of polluting Islam with human agency and thereby contaminating religion through the concrete context of social relationships becomes a potential act of regression that prevents the nation from moving forward. To human rights supporters, there was a tacit assumption that only a direct interpretation from the original sources of Islam, the Quran or the prophetic sunna, and one untouched by arguments laid out by later legal treatises and encyclopedias could act as the new standard by which the Omani national community would be judged and reformed. Moreover, it would need to be a particular mode of scriptural interpretation, one that did not contradict notions of universal equality or democracy in accordance with international law. Their assertions resonate with a globally pervasive modern discourse about Islam, which operates within a religion-culture binary. This binary becomes the lens through which good and bad Islams are sorted and classified by Muslims and non-Muslims, in accordance with how closely they conform to Western liberal values (Rogozen-Soltar 2017; Shryock 2010).

On the other hand, for many Nizwanis, the notion of equality before God and the ideas entailed in the notion of kafā'a in marriage were not paradoxical; the virtues inherent in carrying out the obligations of being a Muslim, such as piety, were not bound up in social status. As one Nizwani put it, "When we go to prayer, we all mix. . . . I would pray next to an Asian worker, a mawlā, and all men. There is no difference. But there are levels taking place through marriage in a sharī'a

community that are not between you and God but are *dunyawī* [worldly] in trying to make a marriage strong and respectable." For many in Nizwa, the idea of
kafā'a as part of tribal or worldly customary ways was integral to "correct" Islamic practice in daily life. The notion of "equivalence" of a potential spouse, a
partner one could respect, was recognized as the constitutive social basis through
which Muslims cultivated their lives and their capabilities—not only for virtuous conduct but also for ethical living. In short, it was generally held that one's
lineage, and all this entailed by way of upbringing, could determine one's ability
to be a good Muslim. This capability becomes an attribute acquired and honed
by the self, through the surrounding network of authorities, institutions, kin, and
neighbors. Since guiding practices and habits differ with the considerable variation in stature, respectability, learning, and ancestry, including that of the spouse,
the notion of social "compatibility" becomes crucial, opening a gateway for the
concerns of a community trying to live up to the ideals of sharī'a as they understand it.

Conclusion

Twentieth- and twenty-first-century Omani history as a public performative has
resulted in fracturing the moral coherence of the sharī'a community. A modern
bureaucratic apparatus, a state-centered Islam, and a national sense of tradition
emerge as alternative grounds for an ethical existence. There is an ethics and politics involved in the creation of a modern state apparatus enshrined by a regime
of history. In Oman, this national narrative has necessitated the leveling of difference through principles of civil and political equality, while enjoining an erasure of the slave trade, its legacy, and a sharī'a community organized along tribal
hierarchical lines. However, the enterprise of organizing a national past has also
created conditions in which the remnants of slavery—as a social status, a mode
of behavior, and a way of life—continue to act as an effective orientation for an
ethical Islam. Being a proper Muslim modern in the nation-state becomes a space
of contradictory modes of argumentation between Islam's canonical texts, the
classical past, and everyday practices in order to reconcile a nationalist ideology
of homogenous citizenship with an unofficial state-sanctioned system of historically acknowledged tribal relationships.

    The survival of fragmented pieces of the slave past, whether in social interac-
tion, a family name, or the cases of kafā'a in marriage, creates tensions between
tribal supporters and human rights supporters in ways that map onto different
modes of conceptualizing the relationship between religion and culture. Both
sides have normative understandings of religion versus culture that define Islam

as an ahistorical, independent set of principles that stand apart from culture, loosely understood as any form of human agency or set of actions. The ways in which human rights supporters distance themselves from those who sanction a tribally organized way of life demonstrate the enormous power wielded by international human rights law, which becomes the lens through which religion, as embodied by the pure, ahistorical sources of the Quran and prophetic sunna, is sorted from culture. In this context, culture is defined as the juristic acts of interpreting the sources, which are construed as tainted—the result of being conditioned by the history of tribal customary ways over centuries. It is this possibility of separating uncontaminated Islam from the dangerous precedent of custom/ culture that spurs many Omanis toward reforming the national tribal landscape into a world order rooted not only in the ideals of a Western liberal civilization but also in a "pure" Islamic civilization that would rearrange the tribal system. For tribal supporters, religion ceases to be an unadulterated core, outside the realm of history, and the only way the ideals of Islam can be fulfilled is through the pragmatics of daily living. This includes cultivating everyday social interactions, modes of behavior, and an "equivalent" marriage that produces a spouse whose lineage, upbringing, and virtue enable the Omani subject to become a proper Muslim.

THE AL-LAWATI AS A HISTORICAL CATEGORY

I have no doubt that we are Omani. If my great-grandfather's grave is in Oman, how can I claim to be from somewhere else?

—al-Lawati interlocutor, Muscat, 2011

One of the most striking exhibits in the *Hall of Land and People* at the new National Museum is an intricately carved blue balcony (figure 7.1). Curiously, no textual panels announce its presence on the exhibit floor; the visitor can only assume its significance fits the overall theme of the hall, "a visual representation of the nation, its past and present—giving forms to patterns of life determined by local resources" (al-Moosavi 2016, 6). However, long-term residents and visitors to the Muscat area are well aware that the balcony is a landmark of the Matrah district, formerly one of most important commercial centers and ports of pre-nahda Oman.

The town of Matrah runs along the beachfront, two miles west of Muscat, surrounded by craggy volcanic hills. A Portuguese fort sits atop a rocky point on the east end of town. According to John Lorimer's *Gazetteer* (1908), Matrah was once the primary destination for trade caravans from the interior and the main loading zone for a variety of goods—staples like rice, piece goods, sugar, oil, iron, and spices from Bombay, as well as dates, dried fish, and other exports. Today, the seafront is flanked by a corniche walkway, and the town is a tourist destination. In the winter and spring, cruise ships disgorge hundreds of people to explore the Matrah souq, widely advertised as one of Oman's oldest commercial centers and the "traditional" souq par excellence. Its "restored" structures feature painted, wooden-beamed ceilings and wind their way through narrow lanes; its stalls' wares range from sacks of spices, perfume oils, and antiques to household goods and ready-made garments. Near the beachfront entrance to the souq, along a line of shops overlooking the shore, lies a crenelated, low-arched gateway; peeking within, one might see two middle-aged guards lounging in chairs.[1] Above the doorway are the words *Sur al-Lawatiya*. It is in this sur (fortified enclosure) that the Muslim al-Lawati community once resided as a prosperous merchant community. Together with the Hindu Banian merchants, members of this community were Oman's intermediaries in the import and export trade. The guards at the main gate keep the Sur al-Lawati inaccessible to anyone not accompanied by a member of the community.

The National Museum's reconstructed balcony is part of the facade of the sur. In the sur itself, a succession of balconies set against high walls and arched windows forms the frontage of a fortified structure of tightly packed one- and two-story houses along the beachfront. One older community member told me that in the 1960s, the sur contained 218 houses of different sizes, including places of congregational prayer. Together, these structures create an architectural aesthetic unique to the Omani builtscape—their bow-arched windows and semienclosed balconies with intricate latticework, sloping roofs, and slender colonnades reveal more elements of traditional Gujarati residential architecture than those of Muscat, with its single-story buildings and unadorned exteriors.

The result is a stone-and-mudbrick enclosure delineating an exclusive, inward-looking community whose two formal entrances were once locked at night. At the same time, the architecture expresses historical ties with other Indian Ocean

FIGURE 7.1. The sur al-Lawati balcony at the National Museum

Photo by the author

coastlines, creating an aesthetic "equivalence" that links these regions (Simpson and Kresse 2008, 20). Scholarship on the Arab Gulf region often links heritage production with technologies of state pedagogy in its efforts to fix the boundaries of a nation. Indeed, the sur is intimately associated with the al-Lawati, constituting the site of their belonging in Oman and the locale for the ritual performances of a collective Shi'i body linked to the Kutch-Sind region of the Indian subcontinent. Yet such a strategic explanation ignores pressing questions regarding how statist narratives domesticate heterogeneous populations and govern social difference.

This chapter explores how official accounts of the past have interpellated the material traces of diasporic communities, specifically this once-fortified enclave of a non-Arab community, as a token of the nation's pluralist history as an Indian Ocean trading power. This is consistent with Oman's expanding culture industry, which since the 1970s has generated history-making practices toward creating an all-encompassing historical narrative framework that assimilates non-Arabs and non-Ibadis into the cultural norms of Omani nationhood. The act of incorporating the sur and its residents into the history of a national people, rooted in "Omani civilization" and a "desectarian Islam," is an inclusionary tactic whose operation involves gaps, disjunctures, and diversity at the core of a unifying history of a sovereign nation. Simultaneously, the Omani state was also regulating its citizen subjects by institutionally sorting them into tribal kinship categories. Lineage distinctiveness anchored to the tribal genealogical histories of the Arabian Peninsula thus became an integral component of national belonging.

The looming presence of the sur emerges as the site of struggle between two distinctive yet interrelated trajectories of historical consciousness—a sovereign Arab and Muslim identity versus one oriented toward a Hyderabadi Shi'a Muslim community and the (publicly unacknowledged) colonizing power that once enabled its prosperity. These are not merely fissures in a nationalist project; they coalesce in points of tension that influence daily social interactions, assuming an important dimension of peoples' lives. In the process, the builtscape of the sur may be understood as a tangible repository of these histories and the residents' daily movements, rhythms, and practices. These living pasts move beyond the cognitive to exert a force over daily life, shaping al-Lawati experiences of being Omani through shifting institutional arrangements of inclusivity and belonging. In their entanglements with each other, both modes of historical consciousness center on what it means to speak of "home," "origins," and "authenticity." These two modalities of understanding the past implicate the ways that the al-Lawati sense of being different from the rest of the population of Oman informs the ways they have participated in public life during the twentieth century. Although the legacy of British informal governance continues to be felt throughout the region, one of the more intensive struggles emerging from that legacy is how the experience of being al-Lawati affects how they feel recognizably Omani through their own sense of history and tradition.

Inasmuch as the sur has been incorporated into state heritage practices, the historicism of a state pedagogy is contingent on the conditions of its contextual enactment (Tambar 2014, 15). When loyalties are questioned or suspicions cast, an alternative historical trajectory is evoked, orienting the al-Lawati in a historical difference forged on the basis of Indian caste, Shi'i geography, and British subjecthood. The informal governance of Oman by the British Raj is an alternative history—one not acknowledged in the official public domain—that opens possibilities for social tensions in the present day. With such an understanding in mind, and through examining ethnographic encounters and archival material, I explore how the Sur al-Lawati's tangible presence has presided over a more entangled history, in which the communal boundaries of this community of merchants and retailers were reconfigured during the twentieth century. Being al-Lawati is an inherently unstable identity and way of life, made up of memories and histories. These accounts have been formulated over the course of the twentieth century, the British Raj in the early part of the century, and the Sultanate of Oman from the 1970s onward—a series of connotations whose potency has come about through the sociopolitical struggles of a particular moment.

Once flanked by two gates and four towers, the Sur al-Lawati has undergone substantial material changes. Only one tower remains, the focus of a restoration project sponsored by the Ministry of Heritage and Culture. Another was "stolen" (in the words of community members) to enable the construction of a house, a third demolished, and the fourth transformed into a coffee shop, whose interior retains the tower's round dimensions. All the houses in the sur are owned or rented to al-Lawati community members, but few live there on a permanent basis. Hundreds of families once resided in the sur, but since the 1970s, most have moved beyond the walls, settling in Muscat's more modern districts, with modern plumbing and other amenities.[2] Built to provide security from Arab attacks and privacy for the women of the community, the enclosure is now the domain of a few scrawny cats and a group of elderly women who have refused to move elsewhere. Even today, however, houses in the sur are privately owned and may not be sold or rented to anyone outside the community.

Thus, unlike the bustling souq next door, since the 1970s the sur's residences and narrow alleys are increasingly empty. Only during the late afternoons and evenings does it come alive, with women (predominantly) and men moving through the narrow lanes to attend the majālis of the many *ma'ātim* in the enclosure, as well as those in the main mosque. This is especially the case during Ramadan, Muharram, and Safar, the important months of Shi'a devotional life, which are closely linked to the mourning rituals and ceremonies of 'āshura, the tenth day of Muharram, which commemorates the martyrdom of Imam Hussein and his followers in the Battle of Karbala (BCE 680). Indeed, the main gate is overshadowed by a bulbous dome and minaret, decorated in the glazed mosaic-faience tilework characteristic of Persian religious architecture. These architectural elements and decorative patterns are the markers of what many consider the most important Shiʿa mosque in Oman, the Masjid Al-Rasool al-Aʿzam.

The al-Lawati as British Subjects

In Lorimer's *Gazetteer*, the al-Lawati are called the Khojas, a term the British considered an Indian caste identification.[3] Many al-Lawati of Oman still use this descriptor among themselves, forming an integral basis of self-understanding, although it has no bearing on their relations with other Omanis (inasmuch as it is unknown to them). The name, and all it connotes, was shaped by nineteenth-century British governance and colonial policy and has had a decisive impact on their sense of self and historical consciousness. The term's significance today is the result of having been deployed as part of colonial endeavors to make religion the all-important and exclusive category of classification in the governance of the British Raj: the promulgation of religion as the primary category supplanted the more contradictory but fluid strands that made up the al-Lawati understanding of what being a Khoja in Oman signified, a matter that will be further expanded on in the next section. Although the Khojas were dispersed as merchants across the commercial and trading centers of the Indian Ocean, especially in East Africa and the Arab-Persian Gulf regions, their distinctive experiences as migrants and settlers in each locale created communities shaped by local social and political imaginaries that informed how knowledge was socially reproduced.

The British assimilated the Khojas of Oman into a metanarrative of history drawn from the Kutch-Sind regions of western India. Linguistically and culturally, they were considered part of a past that incorporated Sind into the worlds of Islam and the interactive exchange of missionary activities, trade networks, and regional relations, based on knowledge and religion that had migrated from eastern lands. In Lorimer's (1908, 2378) words, the Khojas were "a sect of people whose ancestors were Hindus in origin who were converted to and have throughout abided in the faith of the Shiʿa Imami Ismailis and which have always been and still are bound by ties of spiritual allegiance to the hereditary imams of the Ismailis."

Such a narrative had practical effects. When the British juridically designated the Khojas as part of the Nizari Ismaili sect of Islam, in a landmark case settled by the Bombay High Court in 1866, they went from being a caste (a social group based on ties of endogamy, occupation, language, and religious practices) that practiced a uniquely syncretic set of religious practices based on both Hinduism and Islam to being labeled Ismailis according to state mandate.[4] With this legal decision, which centered on the figure of the Aga Khan and his claims to leadership, the Khojas were fixed within a classificatory scheme, with the Arab world at its center. They thus became implicated within the larger Shi'i discursive Islamic tradition through a historical narrative premised on seminal works by scholars of Oriental studies that traced the Khojas back, in unbroken descent, to the Assassin legends of the Middle Ages (Bartle Frere 1876, 430).

As Teena Purohit (2012, 4–5) emphasizes in her analysis of the case, before this ruling the Khojas did not have a single religious identity but employed multiple forms of self-recognition. The schisms in Bombay as a result of the 1866 decision did not merely culminate in the legal consolidation of religious classifications, such as Ismaili, with their accompanying liturgies and ritual texts. As many of my respondents in Oman told me, the prospect of rallying around the definition of Ismaili Muslim was problematic for the Khojas of the Persian Gulf region, producing a set of historical experiences that have rendered them distinct from the rest of the Khoja community and their adherence to Aga Khan as the Ismaili imam. Although many Khojas in Bombay seceded from allegiance to the imam by becoming Sunnis, those in Matrah retained their Shi'a persuasions, formally becoming Ithnā 'Asharī even as they rejected the possibility of being Nizari Ismailis, followers of the Aga Khan.

The British Raj and its mode of governance, particularly its ability to adjudicate and redefine the nature of religion in its domains—exemplified in the 1866 court ruling—undergirded the British understanding and categorization of the Khoja of Oman. For the British, the al-Lawati were a local trading class that had originated in the villages and towns of Upper Sind. Originally Hindu, they were converted in the fifteenth century by Pir Sadrudin, a dā'i (missionary) of the Ismaili Shi'a sect (Bartle Frere 1876, 431). Court records, gazettes, and journals compiled by former British administrators formed the core of representations of the past that defined the Khoja, including the al-Lawati. Through their role in British informal governance of the Gulf region, they were conceptualized by the British through engagements with historical and contemporary events in India. This included such key issues as to whether the Khojas were British subjects, a question that hinged on whether al-Lawati community members' ancestors had migrated to the region before or after the 1840 British conquest of Sind.[5] Lorimer (1915 vol. 1, 1034) states that of the 250 males among the Khoja caste living in Matrah, 120 were British subjects with the rights to British protection and travel passes.[6] Of forty-one families living in other parts of the sultanate, twenty-nine were under British protection. The rest were subjects of the sultan.

Other events shed light on the relationship between the British and the Khojas. In 1895, Arab tribes, led by the al-Harthi—who would have a pivotal role in the establishment of the imamate in 1913—attacked Muscat and occupied it. Sultan Faisal (1888–1913) and his family fled over the roofs of Indian merchants to reach the British Agency. The sultan took refuge in Fort Jalali, and arrangements were made for the protection of British subjects and their property, including notices of nationality affixed to the doors of their houses and godowns (warehouses). At Matrah, the Khojas withdrew to their enclave, which was supplied with a British flag (Major Sadler's report during the rebellion of 1895, R/15/6/37). These British subjects, according to archival material, were all deemed to be Indian merchants, crucial actors in the British imperial enterprise. They were generally considered to have the necessary connections with firms in other cities, such as Bombay, to facilitate business; as financiers and merchants, they were able to exploit the changing economic relationships brought by European-owned trade-carrying steamships in the 1860s (Landen 1967, 132–33). Although most Khojas were petty traders, artisans, and shopkeepers dealing in piece goods, spices, and the like in the early twentieth century, some did business on a large scale, administering the local commercial enterprises of the Gulf region (Lorimer 1908, 1:1034). For example, Khoja merchants were primarily responsible for the export of dates from the groves and plantations of Wadi Sama'il, Oman, and the al-Sharqiyah on steamships from Muscat (Landen 1967, 143).

For the British, the Indian merchants, embodied by the Hindu Banians and the Muslim Khojas of Matrah, were an extension of their rule over British India. They were perceived as intermediaries between Western businesses and Arab society; as managing agents, they provided expertise and facilitated entry into the local economy and exchange networks. Familiar with local politics and social conditions, the resident Indian merchants and their firms became key interlocutors, gaining a virtual monopoly over Omani foreign trade and Muscati business activities (Lorimer 1908, 2:382–83). By the late 1800s, Indian merchants had superseded the Arabs, becoming the primary importers, exporters, retailers, distributors, bankers, shipowners, and government officials (Landen 1967, 139). Their commercial importance and interests, given the sultan of Muscat's dependence on Indian-administered loans and port customs, meant they were a significant force in regional politics, despite being ostensibly apolitical.[7]

Grounded in a mode of governance based on British protection and sultanic ties, the al-Lawati, or Khoja, community was integral to a system that assured the Muscati state a source of credit and the British a pivotal means toward consolidating their economic and political hold over the region. The lynchpin of this system was the British Indian merchant. As John Wilkinson (1987, 69) notes, with the ability to cut off supplies and exports to the interior and to increase customs tax from the main port and the Batinah coastal region, a modus vivendi was reached without recourse to active armed intervention, fortifications, or armed alliances.

The Khoja were therefore not only incorporated into the administrative apparatus of imperial sovereignty but also defined in terms of their orientation toward the British Raj. The Raj became the pivot point around which a sociopolitical geography was built—one that co-opted the Khoja—into a body of knowledge about India's history, religions, and societies. This knowledge informed the practices of governing populations far beyond India, to encompass the empire (Cohn 1996; Metcalf 2007). As Lorimer (1908, 2:1034) observes, "The only non-Khojah admitted into the enclosure are the British officials at Muscat, whom they regard as their *natural* protectors." The Sur al-Lawati came into being as the nexus of trade networks, imperial administration, and historical imaginings.

Memories of Khoja History and Sociality

Even as the al-Lawati community was co-opted into imperial channels of control and surveillance, its mode of life was shaped by local conditions and regional relations transmitted through daily education, devotional practices, and forms of social interaction. Like the Hadrami diasporic settlements across the Indian Ocean lands (Ho 2006, xxi), the Khojas "comported themselves to local arrangements wherever they went . . . entering into relations that were more intimate, sticky and prolonged than the Europeans could countenance."[8] Today, fragmentary conceptions of the past carve out the ancestral space that defines the lifeways of the sur al-Lawati. There are undeniable ruptures in people's understanding of their past, and the details of these shards of memories varied among the many community members I met during my fieldwork. Gaps between textual references and oral memory, between official pedagogy and popular knowledge, marked the impossibility of attaining a comprehensive picture, even as the remembered fragments carried possibilities of animating an ever-present way of living (Das 2007, 6).

The experiences of migration, local trade, business interactions, and political and social ties coalesce, transgressing the boundaries of the community suggested by the British understanding of the Khoja as one grounded in Indian caste and religion. The Khojas' integration into the Omani region was shaped not only by the structures of the British Empire but also by networks of commerce and movements of religious learning, regional mobility, and interaction.

For instance, I met Habib at one of the four-star hotels along Muscat's beachfront. A tall, spare man in his late sixties, wearing the tasseled disdasha and *kumma* that proclaim the Omani citizen, he was nevertheless a striking contrast to the other sheikhs, scholars, and government bureaucrats I had encountered and talked with in Nizwa. It was not merely his beardlessness, although that was one facet; our interaction was the first time my conversation with an Omani took place entirely in English, the first of many similar experiences with community members. Over tea, Habib, considered by many to be an al-Lawati spokesman and elder, explained the community's distinctive history in Oman: "Before the nahda, the government was poor. The sultans were always in need of money. The only source of income was the little bit of export they did. The Lawati, being rich, helped the government, and that is how they got their power." He also recounted stories of legendary community members, such as Bhacker Abdul Latif, once the sheikh of the community, who consolidated and expanded the Haji Bhacker Company (est. 1895), which initially dealt in firearms and pearls, later becoming a leading exporter of fish to Germany and Holland. Today, the Bhacker Haji Abdul Latif Fazul is one of several formidable al-Lawati merchant dynasties exercising a quasi-monopoly over the maritime freight sector in Matrah.[9]

Bhacker Haji Abdul's father had come from Kutch, and the son, equipped with money and intelligence, considered one of the richest men in Matrah in the 1950s, was a close friend of Sultan Said bin Taimur and well respected by the British. His granddaughter, in her late twenties when I spoke with her, told me BBC radio announced the news of Bhacker Abdul Latif's death in 1953, and the flag was flown at half-mast for three days in Muscat. Photographs on company literature and websites, office walls, and family albums show three generations of bearded men wearing Omani garb generally associated with elite tribal leaders: the *bisht* (an outer cloak, usually wool, worn over the disdasha, trimmed with gold) and the masar. As I was told, many also wore the khanjar in their travels through the interior and the Batinah coastal region or in their meetings with Arab tribes. In the sur, though, the dagger was not worn.

To underscore the community's loyalty toward the rulers, my interlocutors often emphasized the sultans' dependence on the al-Lawati community to shore up their perennially shaky finances. The relationship to the sultan was constitutive of their understandings of being subjects to him and being Omani. Such stories were held as part of a community narrative reservoir, in wide circulation and often recounted to me by different sources. For example, when the Arab tribes of the interior invaded Muscat and the cities of Muscat/Matrah were close to being occupied in 1895, I was told it was the al-Lawati merchant community who enabled the sultan to buy off the invading tribal armies. Those momentous events forced Sultan Faisal (1888–1913) to take refuge from the invading tribes in Jalali Fort in Muscat, and the al-Lawati supplied him with food and water brought over in small boats from Matrah. This was also the scenario during the 1913 Ibadi tribal revolt, when the last imamate was established in the interior: an al-Lawati sheikh, Habib Murad, became a legendary figure in the community for freely giving Sultan Taimur the keys to his godown (where his merchandise was stored), telling him to take whatever he needed to thwart the invasion. Another community member, a scholar who has written about the once vibrant social life of the sur, told me Sultan Faisal considered the al-Lawati the "stars" of his country for their riches and their education.

Many from the older generation had memories of the close-knit networks of the 1950s and 1960s that created a distinctive form of sociality in the sur, continually strengthened through interpersonal interactions, religious observances, weddings, and Eid celebrations in the mosques and ma'ātim of the sur. Outside the sur, the men of the community would gather at majālis to hold councils and exchange news, recite Quranic passages during Ramadan, and merely for relaxation and talk. Younger men would stay up all night discussing business in the coffeehouses outside. The mornings and the late afternoons would find the sur empty of men, as they went about their business activities; the only visitors were the Baluchi water boys, who came twice each day to fill the water pots and washing and bathing vessels, and the men who brought firewood for cooking. The gates of the sur were locked at night.

The transregional impact of events in Bombay, the capital of the British Raj, is evident. Colonial officials, personalities such as the Aga Khan and his family, and sectarian dissidents in the distant Bombay Khoja community were all intimately involved in the historical trajectory of the Matrah Khoja community and the events surrounding it, projecting power and meaning over a scalar geography of empire, religious practice, knowledge, and modes of sociality.[10] Earlier regional ties with Khojas in India are recalled through fragments of stories, passed down over the generations, characterized not by commonalities but by division and conflict. A number of the al-Lawati recalled that the main mosque of the sur once housed the *jamā'at khāna* (council hall, once commonly used for Khoja social functions and religious observances; today, the term is used solely to refer to its being a Nizari Ismaili place of worship and congregation).[11] Opinions differ on the role of the Aga Khan and his claim to be the direct heir to the imams of the Middle Ages; among the Khojas in Matrah, his rule in the 1850s is remembered as a time of vociferous arguments and armed fights, culminating in the destruction of the jama'at. One member of the community recalled being told of how a woman of the sur took up all of the vessels and materials related to the jamā'at that were once within the great mosque, went onto the beach, and threw them into the sea. The twenty families who supported the Aga Khan were later asked to leave the sur; the majority became Ithnā 'Asharis (Lorimer 1908, 1:2380).

Once they converted to the Ithnā 'Ashari sect of Shi'a Islam, the Khoja of Matrah became increasingly oriented toward the Arab world. According to community members, Najafi *'ulama'* converted them to the sect sometime in the mid- to late 1800s. The religious practices of the Matrah Khoja community were significantly shaped by ʿulamāʾ from Najaf, such as Sayyid Hassan al-Mosawi, who were formally invited to preside over the community's legal and religious needs in the late nineteenth century (al-Saleh 2015, 35). The building that was once the jamāʿat became an Ithnā ʿAshari mosque, and scholars from Iraq and the Gulf region stayed in the community as teachers over the years to guide the community in Shiʿa doctrines and ritual practices, including, in the words of one informant, "encouraging them to take to Arabic." Today, the community's daily lives are punctuated by the religious practices of the Shiʿa IthnaʿAshari tradition and the devotional activities of scholars and preachers from Bahrain, Saudi Arabia, and Iraq.

Oral and literary accounts recall the khutba (sermon) delivered in Arabic from the minbars of maʿatim and mosques, the flow of Arabic qaṣaʿid (poetry verses) from the rithāʿ (poetry of mourning) of Hussein, Quran recitations, the panegyrics on the Prophet, and the pleasant pre-nadha evenings spent on the beach outside the sur, when the young men competed on knowledge of Arabic poetry.[12] Arabic was used for everyday business interactions. These memories provide an alternative sense of history to one tethered to the Indian subcontinent. These memories forge the sense of a distinctive community that established local ties to the sultanate in response to transformative regional sociopolitical dynamics. They provide evidence of an alternative set of values and practices that dislodge the hegemonic construction of the Khojas of Matrah and their social world, built from the British archives, as one primarily oriented toward the British Raj. Instead, this sense of the past gives way to an understanding of a community whose networks and relationship are less categorical and more porous to imperial governance, religious schisms, and regional rivalry.

At the same time, the Khojas were distinctive in Oman for introducing new modes of education, shaped by their ties to the Raj. By the 1940s, the al-Lawati community had established their own schools in the Matrah area. Unlike the madrasa system of the interior, which emphasized memorization of the Quran and prophetic hadiths, these were organized according to the Lancasterian system: a single headmaster and his abler students as teachers' "assistants" passed on their knowledge for a monthly fee of thirty Indian rupees. The textbooks were primers from Egypt and India, and the focus was on learning English, Arabic, mathematics, and accounting.[13] Most students were the sons of traders and retailers. The Khojas were considered one of the most intellectual of Oman's many ethnic groups because of their command of English, their business acumen, and their ties to the Indian Ocean region and Europe.

Even as the men engaged in trade, pilgrimage to the Shiʿa religious sites in Iraq, and travel across the region—assimilating through dress, language, and behavior—their permanent enclave in Matrah remained socially segregated, especially through endogamous marriage. Although al-Lawati men occasionally married Baluchi or Arab women, I was repeatedly told that before 1970, women invariably married within the community. These practices were solidified in a distinctive daily language, Khojki, based on Sindhi and Katchi, although Arabic was widely used in business, learning, and pleasure. As one community member informed me, thoughtfully, "Because women were not mixing with Arab society, their language of Khojki was purer and less diluted, and they knew more about customs and traditions." In short, women were considered the bearers of al-Lawati distinctiveness in language, religion, and way of life.

Who Are the al-Lawati?

As the Khoja diaspora has been pushed out of British imperial channels of control and encased within the boundaries of nations, myriad social actors have posed this question, overtly and tacitly: Who are the al-Lawati? This question foregrounds the specificity of their historical experiences, which have conditioned their self-understanding and the ways it has been made visible or invisible through Omani national history, normative values, and iconic imagery. As the Khojas have moved out of the sur since the 1970s to settle in the suburbs of Muscat, they have assimilated into national public life and institutional state settings with other Omanis as "equal" citizens in ways that have also made them increasingly conscious of their differences, which undermine the dominant national narrative. Politically "hot" terms, such as *Omani Arab*, *tribe*, and *Islam*, are especially salient in delineating national cultural norms. These categories and what they entail inform how historical perception is structured among the al-Lawati, the effects of which come to the fore as part of daily interactions that have refigured their relationship with the sur.

How the al-Lawati engage with the specificity of their difference within a nationally articulated landscape is influenced by a number of contesting relationships between politics and the past. As elucidated in chapters 3 and 4, the national historical chronicle and its imagery establishes a unifying historical story line, embedded within a homogeneous language of deep rootedness ('arāqa) and the values evoked by the power of labor within Omani territory—its lands and seas—over centuries to build a flourishing nation and way of life. This singular historical experience, according to the state narrative, is the core and distinctiveness of Omani nation building, dissolving ethnic, historical, and religious differences to forge the common denominator on which a national consciousness is built. This denial of social difference is set against strong structural and institutional state governance that has been constitutively undergirded by tribal hierarchy, where the notion of "being Arab" as an originary category is intimately linked to that of *asal* (descent), patrilineal genealogy, and tribal history. This paradoxical state of affairs and the everyday sensibilities it enables generate the ways in which al-Lawati subjectivity is produced.

In a brief footnote to his entry on the Khojas, Lorimer (1908, 2:1035) mentions that in the Sultanate of Oman, the Khojas were known among the Arabs as "Lawatiyah." The term's origins are obscure, but he suggests it may be derived from the word *lota*, the Indian water vessel, which they carried when they first arrived in the region. He notes that the Khojas never called themselves "Lawatiyah" and disliked the name. Whatever the truth of these remarks, a century later the name has become part of normative institutional nomenclature: every citizen linked through the patrilineal line to the Khojas/al-Lawati is officially placed within that category, which is now an officially endorsed "tribal" patronym with all the ensuing legal and administrative documentation that its members would carry.[14]

Changes to the connotation of the term are linked to the wide dissemination of a historical account, which I found in one of the few texts to delve into the question of al-Lawati identity, Jawad al-Khabori al-Lawati's *Al-Adwār al-'Umāniyya fil-Qarra al-Hindiyya: Dawr Banī Sāma b. Lu'ay* (2001). A historian and philosopher, al-Khabori (1913–1984) was an unusual member of the community, more noted for its merchants and artisans. A childhood intimate of Sultan Said bin Taimur, he later went into voluntary exile due to political and religious differences with the community and the sultan.[15] During his years in Bombay and Karachi, he began writing a book on a topic that had often plagued him—the word *al-Lawatiya* and its relationship to Oman. One of his former associates recalled that he was motivated by more than historical curiosity; as a scholar of Arabic literature and history, al-Khabori had been made to feel inferior because he was considered "Indian," whereas he had grown up with an understanding of being "Arab." As his associate recalls, the need to answer this question of identity came to a head when al-Khabori was with a group of Arab tribesmen, and someone asked him about Arab poetry. When Jawad answered the question by providing information that they were not aware of, one of them laughed and said, "See, this Indian chap knew it and we did not know." This type of ethnic division, in the context of growing Arab nationalism in the late 1950s, upset him greatly. Al-Khabori was one of many among the older generation of al-Lawati who felt such anxieties at a time when the imam was in exile and his supporters were rallying around a new movement of Arab nationalism and pressing for full membership in the Arab League.[16]

Another incident during my fieldwork underlines the impact of Arab nationalism during the 1960s among the al-Lawati community. While I was sitting with one of my interlocutors, Mustafa (a retired employee of Petroleum Development Oman), and his wife in their spacious living room, listening to their life experiences, Mustafa pointed to a black-and-white photograph behind me. In front of a grove of date palms stood two rows of men in military garb carrying rifles, a military unit of the Sultan's Armed Forces. All but the British officer wore Middle Eastern kaffiyeh on their heads. The photograph showed Mustafa and his fellow cadets, a mixed group of Arabs, Baluchis, and some al-Lawati serving the sultan under the direction and training of the British in Al Buraimi in 1964. As Mustafa recalled, he enlisted in the 1960s when the spirit of Nasserism was prevalent and there was a strong sense of Arab identity even among the sultan's troops. Localized ways of life were intimately woven into larger regional developments in the Arab world and were inscribing a sharpened sense of ethnic differentiation. The exclusion of the al-Lawati minority from the memories, feelings, and desires embodied in the narrative of Arab nationalism at the time, as Mustafa explained, "made many among the al-Lawati feel 'minus' in their hearts and less than others."[17]

Al-Khabori wrote his work in the 1960s and 1970s, when notions of being Arab and Omani were core conceptions through which to address and resolve the al-Lawati sense of difference and their place in the modern nation-state. His thesis was that the al-Lawati were descendants of the Arab tribe, Banu Samā bin Luw'ay (al-Lawāi'ya). In Oman, he notes, the *ta* has often been used as a substitute for the hamza, in written literature and in conversation, to facilitate pronunciation. With this observation, he assimilates the Khojas into the Arab and tribal traditions and histories of the Arabian Peninsula. In this view, Sind and Kutch are on the margin of a clearly Arab/Muslim trajectory, focusing on movement, conquest, social transformation, and the drift of peoples from west to east and back again, establishing a narrative of return to a home posited as one of pure Arab tribal origin.

This ethnohistory uses Arab primary histories; secondary scholarship in Arabic, Urdu, and English that draws on a range of events, epochs, and sources; oral tales; material features of the landscape; and received wisdom recounted on the shores of Matrah, in coffeehouses and in the majālis, to generate what might be considered a double movement. Even as a historical narrative that forges its understanding of the Khojas through the conception of Hindu origins and caste was marginalized by the advent of a nationalist modernity, another past comes to the fore—disseminated through the spread of ideas and literary texts—rooting the Khojas of Oman in the national landscape as "al-Lawai'ya" by enfolding them within an Arab tribal genealogy. In the narrative, the al-Lawai'ya are part of the early Arab armies that established an Arab-Islamic state in the region of Multan, seamlessly integrating Multan, Sind, and Oman into a historical geography of conquest, religious reform, and mobility. Further migrations by the Banu Sama' occurred in the wake of the conquests of Oman by the Qarmatians in AD 929. The conquest of Multan by Fatimid missionaries in 347 AH / AD 958 was foreshadowed by the conversion of the Bani Sama' to Shi'ism in Bahrain by the Qarmatians. The state's conquest and occupation by Mahmud of Ghazna, in the early eleventh century, ultimately led to the dispersion of the tribe across the Indian subcontinent. Linguistically, that the al-Lawati speak Khojki is attributed to this intermediary period, when they resided in Sind after leaving Oman in the first century AH / seventh century AD, returning to the "mother country" in the 1800s, during the age of Imam Ahmed bin Said Albu Said, as merchants and traders.

Although recounting an Arab genealogy among the al-Lawati community did not originate with al-Khabori, it is most systematically elaborated in his work. Several members of the older generation whom I interviewed recalled the distribution of pamphlets and short works, such as those of Muhammed al-Tawil, predating the nahda, that attempted to trace the al-Lawati to Arab tribal origins through family trees. The undated booklet of Muhammad Taqi Hasan al-ʿUmani adopted an alternative account, suggesting the Lawatiyah were descended from Hakam bin ʾAwanat al-Lat, who commanded the first Arab invasion of the Indian subcontinent and later became governor of Sind (Ward 1987, 73). The assumption of a genealogy linked to the Arab tribes and the early histories of Islamic conversion pervaded across genders and age groups; I often heard variations when talking with members of the community.[18] When I asked a senior educator who worked at the national museum whether she felt her community's history was well represented there, she replied tersely that the al-Lawati were one of the original tribes of Oman—not an ethnic minority.

This assumption was by no means uncontested. A number of community elders voiced reservations at the idea of being Arab. Many felt they were Arabs through their rooted presence in the region, attested to by the presence of age-old gravestones in Rustaq and the longevity of the main mosque and the sur: "If my great-grandfather's grave is in Oman, how can I claim to be from somewhere else?"[19] The sur itself was evidence, often cited as a material testament to the community's long-standing presence in the region. Several people pointed out the date inscribed on the upper panels of the western gate of the sur al-Lawatiya, 1074 AH / AD 1663.[20]

What it meant to be Arab was thus a strong point of contention, with some believing in descent from a singular tribe and others in a more diverse path, in which families from different groups earned the category of "Arab" through their relationships with the region and its people over hundreds of years. One former diplomat told me when I asked about the importance of origin in Oman, "All this talk about roots is highly improper. Everybody comes from somewhere else. The world has been changing for thousands of years. We may have come from Kutch, but we've lived here for centuries and we've become Arabs." Now the possibility of the al-Lawati's being descendants of Arab tribes is also a subject of jocular debate. Some of my interlocutors had done DNA tests. One of these spoke of confronting those who insisted on an Arab tribal origin, claiming that he always informed them, "If you think you are Arab, I will pay for the cost of your DNA test. I will bring you the kit myself."

The terms *Arab* and *tribe* have thus become central in channeling the discussion of history and origin from the complex, overlapping bonds that characterized being a Khoja of Matrah toward internalizing the exclusive boundaries of Omani nation building. In the process, a sense of self is being fabricated through new modes of belonging and ties of affinity. And yet both sides of the debate have been fundamentally shaped by a language of commonality that limits how identities are set and recognized within a bordered national terrain. It was only from a chance remark by a young al-Lawati journalist that I learned it was not until 1981 that the al-Lawati had received their official name. Before that, all documentation, from property deeds to passports, had registered the Khojas as "Hyderabadi." It was unclear whether the change was a government initiative or spearheaded by the community's elders, but it reflected a powerful desire to anchor all those linked to the community to a single tribal (qabīla) name as the organizing basis for government administration. This would bring the community to the fore in terms of a public identity that had specifically Muslim and Arab connotations rather than an Indian tinge.[21]

With al-Khabori's ideas already widely disseminated even before publication of his text, the transformation of the community's name and its standardization to al-Lawati as a "tribe," descended by blood from Usama bin Luʻay, enabled their assimilation into national communal life and modes of governance. In the 1970s, as one scholar in the community informed me, the community "rejected the idea of being Indian, especially as they climbed higher in government circles, ministerial ranks, commerce, industry, and diplomacy."

Regardless of people's conviction, this genealogical emphasis on being Arab has two important effects: it makes it possible for communities of diverse historical experiences to cohabit with each other in new relations of mutuality and ethical engagements. Furthermore, the tribal emphasis further shores up those national historic frameworks rooted in the values of citizenship and ethical principles that draw the boundaries of native versus outsider within the national terrain. In the process, certain forms of collective memory, habits, and geographic senses of belonging, such as those tied to the Indian subcontinent, are increasingly abandoned to embrace others as part of the process of becoming modern Omanis and Arabs (Asad 2003, 180). But this also weakens their autonomy over aspects of a distinctive communal life. Marriages, for example, are no longer endogamous. From rarely leaving the sur before the 1970s, women are increasingly integrated through their schooling and work, enabling more assimilative lifestyles. Lawati men and women now marry outside the community. One businessman informed me, "In my family, my elder brother's son married a woman from Morocco, and the other one, a Khoja. My second brother's son married a woman from the Baharna [Shiʿa from the Gulf region, specifically Bahrain], and his daughter married a Sunni Omani." Although it was rare to marry an Arab from the interior, men and women had married Arabs from the Batinah coastal region and Muscat who were less tribally conscious, as well as other ethnic groups, such as the Baluchis and other Shiʿa ethnic communities.

The exodus from the sur since the 1970s has also dwindled the number of community members who speak Khojki. In the words of a former minister, "The children of most families today don't speak Khojki. Even in my household, my two sons and daughter speak Arabic. In the next ten to fifteen years, few will be able to speak it, and probably no one today knows how to write it anymore. There is no hope of reviving it." Even tombstones are now carved in Arabic rather than Khojki, a practice, I was informed, that only began in the 1970s. In sum, the categories of Hyderabadi and Khoja are increasingly marginal in the histories and lifeworlds they conjure, as a direct result of the community's attempt to embody the cultural and historic norms of Omani citizenship.

Hauntings of a Non-Omani Past

Despite al-Lawati attempts to adapt to the normative framework of Omani history and the values and principles it perpetuates, fractured memories that are unassimilated in the national narrative confront the present, suspended but not forgotten. The difference that defined the Lawati community through their former relationship with the British imperium persists. If the possibility of being an Omani citizen is predicated on being both tribal and Arab, this political subjectivity is also caught in the ethical and political ambiguities of historical entanglements that the al-Lawati are trying to tidy up to create a space for themselves as Omani. This resonates with what an al-Lawati trader from al-Khoborah in the Batinah told me when I asked him about the importance of surnames: "If you are an Omani and your origins are Pakistani and your surname is . . . Khan, the presence of this name will always remain, reminding you and others that you are not originally from Oman but from Pakistan. In the end, an obstacle [ḥājiz] will arise between you." The power of history making grounds itself in the everyday, not merely through the act of naming as Khoja, Hyderabadi, or al-Lawati. These names, as categories, entail a certain historical understanding of the people they are organizing, leading to the reconfiguration of the community's social and religious life. This reordering also generates paradoxes and fissures that manifest in critical differences in the histories and values at the heart of the national narrative (Ivy 1995, 1–29). A binary is constantly in place; the concept of local versus foreign, forged on a platform of histories, becomes the basis for a suite of potent associations linked to the al-Lawati tribe and their past—rich versus poor, Indian versus Arab, exploitative versus in need, miserly versus hospitable, educated versus ignorant, Shi'a versus Ibadi/Sunni Muslim—that structure groups' daily relationships with each other. These are differences established on the basis of origin, occupation, wealth, and social standing.

These designations become part of a continuum that identifies people and places as either more foreign or more local and part of a more or less stable structure of perception. Because most al-Lawati returned to Oman after the lean years of the 1950s and 1960s, they were generally considered to be one of the most qualified groups to construct the country's modern infrastructure. With their command of English and the degrees most had obtained in the Middle East, Pakistan, and India, they were placed in key positions in government, petroleum development, business, industry, and diplomatic circles. However, among Omanis generally, the al-Lawati are characterized not only through the framework of descent, wealth, religion, education, and influence but also through their more tangible mannerisms, style of walking, form of speech, even accents. A good friend from the Batinah region once joked that he could spot the Lawati by the way they communicated with each other, even when he could not hear their conversation.

The local rituals of hospitality in the guest-host exchanges of coffee and dates in the Arab interior—now symbolic of Omani generosity, open-handedness, and magnanimity—have become fraught in a continually felt gap between those who are considered to embody the ideals of Oman in daily practice and those who do not. On many of my visits to al-Lawati households, I was driven there by my friend Abdullah, an Ibadi from Nizwa, who was also a taxi driver. Many times after I left the house, he asked if they had served any food. What was especially noticeable for someone like me, who had been living in the interior, was that dates and coffee were not always offered during my visits. Baked snacks and juice were more the norm, set on a coffee table rather than on a mat on the ground. On some occasions, only a drink was offered. After hearing these deviations from the norm several times, Abdullah mentioned that they were not unusual; the al-Lawati were known to be *bukhalā'* (miserly). At the time, I thought this a personal prejudice. However, I heard Arabs of the interior and the Batinah region use the term *bakhīl* several times to describe the al-Lawati. In my discussions with community members about this issue, a number angrily cited their community's many endowments and causes for good that have benefited all in Oman, such as schools set up in Matrah in the 1940s and 1950s, when there were virtually none. Nonetheless, it could be concluded that the al-Lawati were not considered generous because their hospitality was not recognizable to tribal Arabs as following the norms of national life, as defined by Omani Arab ethical sensibilities and embodied in the ubiquity of the dalla, a national icon.

This perception, structured and cemented by an alternative sense of the past, also informed the trajectory of the Arab Spring protests in February and March 2011. The first protests about corruption among cabinet ministers named non-Arabs and nontribal Omanis, including Maqbool Ali Sultan, a Lawati who was minister of trade and industry at the time. Other names followed, but many al-Lawati still consider protests against this minister to be an expression of generations of resentment and anger that had naturalized into an antipathy against the community, which is perceived as rich, with a monopoly on Oman's business, banking, and trade resources, and ultimately as outsiders and exploiters.

In his work on social and gender inequality in Oman, Khalid al-Azri (2013) notes the effect of ethnic differentiation in the workplace. He interviewed a banker from the interior, who was working at the Omani National Bank. The banker stated in frustration, "This is a bank of al-Lawatiya. . . . Every day I feel that people want to question me. Why are you here? Why don't you go and work in the Ministry of Heritage and Culture or for the secret police" (2013, 51). This example indexes the general perception among Omanis that employment practices and social relationships in the workplace often serve to reinscribe historical ethnic differences. It is a perception informed by the understanding that the al-Lawati still monopolize trade and industry and hold disproportionate economic and political clout.

Murtada, an official at the Ministry of the Interior and at the al-Lawati Awqaf administration, recalled in one of our interviews a conversation with a friend that turned from gentle teasing into a serious argument. His friend had said the al-Lawati were in Oman only as guests of the sultan; they owed their citizenship entirely to his beneficence and were not "real" Arabs, native to the area. Murtada, in great anger, told his companion, a Hinai from the interior, that it was only through his people's support that the sultan had been able to assume power and usher in the nahda. They, the Arabs of the interior, had tried to wage war on his family and overthrow them. As far as he was concerned, the fact that he was born there, had dedicated his entire life to the region, and was going to die there made him an Arab and an Omani. Even in banter with friends, it seemed, these memory fragments seeped through and destabilized the discursive historical framework the state embodies while reinscribing hierarchical ethnic boundaries between Omanis.

The Sur al-Lawatiya Today

Even as the advent of national modernity and the ensuing exodus has transformed the sur into an increasingly marginalized space, it still embodies the distinctiveness of being an Omani citizen of the al-Lawati tribe today. On the one hand, the traditional facades of the old houses facing the corniche are now a focal point of city municipal laws regarding their maintenance and whitewashed color scheme, as the sur has increasingly become the object of state ventures in historic preservation and aesthetics. The facade is increasingly construed as a living testimony to Oman's maritime and pluralist history.

Within the sur, however—a site still prohibited to unaccompanied non-Lawati—a different sense of the past motivates the social practices that now define its spaces. These are the observances of celebration and mourning that define the Shiʻa religious calendar, including those commemorating the martyrdom of Imam Hussein at the Battle of Karbala (tenth of Muharram, or ʻĀshura) in 681, the birth and death anniversaries of the Shiʻa Twelver imams, Eid celebrations, and fasting during Ramadan. During the Shiʻa sacred months of Muharram and Safar, among other religious observances, the abandoned pathways of the sur suddenly come alive with people's hurried movements to and from religious congregational sites, the buzzing of conversation, prayers, readings, and sermons on the histories of the imams, smells of food offerings on many an evening. The sur's fortified enclosure today graphically illustrates the sharpening division—between public and private, politics and religion, desectarian Islam (politically neutralized) and Shiʻa religious practices—that anchors the political rationality of the modern Omani state as a foundation for civil and political equality.[22] Following de Certeau (2011), how the sur is used today embodies another form of belonging, one that maps onto the ways the al-Lawati community perform their understanding of inhabiting Omani citizenship. The sur has become one of a number of spaces where Shiʻa doctrines and observances—which many al-Lawati would consider the essence of their difference from non-Lawati Omanis—as sectarian religious practices, have been tucked away from the public realm of politics into the private realm to maintain a desectarian Islamic public domain.[23]

People still frequent the narrow streets and houses of the sur, but the purpose is increasingly religious in orientation. The old narrow houses have taken on a different kind of significance during the nahda. Although emptied of occupants on most days, most of the houses are havens for family get-togethers, chats with neighbors and friends after religious observances, and for *iftār* (breaking the fast) during Ramadan. Asma, a middle-aged teacher in Muscat, informed me, "I open my house and spend ten days from the first to the tenth of Muharram in the sur. At this time, we go to the *maʻtem* every day for morning, afternoon, and evening majālis. And we use these houses to rest. But I might spend only one night, ʻĀshūra, in the sur."[24]

This plan was common among the men and women I talked with. ʻĀshura was a night whose observances took on an additional importance, as the men participated in the Muharram procession that wound its way through the alleyways of the sur, reenacting the Battle of Karbala through rhythmic poetry, lamentation, and chest beating.[25] For the al-Lawati, the enclave's role has come to embody the emancipation from their public personae as Omani citizens, toward the more private state of membership in the al-Lawati community through the practices of Shi'a Islam. The strong affinity to the sur is due, in part, to its transformation into a wholly private space for Shi'a religious practices.[26]

Despite living outside the sur, families have held on to their properties, and with increased prosperity brought about by state oil wealth, many have acquired more than one house for extended family. Like Nizwa's old quarter (chapter 5), the abandoned houses are gaining value. The sur contains, in the words of a Lawati friend, "some of the most expensive real estate if taken per square meter, comparable to property values in many of the big cities in the world."[27] As in Nizwa, the tangible signs of neglect have been accompanied, in recent years, by a wave of nostalgia, generated by strong affective ties and memories of bygone days. The only way to salvage the old quarter in Nizwa was to transform it into a source of tourism investment. But among the al-Lawati, as one of the community elders told me, "because of sentimental attachment, no Lawati are selling any houses in the sur. In fact, they are building more of them."

Even as memories and histories make a place, a place can also make histories. For many Lawati, a "return" to the sur continues to mark a delineation of the specificity of their mode of belonging in Oman from that of non-Lawati. In response to my question regarding why people came from all over Muscat to attend the ma'ātim (congregational halls), even though there are Shi'a mosques in other districts, Arwa (a woman in her thirties and an official at the Ministry of Tourism who was deeply interested in the history of her community) told me it was the one place where people could speak Khojki to each other. Another friend, who still lived in the Matrah area, thoughtfully replied, "Since we were kids, I have been going to the same ma'tem. There is something spiritual—we call it *ruhānīya* that I feel. I don't get that sense . . . when I go somewhere else." Members of the older generation, who had grown up in the 1960s and 1970s in Muscat and Matrah, often voiced strong sentiments about the sur. One grandmother told me, "I feel that this is like our mother, our earth. We cannot leave. There are other ma'ātim in Muscat, and I do go to them. But for the first ten days of Muharram, I must come to the sur. If I don't come, I feel too uncomfortable."

The sur's two-story houses once had a singular layout—a ground floor comprising an open chamber for cooking and other spaces for washing, and an upper sleeping area. Many of these have been demolished and rebuilt in accordance with the modern emphasis on multiroom construction, with the requisite facilities and corresponding to separate social functions along generational and gender lines. About thirty are completely modern and strikingly different from the older ones, with their crumbling masonry, graffitied fronts, and peeling walls. However, with the state valorizing the al-Lawati building tradition and aesthetics, many of the new houses have been purposefully built to incorporate the overall traditional aesthetics and features for which the sur al-Lawatiya is now renowned. Mustafa, a photographer and member of the community, was planning to create a book of photographs he had taken over the years, capturing the architectural features and decorative motifs that make the sur unique in Oman, many of which have disappeared.

Some twenty houses are permanently occupied by elderly women, widows, or divorcees—women "who never left," in the words of one interlocutor: "They don't want to leave the sur because they have very strong connections with it, since they lived there when they were kids." These women typically reside in a series of rooms upstairs, having transformed their lower chambers into ma'ātim, attended by three or four women who recite the Quran together or read imamate history, doctrinal texts, or poetry. Furthermore, some houses have been donated to al-Lawati awqāf (religious endowments) and transformed into ma'ātim specifically for women to conduct prayers and qirā'at (readings). Converting one's home into a ma'tem was considered a form of acquiring baraka (blessing) from God and a way of "giving the elderly something to do." Muhammad, a community elder and a former general director of the Ministry of Electricity and Water, often stopped to greet the elderly occupants of the sur as he pointed out interesting features from the community. They spoke Khojki with each other, the mother tongue for these last remaining residents of the sur.

Televisions screens on the walls in the two purpose-built ma'ātim for men and women are hooked up for live viewing of the khutba, lectures, and readings taking place during important religious occasions in the main mosque opposite the corniche, frequented only by men of the community. The tables outside many of the small open squares of the quarter, near the main ma'ātim, are staffed during these times by young men who sell CDs, T-shirts, and books on Shi'a doctrine, religious songs, and the sermons and readings of prominent preachers and scholars of the Gulf region, Saudi Arabia, and Iraq arranged in front of them. During the days of mourning for the death of Imam Hussein in the months of Muharram and Safar, the sur is generally covered in large black sheets and black flags, expressive of grief. For celebrations of the birth of an imam, such as one I attended to commemorate Imam Mahdi (869–940), the entrances to the sur and the main pathways to the mosque and the ma'ātim are decorated with strings of colored lights, accompanied by little banners.

An enclave that once delineated the uniqueness of a lifeworld brimming with full-time residence, community celebrations, and economic exchange has been gradually reworked into a vital space of regular religious observances. Through reconfiguring the use of the sur's historical space and contemplating it in terms of Shiʿa religious observances, as well as historical memories, it comes to be considered by the al-Lawati in terms of their own communal sense of being distinctive from the national norm, even as the sur's very presence further entrenches the al-Lawati's affective ties to Oman. This paradox is further exemplified by the presence of Arabic plaques above many doorway lintels or on the walls of houses. These express fundamental Shiʿa tenets, such as "There is no God but God and Muhammad is his Prophet. Ali is the *walī* [friend or helper] of God," or important sayings of Imam Ali (656–661). In the process, the intimate historical connections that tie the al-Lawati community to the Indian subcontinent and the British Raj are obscured, giving way to a space that is increasingly oriented toward the Arab world, even as it is simultaneously directed toward a transregional Shiʿa one.

Conclusion

In the nineteenth and twentieth centuries, the experience of inhabiting the sur was regulated by the al-Lawati's shifting sense of belonging and their own sense of the past, the result of transformative dynamics in state building. Names such as Khoja, Hyderabadi, or al-Lawati were not merely changes of terminology but were embedded within historical orientations that were either marginalized or deployed as a result of regional sociopolitical changes. A pre-oil sense of history—once tied to the British Raj, diasporic relationships with the Khoja communities of India and East Africa, and Indian Ocean trade networks—has been displaced by one oriented toward Shiʿa Twelver networks in the Arab world and Omani nation-state building.

Today, the nation-state's initiatives to monumentalize the sur—in a bid to incorporate its historic and aesthetic significance into an overall historic framework—integrates it into the Omani national idiom. But the process of its incorporation produces its own ambivalences, marking the boundaries of citizenship and its limits. In their dense and many-layered otherness, the al-Lawati's sense of their past and collective memories has been fundamentally informed by state heritage discursive practices on the one hand and its governing logic on the basis of tribes on the other. Even while entrenching a national grammar made up of a rubric determined by "Arab Omani civilization," "tribe," and "Islam," public histories converge to regulate ethnic variability, generating a contested social and political terrain in the process, one that illuminates the limits of pluralism in Oman. This sense of history, its narratives and practices, organizes the cultural, ethical, and religious norms of the Omani nation-state, delineating the framework for establishing the boundaries of the public and private domains.

The values and principles it imparts ultimately inform daily social interactions among the al-Lawati that may, at times, be recast as moments of doubt, suspicion, or downright hostility, rubbing up against state efforts to assert a national homogeneity.

Understanding Omani conceptions of their communal history is more than a matter of determining their veracity; they become modes of perception that structure the community's historic sense of belonging to the region in myriad ways, as an integral part of daily life and making sense of a past that acts as a conduit toward assimilating to and differentiating from the norm in a manner legible to the framework of the nation-state. Being al-Lawati, with all its nuances, is a mode of living constitutively made up of a series of memories and histories. These accounts of the past are contingent on the historical conditions of possibility that have come about through the sociopolitical struggles of a particular moment whether it involved facilitating British imperial rule, dissent within religious sectarian networks, Arab nationalism, or modern state building. The sur and its transformation into a space primarily devoted to Shi'a religious practices embody the al-Lawati sense of being Omani citizens distinct from other Omani communities, while enabling its use in ways consonant with the Omani state's ruling logic on Islam.

CONCLUSION

Cultivating the Past

In a widely cited answer to a question from a Kuwaiti journalist as to how he had managed to unify the heterogeneous Omani population, Sultan Qaboos replied, "Heritage with modernization. And I believe that we have succeeded with this combination" (al-Jarallah 2006).

Why would this combination be an important formula for national unification? The answer may well lie in the wake of protests that overtook key urban centers of Oman in 2011 and 2012. Lambasting the forces of Westernization, the state responded with economic compensation packages and harsh security clampdowns—and slight political reforms. However, in a barrage of symposia and workshops hosted by state institutions, youth groups were organized and an infrastructure planned that would intensify the emphasis on heritage discursive practices and the values and principles they imparted. These were conceived as establishing the ethical conditions for cultivating national histories and goals among citizens, in ways that would allow them to creatively deliberate and act in the face of destabilizing change in the present, while remaining rooted to the ethical space of the nation and steering clear of Islamist attachments to a regressive history.

In explaining the ubiquity of heritage in Euro-America, Rodney Harrison (2013, 3) suggests that there is a "sense of crisis and uncertainty, which has grown in significance in contemporary post-industrial societies . . . in the midst of technological, environmental and social change." This has resulted in a heightened sense of loss and nostalgia, leading to the wholesale acquisition of memories through preserving the outmoded and disused. Although the many forms of heritage in the West could be explained in terms of the threats of losing something invaluable through the shift to postindustrial society, this is not the primary logic of heritage in the Arab world. As Nathalie Peutz (2017) observes, the project of heritage and its systematic dissemination cannot be removed from the overwhelmingly hegemonic operations that carved the Middle East regional landscape into its concomitant nation-states—the impact of European colonial governance, the forms that resistance movements assumed, the subsequent state-building efforts, and the consequences of Euro-American military and cultural imperial ventures as part of a global capitalist economy. The effects of these geopolitical struggles have been felt in the overtly political rise of Islamist movements, sectarianism, and localized human rights activism and through softer power through the wide dissemination of Western television, movies, music, and styles of dress.

In Oman, two kinds of temporal logic have been at work. Most scholars delving into modern nation-state building in Oman have circled around the notion of the nahda—the period that began when Sultan Qaboos bin Said (r. 1970–2020) ascended the throne—heralded as a time of progress that built the foundations of a modern nation-state. This approach generally covers the bulk of material that explores Oman in terms of modern statecraft (see, for instance, Allen 1987; Allen and Rigsbee 2000; Limbert 2010; Riphenburg 1998; Valeri 2009). This is held in strong contrast to the preceding period of poverty, isolation, and tribal conflict that defined the early twentieth century in Oman. Such a temporal framework explains the state's political authority through the impact of the sultan, the feelings of indebtedness he has roused in his subjects, and the modern state infrastructure he has established as the basis for establishing his territorial authority.

On the one hand, the nahda is seen as a sharp break from the immediate past: The introduction and standardization of modernist institutional and infrastructural forces in Oman are entirely different from, and better than, what preceded. Like the narrative of Renaissance-era Europe's recovery from a "barbaric" past, Oman is thought to be reemerging from the dark times that followed the breakup of its maritime empire in East Africa.

On the other hand, there is another temporal logic at stake, one that emphasizes the past in terms of continuity rather than fracture. Since Oman's inception as a modern state in 1970, there has been a propagation of its heritage industry through museums, exhibitions, cultural festivals, and the restoration of its forts, castles, and citadels. Material forms of old mosques, the dalla, and the khanjar saturate the public and private domains and become part of a mode of producing historicities and histories that carve out the spatial and temporal terrain of the nation-state. Material forms and architectures become a standardized public vocabulary, seen on street roundabouts and in educational media, currency, and postage stamps. Historical sites and material objects alike become tethered to fundamental and enduring values of national life—creativity, entrepreneurship, pluralism, hard work, cosmopolitan interaction, and family ties—that come to define the ethical actions of the modern Omani citizen, who must "ingest" the conception of tradition that defines the public domain in order to navigate the unknown shoals of modern living.

Like the rest of the Arab-Persian Gulf region, the explanatory basis of pervasive heritage in Oman tends to reference the rise of a new form of polity—the nation-state, the need to create a new mode of collective consciousness by sociopolitical elites and to mitigate the uncertain effects of rapid modernization brought about by sudden oil wealth. Heritage, in such a scenario, is deemed no more than a fabricated form of history that papers over reality, one moreover that cannot be relied on for any kind of essential truth. The familiar form these public heritage institutions assume—from museums to textbooks—is taken as the work and design of Western professionals and thus purged of any genuine sense of the past. This assumption parallels Pierre Nora's (1989), in which sites of memory once co-opted by the top-down official discourse of the state allow people to invoke the past rather than to genuinely experience it. True memory is lost; that which replaces it, "heritage," is perceived as a form of manipulation that only serves to alienate the populace from "true" memory.

Yet the question remains: Why would the sultan consider heritage and modernization as such a potent combination for establishing unity among a heterogeneous population? Is heritage truly establishing Omani unity, or is it alienating the people of Oman, who are being forged as a collective on the basis of the sultan's benevolence? What if we think of heritage as a constructive force not in terms of its veracity but in terms of its wide-ranging effects.

Heritage as a Force to Reckon With

Dipesh Chakrabarty's (2000) work on "provincializing Europe" brought to our attention that even as metropolitan practices may become constitutive in producing postcolonial modernity in former colonies, they are also inadequate, obliging us to look for histories and their impact in ways that cannot be assimilated to dominant Euro-American models. Echoing these sentiments, I have argued in this book that although Western professionals may have contributed to the entrenchment of globally familiar forms of heritage in Oman (and elsewhere), these were by no means uniform, especially as they were structured to secure very different governance regimes, which selected histories in accordance with the challenges they faced. The conceptualization of time as heritage, in both its representational form and its substantive content, has propagated a highly contingent configuration of ideas and practices about the past. It was formulated to respond to context-specific struggles between different religious and socialist and Western imperial coalitions in the region to secure the institutional bases of a modern, dynastic sultanate.

In tracking the imprint of this history, I realized that official heritage objects and monuments, specifically Nizwa Fort and the dalla, were not always conceived primarily in terms of their symbolic significance. They assumed their taken-for-granted representational roles as symbolic icons through a process of purification that separated them from the ties that had bound them in their utilitarian roles to the Ibadi Imamate and its way of life. Through the pragmatic nature of its administrative, military, and judicial roles, Nizwa Fort facilitated a past that was oriented toward God and divine salvation and grounded in Ibadi doctrine and practice. For the dalla, the status ranking that was part of the hierarchical layout of the sabla and defined its movement around the sabla chamber during the imamate also lubricated the readings and discussion of histories that were held up as moral and ethical yardsticks for assessing the conduct of daily affairs. Both material forms facilitated a mode of history that held that the variegated nature of everyday interactions and relationships could be assessed on the basis of past authoritative and exemplary forms of justice and morality, as embodied by the lives of virtuous forbears such as former imams, as well as the Prophet and his companions.

Accompanying the social and economic transformations in the Omani landscape that were part of nahda era was the transfiguration of these sites and objects into texts. This operation dematerialized the type of work they had once performed, enabling a "liberation" that opened a space for reconfiguring the material of old, occasioning the transformation of boundaries between history, polity, and the public domain, thus enabling the transformation of replacing the Ibadi Imamate into the Sultanate of Oman. As official national heritage, the dalla and Nizwa Fort, among other sites and objects on display, become a mode of history, a set of ethical practices and an aesthetic appreciation that translates into a series of abstract values and principles to substantiate the sultanate. In their embodiment of idealized attributes of civilization and culture, these object forms escape material political and social consequences through inhabiting a transcendent terrain that connects past and present as a continuing plane of transcendental values that are lifted away from the narrow confines of historically specific social, political, and religious practices. Simultaneously, even as abstract values, these suprahistorical ideals have political ramifications in their material embodiment—as coffeepots, architectural elements, water jars, or silver jewelry—since they lend themselves to a depoliticization that naturalizes the national narrative and the accompanying values that these objects now embody, while organizing ethical reflection and action in ways consonant with the national past.

Through heritage practices and its matrix of institutions, infrastructures, and knowledge, the locus of authoritative time in the modern sultanate has transferred from an exemplary past, predicated on divine salvation, to an uncertain future that now tends to rule over the present and calibrates the past into a series of immanent and worldly principles and values. Material forms, whose wide dissemination animates and directs the nation-state, bring into sharp focus the pedagogical practices of knowing this national past as integral to Oman's modernity—a new grammatical foundation laid down by the categories of culture and civilization. In confronting regional challenges, as well as localized regimes of tribal and socioreligious inequalities, this new institutional history has worked to displace the authoritative notion of an elected Ibadi Imamate and its notions of history, religion, and ethics as a recognized source of local knowledge, making way for a nationalized sultanate instead.

The material effects of such a history are an institutionalized conception of culture and civilization, grounded in the telos of becoming Omani through the productivity of laboring the resources of Omani lands and waters. Such an understanding also differentiates the more autochthonous sense of belonging that is tied to citizenship in other Gulf countries, such as Kuwait or UAE (of Bedouin tribal pasts or desert values), toward one that is more expansive and malleable, enabling foreigners to become citizens (at least in theory) if they live in Oman for twenty years and speak Arabic. Unofficially, it was well known that only an elite expatriate group would be allowed citizenship after those twenty years. It was considered a difficult bureaucratic process and one with little transparency. The assumption was that citizenship would go to those deemed to have contributed positively to Oman's prosperity, thus fitting with the historical paradigm propagated by heritage institutions. In reality, it was more often those with the right connections and background.

This premise becomes foundational to the promise of leveling hierarchies, while building political and social unity on the basis of the sameness of citizenship. In the process, through the work of heritage, the forts, the dalla, and the sur al-Lawati have palpable political effects, inasmuch as the pivotal role of Britain's informal governance of the Gulf region has been crowded out of official memory. Tribal genealogies and their hierarchical regimes, which were once imbricated within and deployed imamate rule, have been effaced. Heritage becomes the exemplary public site for (1) the regulation and reconfiguration of Ibadism, still the official sect of Oman, through transcending any kind of sectarian doctrinal specificity; (2) effacing tribal hierarchical socialites; and (3) regulating ethnic variability by absorbing all non-Arab groups into an all-encompassing narrative framework that transforms them into Omanis, while shearing them from historical and cultural specificities that threaten the ongoing construction of a common national grammar. The Ibadi Islam that emerges under the rubric of the modern state has been reworked to one, in the words of Ahmad al-Khalili, the grand mufti of Oman, "where differences between Sunni and Ibadi Muslims are subsidiary issues that are of little eternal consequence and in no way impede Muslim unity" (Hoffman 2004; see also Broucek 2018).

Such history practices summon a notion of culture and civilization that sediments a new, normative understanding of Islam—new modes of marking time and history that define the ethical actions necessary to become a modern Omani. This fits within the calculus of the state, wherein the public domain is organized around national norms for time, language, religion, ethnicity, and citizenship, helping cultivate a unified national ethos and way of life while the private realm secures anomalies, whether in terms of alternative senses of history and memory or sect-specific rituals and practices.

The relationship between materiality, history, and ethics lays the foundations for organizing a new form of envisioning—an eye honed by disciplinary techniques and modes of reasoning that behold a nationalist sensibility and ethical citizenship and are blind to the archaic religious embodiments of history. Using Oman as my case study, I find that the material ways in which the past is referenced, propagated, and argued about as heritage cannot be subsumed within a singular, functional mode of realpolitik reasoning. The ways of reasoning out the past that come about through heritage institutions have a force and a felicity that must be reckoned with in creating a social and political space within which the citizen-subject is actively being cultivated. Discourse and imagery actively hone perception, sensibilities, and emotional attachments in ways that are organizing and reorienting practical modes of daily living.

However Omanis interpret and experience this idealization of the past, such heritage institutions as Nizwa Fort and such objects as the dalla now rest on the authority of a very different grammatical foundation for history and religion—a pre-Islamic evolutionary chronicle. It is on this new ground that Omanis are forced to think through their relationship with the material past of northern Oman, reappropriating and generating their own framings of the past in the process. These are not always compatible with the state's, but they operate in reference to and within the normative understandings of history adduced by and established by the state.

As part of the harsh realities of lived citizenship, many of the people I encountered during my stay in Nizwa were struggling to make ends meet—working more than one job, coping with rising living expenses, and delaying marriage as a result. Their relationship with the city's historic core was continually influenced by a perceived gap between the state's conservation and heritage projects and the ever-present values and attitudes (social solidarity, interpersonal consultation, entrepreneurship) they were thought to carry with them. As I have shown through-out this book, these aspirations, grounded in a valorized past, were continually buffeted by alternative state logics that intervened in daily lives. To the extent that people's sense of material history was informed by heritage discursive practices, it was equally conditioned by the assertion of state power into social life in other ways, including the socioeconomic modernization that had transformed the ur-ban landscape and brought in overseas workers. It also included sanctioning, while subsuming, the Arab tribal structure and creating new tribes (the al-Lawati) as the organizational pivot of a centralized state apparatus, regulating them in ways that characterized their historical relationships with the sultanate and channel-ing their role into that of mediators between the government and the populace.

It was from within the confluence of these competing governing rationales that people's responses emerged as alternative understandings of their ties to major historic sites. For Nizwanis, these ambiguities created a space for critique and ac-tion that evoked a nostalgia for life under the imamate, critiquing the socioeco-nomic changes brought about by the modern state while further entrenching its power in questions of history through privatized restoration and tourism proj-ects that addressed the deleterious impact of the changes. Liberal assumptions of equality among Nizwanis and other Omanis—established through heritage dis-course, citizenship, and the global human rights regime—tangled with the con-tinuing importance of the tribe and genealogical history in social life and marriage. The result was the raising of questions and debates on the conflictual relation-ship between Islam and a tribal hierarchical mode of sociality and the proper place of religion as part of personal status law. For non-Arab communities, such as the al-Lawati, the contradictions between the state's governing rationales (heritage practices versus the tribe) and their accompanying attitudes toward the past cre-ated a space within which al-Lawati sense of history and memory strengthened, becoming a forum for debate in their attempts to entrench their own sense of be-longing in Oman.

The paradigms that national heritage institutions assume may be global, but the history they assume in nation-states—their mode of articulating and mani-festing the past—are historically specific within a changing transregional geopo-litical economy. The struggles and debates they rouse vary with context. Through the management of time, modern state building has organized religious, ethnic, kin-based, and ideological differences. The historical consciousness engendered by such an operation, however, has created its own historically specific set of prob-lems, derived from the paradoxes that modern state governance generated through the creation of a national ethics.

Glossary

ʿadāt wa taqālīd: customs and traditions

aflāj: water channels/canals

ahl al-faḍl: virtuous forebears

ahl al hal wal ʾaqd: elders, scholars, and tribal leaders

ʿālam: scholar

amr bil-maʿruf wa nahy ʾan al-munkar: commanding the right and forbidding the wrong

asal: lineage/descent

aṣali: of the original tribes of Arabia and therefore superior

ʿashā: late evening prayers

athār: traces

awqāf: endowments

bakhīl: miser

dalla: coffeepot

dhow: traditional ship

disdasha: traditional robe worn by men in the Gulf region

fatwa: juridical opinions

fiqh: jurisprudence

firqa: sect

fitna: strife

hadith: words and deeds of the Prophet

harat al-ʿaqr: Nizwa's oldest residential quarter

jihad: decisive confrontation

kafāʿa: compatibility or equivalence (in marriage)

khādim: servant

khanjar: ceremonial dagger

mawlā: client or dependent

nahda: "awakening" or "renaissance"

naṣab: patrilineal descent

qadi: judge

rāshidun: rightly guided

sabl: council/meeting halls

sabla: community gatherings

salat al-ʿasr: late afternoon prayers

shura: consultation

souq: market

sunna: words and deeds of the Prophet and his companions

sur al-Lawati: the fortified enclave of the al-Lawati community

tafsīr: exegetical literature

turāth: heritage

ʿulamāʾ: religious scholars

ʿumma: theologically defined public space

walāʾ: clientage

wali: governor

zakāt: alms tax for the poor

Notes

INTRODUCTION

1. Here, I use the parlance of Kirshenblatt-Gimblett 1998, 19, where exhibit objects are metonymic for an "absent whole that may or may not be recreated."

2. For works on the history of nineteenth- and twentieth-century Oman, see Landen 1967; Peterson 1978; and Jones and Ridout 2015.

3. For the process of purification as the basis of modernity, see Latour 1991.

4. It was also the capital of the imamate under Imam Barakat bin Muhammad bin Ismail al Ismaily (1536–1557) and Yarub bin Belarab bin Sultan (1721–1722).

5. On the "lineage game," see Samin 2015, 11.

6. On heritage practices as part of the legacy of imperial governance and subsequent nation building, see Colla 2007; Shaw 2003; and Bernhardsson 2005.

7. Some scholars argue that conservation is the child of modernity, its ideological other. The assumptions underlying an inexorably changing future allow modernity to develop according to the laws of progress, while "preserving" the age value of monuments as symbolic vestiges of a superseded past (Lowenthal 1985).

8. Sultan Qaboos bin Said does not have a son to succeed him. However, the Al Said royal family would continue to rule under a 1996 succession decree, which states that only Muslim male descendants of the sultan's direct ancestor, Sultan Turki (1871–1888), who are legitimate sons of Omani Muslim parents, may become sultan. A royal family council would convene within three days of the sultan's death to determine the successor. This is what happened when Sultan Qaboos passed away on January 10, 2020. The next day, Sayyid Haitham bin Tariq, the sultan's first cousin was deemed sultan by the royal family. See Valeri 2015 for details.

1. REFORM AND REVOLT THROUGH THE PEN AND THE SWORD

1. The term *sultan* in the Omani context was coined by the British and first used in the Anglo-Muscati treaty of July 31, 1839 (Kelly 1968, 12). A common term in the area, it had never been used as a title for the region's rulers; they were imams or seyyid (the mostly hereditary rulers of the Āl Busa'idi dynasty).

2. Major L. B. H. Haworth, Letter to the Political Resident in the Gulf, May 9, 1917, India Office Records, British Library, IOL/P & S/10/427.

3. For a more comprehensive understanding of the twentieth-century revival of the Ibadi Imamate, see J. Peterson 1976.

4. L. B. H. Haworth Correspondence to the acting Political Resident, Baghdad, March 5, 1919, IOR/15/6/204.

5. Hayworth Correspondence, March 5, 1919, IOR/15/6/204.

6. In a groundbreaking study of the nineteenth- and twentieth-century slave trade, Matthew Hopper (2015) cogently argues that the Suez Canal, the telegraph, and the steamship helped incorporate the Arabian Peninsula into global trade networks. For Oman, these technologies were a primary impetus in expanding the date trade between the Batinah coast and the United States. The London–India telegraph line was originally laid in the Red Sea, with shore stations in the Kuria Muria Islands and in Muscat. This route, opened in 1859, was abandoned in 1865 (Landen 1967, 103–4; Lorimer 1915, 1:601–21).

7. The sultanate had several points of strategic importance: its long coastline on the flanks of the oil tanker route from the Arab-Persian Gulf and near the main shipping route to Karachi and Bombay, its convenience as a landing ground for military aircraft, its potential as a naval base to command the entrance of the Arab-Persian Gulf, its oil potential, and British policies in Persia and Iraq (Bailey 1988, 6:3).

8. Hayworth Correspondence, March 5, 1919, R/15/6/204.

9. It was only from the 1950s, with the discovery of oil in the Arabian Peninsula, that the British directed their attention to the interior.

10. Once leaders of a maritime empire, the sultans of Oman also held territories in East Africa (Zanzibar) and on the Indian coast for the better part of the nineteenth century. The death of Sayyid Saʿid bin Sultan in 1856 led to a controversy between two of his sons, which ended in 1861 with a British-mediated agreement that divided the territory into Oman and Zanzibar, leading to the collapse of Oman's imperial economy.

11. Haworth sums this up neatly in a letter to A. H. Grant: "The life of Oman depends upon the external world. The rice and grain it imports, the clothes it wears, and the wood from which it makes its boats are imported from India while the dates, pomegranates and limes it exports are sold to British subjects and despatched to British ports. It would only be necessary to declare a blockade . . . to bring the tribes to their senses." L. B. H. Haworth, May 17, 1917, India Office Records, British Library, R/15/6/204.

12. In September 1895, Sultan Turkī asked for a loan of $30,000 (Maria Theresa dollars). The British Raj sanctioned a loan of Rs. 60,000, at 4.5 percent interest, repayable from the Zanzibar subsidy. Most of this was needed to pay off loans that had been used to buy off invaders in the 1894 Arab tribal invasions of Muscat and Matrah.

13. All slaves who had been forcibly imported after that date could be set free, because the slave trade was already illegal, and granted manumission certificates. They could apply for protection to the British consulate in Muscat or on a British vessel or by entering India or another British territory. Slaves imported before 1873 were occasionally liberated when it was shown they had been treated badly or no one appeared to claim them. In Muscat, when a runaway slave was returned, the slaveholder was required to sign an agreement swearing he would treat the enslaved person with kindness (Lorimer 1915, 2:2488–90).

14. The treaty paved the way to 60,000 Maria Theresa dollars (Landen 1967; Lorimer 1915, 2:2475–516; Townsend 1977, 42–46) that became part of an annual subsidy (the Canning Award), a vital part of the sultan's annual revenues and ultimately a means for the British to maintain some control over the ruler's actions.

15. This was discontinued in 1937, despite a personal appeal by Sultan Said bin Taimur to the viceroy of India (Bailey 1988, 7:4).

16. The munitions subsidy was personal to Sultan Taimur, but the arms traffic subsidy continued for three years under Sultan Said bin Taimur to prevent the financial collapse of the state. At the treaty's expiration, the political resident recommended it continue through 1935, on condition that the funds would be spent on social services, such as sanitation and school construction. The subsidy ceased on January 1, 1936, although the sultan pressed for its renewal (British Foreign Office 1987, 2:186).

17. Haworth Correspondence to Deputy Political Resident of the Persian Gulf, Bushire, January 23, 1918, India Office Records, British Library, R/15/6/48.

18. I am indebted to Charles Hirschkind (2006) for this interpretation.

19. Despite the Ministry of Heritage and Culture's much-publicized efforts to print all Ibadi literature, this work is difficult to obtain through official channels. This might be due to al-Salimi's perspective on the Al Bu Said dynasty and overt aims to revive the Ibadi Imamate. However, its importance made it possible to obtain photocopies: it is known to almost every Omani; many have private copies that circulate.

20. For a better understanding of the nineteenth-century Ibadi movement as part of the nahda, see Ghazal 2010, 1–36.

21. Modern Ibadi historians are generally in accord with the notion that history writing was not an active field among Ibadi 'ulamā' (A. al-Lawati 2003, 99–107; N. al-Salimi 1961, 4). The primary literatures were in the domains of Quran and hadith exegesis and Ibadi jurisprudence. Histories and biographical literature are few and far between; al-Salimi's work thus has special value as a scholarly history that comprehensively chronicles Oman's past from the Jahiliyya/pre-Islamic period to the first decade of the twentieth century.

22. For an overall understanding of the historiographical compilation of al-Salimi's tuhfat, see Coppola 2017.

23. And yet it could also be argued that there was a profound fascination with such figures as Alexander the Great, who suffused the intellectual life of British India through archaeological works, histories, and periodicals, as well as the private letters of colonial administrators, scholars, and travelers. His military exploits did become an exemplar for the British, who saw themselves as emulating his footsteps as a European conqueror in pursuing grand military conquests and personal glory while proving his superiority over Asiatics (Hagerman 2009).

24. For a more detailed explanation of these patterns in Islamic historiography, see Robinson 2003.

25. According to a footnote in my copy of the tuhfat (N. al-Salmi 1961, 1:325), this saying has been handed down from some of the earliest imams.

26. For work that tries to strip away the standardized and idealized perspective of the Ibadi golden age to emphasize the political and tribal conflicts beneath, see Wilkinson 1987 and 2010.

27. Haworth Correspondence, March 5, 1919, IOR/15/6/204.

28. Haworth Correspondence, March 5, 1919, IOR/15/6/204.

29. Haworth Correspondence, March 5, 1919, IOR/15/6/204.

30. L. B. H. Haworth, Letter to Deputy Secretary to the Government of India, October 30, 1917, India Office Records, British Library, IOR/15/6/48.

31. Haworth Correspondence to Deputy Political Resident of the Persian Gulf, Bushire, January 23, 1918, India Office Records, British Library, R/15/6/48.

32. In his correspondence to the Deputy Political Resident of the Persian Gulf, Bushire, December 20, 1917, India Office Records, British Library, R/15/6/48, Haworth concludes that "it is doubtful whether any oriental country can rule itself. They are unfit and govern themselves in contact with European powers."

2. NIZWA FORT AND THE *DALLA* DURING THE IMAMATE

1. It was also the capital of the imamate under Imam Barakat bin Muhammad bin Ismail al Ismaily (1536–1557) and Yarub bin Belarab bin Sultan (1721–1722).

2. The aflāj (sing. *falaj*), now part of a World Heritage Site, are a complex series of water channels that use gravity to channel water over long distances, usually from sources at the base of the Hajar Mountains.

3. Saif was one of many thousands of people who migrated out of Oman to live, study, and work in Saudi Arabia, the Gulf countries, Iraq, and Pakistan in the late 1950s and 1960s, from the end of the imamate into the pre-nahda civil war era.

4. For more on the fort's physical layout, see D'Errico 1998; Gaube, al-Salimi, and Korn 2008; Cabinet of the Deputy Prime Minister 2008, 120–41; and Dinteman 1993.

5. For a detailed discussion of the fort and city, see al-Farsi 1994 and Literary Symposium in Nizwa 2001.

6. For more information on the Ibadi sectarian tradition of Oman, see Wilkinson 1987 and Gaiser 2010.

7. For elaboration on how the imamate tradition was anchored to an unchanging representation and organization of history, see Wilkinson 1987, 7. Wilkinson explains how the need to maintain the Prophet's community, the golden age, as the model to strive for, opened a space of experience in which the present was considered continuous with the past. That which connected past and present was a modular way of being, grounded in the ethical norms embodied by the Prophet and his companions and the community they established in Medina.

8. For an exploration of the role of history in Omani fiqh and doctrine, see al-Jaludi 2003; A. al-Lawati 2003; and Wilkinson 1987.

9. For more information on Islamic historiography, see T. Khalidi 1994; Robinson 2002; and Rosenthal 1968.

10. The term *sīra* (pl. *siyār*) had different connotations outside the Omani region, in the tradition of Islamic historiography, where it generally alluded to a focus on the documentation of the life of the Prophet and, later, to biographical dictionaries. In Oman, it was generalized to include epistles, edicts, and juridical opinions as well as life histories. The term *sīra* began assuming biographical connotations only in the 1600s, with "the first biography of Omani literature" of Ya'rubī Imam, Nasir bin Murshid al-Ya'rubī (1624–1649). This notion of sīra alluded to the idea of a path to follow and emulate. See Khalidi 1994 for details on the development of the sīra in Arabic and Persian historiography. For an exploration of the Omani siyar, see N. al-Salimi 2010; Wilkinson 1992; A. al-Lawati 2003; and al-Jaludi 2003.

11. The Siffin arbitration is generally considered to have led to the emergence and consolidation of the different sects of Islam: the Shi'a, Sunni, and Khawāraj.

12. For more insight into siyar as fiqh works, see N. al-Salimi 2010 and Wilkinson 1978. These individual manuscripts only began to be compiled into collections from the seventeenth century onward.

13. Personal communication with legal consultants in the Nizwa governor's office, November–December 2010.

14. This phrase, part of the *bai'a* (oath of fealty) that established a new imam, is mentioned repeatedly in N. al-Salimi 1961.

15. A series of informal interviews and conversations with older religious scholars in their seventies and eighties, members of Nizwa families with centuries-old reputations for scholarship and piety, and the custodians of Nizwa Fort during my ethnographic fieldwork in 2010–2011 and the summers of 2015 and 2016.

16. There is no mention of who the sheikh was. There is, however, mention that this man was a scholar and teacher who taught the imam's son, Badr. From the tone of the letter, he was an influential man. This letter is from the National Records and Archive Authority, Muscat, Oman, O.M.NRAA.A.3.2.2.

17. In Limbert's (2010, 63–64) work, coffee is thought to be a luxury item for elites prior to the nahda, so it is rather curious that she also explains that coffee played such an integral role in social interaction that those who could not afford it when, for example, there was a death in the family would have neighbors and wealthier kin provide some. According to my informants, wealthier men in the sabla took turns providing coffee and dates, or the sabla had a *waqf* (endowment) to supply these needs.

18. This work by Sheikh Darwish bin Jum'a al-Mahruqi (1611–1676) is a collection of practical sermons for living a virtuous life, Ibadi doctrine, and jurisprudence.

19. Women had their own gatherings in the dahliz or in narrow side streets, sitting after 'asr (late afternoon) under the shadow of the trees between houses. These gatherings

became more private in the late 1990s, as women took turns meeting in each other's houses (Limbert 2010, 46–82).

20. The harat al-'aqr, as the oldest, largest, and most important of Nizwa's residential quarters, was said to have five public sabl rather than the one or two found in the smaller hārāt.

21. Limbert (2010, 46–80) makes a similar argument regarding visiting groups of women in Bahla during her fieldwork.

22. Certain occupations were closely linked to tribal lineage, inasmuch as certain kinds of work were relegated to those descended from enslaved people.

23. For writings that relate how authoritative accounts of the Prophet's life enter popular culture and daily life, see Berkey 2001 and Asani 1995.

24. None of my interlocutors ever mentioned that the mass adoption of television had resulted in the end to the central mediating role of the sabla as part of their daily routines. Television was a key site for heritage construction, especially through documentary programs in the 1970s and 1980s. However, much of the information imparted through television was part of the standardized logic and language disseminated by other forms of heritage media, including print media, official publications, urban landscapes, museums, exhibits, and textbooks. In the late 1990s and 2000s, Omani television had become of secondary interest to the rival attractions of satellite television channels and their offerings of Indian soap operas, South Korean dramas, and Hollywood fare.

3. MUSEUM EFFECTS

1. According to the Foreign and Commonwealth Office Archives, this included the opening (in Muscat) of Khoula Hospital, of two new gates designed by the Iraqi architect Professor Makiya, and of Port Qaboos. Foreign and Commonwealth Office Archives, FCO 8/2454, Report on National Day Celebrations by D. E. Tatham to J. R. Young Esq., British Embassy, Muscat, November 24, 1974.

2. Details of the reconfigured museum, which is very similar to the original, at least on the ground floor, are found in my dissertation (Sachedina 2013). The upper floor in the new layout was dedicated to the life cycle, another familiar model in the ethnographic museum world.

3. The zaygra are wells based on a pulley system powered by animals. The aflāj system, used throughout Oman for irrigation and water supply, especially in the interior, involves a series of surface and underground canals that tap into the water table, thought to date back two thousand to twenty-five hundred years.

4. In their focus on the relationship between power and knowledge, museum scholars have explored the constitutive political bases for museum and exhibit construction, the "invention of tradition" to legitimize elite interests, and the nature and impact of ethnographic authority (in terms of institutions and actors and their underlying assumptions). By no means an exhaustive list, some of the most notable are Ames 1995; Bennett 1995; Clifford 1998; Dudley 2009; Karp and Lavine 1991; Karp et al. 2006; Kirshenblatt-Gimblett 1998; and Pieprzak 2010.

5. See M. Al-Belushi 2008 for more information on the history of the institutionalization of heritage in the Sultanate of Oman. According to meeting reports, in the early 1970s, the Historical Association of Oman was also restoring Jabrin Fort, an old imamate stronghold, and preparing to introduce archaeological teams into the country, such as the Danish teams that went on to do survey work in the North and carried out extensive research on the archaeological sites of the Bat area in Ibri, in the Dhahirah region.

6. "Voice of the Arabs" (Ṣaut al-'Arab) was one of the most prominent transnational Egyptian Arabic-language radio services. It was a primary means by which Egyptian president Jamal Abdel Nasser (1956–1970) disseminated his ideas on anti-imperialism,

pan-Arabism, national socialism, and revolution across the Arab world. Omanis received these ideas through smuggled radios in Oman or as part of their experiences of exile in Arab countries and beyond.

7. Extract from Summary of World Broadcasts, September 23, 1958, FO 371/126874 /1015/6.

8. This was a direct result of the imamate leadership's being deeply subject to the currents of Arab nationalism.

9. Although both movements were socialist, NDFLOAG formed in Dubai and was considered an intellectual student movement oriented toward northern and central Oman; PFLOAG was considered a larger, more rural guerilla group based in the Dhufar region and South Yemen. NDFLOAG was thought to be more Ba'athist and more aware of transregional revolutionary theory, "imbued with the spirits of Castro and Guevara" (Takriti 2013, 169). The groups eventually joined forces in 1971 (Takriti 2013).

10. BCG (Crawford) to Foreign Office, Arabian Department, June 17, 1970, National Archives, London UK—Foreign Office Records FCO 8/1422.

11. The term *Oman* continued to refer to the interior, the former imamate domain, into the 1980s (Clements 1980; Darlow and Fawkes 1976; Skeet 1992).

12. This understanding of objects becoming entextualized as part of the "museum effect" is deeply influenced by the writings of, for example, Svetlana Alpers (1991), Tony Bennett (1995), and Webb Keane (2005). As Crispin Paine (2013, 2) puts it, "an object comes into a museum, it becomes a museum object. It acquires . . . a new personality which completely overlays its previous one."

13. *'Umān* was a government newspaper, published directly by the Ministry of Information. *Al-Waṭan* was a private paper but under the close supervision of the Ministry of Information.

14. *Umān*, March 19, 1973; June 24, 1976; April 12, 1978; November 18, 1980.

15. *'Umān*, November 18, 1980.

16. Eickelman (1989) notes that after the seizure of the Great Mosque in Mecca on September 20, 1979, uniformed police were stationed outside Nizwa's congregational mosque. According to his informants, there was a real fear that people in the interior wanted the imamate restored.

17. As Marc Valeri (2015, 20) notes, although Oman may have been considered a haven of stability during turbulent times in the Middle East, it has "always perceived political instability in the region as a factor threatening its own internal security."

18. To my knowledge, no official census has ever been taken (the issue is too contentious), but there is a general understanding that Ibadis make up a little less than 50 percent, with Sunnis growing in number.

19. Eickelman (1987) mentions this desectarian emphasis on Islamic education; Valeri (2009) and Limbert (2007) have discussed a desectarian mode of Islam that has become an integral part of citizenship cultivation.

20. In his examination of Ibadi official discourse of recent years, James Broucek (2018, 328) argues that Ibadism today has been reconfigured in ways that make it commensurate with other Islamic sects, creating an "ecumenical Ibadi theology" that justifies its authority on the basis of being "traditional." Through a selective interpretation of the Quran and prophetic sunna, official discourse emphasizes the specificity of the Ibadi section on the basis of apolitical theological questions that create a common ground with other Islamic sectarian traditions rather than boundaries of association and disassociation that demarcate its specificity. The result today is an Ibadi sect that has shorn off its doctrinal, theological, and juridical specificity, including the imamate, to create a common baseline that emphasizes toleration and unity rather than competing doctrinal understandings of political and juridical governance.

21. In UAE, foreign nationals make up 81 percent; in Qatar, 88 percent. In Bahrain, foreign workers make up 40 percent (Exell 2016, 14–15). See http://gulfmigration.eu /oman-population-by-nationality-omani-non-omani-at-dates-of-census-1993-2003 -2010/ (accessed March 21, 2018).

22. For details on demographic information in Oman in terms of citizens versus expatriates, the following website is available: https://www.ncsi.gov.om/Pages/IndicatorDetails .aspx?ItemID=m3J5yY5QxUbEvHhsfc8KuQ%3d%3d (accessed April 2018).

23. All members were Omani and had Western education backgrounds. The Spanish firm Acciona Producciones y Diseño designed the museum's interiors, and international museum organizations such as the Tate Gallery, Victoria and Albert Museum, and the Smithsonian Institution assisted in organizing collections management, the learning center, and guide training.

24. This model of Islam resonates with Jessica Winegar's (2008, 665) argument that exhibitions on Islam in the post-9/11 United States become part of an exhibitionary regime that seeks to provide an idealized model of values commensurable to a secular liberal ethos.

25. Qatar National Museum opened in 1975. The new national museum is still under construction, so it is not possible to compare with Oman's museums (Exell 2016, 29–33).

26. Extract from Summary of World Broadcasts, August 26, 1958, Foreign Office, National Archives, London, FO 371/126874/1015/6.

27. In 2007, a new decree shifted Qatar's national day from September 3 (British independence in 1971) to December 18. This was to commemorate Sheikh Jasim's founding of the state of Qatar in 1878, giving Qatar more longevity (ninety-three years) as a nation-state (Maziad 2016, 134–35).

4. ETHICS OF HISTORY MAKING

1. This understanding of heritage is taken from Kirshenblatt-Gimblett 2004.

2. The importance of heritage discourse practices in solidifying national identity in the Gulf as part of state engineering efforts has been explored by Davis and Gavrielides 1990; Khalaf 1999, 2000, and 2008; Vora 2013; Cooke 2014; Rugh 2007; and Kanna 2011.

3. Some of the foremost writings on Middle East heritage and politics present variations of these perspectives, which are often discussed together: Erskine-Loftus, Hightower and al-Mulla 2016; J. E. Peterson 2016; Koch 2015; Exell and Wakefield 2016; Exell 2016.

4. For more on the emergence of this aesthetic, see Damluji 1998.

5. Sultan Hamdoon al-Harthy, interview with author, May 7, 2017.

6. The second chapter of a 2000 declaration by the Ministry of Regional Muncipalities, Environment and Water Resources (No. 2000/4, article 23) is titled "Architecture and Artistic Conditions of Buildings" and states, "Architectural designs of all Buildings should be according to Arab and Islamic architecture style" (Hegazy 2010, 5).

7. Although these topics are mentioned for every grade, they appear in greater detail in the Ministry of Education's social studies textbooks for seventh graders (2007, Part 1, 10–15) and eleventh graders (2006, 20–24).

8. These explanations appear in greater detail in the eleventh-grade textbook (Ministry of Education 2006, 66).

9. There are exceptions. For relaxing excursions or sports, Western clothes are often worn, but these acts are allocated to the personal or private domain.

10. According to Valeri (2015), the protesters renamed Globe Roundabout as Maydan al-Iṣlāḥ, (Reform Square), recalling their calls for reform of the state rather than its overthrow, as was the case in Syria, Tunisia, or Egypt. However, Sohar's protests were in world headlines on February 27, 2011, and April 1, when violent clashes between protestors and police armed with teargas canisters and rubber bullets led to the death of two demonstrators. Until then, protests in Muscat and other smaller regional centers and towns in Oman had been peaceful.

11. A youth discussion forum that was held in January 2011 by a youth group, Youth Vision (Ru'yat Ash-Shabāb), which was funded by the state.

12. A discussion forum sponsored by the Majlis al Dawla (State Council) on April 16–17, 2012.

13. Another symposium, sponsored by the Ministry of Endowments and Religious Affairs on June 2–4, 2012. It recommended the launch of national programs and the development of studies that would strengthen values, morals, and emotional ties with citizenship to limit what was considered to be "negative conduct" (al-maẓāhar al-salbiya).

14. A symposium organized by the Ministry of Higher Education in April 2013.

15. This symposium was organized by the state body National Council for Human Rights, in cooperation with the National Youth Council, in September 2013.

16. This refers to a series of events during the Sohar demonstrations in February 2011. These included the blocking of trucks entering the port of Sohar and the looting and arson attack of the Lu Lu Hypermarket. The demonstrators also targeted the governor's office and a police station, setting them on fire. In response, the police fired rubber bullets into the crowds surrounding Globe Roundabout, which led to one death (Worrall 2012, 99–100).

17. The protests are generally considered to have spread primarily due to the use of text messaging, as well as Facebook, Twitter, YouTube, WhatsApp, social forums, blogs, and such chatrooms as Sablat Al-'Arab. These were considered to be one of the most prominent means for organization and discussion. This phenomenon echoes the beginnings of protests, sit-ins, and demonstrations in other parts of the Arab world.

18. The Majlis ad Dawla is appointed for a three-year term. Its primary role is to relay the interests of the local communities to the central government and vice versa, acting as an intermediary body. Primarily advisory, its members (unlike those of the Majlis al Shura) are not elected by the people; they are directly appointed by the sultan and include tribal elders, intellectuals, and dignitaries.

5. NIZWA, CITY OF MEMORIES

1. The text of the final judgment and sentencing of those involved was published in all three Arabic dailies, 'Umān, al-Waṭan, and al-Shabība, on May 3, 2005.

2. When asked about mass arrests in the early 1970s, Nizwanis frequently explained it in words similar to those of one Nizwani friend: "At the time, Omanis felt the son [Sultan Qaboos bin Said] would not be better than the father [Sultan Said bin Taimur] . . . in terms of tyranny and oppression."

3. The tanur, like the sabla, is another public building and considered an example of communal living and a cooperative way of life in Omani heritage discourse. The tanur is an underground pit, usually used for Eid celebrations when the residents of the hara come to specific areas of the neighborhood, bringing the household meat to roast. In Nizwa, in the Sifala (lower town) area, it is usually soaked in spices and then wrapped in palm fronds to be put into the tanur.

4. Although Ibadi Islam is no longer emphasized as Oman's official sect, the Grand Mufti of Oman, Sheikh Ahmed bin Hamad al Khalili, is an Ibadi scholar. Students of religious institutes of higher education and sharī'a (now relegated to the domain of personal status or family law) are predominantly trained in a reconfigured understanding of Ibadi law and doctrine.

5. For more on the relationship between the propagation of a "neutral" Islam as part of state religiosity and its cultivation of comportment and individual morality as civic virtues, see Limbert 2007 and Eickelman 1989.

6. The idea of consultation and formal election, though nominal at times, was of crucial importance to Ibadi doctrinal tradition and set in contrast to the sultans, who were thought to have seized their power, imposing their rule on the people (N. al-Salmi 1961, vol. 2).

7. This term appears in the eleventh-grade social studies textbook (Ministry of Education 2006) to explain the role of the "civilizational trajectory of Oman" in the study of the "Omani personality."

8. At one time, the qursh fransi (Maria Theresa dollar) was a standard currency of Oman. One qursh was roughly 110 baisa, and 1,000 baisa today is equal to OR 1 ($2.60).

6. NIZWA'S LASTING LEGACY OF SLAVERY

1. Oman's share in the date plantation economy was relatively small, compared to Iraq, for example, but was considered a dynamic force in the creation of a global trade network, especially in carving a niche in the US date market in the 1800s. The first American export company, W. J. Towell, formed in 1866 specifically to ship Omani fardh dates to New York (Bhacker 1992; Hopper 2008).

2. The global export of dates from Oman to the United States ended in the 1930s, due to successful American attempts to grow date offshoots from the Arabian Peninsula and Iraq in California. This led to the collapse of the date export trade, a key factor in ending the slave trade in East Africa to the Gulf (Hopper 2015, 181–91).

3. This treaty also arranged for the manumission of any persons who could prove that they had been captured subsequent to the signature of treaty.

4. Although there are no pearling banks along Muscat or its coastal regions, a large number of Omanis from the Batinah (almost five thousand, of whom one thousand were believed to be slaves) migrated seasonally to the Trucial coast (today's Emirates) to participate in the pearl-diving season (R/15/1/230; R/15/2/601).

5. In a report issued by the British Political Resident, Bushire, Iran to the India Office (July 20, 1935, R/15/1/228); In a report on "Domestic Slavery in the Persian Gulf" from the Honourable Liet-Colonel H.V. Biscoe, Political Resident of the Persian Gulf to the Foreign Secretary to the government of India, New Delhi (March 18, 1930, R/15/1/230). In an anonymous note entitled "Minute file xiii/3", July 23, 1948, R/15/1/234. This is also mentioned by Bertram Thomas, the finance minister and wazir to Sultan Taimur (1913–1932), who notes that slaves can mingle freely in the community to which they belong and could be manumitted if they wanted to since it was "universally known throughout the Gulf that the British authorities do grant manumission to any slave applying for it." (R/15/2/601).

6. These observations are echoed in a letter from A. P. Trevor to E. B. Howell: "From my own knowledge and experience, that in the vast majority of cases, slaves round the coast of the Persian Gulf are well treated and live comfortably, being for all practical purposes much better off than they would be as free men." Honourable Lieutenant-Col. A. P. Trevor, Political Resident in the Persian Gulf to the Honourable E. B. Howell, Foreign Secretary to the Government of India, March 27, 1922, IOR R/15/1/222.

7. According to a report on the DOMESTIC SLAVERY IN THE PERSIAN GULF (from the Honourable Liet-Colonel H.V. Biscoe, Political Resident in the Persian Gulf to the Foreign Secretary of the Government of India, New Delhi), Bushire, March 18, 1930, IOR R/15/1/230.

8. Thomas goes on to explain that among the fifty-four slaves manumitted in the Oman region in 1934, the reason was not a desire for freedom in itself but ill treatment of some kind by the slaveholder. He generally observes that those seeking manumission were those who had recently been enslaved.

9. The mawāli category is rather broad, in that it included smaller Arab tribes and foreign peoples who had, in the past, resorted to larger and more powerful tribal groupings for protection and to acquire rights as members of a community. These groups include the bayāsira, whose origins are rather murky, with ideas about their ancestry ranging from descendance from the region's original inhabitants to being migrants from Hadrawmawt.

It also included the *zuti*, thought to have descended from prisoners of war who became clients of Arab tribes, facilitating their assimilation. What all these groups had in common was that they were mawāli clients of Arab tribes; their ancestry was therefore incorporated into Arab genealogies. Their inability to trace their origins rendered them hierarchically lower, unlike even the most ordinary "pure" (*aṣli*) Arabs, who, I was told, could at least trace their lineage back ten generations, even if they were not the descendants of kings or the Prophet's family.

10. The terms *mawlā* (client) and *khādim* (servant) are used almost interchangeably at this point among Omanis. And it is hard to differentiate between the two, especially as all slaves eventually when manumitted became clients in assuming the tribal lineage of their patrons and in perpetuating the patron-client relationship until 1970.

11. In his work on Sohar, Fredrik Barth (1983, 228) mentions a sultanic decree in which, people informed me, the sultan had declared, "They are free people. No one can say that they are good or bad. . . . The *wāli* can punish any man who calls another *khādim*, and they should no more say *habib* to others."

12. Marc Valeri (2013, 267–77) comes to the same conclusion in his analysis of the relationship between the modern Omani state and the tribes. Even as the modern nation-state and its laws are established on the basis of a homogenous citizenry, it works to manage the tribes in accordance with its priorities and historical relationships with them.

13. Andrew Shryock (1997, 262–76) also examines this emphasis on noble lineage, pure bloodlines, and good behavior, in the context of the Jordanian Arab tribes who claim origins in the Arabian Peninsula.

14. As an alternative to a rigidly circumscribed official mass media, online social forums had become increasingly vociferous spaces for debate and commentary among those considered to belong to the nahda generation (those born and shaped by the infrastructure of modernity introduced since 1970). However, these forums were removed in the months following the Arab Spring protests of 2011.

15. Most of these threads are defunct, since their removal by the government following the Arab Spring protests.

16. This should not be mistaken for the *al* that characterizes many family names in the Arab world, including Oman. This *Aal* is a designation and prefix of only a handful of the most powerful Arab tribes in the region, including the royal family (Aal Said), and is considered synonymous with honor and nobility in the region, hence the discomfiture of the council.

17. According to Abdullah Aal Tuwaiya and others conversant with the case, members of the al-Harthi tribe pressured the Ministry of the Interior to displace the Tuwaiya name altogether. Said, one of the few in the family to retain the surname al-Harthi, also reached one of the highest rungs in the Omani state. Said was editor in chief of the *Oman Observer*, an English-language newspaper, and later became undersecretary at the Ministry of Information. His brother, Abdullah, maintained that part of the reason for these promotions was that he was considered an al-Harthi.

18. This argument is cited in a letter (dated July 16, 2011) between the al-Tuwaiya and their lawyer, Curtis F. J. Doebbler, and was part of an email correspondence between me and Abdullah al-Tuwaiya.

19. In 2011, Muhammad bin Ahmad Hasan al-Quḍat conducted a statistical survey on Oman's governorates to explore which region was more likely to place importance on the issue of lineage. The interior (*dhakhiliya*) region, where Nizwa is situated, ranked highest, with 90 percent of respondents stressing the importance of lineage (al-Quḍat 2011, 50).

20. Khalid Al-Azri's (2013, 42–43) work includes a debate between Imam Abu Muhammad Sa'id al-Khalili (d. around 1871) and a powerful tribal leader and prominent Ibadi scholar Isa bin Salih al-Harthi on the criteria that determine the deployment of

kafāʿa. Al-Khalili insists that the only criterion that could be allowed was lineage. Al-Harthi, citing another prominent scholar, Shaykh Muhna b. Khalfan b. Mohammed (d. 1835), insisted "one should be equal to the woman in everything: lineage, followed by religion, property and then her beauty" (Al-Azri 2013, 44). Imam al-Khalili retorts that beauty is a criterion that is "immeasurable." He qualifies this by referencing a historical account of the Prophet's uncle's son Ibn Abbas, who was blind and would not have been able to marry under such conditions.

21. For an illuminating discussion on the legal conflicts around the codification of kafāʾa and its social consequences in Omani society, see al-Azri 2013.

22. A 2010 sultanic decree (55) allows a woman of eighteen years to appeal her guardian's refusal of a potential marriage partner; in such cases, the judge acts as a substitute guardian. Justifiable reasons for a guardian to refuse include kafāʾa, but determining kafāʾa is up to the court. If the court determines lack of equivalence between marriage partners due to lack of higher lineage on the part of the husband, the appeal could be refused. Equivalence is considered an attribute the man (not the woman) must prove; the husband is not hurt if his wife is "lower" than him, since his children will assume his name.

23. This hadith, which has provoked a great deal of controversy in human rights circles, is found in the Ibadi hadith collection of Imam al-Rabiʿ (al-Jami al-Sahih). Other prophetic traditions were quoted to me to legitimize applying the conditions of kafāʾa on a marriage. One states, "Arabs are the akfaʾ of Arabs and Quraysh are the akfaʾ of the Quraysh." "The people of one tribe or one family would be akfaʾ among themselves, and people of one race would be akfaʾ among themselves." Both these hadiths have been used in cases of divorce (Al-Azri 2013, 55–56).

24. This verse could be interpreted as validating the equality of mankind: "Oh Mankind, we created you from a single [pair] of male and female and made you into nations and tribes, that you may know each other" (49:13). The same verse was used by many of my interlocutors to prove a tribally organized community was sanctioned by God.

25. The Ministry of Endowments and Religious Affairs banned the book (according to Hamid) for its criticism of Ibadi sharīʿa. However, it was intensively debated online, instigating broad opposition between those who considered discrimination based on lineage as antithetical to Islam and the many who still considered the importance of tribe and lineage. In debating intermarriage between tribal and ethical groups, one participant stated, "Whoever wants to be a relative in marriage to slaves, they can do so, but there is no need to trouble us" (al-Azri 2013, 60–61).

26. The prophetic sunna, although considered one of two primary sources of sharīʿa, was too contested to be clear evidence. There were doubts about which hadiths were genuine and debates on their interpretation, especially because they were textualized versions of an oral tradition.

7. THE AL-LAWATI AS A HISTORICAL CATEGORY

1. The second gateway is on the opposite end on the land side of the sur and is called the Gate of the Dead. Funerals once passed through this gate toward the cemetery.

2. According to Lorimer (1908, 1034), most of the al-Lawati community, who also call themselves Khojas, lived in Matrah (at the time numbering 1,080). There were and are families living along the Batinah coast, who were engaged in the trade networks and retail business. In 1908, 125 people lived in al-Khaborah on the Batinah and 30 in the cities of Sohar and Suwaiq. A considerable number also lived in Trucial Oman (now part of UAE) and Iran. Estimates of the population since 1970 are between 5,000 and 10,000; most still live in Matrah and the Batinah coast in al-Khabora, Saham, Barka, and Masnaʾa (J. Peterson 2004, 42–43).

3. Volume 2 of Lorimer's *Gazetteer* is dedicated to the geography and statistical analysis of the Gulf region, and its entries are arranged alphabetically; the al-Lawati are placed

under "K" for "Khojah sect." The entry merely notes that in the Sultanate of Oman, the Khojas are known to the Arabs as "Lawatiyah" and that they are also commonly spoken of as Hyderabadis, owing to the fact that many came as migrants from Hyderabad, Sind. A number of them came from Kutch and Kathiwar.

4. The Aga Khan Case, as it was called, concerned a suit filed by leaders of the Khoja caste against the Aga Khan, an exiled Persian nobleman who had allied himself to the British by assisting their conquest of Sind. This case was ostensibly a property dispute, since the Aga Khan claimed to be the religious leader of the Khojas. Although many considered him a source of guidance and personage of veneration, some elders opposed his presence in the community, since he demanded control of communal property and caste affairs, as well as payments of revenues and tithes. During the trial, the presiding judge, Justice Arnold, found it necessary to determine the Khojas' religious identity before he could resolve the issue of property ownership. The plaintiffs argued that the property belonged only to members of the caste who were Sunnis, and since the Aga Khan was not a Khoja, he had no right to intervene. However, Khoja religious poetry, the Quran, and Oriental scholarship on Persian history and Shi'a Islam were used to prove the Khojas and the Aga Khan were, in fact, Shi'a, specifically Shi'a Nizari Ismaili. The judge found that the Khoja were Ismaili and, therefore, that the property of the caste did belong to the Aga Khan, as their living imam, believed to be the direct descendant of Ali bin Abi Talib and the Prophet's daughter, Fatima Az-Zahra (Asani 2011, 95–129; Purohit 2012).

5. The entire question of British extraterritorial jurisdiction was one of contentious debate. In Muscat in 1858, Sultan Thawaini received a guarantee from the British that those Lawati/Khojas who were settled in Oman before the British occupation of Sind in 1840 would not be regarded as British subjects (Bhacker 1992, 172). Sultan Turki ibn Said maintained that the entire Khoja community were his subjects, and it was with great reluctance that he conceded in 1873 and 1876 that the Khojas, like the Hindus, were due British protection (Landen 1967, 230). In his writings on Oman, Sir Percy Cox, political agent and consul at Muscat (1899–1904), remarks that communities of British Indians, which included the Hindu Banians and the "Muhammadans of Khoja persuasion, descendants of immigrants from Sind and disciples of H. H. the Aga Khan or recent seceders from his faith, that it was the duty of the British representative to look after and occasionally visit" (as cited in Ward 1987, 299).

6. The benefits of British protection were the following: exemption from private property searches, exemption from local taxes, right of full discharge from creditors if bankrupt, British assistance in debt recovery, British official representation in any local trial, and exemption from direct interference by local authorities. Those who were British subjects or British protected could also obtain the assistance of the British diplomatic service for reparations for any damage or losses incurred during an attack by the local population (Allen 1981, 52). It is generally thought that this close association with the British may have been one of the primary reasons for the sacking and burning of Khoja and Banian shops in the course of various raids on Muscat and the Batinah coast. They were often viewed as British agents, giving rise to negative consequences that still reverberate today.

7. By the mid-nineteenth century, it became increasingly clear that the Banian and, to a lesser degree, the Khoja merchants were, through British authoritative sanction, in almost complete control of state finances as creditors, as well as of loans in East Africa and Oman (Hamilton 2010, 149; Landen 1967).

8. Although several al-Lawati elders believe their migration and settlement in the region occurred no less than three hundred years ago, based on a date inscribed on the upper panels of the western gate of the Sur al-Lawati of 1074 AH / AD 1663, scholars generally date their arrival in Oman to the late eighteenth century. Noting that the alternative name for the al-Lawati/Khojas is Hyderabadi, these scholars assume merchants who had estab-

lished themselves in Hyderabad, Sind, which was built in 1768, would have arrived in the Muscat region only after that date, playing an important role in the trade of the western Indian Ocean from that time. It is generally thought that the al-Lawati migrated and settled in Oman in waves between the late eighteenth and late nineteenth centuries (Allen 1981; Pradhan 2013).

9. For more on the economic and political power of the leading al-Lawati families, see Valeri 2010.

10. In his appendices, Lorimer (1908, 1:2379) notes that in 1885, the government of India refused to interfere on behalf of Imami Khojas, who had been dispossessed of the use of the original Khoja *jamāʿat*. There were arguments they were entitled to it under the 1866 Bombay High Court decision, but there was a sense that it would be a somewhat irrelevant exercise, since only twenty families had been ousted and had, in the end, been allowed to build a new jamāʿat for Imami Ismailis outside the sur. In 1886, Lorimer reports, the government was looking into complaints that certain Khoja women in Matrah were being abused by their husbands to coerce them to join the Ithnāʾ ʿAshari community and renounce allegiance to the Aga Khan. It turned out only one was so abused.

11. It is clear throughout the oral accounts I heard from community members, as well as those written by colonial authorities, that the Khojas were mostly Shiʿa, although some were and still are Sunni. Henry Bartle Frere (1876, 431), for example, mentions that the Aga Khan attended the majālis during the months of Muharram and Safar to listen to the *qiraʿat*, or narrative accounts of the Battle of Karbala, and preside over the distribution of water mixed with the holy dust of Karbala. Thousands, according to Bartle Frere (435), also went on pilgrimage to Karbala. The legal proceedings initiated on behalf of the Aga Khan in 1866 led to the formal administrative and doctrinal schism that ultimately divided the Khojas of Matrah and elsewhere into Ithnāʾ ʿAshari Shiʿas and Imami Ismaili Shiʿas. Many families among the al-Lawati are still divided between the two Shiʿa sects, but today all al-Lawati of Oman are overtly Shiʿa Ithināʾ Ashari.

12. Two of the most noteworthy are Jawad al-Khabori's *Al-Adwār al-ʿUmaniyya fil-Qarra al-Hindiyya: Dawr Banī Sāma b. Luʾay* (The Omani role in the Indian subcontinent) (2001) and Mohsin bin Jumʿa bin Muhammad al-Lawati's *sur al-Lawati (2010)*. Both are virtually impossible to get in bookstores yet are widely disseminated among community members. Recent memoires include Baqer bin Muhammad Al-Saleh's (2015) and Mustafa bin Mukhtār al-Lawati's (2016).

13. These schools are closely associated with the al-Lawati community but were open to all in the Matrah region; some Baluchis and Arabs attended classes.

14. Some families have refused to change their surnames to al-Lawati, preferring their family names over a tribal emphasis. These family names are generally known to be from the al-Lawati community and generally considered to be of obvious Indo-Pakistan origin.

15. According to the preface to al-Khabori's biography by the scholar Mohsin al-Jumʿa, al-Khabori was a "milk brother" to Sultan Said bin Taimur, a fostered kin relationship referring to the fact that al-Khabori's mother also nursed the sultan. Sultan Said spent many of his childhood days at the sur, and al-Khabori often stayed in the palace.

16. By the late 1950s, the imam and his supporters were no longer considered leaders of an isolated Ibadi state, carrying on the inheritance of an imamate established in 1913 by local historical and political dynamics. Actively supported by the Arab League, they were construed as a legitimate Arab state whose rights to sovereignty were being suppressed by a Western imperial power and its puppet, the sultan of Muscat (J. Peterson 1978; Rabi 2006).

17. Sultan Said himself, although proud of his Ibadi background, was not really interested in orienting Oman to the Arab world. He had stronger relationships with Pakistan and India (Rabi 2006).

18. A number of recent memoires, including Baqer bin Muhammad Al-Saleh's *Sur Al-Lawatiya fī Matrah* (2015) and Mustafa bin Mukhtār al-Lawati's *Tajāribī ṭaya Az-Zaman* (2016), espouse similar views about the origins of the al-Lawati, attesting to this theory's wide dissemination.

19. In an unpublished analysis, Harith al-Kharusi (2012) studied the ten graves in Rustaq. They are unmarked but, according to al-Kharusi, appear to have been made at the same time, given their stylistic similarities. People living nearby generally attribute them to the al-Lawati.

20. It is possible that the gate was once part of a Portuguese garrison, recorded as having been established in the area in the seventeenth century (Damluji 1998; J. Peterson 2004), and reused in building the sur al-Lawati in the late eighteenth / early nineteenth century. The oldest house in the sur dates back 150 years (Damluji 1998, 174), rendering the sur's material history rather vague.

21. Eickelman (1989, 14) notes how some members of the community laughed at the prospect of having their leaders designated as sheikhs, as if they were a tribe. He also details the role of the community's council as intermediaries between their people and the government to defuse religious tensions in the aftermath of the Iranian Revolution in 1979 (see also S. S. al-Hashimi 2015, 137–40) and to resolve administrative issues in the mid-1980s.

22. Valeri (2010) details regular arrests and imprisonment of members of the Shiʿi population, including from among the al-Lawati, since the 1980s as the result of a sense of impending threat to Omani national security. Those detained were accused, at the very least, of crossing the boundaries between the public and private and trying to politicize their religious activities. In 1997, a number of Shiʿa were arrested and accused of "action against the security of the state" (Valeri 2010, 261) by transmitting important documents to Iran and trying to establish an Islamic regime.

23. Other Shiʿa mosques in the Muscat area include Masjid Jafar as-Sadiq in Ruwi and Masjid Ibrahim al Khalili in Ghubra.

24. ʿĀshūra is the day of mourning that is sacred to the Shiʿa. It is the anniversary of Imam Hussein's martyrdom at Karbala.

25. This procession used to involve self-flagellation; one of my guides remarked that the houses along the way were often streaked with blood. The Omani government has banned the practice.

26. According to Valeri (2010, 258), in 2006 and 2007 the government did allow the al-Lawati to hold the Muharram procession outside the sur, where it wound its way through the back streets of Nazimuja (the neighborhood behind the sur) toward the corniche on the seashore front of the sur (a crowded venue in Muscat). This rendered the procession a rather public display. But in 2008, it was forbidden for the procession to move onto the seashore again. According to Valeri, the reasons for these decisions might have had to do with the "apparent Shiʿi regional revival" at the time, especially in Iraq and Saudi Arabia.

27. I was told that a place of only twenty square meters could go for as much as 20,000 OR ($60,000).

Bibliography

Abu El-Haj, Nadia. 2001. *Facts on the Ground: Archaeological Practice and Territorial Self-Fashioning in Israeli Society.* Chicago: University of Chicago Press.

———. 2012. *The Genealogical Science: The Search for Jewish Origins and the Politics of Epistemology.* Chicago: University of Chicago Press.

Agrama, Hussein Ali. 2010. "Ethics, Tradition, Authority: Towards an Anthropology of the Fatwa." *American Ethnologist* 37 (1): 2–18.

———. 2012. *Questioning Secularism: Islam, Sovereignty and the Rule of Law in Modern Egypt.* Chicago: University of Chicago Press.

Allen, Calvin. 1981. "The Indian Merchant Community of Masqat." *Bulletin of the School of Oriental and African Studies* 44 (1): 39–53.

———. 1987. *Oman: The Modernization of the Sultanate.* Boulder, CO: Westview.

Allen, Calvin, and W. Lynn Rigsbee. 2000. *Oman under Qaboos: From Coup to Constitution, 1970–1996.* London: Frank Cass.

Al-'Ansi, Saud bin Salim. 1991. *Al-'Adat al-'Umaniyya.* Muscat, Oman: Ministry of National Heritage and Culture.

Al-Askari, Suleiman. 1984. "Study on Kashf al-Ghumma attributed to Sirhan bin Said al Azkawi." PhD diss., University of Manchester.

Al-Azri, Khalid. 2010. "Change and Conflict in Contemporary Omani Society: The Case of *Kafa'a.* In Marriage." *British Journal of Middle East Studies* 37 (2): 121–37.

———. 2013. *Social and Gender Inequality in Oman: The Power of Religious and Political Tradition.* London: Routledge.

Al-Belushi, Khamis bin Karim. 2011. "Youth between Heritage and the Present!" *Oman Daily* (Arabic newspaper), March 20, 2011.

Al-Belushi, Mohammed Ali K. 2008. "Managing Oman's Archaeological Resource: Historical Perspectives." *Public Archaeology* 17 (3): 149–73.

Al-Duri, Abd al-Aziz. 1983. *The Rise of Historical Writing among the Arabs.* Princeton, NJ: Princeton University Press.

Al-Farsi, Nasir Bin Mansoor. 1994. *Nizwa 'abr al-ayām* [Nizwa across time]. Nizwa, Oman: Administrative Association of Nizwa.

Al-Hadad, Fathi Abdul Aziz. n.d. *Al-Siyāha fi Sultanate 'Uman* [Tourism in the Sultanate of Oman]. Muscat, Oman: Al-Damri Library.

Al-Hajri, Hilal. 2006. *British Travel Writing in Oman: Orientalism Reappraised.* Bern, Switzerland: Peter Lang.

Al-Hashimi, Mubarak bin Saif bin Said. n.d. *Imām Nur al-Din al-Sālmī wa Arā'ho fi lūhiyāt.* Muscat, Oman: Maktabat al-Dāmri.

Al-Hashimi, Said bin Muhammad. 2007. *The Intellectual Life in Oman during the 13th Century A.H. / 19th century A.D.* Riyadh: Saudi Historical Society.

———. 2009. *Sheikh Amir bin Khamis al-Maliki: His Life and Works 1863–1928.* Kuwait: University of Kuwait Academic Publication Council.

Al-Hashimi, Said Sultan. 2015. *'Umān: al-Insān wal Sulta.* Beirut: Centre for the Studies on the Arab Union.

Al-Hibri, Tayeb. 2010. *Parable and Politics in Early Islamic History: The Rashidun Caliphs.* New York: Columbia University Press.

Al-Izkawi, Sheikh Sirhan bin Said. 2006. *Kashf al-Ghumma: al-jāmaʿ li akhbār al-umma*. Beirut: Dar al Bārudi.

Al-Jāludi, ʾAlyān. 2003. "Al-Siyar al-ʾUmaniya Maṣdaran li Tārikh ʾUman." In *ʿAmāl al-multaqa al-ʾilmi al-thani hawla maṣādar at-tarīkh al-ʾumāni* [Proceedings of the second scholarly symposium on Omani historical sources], edited by Hasan al-Malakh and Ibrahim Bahaz, 15–55. Amman, Jordan: University of Al Bayt.

Al-Jāmiʿī, Abdul Hamid. 2003. *Al-Kafaʾa wal Mashrūʿ al-Ilhī fī al-ʿalam* [Kafaʾa and God's plan in the world]. Beirut: Al-Fikr Al-ʾArabi.

Al-Jarallah, Ahmad. 2006. "His Majesty the Sultan in a Wide-Ranging Interview to Kuwait's *Al Siyassa Daily*." http://www.chamberoman.com/pdf/alghorfa_jan_feb06 /special_interview.pdf.

Al-Khabori Al-Lawati, Jawad. 2001. *Al-Adwār al-ʿUmaniyya fil-Qarra al-Hindīyya: Dawr Banī Sāma b. Luʿay* [The role of the Omani in the Indian subcontinent]. Beirut: Dar al-Nubalā.

Al-Khaḍuri, Salem Muhammad Khamis. 2004. *At-Tanimīya wat Tahdith fī al-mujtamaʿ al-ʿumani al-muʿāṣar* [Growth and modernization in contemporary Omani society]. Alexandria, Egypt: Dar al-Maʿrifa al-Jāmʿīya.

Al-Kharusi, Harith. 2012. "Qubūr al-Qabīla al-Lawātiya fi Wilāyat al-Rustāq." Unpublished paper.

Al-Lawati, Ali. 2003. "Kutub al-Ansāb wa al-Siyar al-ʾUmāni baina al-Fiqh wal Tārikh." In *ʿAmāl al-multaqa al-ʿilmi al-thani hawla maṣādar at-tarīkh al-ʿumāni* [Proceedings of the second scholarly symposium on Omani historical sources], edited by Hasan al-Malakh and Ibrahim Bahaz, 99–107. Amman, Jordan: University of Al Bayt.

Al-Lawati, Malallah bin Ali bin Habib. 1984. *Outline of the History of Oman: Supplement of UNESCO's Silk Road Project*. Muscat: Mazoon Printing.

Al-Lawati, Mohsin bin Jumʿa bin Muhammad. 2010. *Sur al-Lawāti*. Beirut: Dar al Mahaja.

Al-Lawati, Mustafa bin Mukhtar. 2016. *Tijāribī ṭai Az-Zaman: Sirat Dhātiya maʿa akhbār Az-Zamān*. Muscat: al-Ruʿyā.

Al-Malakh, Hassan, and Ibrahim Bahaz, eds. 2002. *ʿAmal al-Multaqa al-ʿIlmi al-Awwal hawla maṣādar at-tarīkh al-ʿumāni* [Proceedings of the first scholarly symposium on Omani historical sources]. Amman, Jordan: University of Al Bayt.

———. 2003. *ʿAmāl al-multaqa al-ʿilmi al-thani hawla maṣādar at-tarīkh al-ʿumāni* [Proceedings of the second scholarly symposium on Omani historical sources]. Amman, Jordan: University of Al Bayt.

Al-Maamiry, Ahmed Hamoud. 1980. *Oman and Ibadhism*. New Delhi: Lancers Books.

Al-Maʿmari, Saif bin Nassar. 2016. *Al-Muwāṭina fī ʿUmān: Huwīya wa Qiyam wa Taḥaddiyāt* [Citizenship in Oman: identity, values, and challenges]. Muscat, Oman: Dār al-Warāq.

Al-Masruri, Muhammad bin Hamad bin Ali. 2014. *Majālis al-ʿamma wa daurha fī taʿzīz qiyam*. Muscat, Oman: State Council.

Al-Moosavi, Jamal. 2016. *The National Museum Sultanate of Oman: Highlights*. London: Scala Arts.

Al-Nakib, Farah. 2016. *Kuwait Transformed: A History of Oil and Urban Life*. Stanford, CA: Stanford University Press.

Al-Quḍāt, Muhammad Ahmad Hassan. 2011. "The Problems which Marriage Confronts in the Sultanate of Oman and Its Educational Effects: A Civic Study." *Al-Kalima: Monthly Journal* 47 (March): 33–60.

Al-Rasheed, Madawi, and Robert Vitalis, eds. 2004. *Counter Narratives: History, Contemporary Society and Politics in Saudi Arabia and Yemen*. New York: Palgrave Macmillan.

Al-Saifi, Muhammad bin Abdullah bin Said bin Nasser. 2008. *Al-Namīr: Hikāyāt wal Riwāyāt*, vol. 3. Muscat, Oman; Maktaba wa Tajīlāt Ghhāyat al-Murad.
——. 2015. *Al-Salwa: fi Tarikh Nizwa*. 6 vols. Muscat, Oman: Ministry of Heritage and Culture.
Al-Saleh, Baqer bin Muhammad. 2015. *Sur al-Lawatiya fi Matrah*. Muscat, Oman.
Al-Salimi, Abdulrahman S. 2010. "Identifying the Omani Siyar." *Journal of Semitic Studies* 55 (1): 115–62.
——. 2012. "Trends in Religious Reform on the Arabian Peninsula." *Hemispheres* 27:161–73.
Al-Salmi, Muhammad ibn Abdullah. 1998. *Nahḍat al-ʿAyān bi ḥurriyat al-ʿuman*. Beirut: Dar al-Jil.
Al-Salmi, Nur al-Din. 1914. *Talqin al- ṣibīyān*. Muscat, Oman: House of Islamic Books.
——. 1961. *Tuḥfat al-Aʿyān bi-Sīrat Ahl ʿUman*. 2 vols. Cairo: Dar al Kitab al-ʿArabi.
——. 1989. *Jawhar al-Nizam*. Muscat, Oman: Ministry of National Heritage and Culture.
Al-Shukaili, Ibrahim bin Muhammad bin Hāmad. 2013. *Madrasat al-Imam: Muhammad bin ʿAbd Allah al-Khalili*. Muscat, Oman: Ministry of Endowments and Religious Affairs.
Aal-Tuwaiya, Salem. 2007. "An Entry into Racial Discrimination in Oman," report submitted to social media forum. http://www.farrq.net/forums/showthread.php?t=137.
al-Yahmadi, Nasir. 2011. "How Do We Harmonize Our Heritage with the Spirit of the Age?" *Oman Daily Newspaper* (Arabic), March 9, 2011.
Ahmad, Attiya. 2017. *Everyday Conversions: Islam, Domestic Work, and South Asian Migrant Workers in Kuwait*. Durham, NC: Duke University Press.
Alpers, Edward A. 2000. "Recollecting Africa: Diasporic Memory in the Indian Ocean World." *African Studies Review* 43 (1): 83–99.
Alpers, Svetlana. 1991. "The Museum as a Way of Seeing." In *Exhibiting Cultures: The Poetics and Politics of Museum Display*, edited by Ivan Karp and Steven D. Lavine, 25–33. Washington, DC: Smithsonian Institution.
Ames, Michael. 1986. *Museums, the Public, and Anthropology: A Study in the Anthropology of Anthropology*. Vancouver: University of British Columbia Press.
——. 1995. *Cannibal Tours and Glass Boxes: The Anthropology of Museums*. Vancouver: University of British Columbia Press.
Anderson, Benedict. 1991. *Imagined Communities*. Princeton, NJ: Princeton University Press.
Anthony, John Duke. 1976. *Historical and Cultural Dictionary of the Sultanate of Oman and the Emirates of Eastern Arabia*. Metuchen, NJ: Scarecrow.
Appadurai, Arjun, ed. 1986. *The Social Life of Things: Commodities in Cultural Perspective*. Cambridge: Cambridge University Press.
——, ed. 1988. *The Social Life of Things: Commodities in Cultural Perspective*. Cambridge: Cambridge University Press.
Appadurai, Arjun, and Carole A. Breckenridge. 1992. "Museums Are Good to Think: Heritage on View in India." In *Museums and Communities: The Politics of Public Culture*, edited by Ivan Karp, Christine Mullen Kreamer, and Steven Levine, 34–55. Washington, DC: Smithsonian Institution.
Arendt, Hannah. 1961. *Between Past and Present*. London: Penguin Books.
Arkoun, Mohammed. 1990. "The Meaning of Cultural Conservation in Muslim Societies." In *Architectural and Urban Conservation in the Islamic World*, edited by Abu H. Imamuddin and Karen R. Longeteig, 25–33. Geneva: Aga Khan Trust for Culture.
Asad, Talal. 1973. "Two European Images of Non-European Rule." *Economy and Society* 2 (3): 263–77.
——. 1986. *The Idea of Anthropology of Islam*. Occasional Paper Series. Washington, DC: Georgetown University Press for Contemporary Arab Studies.

———. 1992. "Conscripts of Western Civilization." In *Dialectical Anthropology: Essays in Honour of Stanley Diamond*. Vol. 1, *Civilization in Crisis: Anthropological Perspectives*, edited by Christine Ward Galley, 333–51. Tallahassee: University of Florida Press.

———. 1993. *Genealogies of Religion: Discipline and Reasons of Power in Christianity and Islam*. Baltimore: Johns Hopkins University Press.

———. 2003. *Formations of the Secular: Christianity, Islam, Modernity*. Stanford, CA: Stanford University Press.

Asani, Ali. 1995. *Celebrating Muhammad: Images of the Prophet in Popular Muslim Poetry*. Columbia: University of South Carolina Press.

———. 2011. "From Satpanthi to Ismaili Muslim: The Articulation of Ismaili Khoja Identity in South Asia." In *A Modern History of the Ismailis: Continuity and Change in a Muslim Community*, edited by Farhad Daftary, 95–129. London: I. B. Tauris.

Athamina, Khalil. 1992. "Al-Qasas: Its Emergence, Religious Origin and its Socio-Political Impact on Early Muslim Society." *Studia Islamica* 76:53–74.

Bailey, Ronald W., ed., 1988. *Records of Oman, 1867–1947*. 7 vols. Farnham Common, UK: Archive Editions.

———, ed. 1992. *Records of Oman, 1867–1960*. 12 vols. Cambridge: Cambridge University Press, Archive Editions.

Barringer, Tim, and Tom Flynn, eds. 1988. *Colonialism and the Object: Material Culture and the Museum*. London: Routledge.

Barth, Fredrik. 1983. *Sohar: Culture and Society in an Omani Town*. Baltimore: Johns Hopkins University.

Bartle Frere, Henry. 1876. "The Khojas: The Disciples of the Old Man of the Mountain," part 1 and 2. *Macmillan's Magazine* 34 (May/October): 342–50, 430–38.

Bauman, Richard, and Charles Briggs. 2003. *Voices of Modernity: Language Ideologies and the Politics of Inequality*. Cambridge: Cambridge University Press.

Bendix, Regina F., Aditya Eggert, and Arnika Peselmann. 2012. *Heritage Regimes and the State: Göttingen Studies in Cultural Property* vol. 6. Göttingen: University of Göttingen.

Benjamin, Walter. 1968. "The Work of Art in the Age of Mechanical Reproduction." In *Illuminations*, edited by Hannah Arendt, 217–253. London: Fontana.

———, ed. 1989. *The Problems of Modernity*. London: Routledge.

Bennett, Tony. 1995. *The Birth of the Museum: History, Theory, Politics*. London: Routledge.

———. 2006. "Exhibition, Difference and the Logic of Culture." In *Museum Frictions: Public Cultures/Global Transformations*, edited by Ivan Karp, Corinne A. Kratz, Lynn Szwaja, and Tomas Ybarra-Frausto, 46–70. Durham, NC: Duke University Press.

Bergson, Henri. 1990. *Matter and Memory*. London: Zone Books.

Berkey, Jonathan B. 1992. *The Transmission of Knowledge in Medieval Cairo: A Social History of Islamic Education*. Princeton, NJ: Princeton University Press.

———. 2001. *Popular Preaching and Religious Authority in the Medieval Middle East*. Seattle: University of Washington Press.

Bernhardsson, Magnus T. 2005. *Reclaiming a Plundered Past: Archaeology and Nation Building in Modern Iraq*. Austin: University of Texas Press.

Betts, Paul, and Corey Ross. 2015. *Heritage in the Modern World: Historical Preservation in Global Perspective*. Oxford: Oxford University Press.

Bhaba, Homi. 1990. "DessemiNation: Time, Narrative and the Margins of the Modern Nation." In *Nation and Narration*, edited by H. Bhabha, 291–322. London: Routledge.

———. 1996. *The Location of Culture*. New York: Routledge.

Bhacker, Redha. 1992. *Trade and Empire in Muscat and Zanzibar: Roots of British Domination*. London: Routledge.

Bissell, William Cunningham. 2005. "Engaging Colonial Nostalgia." *Cultural Anthropology* 20 (2): 215–48.

Blyth, Robert J. 2003. *The Empire of the Raj: India, Eastern Africa and the Middle East, 1858–1947*. London: Palgrave-Macmillan.

Boddy, Janice. 2007. *Civilizing Women: British Crusades in Colonial Sudan*. Princeton, NJ: Princeton University Press.

Boyarin, Jonathan, and Charles Tilly. 1994. *Remapping Memory: The Politics of Time/Space*. Minneapolis: University of Minnesota Press.

Boym, Svetlana. 2001. *The Future of Nostalgia*. New York: Basic Books.

Breckenridge, Carol. 1989. "The Aesthetics and Politics of Colonial Collecting: India at World Fairs." *Comparative Studies in Society and History* 31 (2): 195–216.

Briggs, Charles L. 1996. "The Politics of Discursive Authority in Research on the Invention of Tradition." *Cultural Anthropology* 11 (4): 435–69.

British Foreign Office.1987. *Persian Gulf Historical Summaries 1907–1953*, 4 vols. Cambridge: Archive Editions.

Broucek, James. 2018. "Generic Islam? Official Religious Discourse in the Sultanate of Oman." In *Oman, Ibadism and Modernity*, edited by Abdul Rahman al-Salimi and Reinhard Eisener, 325–36. New York: Georg Olms Verlag.

Brown, Daniel 1996. *Rethinking Tradition in Modern Islamic Thought*. Cambridge: Cambridge University Press.

Brown, Wendy. 2001. *Politics out of History*. Princeton, NJ: Princeton University Press.

———. 2006. *Regulating Aversion: Tolerance in the Age of Identity and Empire*. Princeton, NJ: Princeton University Press.

Butler, Beverly. 2003. "Egyptianizing the Alexandrina: The Contemporary Revival of the Ancient Mouseion/Library." In *Imotep Today: Egyptianizing Architecture*, edited by C. Price and J. M. Humbert, 257–302. London: UCL Press.

Butler, Judith. 1993. *Bodies that Matter: On the Discursive Limits of "Sex."* New York: Routledge.

Cabinet of the Deputy Prime Minister. 2008. *Forts and Castles of Oman*. Muscat, Oman: Council of Ministers.

Cain, P. J., and Anthony G. Hopkins. 1993. *British Imperialism: Innovation and Expansion*. London: Longman.

Calasso, Giovanna. 1994. "Universal History, Local History, National History, Recent Theoretical and Methodological Contributions on Islamic Historiography." In *Proceedings of International Conference, 23–27 November 1992: The East and the Meaning of History, Studi Orientali, vol. XIII*, 199–219. Rome: Bardi Etitore.

Campbell, Colin. "Detraditionalization: Character and the Limits to Agency." In *Detraditionalization*, edited by Paul Heela, Scott Lash, and Paul Morris, 149–71. Oxford: Blackwell.

Carapico, Sheila. 2004. "Arabia Incognito: An Invitation to Arabian Peninsula Studies." In *Counter-Narratives: History, Contemporary Society and Politics in Saudi Arabia and Yemen*, edited by Madawi al-Rasheed and Robert Vitalis, 11–33. New York: Palgrave Macmillan.

Carruthers, Mary. 1990. *The Book of Memory: A Study of Memory in Medieval Culture*. Cambridge: Cambridge University Press.

Carter, J. R. L. 1982. *Tribes in Oman*. London: Peninsular.

Carvounas, David. 2002. *Diverging Time: The Politics of Modernity in Kant, Hegel and Marx*. New York: Lexington Books.

Chakrabarty, Dipesh. 1992. "The Death of History? Historical Consciousness and the Culture of Late Capitalism." *Public Culture* 4 (2): 47–65.

——. 1997. "The Time of History and the Times of Gods." In *The Politics of Culture in the Shadow of Capital*, edited by Lisa Lowe and David Lloyd, 35–60. Durham, NC: Duke University Press.

——. 2000. *Provincializing Europe: Postcolonial Thought and Historical Difference*. Princeton, NJ: Princeton University Press.

Chamberlain, Michael. 1994. *Knowledge and Social Practice in Medieval Damascus, 1190–1350*. Cambridge: Cambridge University Press.

Chatterjee, Partha. 1986. *Nationalist Thought and the Colonial World: A Derivative Discourse*. Minneapolis: University of Minnesota Press.

——. 1993. *The Nation and Its Fragments: Colonial and Postcolonial Histories*. Princeton, NJ: Princeton University Press.

——. 1998. "Secularism and Toleration." In *Secularism and Its Critics*, edited by Rajeev Bhargava, 345–79. New Delhi: Oxford University Press.

Chatty, Dawn. 1996. *Mobile Pastoralists: Development Planning and Change in the Sultanate of Oman*. New York: Columbia University Press.

——. 2009. "Rituals of Royalty and the Elaboration of Ceremony in Oman: View from the Edge." *International Journal of Middle East Studies* 41:39–58.

Cheah, Peng. 2003. *Spectral Nationality: Passages of Freedom from Kant to Postcolonial Literatures of Liberation*. New York: Columbia University Press.

Cheah, Peng, and Bruce, Robbins, eds. 1998. *Cosmopolitics: Thinking and Feeling beyond the Nation*. Minneapolis: University of Minnesota Press.

Choay, Francoise. 2001. *The Invention of the Historic Monument*. New York: Cambridge University Press.

Choueiri, Youssef M. 2003. *Modern Arab Historiography: Historical Discourse and the Nation-State*. London: Routledge Curzon.

Cinar, Alev. 2001. "National History as a Contested Site: The Conquest of Istanbul and Islamist Negotiations of the Nation." *Comparative Studies in Society and History* 43 (2): 364–91.

Clarence-Smith, William G. 2006. *Islam and the Abolition of Slavery*. Oxford: Oxford University Press.

——. 2008. "Islamic Abolitionism in the Western Indian Ocean c. 1800." Paper presented at the Slavery and the Slave Trades in the Indian Ocean and Arab Worlds: Global Connections and Disconnections conference, Yale University, November 7–8, 2008. http://www.yale.edu/glc/indian-ocean/hopper.pdf.

Cleere, H. 1996. "Uneasy Bedfellows: Universality and Cultural Heritage." In *Destruction and Conservation of Cultural Property*, edited by P. Stone and J. Thomas, 22–29. London: Routledge.

Clements, F. A. 1980. *Oman, the Reborn Land*. London: Longman.

Clifford, James. 1988. *The Predicament of Culture: Twentieth Century Ethnography, Literature and Art*. Cambridge, MA: Harvard University Press.

Cohn, Bernard. 1987. *An Anthropologist among the Historians and Other Essays*. Oxford: Oxford University Press.

——. 1996. *Colonialism and Its Forms of Knowledge: The British in India*. Princeton, NJ: Princeton University Press.

Cole, Jennifer. 2001. *Forget Colonialism? Sacrifice and the Art of Memory in Madagascar*. Berkeley: University of California Press.

Colla, Elliott. 2007. *Conflicted Antiquities: Egyptology, Egyptomania, Egyptian Modernity*. Durham, NC: Duke University Press.

Connerton, Paul. 2003. *How Societies Remember*. Cambridge: Cambridge University Press.

Coombes, Annie E. 2003. *History after Apartheid: Visual Culture and Public Memory in a Democratic South Africa*. Durham, NC: Duke University Press.

Cook, Michael. 2000. *Commanding Right and Forbidding Wrong in Islamic Thought*. Cambridge: Cambridge University Press.

Cooke, Miriam. 2014. *Tribal Modern: Branding New Nations in the Arab Gulf*. Berkeley: University of California Press.

Coppola, Anna Rita. 2017. "Omani Historiography between Tradition and Modernity: Nūr al-Dīn al-Sālimī and his Tuḥfa." In *Today's Perspectives on Ibadi History*, edited by Reinhard Eisener, 293–309. Hildesheim, Germany: Georg Olms Verlag.

Crone, Patricia. 2004. *God's Rule: Government and Islam*. New York: Columbia University Press.

Crary, Jonathan. 1990. *Techniques of the Observer: On Vision and Modernity in the Nineteenth Century*. Cambridge, MA: MIT Press.

———. 2001. *Suspensions of Perception: Attention, Spectacle and Modern Culture*. Cambridge, MA: MIT Press.

Damluji, Salma, ed. 1998. *The Architecture of Oman*. Reading, UK: Ithaca.

Darlow, Michael, and Richard Fawkes. 1976. *The Last Corner of Arabia*. London: Namara.

Das, Veena. 2007. *Life and Words: Violence and the Descent into the Ordinary*. Berkeley: University of California Press.

———. 2015. "What Does Ordinary Ethics Look Like?" In *Four Lectures on Ethics: Anthropological Perspectives*, by Michael Lambek, Veena Das, Didier Fassin, and Webb Keane, 53–127 Chicago: Hau Books.

Davis, Eric, and Nicolas Gavrielides, eds. 1991. *Statecraft in the Middle East: Oil, Historical Memory and Popular Culture*. Miami: Florida International University Press.

Davis, Kathleen. 2008. *Periodization and Sovereignty: How Ideas of Feudalism and Secularization Govern the Politics of Time*. Philadelphia: University of Pennsylvania Press.

Davis, N. Z., and Starn, R. 1989. "Introduction," in "Memory and Counter Memory." Special issue, *Representations* 26:1–6.

De Certeau, Michel. 1988. *Writing of History*. New York: Columbia University Press.

———. 2011. *The Practice of Everyday Life*. Berkeley: University of California Press.

De Cesari, Chiara. 2019. *Heritage and the Cultural Struggle for Palestine*. Stanford: Stanford University Press.

Deeb, Lara. 2006. *An Enchanted Modern: Gender and Public Piety in Shi'i Lebanon*. Princeton, NJ: Princeton University Press.

D'Errico, Enrico. 1998. "Old Muscat and Its Fortifications." In *The Architecture of Oman*, edited by Salma Samar Damluji, 140–47. Reading, UK: Ithaca.

De Jong, Ferdinand, and Michael Rowlands, eds. 2007. *Reclaiming Heritage: Alternative Imaginaries of Memory in West Africa*. Walnut Creek, CA: Left Coast.

Deleuze, Gilles, and Felix Guattari. 1977. "Signature Event Context." *Glyph* 1:172–97.

———. 1980. *A Thousand Plateaus*. London: Continuum.

Derrida, Jacques. 2002. *Ethics, Institutions and the Right to Philosophy*. Translated by P. Pericles Trifonas. New York: Rowman & Littlefield.

Dinteman, Walter. 1993. *Forts of Oman*. London: Motivate.

Dirks, Nicholas. 1990. "History as a Sign of the Modern." *Public Culture* 2 (2): 25–32.

Dorr, Marcia, and Neil Richardson. 2005. *Craft Heritage of Oman*. 2 vols. London: Motivate.

Dreyfus, Hubert L., and Paul Rabinow. 1982. *Michel Foucault: Beyond Structuralism and Hermenutics*. Chicago: University of Chicago Press.

Dudley, Sandra. 2009. *Museum Materialities*. London: Routledge.

Duncan, Carol. 1995. *Civilising Rituals inside Public Art Museums*. London: Routledge.

Eickelman, Dale. 1978. "The Art of Memory: Islamic Education and Its Social Reproduction." *Comparative Studies in Society and History* 20:485–516.

———. 1985. *Knowledge and Power in Morocco*. Princeton, NJ: Princeton University Press.

———. 1987. "Ibadism and the Sectarian Perspective." In *Oman: Economic, Social and Strategic Developments*, edited by B. R. Pridham, 31–50. London: Croon Helm.

———. 1989. "National Identity and Religious Discourse in Contemporary Oman." *International Journal of Islamic and Arabic Studies* 6 (1): 1–20.

———. 1992. "Mass Higher Education and the Religious Imagination in Contemporary Arab Societies." *American Ethnologist* 19 (4): 643–55.

Eickelman, Dale, and James Piscatori. 1996. *Muslim Politics*. Princeton, NJ: Princeton University Press.

Eisener, Reinhard, ed. 2017. *Today's Perspectives on Ibadi History*. New York: Georg Olms Verlag.

Eisenstadt, Shmuel Noah. 1973. *Tradition, Change and Modernity*. New York: Wiley.

El-Amrousi, Mohammed, and John Biln. 2010. "Muscat Emerging: Tourism and Cultural Space." *Journal of Tourism and Cultural Change* 8 (4): 254–66.

Ennami, Amr Khlifa. 1972. *Studies in Ibadhism*. Tripoli: University of Libya Press.

Erskine-Loftus, Pamela, Mariam Ibrahim Al-Mulla, and Victoria Hightower. 2016. *Representing the Nation: Heritage, Museums, National Narratives and Identity in the Arab Gulf States*. London: Routledge.

Exell, Karen. 2016. *Modernity and the Museum in the Arabian Peninsula*. London: Routledge.

Exell, Karen, and Sarina Wakefield, eds. 2016. *Museums in Arabia: Transnational Practices and Regional Processes*. London: Routledge.

Fabian, Johannes. 2014. *Time and the Other: How Anthropology Makes Its Object*. New York: Columbia University Press.

Facey, William. 1979. *Oman: A Seafaring Nation*. Sultanate of Oman: Ministry of National Heritage and Culture.

Forty, Adrian, and Susanne Küchler, eds. 2001. *The Art of Forgetting*. London: Bloomsbury Academic.

Freamon, Bernard K. 2008. "Straight, No Chaser: Slavery, Abolition and the Modern Muslim Mind." Paper presented at the Slavery and the Slave Trades in the Indian Ocean and Arab Worlds: Global Connections and Disconnections conference, Yale University, November 7–8, 2008. http://www.yale.edu/glc/indian-ocean/hopper.pdf.

Frei, Hans W. 1974. *The Eclipse of Biblical Narrative: A Study in Eighteenth and Nineteenth Century Hermeneutics*. New Haven, CT: Yale University Press.

Fritzche, Peter. 2004. *Stranded in the Present: Modern Time and the Melancholy of History*. Cambridge, MA: Harvard University Press.

Forster, Kurt W. and Diane Ghirardo. "The Modern Cult of Monuments: Its Character and Its Origins." *Oppositions* 25:21–51.

Fortier, Anne-Marie. 1999. "Re-Membering Places and the Performance of Belonging(s)." *Theory, Culture and Society* 16 (2): 41–64.

Foucault, Michel. 1977. *Discipline and Punish: The Birth of the Prison*. Translated by Alan Sheridan. New York: Pantheon.

———. 1991. "Politics and the Study of Discourse." In *The Foucault Effect: Studies in Governmentality*, edited by G. Burchell, C. Gordon, and P. Miller, 53–72. Chicago: University of Chicago Press.

Fowle, Major T. C. 1932. Report regarding abdication plan of Sayyid Taimur bin Faisal (1913–1932), written by British Consul and Political Agent, Major T.C. Fowle, December 28, 1929–June 6, 1932. London: British Library, India Office Records.

Fox, John W., Nada Mourtada Sabbah, and Mohammed Al Mutawa, eds. 2006. *Globaliza-tion and the Gulf*. London: Routledge.

Fromherz, Allen J. 2012. *Qatar: A Modern History*. Washington, DC: Georgetown University Press.

Gaube, Heinz, Abdulrahman al-Salmi, and Lorenz Korn, eds. 2008. *Islamic Art in Oman*. Muscat, Oman: Al Roya.

Gaiser, Adam R. 2010. *Muslims, Scholars, Soldiers: The Origin and Elaboration of the Ibadi Imamate Traditions*. Oxford: Oxford University Press.

Geismar, Haidy. 2015. "Anthropology and Heritage Regimes." *Annual Review of Anthropology* 44: 71–85.

Gordin, Michael D., Helen Tilley, and Gyan Prakash, eds. 2010. *Utopia/Dystopia: Conditions of Historical Possibility*. Princeton, NJ: Princeton University Press.

General Directorate for Handicrafts. 2009. *Omani Crafts: Documentary Study*. Muscat, Oman: General Directorate for Handicrafts.

Ghazal, Amal. 2010. "Debating Slavery and Abolition in the Arab Middle East." In *Slavery, Islam and Diaspora*. Edited by Behnaz A. Marzai, Ismael Musa Montana and Paul E. Lovejoy. Trenton, NJ: Africa World Press.

———. 2010. *Islamic Reform and Arab Nationalism: Expanding the Crescent from the Mediterranean to the Indian Ocean (1880s–1930s)*. London: Routledge.

Ghubash, Hussain. 2006. *Oman—the Islamic Democratic Tradition*. Translated by Mary Turton. London: Routledge.

Gilsenan, Michael. 1982. *Recognizing Islam: Religion and Society in the Modern Arab World*. New York: Pantheon Books.

Glassman, Jonathan. 2010. "Racial Violence, Universal History and Echoes of Abolition in Twentieth Century Zanzibar." In *Abolitionism and Imperialism in Britain, Africa and the Atlantic*, edited by Derek R. Peterson, 175–206. Athens: Ohio University Press.

Gledhill, John. 2000. *Power and Its Disguises: Anthropological Perspectives on Politics*. London: Pluto.

Graz, Liesl. 1982. *The Omanis: Sentinels of the Gulf*. London: Longman.

Green, Nile. 2011. *Bombay Islam: The Religious Economy of the West Indian Ocean, 1840–1915*. Cambridge: Cambridge University Press.

Hacking, Ian. 1995. *Rewriting the Soul: Multiple Personality and the Sciences of Memory*. Princeton, NJ: Princeton University Press.

———. 2002. *Historical Ontology*. Cambridge, MA: Harvard University Press.

Hagerman, Christopher A. 2009. "In the Footsteps of the Macedonian Conqueror: Alexander the Great and British India." *International Journal of the Classical Tradition* 16 (3/4): 344–92.

Halbwachs, M. (1950) 1992. *On Collective Memory*. Chicago: Chicago University Press.

Hallam, Elizabeth, and Brian Street. 2000. *Cultural Encounters: Representing Otherness*. London: Routledge.

Hall, S. 2003. "Whose Heritage? Unsettling the Heritage." *Third Text* 49:1–12.

Hamilton, Alaistair. 2010. *An Arabian Utopia: The Western Discovery of Oman*. London: Arcadian Library in Association with Oxford University Press.

Hansen, Thomas Blom, and Finn Stepputat, eds. 2001. *States of Imagination: Ethnographic Explorations of the Postcolonial State*. Durham, NC: Duke University Press.

Harootunian, Harry D. "The Benjamin Effect: Modernism, Repetition and the Path to Different Cultural Imaginaries." In *Walter Benjamin and the Demands of History*, edited by Michael P. Steinberg, 62–88. Ithaca, NY: Cornell University Press.

Harrison, David, and Michael Hitchcock, eds. 2005. *The Politics of World Heritage: Negotiating Tourism and Conservation*. Clevedon, UK: Channel View.

Harrison, Paul Wilberforce. 1940. *Doctor in Arabia.* New York: Robert Hale.

Harrison, Rodney. 2013. *Heritage: Critical Approaches.* London: Routledge.

Hartog, François. 2003. *Regimes of Historicity: Presentism and Experiences of Time.* New York: Columbia University Press.

Hawley, Donald. 1977. *Oman and Its Renaissance.* London: Stacey International.

Healy, Abigail. 2018. "On Our Rador: Nizwa, Oman's Ancient Capital." *TTG Media,* February 7, 2018. https://www.ttgmedia.com/news/features/on-our-radar-nizwa -omans-ancient-capital-13140.

Healy, Chris. 1997. *From the Ruins of Colonialism: History as Social Memory.* Cambridge: Cambridge University Press.

Heelas, Paul, Scott Lash, and Paul Morris, eds. 1996. *Detraditionalization.* Oxford: Blackwell.

Hegazy, Soheir M. 2015. "Cultural Sustainability between Tradition and Contemporary Omani Residences—a Comparative Case Study." *European Journal of Sustainable Development* 4 (2): 185–204.

Heidegger, Martin. 1977. *The Question Concerning Technology and Other Essays.* New York and London: Garland.

——. 2010. "The Omani Architectural Heritage: Identity and Continuity." In *Heritage 2010: Heritage and Sustainable Development,* 2 vols., edited by Rogèrio Amoêda, Sèrgio Lira, and Cristina Pinheiro, 1341–1351. Lisbon: Green Lines Institute.

Held, David, and Kristian Ulrichsen, eds. 2012. *The Transformation of the Gulf: Politics, Economies and the Global Order.* London: Routledge.

Herzfeld, Michael. 1986. *Ours Once More: Folklore, Ideology and the Making of Modern Greece.* New York: Pella.

——. 1991. *A Place in History: Social and Monumental Time in a Cretan Town.* Princeton, NJ: Princeton University Press.

——. 2004. *The Body Impolitic: Artisans and Artifice in the Global Hierarchy of Value.* Chicago: University of Chicago Press.

Hirschkind, Charles. 1991. "Egypt at the Exhibition: Reflections on the Optics of Colonialism." *Critique of Anthropology* 11 (3): 279–98.

——. 1996. "Heresy or Hermeneutics: The Case of Nasr Hamid Abu Zayd." *Stanford Humanities Review* 5 (1): 35–49.

——. 1997a. "Conceptual Challenges to Understanding Islamic Movements: Questions in Tradition, History and Modernity." Unpublished manuscript., Department of Anthropology, University of California, Berkeley.

——. 1997b. "What Is Political Islam?" *Middle East Research and Information Project* 27 (4): 12–15.

——. 2001a. "The Ethics of Listening: Cassette-Sermon Audition in Contemporary Egypt." *American Ethnologist* 28 (3): 623–49.

——. 2001b. "Tradition, Myth and Historical Fact in Contemporary Islam." *ISIM Newsletter* 8: 18–18.

——. 2006. *The Ethical Soundscape: Cassette Sermons and Islamic Counterpublics.* New York: Columbia University Press.

Hirschkind, Charles, and David Scott, eds. 2006. *Powers of the Secular Modern: Talal Asad and his Interlocuters.* Stanford, CA: Stanford University Press.

Ho, Enseng. 2006. *The Graves of Tarim: Genealogy and Mobility across the Indian Ocean.* Berkeley: University of California Press.

Hobsbawm, Eric, and Terence Ranger, eds. 1983. *The Invention of Tradition.* Cambridge: Cambridge University Press.

Hoffman, Valerie. 2004. "The Articulation of Ibadi Identity in Modern Oman and Zanzibar." *Muslim World* 94 (2): 201–16.

——. 2012. *The Essentials of Ibadi Islam.* Syracuse, NY: Syracuse University Press.

Hoggart, Richard. 1978. *An Idea and Its Servants: UNESCO from Within*. London: Chatto & Windus.

Hollywood, Amy. 2002. "Performativity, Citationality, Ritualization." *History of Religions* 42 (2): 93–115.

Hopper, Matthew S. 2008. "Slaves of One Master: Globalization and the African Diaspora in Arabia in the Age of Empire." Paper presented at the Slavery and the Slave Trades in the Indian Ocean and Arab Worlds: Global Connections and Disconnections conference, Yale University, November 7–8, 2008. http://www.yale.edu/glc/indian-ocean /hopper.pdf.

——. 2015. *Slaves of One Master: Globalization and Slavery in Arabia in the Age of Empire*. New Haven, CT: Yale University Press.

Hopwood, Derek, ed. 1972. *The Arabian Peninsula: Society and Politics*. London: George Allen and Unwin.

Horne, Donald. 1984. *The Great Museum: The Re-presentation of History*. London: Pluto.

Humble, Kate. 2015. "Humble Oman" *Independent* (London), May 13, 2015.

Hylland-Ericksen, T. 2001. "Between Universalism and Relativism: A Critique of the UNESCO Concept of Culture." In *Culture and Rights*, edited by J. Lowen, M. B. Dember, and R. Wilson, 127–148 Cambridge: Cambridge University Press.

Ivy, Marilyn. 1995. *Discourses of the Vanishing: Modernity, Phantasm, Japan*. Chicago: University of Chicago Press.

Jeong, Hae Wong. 2016. "National Identity and Performativity at Bahrain National Museum." In *Representing the Nation: Heritage, Museums, National Narratives and Identity in the Arab Gulf States*, edited by Pamela Erskine-Loftus, Victoria Penziner Hightower, and Mariam Ibrahim al-Mulla, 162–175. London: Routledge.

Johansen, Baber. 1999. *Contingency in a Sacred Law: Legal and Ethical Norms in the Muslim Fiqh*. Leiden, Netherlands: Brill.

Johnson, N. 1995. "Cast in Stone: Monuments, Geography and Nationalism." *Society and Space* 13 (1): 51–65.

Jokilehto, Jukka. 1999. *A History of Architectural Conservation*. Amsterdam: Elsevier.

Jones, Calvert. 2017. *Bedouins into Bourgeois: Remaking Citizens for Globalization*. Cambridge: Cambridge University Press.

Jones, Jeremy, and Nicholas Ridout. 2015. *A History of Modern Oman*. Cambridge: Cambridge University Press.

Joyce, Miriam. 1995. *The Sultanate of Oman: A Twentieth Century History*. Westport, CT: Praegar.

Jwaidah, Albertine, and Cox, J. W. 1989. "The Black Slaves of Turkish Arabia during the Nineteenth Century." In *The Economics of the Indian Ocean Slave Trade in the Nineteenth Century*, edited by William G. Clarence Smith, 45–59 London: Frank Cass.

Kanna, Ahmed. 2011. *Dubai: The City as Corporation*. Minneapolis: University of Minnesota Press.

Kaplan, Sam. 2006. *Education and the Politics of National Culture in Post-1980 Turkey*. Stanford, CA: Stanford University Press.

Karp, I., and S. D. Lavine, eds. 1991. *Exhibiting Cultures: The Poetics and Politics of Museum Display*. Washington, DC: Smithsonian University Press.

Karp, Ivan, Corinne A. Kratz, Lynn Szwaja, and Tomas Ybarra-Frausto, eds. 2006. *Museum Frictions: Public Cultures / Global Transformations*. Durham, NC: Duke University Press.

Kashani-Sabet, Firoozeh. 1999. *Frontier Fictions: Shaping the Iranian Nation, 1804–1946*. Princeton, NJ: Princeton University Press.

Keane, Webb. 2003. "Semiotics and the Social Analysis of Material Things." *Language and Communication* 23:409–425.

——. 2005. "Signs Are Not the Garb of Meaning: On the Social Analysis of Material Things." In *Materiality*, edited by D. Miller, 182–206. Durham, NC: Duke University Press.

——. 2007. *Christian Moderns: Freedom and Fetish in the Mission Encounter*. Berkeley: University of California Press.

——. 2008. "The Evidence of the Senses and the Materiality of Religion." *Journal of the Royal Anthropological Institute* 14 (s1): s110–27.

——. 2015. "Varieties of Ethical Stance." In Michael Lambek, Veena Das, Didier Fassin, and Webb Keane, *Four Lectures on Ethics: Anthropological Perspectives*, 127–75 Chicago: Hau Books.

———. 2016. *Ethical Life: Its Natural and Social Histories*. Princeton: Princeton University Press.

Kelly, J. 1968. *Britain and the Persian Gulf 1795–1880*. Oxford: Clarendon.

——. 1972. "A Prevalence of Furies: Tribes, Politics and Religion in Oman and Trucial Oman." In *The Arabian Peninsula: Society and Politics*, edited by D. Hopwood, 107–41. London: Allen Unwin.

——. 1976. "Hadrawmaut, Oman, Dhofar: The Experience of Revolution." *Middle East Studies* 12 (2): 213–20.

Ketelaar, James E. 2006. "The Non Modern Confronts the Modern: Dating the Buddha in Japan." *History and Theory* 45 (December): 62–79.

Khalaf, Sulayman. 2000. "Poetics and Politics of Newly Invented Traditions in the Gulf: Camel Racing in the United Arab Emirates." *Ethnology* 39 (3): 243–61.

——. 2002. "Globalization and Heritage Revival in the Gulf: An Anthropological Look at Dubai Heritage Village." *Journal of Social Affairs* 19 (75): 277–306.

——. 2008. "The Nationalisation of Culture: Kuwait's Invention of Pearl Diving Heritage." In *Popular Culture and Political Identity in the Arab Gulf States*, edited by Alanoud Alsharekh and Robert Springborg, 40–71. London: Saqi and London Middle East Institute, SOAS.

Khalidi, Rashid. 1997. *Palestinian Identity: The Construction of National Consciousness*. New York: Columbia University Press.

Khalidi, Tarif. 1994. *Arabic Historical Thought in the Classical Period*. Cambridge: Cambridge University Press.

Kirshenblatt-Gimblett, Barbara. 1998. *Destination Culture: Tourism, Museums, and Heritage*. Berkeley: University of California Press.

——. 2000. "The Museum as Catalyst." Keynote address at Museum 2000: Confirmation on Challenge, Vadstena, Sweden, September 29, 2000..

——. 2004. "From Ethnology to Heritage: The Role of the Museum." SIEF Keynote address at the Eighth Congress of the International Society for Ethnology and Folklore, Marseilles, France, April 26–30, 2004.

——. 2006. "World Heritage and Cultural Economics." In *Museum Frictions: Public Cultures/Global Transformations*, edited by Ivan Karp, Corinne A. Kratz, Lynn Szwaja, and Tomas Ybarra-Frausto, 161–203. Durham, NC: Duke University Press.

Kite, Stephen. 2002. "Aesthetics of Oman's Traditional Architecture." *Journal of Oman Studies* 12:133–55.

Klein, K. L. 1998. "On the Emergence of Memory in Historical Discourse." *Representations* 69:127–50.

Koch, Natalie. 2015. "Gulf Nationalism and the Geopolitics of Constructing Falconry as a 'Heritage Sport.'" *Studies in Ethnicity and Nationalism* 15 (3): 522–37.

Koselleck, Reinhart. 2002. *The Practice of Conceptual History: Timing, History, Spacing Concepts*. Stanford, CA: Stanford University Press.

——. 2004. *Futures Past: On the Semantics of Historical Time*. New York: Columbia University Press.

Kreps, Christina E. 2003. *Liberating Culture: Cross-Cultural Perspectives on Museums, Curation and Heritage Preservation*. London: Routledge.

La Capra, Dominick.1985. *History and Criticism*. Ithaca, NY: Cornell University Press.

Lambek, Michael. 2010. *Ordinary Ethics: Anthropology, Language and Action*. New York: Fordham University Press.

Lamprokos, Michele. 2005. "Rethinking Cultural Heritage: Lessons from Sanaʿa, Yemen." *Traditional Dwellings and Settlements Review* 16 (2): 17–37.

Landen, Robert Geran. 1967. *Oman since 1856: Disruptive Modernization in a Traditional Arab Society*. Princeton, NJ: Princeton University Press.

Latour, Bruno. 1991. *We Have Never Been Modern*. Translated by Catherine Porter. Cambridge, MA: Harvard University Press.

Le Goff, Jacques. 1992. *History and Memory*. New York: Columbia University Press.

Limbert, Mandana. 1999. "Placing Tradition: The Geo-poetics of Town and Country in Oman." *Journal of Mediterranean Studies* 9 (2): 300–318.

———. 2007. "Oman: Cultivating Good Citizens and Religious Virtue." In *Teaching Islam: Textbooks and Religion in the Middle East*, edited by Eleanor Abdella Doumato and Gregory Starrett, 103–24. New York: Lynne Rienner.

———. 2008. "In the Ruins of Bahla: Reconstructed Forts and Crumbling Walls in an Omani Town." *Social Text* 26 (2): 83–103.

———. 2010. *In the Time of Oil: Piety, Memory and Social Life in an Omani Town*. Stanford, CA: Stanford University Press.

Linke, Uli. 1990. "Folklore, Anthropology, and the Government of Social Life." *Comparative Studies in Society and History* 32 (1): 117–48.

———. 2001. "The Senses of Water in an Omani Town." *Social Text* 19 (3): 35–55.

Literary Symposium in Nizwa. 2001. *Nizwa ʾabr at-tarikh* [Nizwa across the ages]. Muscat, Oman: Ministry of Heritage and Culture.

Lockman, Zachary. 2004. *Contending Visions of the Middle East: The History and Politics of Orientalism*. Cambridge: Cambridge University Press.

Longva, Anh Nga. 1997. *Walls Built on Sand: Migration, Exclusion and Society in Kuwait*. Boulder, CO: Westview.

Lorimer, John G. 1915. *Gazetteer of the Persian Gulf, Oman and Central Arabia*. 2 vols. Calcutta, India: Superintendent Government Printing.

Lowenthal, David. 1985. *The Past Is a Foreign Country*. Cambridge: Cambridge University Press.

———. 1996. *Possessed by the Past: The Heritage Crusade and the Spoils of History*. New York: Free Press.

MacCannell, D. (1978) 1989. *The Tourist: A New Theory of the Leisure Class*. London: Macmillan.

MacIntyre, Alasdair. 1984. *After Virtue*. Notre Dame, Indiana: Notre Dame University.

Maclean, Matthew. 2016. "Time, Space and Narrative in Emirati Museums." In *Representing the Nation: Heritage, Museums, National Narratives and Identity in the Arab Gulf States*, edited by Pamela Erskine-Loftus, Victoria Penziner Hightower, and Mariam Ibrahim al-Mulla, 191–205. London: Routledge.

Makdisi, Saree. 1996. *Romantic Imperialism: Universal Empire and the Culture of Modernity*. Cambridge: Cambridge University Press.

Mahmood, Saba. 2005. *Politics of Piety: The Islamic Revival and the Feminist Subject*. Princeton, NJ: Princeton University Press.

———. 2006. "Secularism, Hermeneutics and Empire: The Politics of Islamic Reformation." *Public Culture* 18 (2): 323–347.

———. 2009. "Religion Reason and Secular Affect: An Incommensurable Divide?" In *Is Critique Secular? Blasphemy, Injury and Free Speech*, 64–101. Townsend Papers in the Humanities No. 2. Berkeley, CA: UC Berkeley, Townsend Center for the Humanities.

——. 2012. "Sectarian Conflict and Family Law in Contemporary Egypt." *American Ethnologist* 39 (1): 54–62.

Mamdani, Mahmood. 1996. *Citizen and Subject: Contemporary Africa and the Legacy of Late Colonialism*. Princeton, NJ: Princeton University Press.

Makdisi, Saree. 2014. *Making England Western: Occidentalism, Race and Imperial Culture*. Chicago: University of Chicago Press.

Markovits, Claude. 1999. "Indian Merchant Networks outside India in the Nineteenth and Twentieth Centuries: A Preliminary Survey." *Modern Asian Studies* 33 (4): 883–911.

Massad, Joseph. 2001. *Colonial Effects: The Making of National Identity in Jordan*. New York: Columbia University Press.

Masuzawa, Tomoko. 2005. *The Invention of World Religions*. Chicago: University of Chicago Press.

Matsuda, Matt K. 1996. *The Memory of the Modern*. New York: Oxford University Press.

Maziad, Marwa. 2016. "Qatar: Cultivating 'the Citizen' of the Futuristic State." In *Representing the Nation: Heritage, Museums, National Narratives and Identity in the Arab Gulf States*, edited by Pamela Erskine-Loftus, Victoria Penziner Hightower, and Mariam Ibrahim al-Mulla, 123–41. London: Routledge.

McBrierty, Vincent, and Mohammad Zubair. 2004. *Oman: Ancient Civilisation, Modern Nation; Towards a Knowledge and Service Economy*. Dublin: Trinity College Press; Muscat, Oman: Bait al-Zubair Foundation.

Mehta, Uday. 1999. *Liberalism and Empire: A Study in Nineteenth Century British Liberal Thought*. Chicago: University of Chicago Press.

Meisami, Julie Scott. 1999. *Persian Historiography: To the End of the Twelfth Century*. Edinburgh: Edinburgh University Press.

Messick, Brinkley. 1993. *The Calligraphic State: Textual Domination and History in a Muslim Society*. Berkeley, CA: University of California Press.

Metcalf, Thomas R. 2007. *Imperial Connections: India in the Indian Ocean Arena, 1860–1920*. Berkeley: University of California Press.

Michalski, Sergiusz. 1998. *Public Monuments: Art in Political Bondage, 1870–1997*. London: Reaktion Books.

Miles, S. B. 1901. "Across the Green Mountains of Oman." *Geographical Journal* 18 (5): 465–98.

——. 1910. "On the Border of the Great Desert: A Journey in Oman." *Geographical Journal* 36 (2): 159–178.

Miller, Daniel, ed. 1995. *Worlds Apart: Modernity through the Prism of the Local*. London: Routledge.

Ministry of Education. 2003. *Social Studies Textbook: Fifth Grade*. 2 parts. Muscat, Oman: Ministry of Education.

——. 2006. *Social Studies Textbook Our Country: Eleventh Grade*. Muscat, Oman: Ministry of Education.

——. 2007. *Social Studies Textbook: Seventh Grade*. 2 parts. Muscat, Oman: Ministry of Education.

Ministry of Heritage and Culture. 1990. *Papers Submitted at the International Seminar on the Silk Roads Held at Sultan Qaboos University, Muscat, Sultanate of Oman, 20–21 November 1990*. Muscat: Ministry of Heritage and Culture.

——. 2001. *An-Nadwa al-Thalitha lil Turath al-sh'abi, 24–26 December 2001* [The third symposium for popular heritage, 24–26 December 2001]. Muscat, Oman: Ministry of Heritage and Culture.

——. 2002. *The Omani Museum*. 2nd ed. Sultanate of Oman: Ministry of Heritage and Culture.

——. 2003. *Bahla, Bat and the Frankincense Trade Route in the World Heritage List*. Muscat, Oman: Ministry of Heritage and Culture.

Ministry of Information. 2005a. *The Royal Speeches of His Majesty Sultan Qaboos bin Said 1970–2005*. Muscat, Oman: Ministry of Information.

——. 2005b. *Masīrat al-Khayr*. Muscat, Oman: Ministry of Information.

——. 2009. *Oman*. Muscat, Oman: Ministry of Information.

Ministry of National Heritage and Culture. 1989. *The Omani Museum*. Muscat, Oman: Ministry of Heritage and Culture.

——. 1991. *Mashruʿ Munaẓamat al-Tarbiya wal Thaqafa wal ʾulum "UNESCO" li dirāsa ṭuruq al-harīr*. Muscat, Oman: Ministry of Heritage and Culture.

Mitchell, Timothy. 1988. *Colonising Egypt*. Berkeley: University of California Press.

——. 1989. "World as Exhibition." *Comparative Studies of Society and History* 31 (2): 217–36.

——, ed. 2000. *Questions of Modernity*. Minneapolis: University of Minnesota Press.

——, ed. 2002. *Rule of Experts: Egypt, Techno-Politics, Modernity*. Berkeley: University of California Press.

Moore, Donald S., Jake Kosek, and Anand Pandian, eds. 2003. *Race, Nature and the Politics of Difference*. Durham, NC: Duke University Press.

Morris, James. 1957. *Sultan in Oman*. New York: Pantheon Books.

Mory, Abdullah M. 1975. "Changes in the Economy and Political Attitudes and the Development in Culture on the Coast of Oman between 1900–1940." *Arabian Studies* 2:167–78.

Muʿammar, Ali Yahya. 2007. *Ibadism in History: The Emergence of the Ibadi School*, vol. 1. Muscat, Oman: Ministry of Awqaf and Religious Affairs.

Musitelli, Jean. 2002. "World Heritage, between Universalism and Globalization." *International Journal of Cultural Property* 11 (2): 323–36.

Nancy, Jean-Luc. 1991. *The Inoperative Community*. Minneapolis: University of Minnesota Press.

Nelson, Robert S., and Margaret Olin. 2003. *Monuments and Memory: Made and Unmade*. Chicago: University of Chicago Press.

Newbury, Colin. 2003. *Patrons, Clients and Empire: Chieftaincy and Over-Rule in Asia, Africa and the Pacific*. Oxford: Oxford University Press.

Nora, Pierre. 1989. "Between Memory and History: *les lieu de memoires*." *Representations* 26 (Spring): 1–10.

Noth, Albrecht. 1994. *The Early Arabic Historical Tradition*. Princeton, NJ: Princeton University.

Onley, James. 2007. *Arabian Frontier of the British Raj: Merchants, Rulers, and the British in the Nineteenth Century Gulf*. Oxford: Oxford University Press.

Onley, James, and Sulayman Khalaf. 2006. "Shaikhly Authority in the Pre-Oil Gulf: An Historical-Anthropological Study." *History and Anthropology* 17 (3): 189–208.

Owtram, Francis. 2004. *A Modern History of Oman: Formation of the State since 1920*. London: I. B. Tauris.

Ozyurek, Esra. 2006. *Nostalgia for the Modern: State Secularism and Everyday Politics in Turkey*. Durham, NC: Duke University Press.

——. 2004. "Miniaturizing Ataturk: Privatization of State Imagery and Ideology in Turkey." *American Ethnologist* 31 (3): 374–91.

Paine, Crispin. 2013. *Religious Objects in Museums: Private Lives and Public Duties*. London: Bloomsbury.

Pandian, Anand. 2008. "Tradition in Fragments: Inherited Forms and Fractures in the Ethics of South India." *American Ethnologist* 35 (3): 466–80.

———. 2009. *Cultivating Virtue in South India: Crooked Stalks*. Durham, NC: Duke University Press.

Pandian, Anand, and Daud Ali, eds. 2010. *Ethical Life in South Asia*. Bloomington: Indiana University Press.

Parry, Geraint. 1982. "Tradition, Community and Self-Determination." *British Journal of Political Science* 12 (4): 399–419.

Patterson, Orlando. 1982. *Slavery and Social Death: A Comparative Study*. Cambridge, MA: Harvard University Press.

Persian Gulf Political Residency. 1873–1957. *Persian Gulf Administrative Reports on the Persian Gulf Political Residency and Muscat Political Agency*. 11 vols. Cambridge: Archive Editions.

Peterson, Derek, ed. 2010. *Abolitionism and Imperialism in Britain, Africa and the Atlantic*. Athens: Ohio University Press.

Peterson, J. E. 1976. "The Revival of the Ibadi Imamate in Oman and the Threat of Muscat." *Arabian Studies* 3:165–88.

———. 1978. *Oman in the Twentieth Century: Political Foundations of an Emerging State*. New York: Croom Helm.

———. 2004. "Oman's Diverse Society: Northern Oman." *Middle East Journal* 58 (1): 31–51.

———. 2007. *Oman's Insurgencies: The Sultanate's Struggle for Supremacy*. London: Saqi.

———, ed. 2016. *The Emergence of the Gulf States: Studies in Modern History*. London: Bloomsbury.

Peutz, Nathalie. 2017. "Heritage in the (Ruins)." *International Journal of Middle East Studies* 49 (4): 721–28.

———. 2018. *Islands of Heritage: Conservation and Transformation in Yemen*. Stanford, CA: Stanford University Press.

Phillips, Mark Salber, and Gordon Schochet, eds. 2004. *Questions of Tradition*. Toronto: University of Toronto Press.

Pickering, Michael. 2004. "Experience as Horizon: Koselleck, Expectation and Historical Time." *Cultural Studies* 18 (2/3): 271–89.

Pieprzak, Katarzyna. 2010. *Imagined Museums: Art and Modernity in Postcolonial Morocco*. Minneapolis: University of Minnesota Press.

Pitts, Jennifer. 2006. *The Rise of Imperial Liberalism in Britain and France*. Princeton, NJ: Princeton University Press.

Pocock, J. G. A. 1989. *Politics, Language and Time: Essays on Political Thought and History*. Chicago: University of Chicago Press.

Povinelli, Elizabeth. 2002. *The Cunning of Recognition: Indigenous Alterities and the Making of Australian Multiculturalism*. Durham, NC: Duke University Press.

Pradhan, Samir. 2013. "Oman-India Relations: Exploring the Long-Term Migration Dynamics." In *Regionalizing Oman: Political, Economic and Social Dynamics*, edited by Steffen Wippel, 107–127. London: Springer.

Prakash, Gyan. 1990. "Writing Post-Orientalist Histories of the Third World: Perspectives from Indian Historiography." *Comparative Studies in Society and History* 32 (2): 383–408.

———. 2002. "The Colonial Genealogy of Society: Community and Political Modernity in India." In *The Social in Question: New Bearings in History and Social Sciences*, edited by Patrick Joyce, 81–96. London: Routledge.

Pridham, B. R. 1986. "Oman: Change or Continuity." In *Arabia and the Gulf: From Traditional Society to Modern States*, edited by I. R. Netton, 132–55. London: Croom Helm.

——, ed. 1987. *Oman: Economic, Social and Strategic Developments*. London: Croom Helm.

Public Authority for Craft Industries. 2009. *Omani Crafts: A Documentary Study*. Muscat, Oman: Public Authority for Craft Industries.

Purohit, Teena. 2012. *The Aga Khan Case: Religion and Identity in Colonial India*. Cambridge, MA: Harvard University Press.

Rabi, Uzi. 2006. *The Emergence of States in a Tribal Society: Oman under Said bin Taymur, 1932–1970*. Portland, OR: Sussex Academic.

Radstone, S. 2000. *Memory and Methodology*. Oxford: Berg.

Rajchman, John. 1988. "Foucault's Art of Seeing." *October* 44 (Spring): 88–117.

Ranciere, Jacques. 1994. *The Names of History: On the Poetics of Knowledge*. Minneapolis: University of Minnesota Press.

——. 2004. *The Politics of Aesthetics*. London: Continuum.

Ratnapalan, Laavanyan. 2008. "E. B. Tylor and the Problem of Primitive Islam." *History and Anthropology* 19 (2): 131–42.

Reid, Donald M. 2002. *Whose Pharaohs? Archaeology, Museums, and Egyptian National Identity from Napoleon to World War I*. Berkeley: University of California Press.

Ricoeur, Paul. 2004. *Memory, History, Forgetting*. Translated by Kathleen Blamey and David Pellauer. Chicago: University of Chicago Press.

Riphenburg, Carole. 1998. *Oman: Political Development in a Changing World*. Westport, CT: Praeger.

Risnicoff de Gorgas, Mónica. 2001. "Reality as Illusion: The Historic Houses that Become Museums." *Museum International* 53 (2): 10–15.

Robinson, Chase F. 2003. *Islamic Historiography (Themes in Islamic History)*. Cambridge: Cambridge University Press.

Rogozen-Soltar, Mikaela H. 2017. *Spain Unmoored: Migration, Conversion and the Politics of Islam*. Bloomington: Indiana University Press.

Rose, Nikolas. 1996. "Assembling the Modern Self." In *Rewriting the Self: Histories from the Renaissance to the Present*, edited by Roy Porter, 224–249. London: Routledge.

Rosenthal, Franz. 1968. *A History of Muslim Historiography*. Leiden, Netherlands: E. J. Brill.

Ruete, E. 1998. *Memoirs of an Arabian Princess from Zanzibar*. Zanzibar: Gallery.

Rugh, Andrea. 2007. *Political Culture of Leadership in the United Arab Emirates*. London: Palgrave Macmillan.

Sachedina, Amal. 2011. "The Nature of Difference: Forging Arab Asia at the American Museum of Natural History." *Museum Anthropology* 34 (2): 142–55.

——. 2013. "Of Living Traces and Revived Legacies: Unfolding Futures in the Sultanate of Oman." PhD diss., University of California, Berkeley. Ann Arbor: ProQuest/UMI.

——. 2019a. "The Nizwa Fort: Transforming Ibadi Islam Through Heritage in Oman." *Comparative Studies in South Asia, Africa and the Middle East* 39 (2): 328–43.

——. 2019b. "The Politics of the Coffee Pot: Its Changing Role in History Making and the Place of Religion in the Sultanate of Oman." *History and Anthropology* 30 (3): 233–55.

Sachedina, Z, and A. Daud 2015. "The Origins of the Lawati" Unpublished paper.

Said, Edward W. 1978. *Orientalism*. New York: Pantheon Books.

——. 2000a. "Geopoetics: Space, Place, and Landscape." *Critical Inquiry* 26 (2): 173–74.

——. 2000b. "Invention, Memory, and Place." *Critical Inquiry* 26 (2): 175–92.

Said, Ibrahim Ahmed. n.d. *Nizwa: Madinat al-tarīkh wa al-haḍarat wa al-inṭilāq* [Nizwa: a city of history, civilization and liberty]. Muscat, Oman: Royal Diwan Court.

Salamandra, Christa. 2004. *A New Old Damascus: Authenticity and Distinction in Urban Syria*. Bloomington: Indiana University Press.

Saldanha, J. A. 1906. *Persian Gulf Precis 1903–1908*, vol. 3 (of 8 vols.). Cambridge: Archive Editions.

Saleh Nasser, Muhammad. 2003. "Sheikh al-Salmi, al-Mu'arrikh." In *'Amāl al-multaqa al-'ilmi al-thani hawla maṣādar at-tarīkh al-'umāni* [Proceedings of the second scholarly symposium on Omani historical sources], edited by Hasan al-Malakh and Ibrahim Bahaz, 321–39. Amman, Jordan: University of Al Bayt, 2003.

Salomon, Noah. 2016. *For Love of the Prophet: An Ethnography of Sudan's Islamic State.* Princeton, NJ: Princeton University Press.

Salvatore, Armando. 1999. *Islam and the Political Discourse of Modernity.* Reading, UK: Ithaca.

Samin, Nadav. 2015. *Of Sand and Soil: Genealogy and Tribal Belonging in Saudi Arabia.* Princeton, NJ: Princeton University Press.

———. 2016. "Da'wa, Dynasty and Destiny in the Arab Gulf." *Comparative Studies in Society and History* 58 (4): 935–54.

Sandell, Richard. 2007. *Museums, Prejudice and the Reframing of Difference.* London: Routledge.

Schielke, Samuli. 2015. *Egypt in the Future Tense: Hope. Frustration and Ambivalence before and after 2011.* Bloomington and Indianapolis: University of Indiana.

Scholz, Fred. 2014. *Muscat Then and Now: Geographical Sketch of a Unique Arab Town.* Muscat, Oman: Ministry of Heritage and Culture.

Scott, David. 1999. *Refashioning Futures: Criticism after Postcoloniality.* Princeton, NJ: Princeton University Press.

Scott, Joan W. 1991. "The Evidence of Experience." *Critical Inquiry* 17 (4): 773–97.

Shapiro, Gary. 2003. *Archaeologies of Vision: Foucault and Nietzsche on Seeing and Saying.* Chicago: University of Chicago Press.

Sharkey, Heather. 2003. *Living with Colonialism: Nationalism and Culture in the Anglo-Egyptian Sudan.* Berkeley: University of California Press.

Shaw, Wendy M. K. 2003. *Possessors and Possessed: Museums, Archaeology, and the Visualization of History in the Late Ottoman Empire.* Berkeley: University of California Press.

Sheriff, Abdul. 1987. *Slaves, Spices and Ivory in Zanzibar.* Athens: Ohio University Press.

———. 2005. "The Slave Trade and Its Fallout in the Persian Gulf." In *Abolition and Its Aftermath: Indian Ocean, Africa and Asia*, edited by Gwyn Campbell, 103–120. London: Routledge.

Sherman, Daniel J., and Irit Ragoff, eds. 1994. *Museum Culture: Histories, Discourses, Spectacles.* Minneapolis: University of Minnesota Press.

Sherwood, Seth. 2005. "Oman, Where Palms Not High Rises Form the Skyline" *New York Times*, May 8, 2005.

Shryock, Andrew. 1997. *Nationalism and the Genealogical Imagination: Oral History and Textual Authority in Tribal Jordan.* Berkeley: University of California Press.

———. 2000. "Dynastic Modernism and Its Contradictions: Testing the Limits of Pluralism, Tribalism and King Hussein's Example in Hashemite Jordan. *Arab Studies Quarterly* 22 (3): 57–79

———, ed. 2004a. *Off Stage on Display: Intimacy and Ethnography in the Age of Public Culture.* Stanford, CA: Stanford University Press.

———. 2004b. "The New Jordanian Hospitality: House, Host and Guest in the Culture of Public Display." *Comparative Studies of Society and History* 46 (1): 35–62.

———. 2010. *Islamophobia/Islamophilia: Beyond the Politics of Enemy and Friend.* Bloomington: Indiana University Press.

Silberman, Neil Asher. 1989. *Between Past and Present: Archaeology, Ideology, and Nationalism in the Modern Middle East.* New York: H. Holt.

Silverstein, Michael, and Greg Urban, eds. 1996. *Natural Histories of Discourse.* Chicago: University of Chicago Press.

Simmons, Gail. 2011. "Oman: Journey to a Mountainous Heart." *Telegraph* (London), November 22, 2011.

Simpson, Edward, and Kai Kresse, eds. 2008. *Struggling with History: Islam and Cosmopolitanism in the Western Indian Ocean.* New York: Columbia University Press.

Sirhan, Sirhan ibn Said. 1984. *Annals of Oman to 1728.* Translated and annotated by E. C. Ross. New York: Oleander.

Skeet, Ian. 1992. *Oman: Politics and Development.* London: Macmillan.

Skovgaard-Peterson, Jakob. 1997. *Defining Islam for the Egyptian State Muftis and Fatwas of the Dar al-Ifta.* Leiden, Netherlands: Brill.

Smith, Laurajane. 2006. *The Uses of Heritage.* London: Routledge.

Starrett, Gregory.1998. *Putting Islam to Work: Education, Politics and Religion Transformation in Egypt.* Berkeley: University of California Press.

Stein, Rebecca L., and Ted Swedenburg. 2004. "Popular Culture, Relational History and the Question of Power in Palestine and Israel." *Journal of Palestine Studies* 33 (4): 5–20.

Steinberg, Michael P., ed. 1996. *Walter Benjamin and the Demands of History.* Ithaca, NY: Cornell University Press.

Steinmetz, George, ed. 1999. *State/Culture: State Formation after the Cultural Turn.* Ithaca, NY: Cornell University Press.

Steward, Kathleen. 1988. "Nostalgia—a Polemic." *Cultural Anthropology* 3 (3): 227–41.

———. 2007. *Ordinary Effects.* Durham and London: Duke University Press.

Stewart, Susan. 1993. *On Longing: Narratives of the Miniatures, the Gigantic, the Souvenir, the Collection.* Durham, NC: Duke University Press.

Stout, Jeffrey. 2004. *Democracy and Tradition.* Princeton, NJ: Princeton University Press.

Sturken, Marita. 2007. *Tourists of History: Memory, Kitsch, and Consumerism from Oklahoma City to Ground Zero.* Durham, NC: Duke University Press.

Takriti, Abdel Razzaq. 2013. *Monsoon Revolution: Republicans, Sultans and Empires in Oman, 1965–1976.* Oxford: Oxford University Press.

Tambar, Kabir. 2014. *The Reckoning of Pluralism: Political Belonging and the Demands of History in Turkey.* Stanford, CA: Stanford University Press.

Thomas, Bertram. 1931. *Alarms and Excursions in Arabia.* London: Thomas Press.

Townsend, John. 1977. *Oman: The Making of the Modern State.* London: Croom Helm.

Troillot, Michel-Rolph. 1995. *Silencing the Past: Power and the Production of History.* Boston: Beacon.

Turtinen, Jan. *Globalising Heritage: On UNESCO and the Transnational Construction of a World Heritage.* Stockholm: Stockholm Center for Organizational Research.

Umān newspaper, 1973–1980. Articles published March 19, 1973; June 24, 1976; April 12, 1978; November 18, 1980.

Urban, Greg. 1996. "Entextualization, Replication and Power." In *Natural Histories of Discourse*, edited by Michael Silverstein and Greg Urban, 21–44. Chicago: University of Chicago Press.

Valeri, Marc. 2009. *Oman: Politics and Society in the Qaboos State.* London: Hurst.

———. 2010. "High Visibility, Low Profile: The Shi'a in Oman under Sultan Qaboos." *International Journal of Middle East Studies* 42:251–68.

———. 2015. "Simmering Unrest and Succession Challenges in Oman." Carnegie Endowment for International Peace (website), January 28, 2015. https://carnegieendowment .org/2015/01/28/simmering-unrest-and-succession-challenges-in-oman-pub -58843.

Van der Veer, Peter. 2001. *Imperial Encounters: Religion and Modernity in India and Britain.* Princeton, NJ: Princeton University Press.

Van der Veer, Peter, and Hartmut Lehmann, eds. 1999. *Nation and Religion: Perspectives on Europe and Asia.* Princeton, NJ: Princeton University Press.

Vejdani, Farzin. 2015. *Making History in Iran: Education, Nationalism and Print Culture.* Stanford, CA: Stanford University Press.

Vogel, Frank E. 2003. "The Public and Private in Saudi Arabia: Restrictions on the Powers of Committees for Ordering the Good and Forbidding the Evil." *Social Research: An International Quarterly* 70 (3): 749–68.

Vom Bruck, Gabriele. 2005. *Islam, Memory and Morality in Yemen: Ruling Families in Transition.* New York: Palgrave Macmillan.

Vora, Neha. 2013. *Impossible Citizens: Dubai's Indian Diaspora.* Durham, NC: Duke University Press.

Walsh, Kevin. 1992. *The Representation of the Past: Museums and Heritage in the Post-Modern World.* London: Routledge.

Ward, Philip. 1987. *Travels in Oman: On the Track of Early Explorers.* New York: Oleander.

Wedeen, Lisa. 2008. *Peripheral Visions: Publics, Power and Performance in Yemen.* Chicago: University of Chicago Press.

Weidman, Amanda J. 2006. *Singing the Classical, Voicing the Modern: The Postcolonial Politics of Music in South India.* Durham, NC: Duke University Press.

White, Hayden. 1978. *Tropics of Discourse: Essays in Cultural Criticism.* Baltimore: Johns Hopkins University Press.

——. 1987. *The Content of the Form: Narrative, Discourse and Historical Representation.* Baltimore: Johns Hopkins University Press.

Wilkinson, John C. 1971. "The Oman Question: The Background to the Political Geography of South-East Arabia." *Geographical Journal* 137 (3): 361–71.

——. 1972. "The Origins of the Omani State." In *The Arabian Peninsula: Society and Politics*, edited by Derek Hopwood, 67–88. London: George Allen and Unwin.

——. 1976. "The Ibadi Imama." *Bulletin of the School of Oriental and African Studies* 39 (3): 535–51.

——. 1985. "Ibadi Hadith: An Essay in Normalization." *Der Islam* 62 (2): 231–59.

——. 1987. *The Imamate Tradition of Oman.* Cambridge: Cambridge University Press.

——. 2010. *Ibāḍism: Origins and Early Development in Oman.* Oxford: Oxford University Press.

Willis, John M. 2009. "Making Yemen Indian: Rewriting the Boundaries of Imperial Arabia." *International Journal of Middle East Studies* 41:23–38.

Winegar, Jessica. 2008. "The Humanity Game: Art, Islam and the War on Terror." *Anthropological Quarterly* 81 (3): 651–81.

Wingate, Sir Ronald. 1959. *Not in the Limelight.* London: Hutchinson.

Witz, Leslie. 2006. "Transforming Museums on Postapartheid Tourist Routes." In *Museum Frictions: Public Cultures / Global Transformations*, edited by Ivan Karp, Corinne A. Kratz, Lynn Szwaja, and Tomas Ybarra-Frausto, 107–135. Durham. NC: Duke University Press.

Worrall, James. 2012. "Oman: The 'Forgotten' Corner of the Arab Spring." *Middle East Policy* 19 (3): 98–115.

——. 2014. *State Building and Counter Insurgency in Oman.* London: I. B. Tauris.

Yates, Francis. 1966. *The Art of Memory.* Chicago: University of Chicago Press.

Yudice, George. 2004. *The Expediency of Culture: Uses of Culture in the Global Era.* Durham, NC: Duke University Press.

Yurchak, Alexei. 2006. *Everything Was Forever, until It Was No More: The Last Soviet Generation.* Princeton, NJ: Princeton University Press.

Ziadeh, Farhat J. 1957. "Equality (*Kafa'a*) in the Muslim Law of Marriage." *American Journal of Comparative Law* 6 (4): 503–17.

Zubair Corporation. 2008. *A Journey through Time.* Muscat, Oman: Baz.

Index

Page numbers in italic refer to figures.

CPSIA information can be obtained
at www.ICGtesting.com
Printed in the USA
LVHW112256280821
696353LV00016B/1749